COMPARATIVE FOUNDATIONS OF A EUROPEAN LAW OF SET-OFF AND PRESCRIPTION

The emergence of a European private law is one of the great issues on the legal agenda of our time. Among the most prominent initiatives furthering this process is the work of the Commission on European Contract Law ('Lando Commission'). The essays collected in this volume have their origin within this context. They explore two practically very important topics which have hitherto been largely neglected in comparative legal literature: set-off and 'extinctive' prescription (or limitation of actions). Professor Zimmermann lays the comparative foundations for a common approach which may provide the basis for a set of European principles.

At the same time, the essays provide practical examples of the arguments that can be employed in the process of harmonizing European private law on a rational basis: they consider the comparative experiences in the various modern legal systems, they explore the extent to which there is a common core of values, rules and concepts, they explain existing differences and they analyse the direction in which the international development is heading.

The introduction to the present volume discusses the terms of reference of the Lando Commission that has set itself the task of elaborating a 'restatement' of European contract law and places its work within the wider context of the Europeanization of private law.

REINHARD ZIMMERMANN is Professor of Law at the University of Regensburg. Among his many publications are *The Law of Obligations: Roman Foundations of the Civilian Tradition* (1990/1996) and *Roman Law, Contemporary Law, European Law: The Civilian Tradition Today* (2001). Co-edited volumes include *Good Faith in European Contract Law* (2000) and *A History of Private Law in Scotland* (2000).

COMPARATIVE FOUNDATIONS OF A EUROPEAN LAW OF SET-OFF AND PRESCRIPTION

REINHARD ZIMMERMANN

University of Regensburg

CAMBRIDGE
UNIVERSITY PRESS

CAMBRIDGE UNIVERSITY PRESS
Cambridge, New York, Melbourne, Madrid, Cape Town, Singapore,
São Paulo, Delhi, Dubai, Tokyo, Mexico City

Cambridge University Press
The Edinburgh Building, Cambridge CB2 8RU, UK

Published in the United States of America by Cambridge University Press, New York

www.cambridge.org
Information on this title: www.cambridge.org/9780521184076

First published 2002
First paperback edition 2010

A catalogue record for this publication is available from the British Library

ISBN 978-0-521-81461-4 Hardback
ISBN 978-0-521-18407-6 Paperback

Cambridge University Press has no responsibility for the persistence or
accuracy of URLs for external or third-party internet websites referred to in
this publication, and does not guarantee that any content on such websites is,
or will remain, accurate or appropriate.

CONTENTS

v

Contents

PREFACE

Comparative legal scholarship in the twentieth century has been dominated by private law; within private law by the law of obligations; within the law of obligations by tort/delict and contract; and within contract by a standard range of topics including conclusion of contract, validity, breach of contract and third-party rights. The magisterial treatise by Zweigert and Kötz both reflected and largely determined that agenda. That treatise has prepared the ground for intense scholarly discussions on offer and acceptance, causa and consideration, specific performance, frustration and privity, to mention some examples. At the same time, however, even within the law of obligations a number of topics not discussed by Zweigert and Kötz have received only scant attention. Set-off and (negative) prescription/limitation of claims are among those topics. Conditions, substitution of debtors and plurality of debtors or creditors might also be mentioned. Even the great *International Encyclopedia of Comparative Law* neglects these topics. One can only speculate about the reasons. Is it because they offer 'fearsome technicalities but few issues that really stir the blood' (Rory Derham, *Set-off*, 2nd edn, 1996, VII)?

The three essays collected in this booklet attempt to explore two of these hitherto comparatively neglected areas. They originated within the context of the Commission on European Contract Law ('Lando Commission'). First drafts of all three papers were submitted as 'position papers' for that commission. The approach adopted towards the two topics covered by them is slightly different. The chapter on set-off is based on as many legal systems of the European Union as were accessible to me. The framework for the two prescription papers is both wider and narrower. Fewer legal systems of the European Union have been taken into consideration. But an attempt has been made to integrate the wider international trends and developments. For the private law of the European Union cannot be looked at in isolation. Thus, obviously, the Uncitral Convention had to be considered. But even legal systems as far away as Québec or South Africa can offer interesting perspectives, not only because both legal systems once inherited their private laws from Europe but also particularly in view of the fact that in reforming their prescription laws they have taken account of the experiences gathered in Europe (and elsewhere). I have benefited very much from the critical discussion of my papers in the commission, from advice on matters of content and style by Hugh Beale and Roy Goode, and from a very intensive discussion on the law of prescription at a meeting of a small working party consisting of Ole Lando, Ulrich Drobnig, Hugh Beale and Ewoud Hondius at Goodhart Lodge in Cambridge. I am very grateful to all my colleagues on the commission and in that working party. At the same time, it must be emphasized that the views expressed in these papers in no way commit or prejudice the commission. Earlier versions of two of the three chapters have appeared in Germany.

At the same time, these chapters constitute practical exercises in the Europeanization of private law. The emergence of a European private law is one of the great issues on the legal agenda of our time. Much has been written about it. In particular, there has been considerable discussion as to the approach to be adopted. I do not think that there is only one approach. As in early nineteenth-century Germany this is the hour of legal scholarship; and legal scholarship both requires and encourages a stimulating diversity of outlook and approach. Many different paths will be, and will have to be, explored. The same method may not prove fruitful for all problems. In many instances we will find a common core of values, rules and concepts. In others we can discern, by looking beyond our national borders, a European or even international development clearly heading in a particular direction. It may be helpful to demonstrate that differences between two or more legal systems are not as great as is commonly presumed; or that an approach prevailing in another country has also once prevailed in ours. It may be necessary, occasionally, to remove ideological preconceptions that have become firmly entrenched in more than one hundred years of national legal scholarship. Often we will be able to learn from past experiences, equally often from the experiences in other countries. Such experiences will provide arguments for making a rational choice between conflicting solutions. Sometimes we will also find that for a long time we have been caught up in thinking patterns of the past. Any enlargement of the lawyer's horizon, as Ernst Rabel has said, will bear reward. The three essays collected in this volume attempt to prove the truth of this statement. They neither follow nor develop a master-method. But they provide practical examples for the arguments sketched in the previous sentences.

I had the great privilege of spending the academic year 1998/9 as A. L. Goodhart Professor of Legal Science in the University of Cambridge and as a Fellow of St John's College, Cambridge. I am very grateful to my friends and colleagues both in the Faculty of Law and at St John's for having invited me and for making my time in Cambridge so memorable and enjoyable. I first learnt about the Goodhart Chair when I read the preface of Raoul van Caenegem's famous book on *Judges, Legislators and Professors: Chapters in European*

Legal History. It is based on a course of lectures given as Goodhart Professor in 1984/5. A few years later John Fleming also published his Goodhart Lectures for 1987/8 under the title *The American Tort Process*. The modest and preliminary reflections in this volume are quite different in scope and ambition from these predecessor volumes. Like them, however, the present collection of essays is inspired by the desire to establish a small token of my gratitude. It can only claim the title of 'Goodhart Lectures' in a very liberal sense of the word; for while the course I taught in 1998/9 in Cambridge did cover the work of the Contract Law Commission as well as my thoughts on set-off and prescription, it extended far beyond these topics in that it dealt with the development of European private law in general. But much of my time in Cambridge in the course of spring and summer 1999 was devoted to the preparation of the material presented in this volume.

Among my friends in Cambridge I am particularly grateful to David Johnston and Neil Andrews for sharing their thoughts on prescription with me. I also wish to record my thanks to Catherine Maxwell (Cape Town/Regensburg) and Oliver Radley-Gardner (Oxford/Regensburg) for their help in preparing this volume.

GOODHART LODGE
Summer 1999

ABBREVIATIONS

ABGB	Allgemeines bürgerliches Gesetzbuch
AC	Appeal Cases
Amb.	Ambler's Chancery Reports
AO	Abgabenordnung
AtomG	Atomgesetz
B & S	Best & Smith's Queen's Bench Reports
BGB	Bürgerliches Gesetzbuch
BGB-KE	Bürgerliches Gesetzbuch, Kommissionsentwurf (draft of the German law of prescription submitted by the commission charged with the reform of the law of obligations)
BGB-PZ	Bürgerliches Gesetzbuch, Peters and Zimmermann (draft of the German law of prescription submitted by Frank Peters and Reinhard Zimmermann at the request of the German minister of justice)
BGH	Bundesgerichtshof
BGHZ	Entscheidungen des Bundesgerichtshofs in Zivilsachen
Burr.	Burrow's King's Bench Reports
BW	Burgerlijk Wetboek
CISG	Convention for the International Sale of Goods
DLR	Dominion Law Reports
ECJ	European Court of Justice
ER	English Reports
HaftpflG	Haftpflichtgesetz
Hare	Hare's Chancery Reports
HGB	Handelsgesetzbuch
HL	House of Lords

List of abbreviations

HR	Hoge Raad
Jac & W	Jacob & Walker's Chancery Reports
Lev	Levinz's King's Bench and Common Pleas Reports
LuftVG	Luftverkehrsgesetz
OJEC	Official Journal of the European Communities
OR	Bundesgesetz über das Obligationenrecht
PECL	Principles of European Contract Law
PflVersG	Pflichtversicherungsgesetz
PIQR	Personal Injuries and Quantum Reports
PrALR	Preußisches Allgemeines Landrecht
RabelsZ	*Rabels Zeitschrift für ausländisches und internationales Privatrecht*
SC	Session Cases
SCR	Supreme Court Reports
StVG	Straßenverkehrsgesetz
Willes	Willes Common Pleas Reports, ed. Dunford
WLR	Weekly Law Reports
ZGB	Schweizerisches Zivilgesetzbuch
ZGB (GDR)	Zivilgesetzbuch (German Democratic Republic)
ZPO	Zivilprozeßordnung

INTRODUCTION: TOWARDS A RESTATEMENT OF THE EUROPEAN LAW OF OBLIGATIONS

I THE EUROPEANIZATION OF PRIVATE LAW AND LEGAL SCHOLARSHIP

One of the most significant legal developments of our time has been the gradual emergence of a European private law.[1] This process was driven, initially, by the regulations and directives issued by the competent bodies of the European Union[2] and by the decisions of the European Court of Justice.[3] Our general frame of mind, however, has long

---

[1] See, e.g., the contributions to Nicolò Lipari (ed.), *Diritto Privato Europeo* (1997); Arthur Hartkamp, Martijn Hesselink et al., *Towards a European Civil Code* (2nd edn, 1998); Thomas G. Watkin (ed.), *The Europeanisation of Law* (1998) (also covering other areas of the law); Peter-Christian Müller-Graff (ed.), *Gemeinsames Privatrecht in der europäischen Gemeinschaft* (2nd edn, 1999); Martin Gebauer, *Grundfragen der Europäisierung des Privatrechts* (1998); Jan Smits, *Europees Privaatrecht in wording* (1999); Arthur Hartkamp, 'Perspectives for the Development of a European Civil Law', in Mauro Bussani and Ugo Mattei (eds.), *Making European Law: Essays on the 'Common Core' Project* (2000), pp. 39ff.; on contract law, see Jürgen Basedow, 'The Renascence of Uniform Law: European Contract Law and Its Components', (1998) 18 *Legal Studies* 121ff.

[2] For a collection of all directives (and other relevant texts) affecting the law of obligations, see Reiner Schulze and Reinhard Zimmermann (eds.), *Basistexte zum europäischen Privatrecht* (2000); see also Stefan Grundmann, *Europäisches Schuldvertragsrecht* (1999).

[3] On the importance of which see, for instance, the contributions by David A. O. Edward and Lord Mackenzie Stuart, both in David L. Carey Miller and Reinhard Zimmermann (eds.), *The Civilian Tradition and Scots Law* (1997), pp. 307ff., 351ff.; W. van Gerven, 'ECJ Case-Law as a Means of Unification

---

remained untouched by these developments; it is still predominantly moulded by the national systems of private law. Only comparatively recently has the perception been gaining ground that considerable efforts are required to overcome this somewhat anachronistic discrepancy; and that a new European legal culture can emerge, organically, only by an interaction of several, hitherto largely separate, disciplines: European community law and modern private law doctrine, comparative law[4] and legal history.[5] Also to be taken into account is the uniform private law based on international conventions and covering important areas of commercial law.[6] In a programmatic article published in 1990, Helmut Coing called for a 'Europeanization of Legal Scholarship',[7] and he drew attention to the *ius commune* as a historical, and to the private law of the United States as a modern, model. In the meantime, some measure of progress has been made. Legal periodicals have been established that pursue the objective of promoting the development of a European private law;[8] textbooks have been written that analyse particular areas of private law under a genuinely

---

of Private Law?', (1997) 5 *European Review of Private Law* 293ff.; most recently, see the analysis by Martin Franzen, *Privatrechtsangleichung durch die europäische Gemeinschaft* (1999), pp. 291ff.

[4] See, e.g., Hein Kötz, 'Rechtsvergleichung und gemeineuropäisches Privatrecht', in Müller-Graff (n. 1) 149ff.; Abbo Junker, 'Rechtsvergleichung als Grundlagenfach', (1994) *Juristenzeitung* 921ff.

[5] See, e.g., Reinhard Zimmermann, 'Das römisch-kanonische *ius commune* als Grundlage europäischer Rechtseinheit', (1992) *Juristenzeitung* 8ff.

[6] See, e.g., Jan Ramberg, *International Commercial Transactions* (1997), and the contributions in Franco Ferrari (ed.), *The Unification of International Commercial Law* (1998).

[7] Helmut Coing, 'Europäisierung der Privatrechtswissenschaft', (1990) *Neue Juristische Wochenschrift* 937ff.

[8] The first ones were *Zeitschrift für Europäisches Privatrecht* and *European Review of Private Law*; both started to appear in 1993.

European perspective and deal with the rules of German, French or English law as local variations of a general theme;[9] ambitious research projects have been launched that attempt to find a 'common core' of the systems of private law prevailing in Europe;[10] more and more law faculties in Europe attempt to attain a 'Euro'-profile by establishing integrated courses and programmes with European partner faculties, or by setting up chairs in European private law or European legal history; bold schemes like the establishment of a European law school[11] or even of a European Law Institute are being discussed;[12] and so forth. Twenty years ago, all this was hardly imaginable.

---

[9] See the programme sketched by Hein Kötz, 'Gemeineuropäisches Zivilrecht', in *Festschrift für Konrad Zweigert* (1981), p. 498, and now implemented in Hein Kötz, *European Private Law*, vol. I (1997, transl. T. Weir); see also Christian von Bar, *The Common European Law of Torts*, vol. I (1998), vol. II (2000); Filippo Ranieri, *Europäisches Obligationenrecht* (1999). For the historical background, see Helmut Coing, *Europäisches Privatrecht*, vol. I (1985), vol. II (1989); Reinhard Zimmermann, *The Law of Obligations: Roman Foundations of the Civilian Tradition* (1990, paperback edn 1996).

[10] On the Trento 'common core' project, see the contributions in Bussani and Mattei (n. 1). The first volume to have appeared is Reinhard Zimmermann and Simon Whittaker (eds.), *Good Faith in European Contract Law* (2000).

[11] For proposals for a Europeanization of legal education, see Axel Flessner, 'Rechtsvereinheitlichung durch Rechtswissenschaft und Juristenausbildung', (1992) 56 *RabelsZ* 243ff.; Gerard-René de Groot, 'European Legal Education in the Twenty-First Century', in Bruno de Witte and Caroline Forder (eds.), *The Common Law of Europe and the Future of Legal Education* (1992), pp. 7ff.; Hein Kötz, 'Europäische Juristenausbildung', (1993) 1 *Zeitschrift für Europäisches Privatrecht* 268ff.; Roy Goode, 'The European Law School', (1994) 13 *Legal Studies* 1ff.

[12] Werner Ebke, 'Unternehmensrechtsangleichung in der Europäischen Union: Brauchen wir ein European Law Institute?', in *Festschrift für Bernhard Großfeld* (1999), pp. 189ff.

II THE COMMISSION ON EUROPEAN CONTRACT LAW

1 *First commission*

A particularly interesting initiative that has been taken, in this context, was the establishment of a Commission on European Contract Law. It came into being as a result of a private initiative but its work has been financially supported, for many years, by the Commission of the European Communities. The Contract Law Commission (which consisted initially of about fifteen lawyers drawn from all member states of the European Union) has set itself the task of working out Principles of European Contract Law and laying them down in a code-like form. For it was realized, at the outset, that the Rome Convention on the Law Applicable to Contractual Obligations was inadequate to ensure the smooth functioning of an internal market as envisaged by Art. 8 a of the EEC Treaty. Thus, already in 1976, Ole Lando called for a European Uniform Commercial Code.[13] In the course of two subsequent symposia in Brussels in 1980 and 1981 the commission constituted itself and decided on its schedule of work. By 1990, it had met twelve times in various European cities. It was chaired by Ole Lando of the Copenhagen Business School. England was represented by Roy Goode and, since 1987, Hugh Beale, Scotland by Bill Wilson. As the European Community increased, so did the Commission on European Contract Law: members for Spain, Portugal and Greece were co-opted. In 1995, after more than fourteen years of work, the first

---

[13] Ole Lando, 'Unfair Contract Clauses and a European Uniform Commercial Code', in Mauro Cappelletti (ed.), *New Perspectives for a Common Law of Europe* (1978), pp. 267ff.

volume of the *Principles of European Contract Law* was published.[14] The preface lists all members of the commission and describes the working method that was adopted. The volume consists of an introductory overview which sets out the objectives pursued by the Principles and outlines their main content. This is followed by the text of the fifty-nine articles in which these Principles are laid down. The main part is made up of comments which have been drafted for every article; in addition, in most cases short comparative notes have been included. The volume is written in English; the provisions themselves, however, have also been translated into French. The Principles were subdivided into four chapters: the first containing 'general provisions', the second dealing with 'terms and performance of the contract' and the third and fourth being devoted to 'non-performance'.[15]

---

[14] Ole Lando and Hugh Beale (eds.), *Principles of European Contract Law*, Part I (1995). A French translation of the entire volume appeared in 1997: Isabelle de Lamberterie, Georges Rouhette and Denis Tallon (eds.), *Les principes du droit européen du contrat*. A German translation of the articles was published in (1995) 3 *Zeitschrift für Europäisches Privatrecht* 864ff.

[15] For comment, see Ole Lando, 'Principles of European Contract Law: An Alternative to or a Precursor of European Legislation?', (1992) 56 *RabelsZ* 261ff.; Lando, 'Is Codification Needed in Europe? Principles of European Contract Law and the Relationship to Dutch Law', (1993) 1 *European Review of Private Law* 157ff.; Ulrich Drobnig, 'Ein Vertragsrecht für Europa', in *Festschrift für Ernst Steindorff* (1990), pp. 1141ff.; Hugh Beale, 'Towards a Law of Contract for Europe: The Work of the Commission on European Contract Law', in Günter Weick (ed.), *National and European Law on the Threshold to the Single Market* (1993), pp. 177ff.; Oliver Remien, 'Möglichkeiten und Grenzen eines europäischen Vertragsrechts', in (1991) *Jahrbuch Junger Zivilrechtswissenschaftler* 103ff.; Reinhard Zimmermann, 'Konturen eines Europäischen Vertragsrechts', (1995) *Juristenzeitung* 477ff.; and see the contributions to Hans-Leo Weyers (ed.), *Europäisches Vertragsrecht* (1997) and to the *Festskrift til Ole Lando* (1997).

2 *Second and third commissions*

By the time Part I of the Principles was published, a second commission had constituted itself and had started work on formation of contracts, validity, interpretation and agency. Since its inaugural meeting in 1992 the second commission has met eight times; it concluded its deliberations in 1996. Over the course of time, it has been joined by members for Austria, Sweden and Finland. Once again, the task of editing the work produced by the commission was undertaken by Ole Lando and Hugh Beale.[16] At the same time, Part I was slightly revised and amended. The volume published early in 2000, therefore, contains a consolidated version of Parts I and II. As a result, the numbering of the articles contained in volume I has changed, a fact which has occasionally caused slight irritation. In view of the way in which the Principles have originated this was, however, unavoidable. In its new version the Principles contain 131 articles organized into nine chapters; for the rest the structure of the volume corresponds to that of its forerunner.[17]

In the course of the final meeting of the second commission, a third commission was created which started its work in December 1997 in Regensburg. The topics under consideration are plurality of debtors and creditors, assignment of claims, substitution of debtor and transfer of contract, set-off, prescription, illegality, conditions and capitalization of interests. The third commission thus moves into a number

---

[16] Ole Lando and Hugh Beale (eds.), *Principles of European Contract Law*, Parts I and II (2000). French and German translations of the entire volume are in preparation. For a German translation of the text of the articles, see Schulze and Zimmermann (n. 2) III.10.

[17] For comment, see Reinhard Zimmermann, 'Die "Principles of European Contract Law", Teile I und II', (2000) 8 *Zeitschrift für Europäisches Privatrecht* 391ff. and the contributions to (2000) *Nederlands Tijdschrift voor Burgerlijk Recht* 428ff.

of fields which have largely been neglected in comparative legal literature. In addition, some of the topics mentioned go beyond the area of contract law; they would be classified as belonging to the general law of obligations, or even the general part of private law, in Germany. The third commission is partly identical with the second (as was the second with the first); it numbers twenty-three members (plus observers from Norway and Switzerland). It is hoped that the results of the work of the third commission will be published in 2002 or 2003. The studies contained in the present volume have their origin in the context of that third commission.

III OBJECTIVES OF THE PRINCIPLES OF EUROPEAN CONTRACT LAW

The structure of what is now the consolidated version of Parts I and II shows that the Principles have been inspired by the idea of the American Restatements.[18] Like the Restatements, the Principles of European Contract Law are not aimed at becoming law that is directly applicable. Rather, according to the statement of their authors,[19] the Principles are intended (i) to facilitate cross-border trade within Europe by providing contracting parties with a set of rules which are independent of the peculiarities of the different national legal systems and on which they can agree to subject their transaction; (ii) to offer a general conceptual and systematic basis for the further harmonization of contract law within

---

[18] On which see, e.g., Konrad Zweigert and Hein Kötz, *An Introduction to Comparative Law* (3rd edn, 1998, transl. Tony Weir), pp. 251f.; W. Gray, 'E pluribus unum? A Bicentennial Report on Unification of Law in the United States', (1986) 50 *RabelsZ* 119ff.; James Gordley, 'European Codes and American Restatements: Some Difficulties', (1981) 81 *Columbia Law Review* 140ff.

[19] Lando and Beale (n. 16) xxi ff.

the European Union (the editors refer to an 'infrastructure for community laws governing contracts'); (iii) to mediate between the traditions of the civil law and the common law; (iv) to give shape to and to specify a modern European *lex mercatoria*; (v) to be a source of inspiration for national courts and legislatures in developing their respective contract laws; and finally (vi) to constitute a first step towards the codification of European contract law. Several of these objectives have also been pursued and have, at least partly, been achieved by the American Restatements. However, the Principles differ from the American Restatements in at least one important point. For while the Restatements were designed to lay down the law as it was currently applied, by means of a set of concise, clearly structured and easily comprehensible rules, the Principles, to a much greater extent, aim at harmonization of the law, i.e., from the point of view of the national legal systems, at reform and development of the law. But it is easy to exaggerate this contrast. For in spite of their common roots in the English common law, the legal systems of the various American states are nowadays probably less uniform than is often thought;[20] and thus the Restatements do not merely have a declaratory function, solely 'identifying' the common American private law. On the other hand, of course, the European systems of contract law have been characteristically moulded by a common tradition and, as a result, are based on common systematic, conceptual, doctrinal and ideological foundations which may be hidden behind, but have not been obliterated by, the scree material piled up in the course of the nationalization of legal development over the

---

[20] See Gray, (1986) 50 *RabelsZ* 111ff.; Mathias Reimann, 'Amerikanisches Privatrecht und europäische Rechtseinheit: Können die USA als Vorbild dienen?', in Reinhard Zimmermann (ed.), *Amerikanische Rechtskultur und europäisches Privatrecht: Impressionen aus der Neuen Welt* (1995), pp. 132ff.

past two hundred years.[21] Thus, the editors of Parts I and II of the Principles expressly refer to a common core of contract law of all the member states of the European Union which has to be uncovered and which may still provide the basis for a modern set of rules. All in all, however, they concede that this is a somewhat more 'creative' task than that tackled by the draftsmen of the American Restatements.[22] The three essays collected in this volume will provide examples of uncovering a common core, of attempting to reconcile different approaches and of situations where a rational choice between conflicting solutions has to be made.

IV THE IDEA OF CODIFICATION TODAY

Parts I and II of the Principles were drafted at a time when the notion of codification has, once again, been gaining considerable attention.[23] Contrary to a view that used to be widely held, it has become increasingly clear that the idea of

---

[21] See Reinhard Zimmermann, '"Heard melodies are sweet, but those unheard are sweeter..."': Conditio tacita, implied condition und die Fortbildung des europäischen Vertragsrechts', (1993) 193 *Archiv für die Civilistische Praxis* 122ff., 166ff.; Zimmermann, 'Roman Law and European Legal Unification', in Hartkamp, Hesselink et al. (n. 1) 21ff.; Rolf Knütel, 'Rechtseinheit in Europa und römisches Recht', (1994) 2 *Zeitschrift für Europäisches Privatrecht* 244ff.; Eugen Bucher, 'Recht – Geschichtlichkeit – Europa', in Bruno Schmidlin (ed.), *Vers un droit privé commun? Skizzen zum gemeineuropäischen Privatrecht* (1994), pp. 7ff.

[22] Lando and Beale (n. 16) xxvi.

[23] Rodolfo Sacco, 'Codificare: modo superato di legiferare?', (1983) *Rivista di diritto civile* 117ff.; Karsten Schmidt, *Die Zukunft der Kodifikationsidee: Rechtsprechung, Wissenschaft und Gesetzgebung vor den Gesetzeswerken des geltenden Rechts* (1985); Franz Bydlinski, Theo Mayer-Maly and Johannes W. Pichler (eds.), *Renaissance der Idee der Kodifikation* (1992); Shael Herman, 'Schicksal und Zukunft der Kodifikationsidee in Amerika', in Zimmermann (n. 20) 45ff.; Reinhard Zimmermann, 'Codification: History and Present Significance of an Idea', (1995) 3 *European Review of Private Law* 95ff.; and see the symposium 'Codification in the Twenty-First Century', (1998) 31 *University of California at Davis Law Review* 655ff.

codifying the law is not at all outdated. In view of the growing particularization of modern legal scholarship,[24] and the hectic activity of the modern legislature, legal systems require this kind of intellectual focus today more than ever before. This realization, for example, has prompted the Dutch legislature to recodify the entire system of Dutch private law. After a long period of deliberation and comparative studies, central parts of the new Burgerlijk Wetboek came into force in 1992. Thus, the Netherlands possesses, at least in the field of the law of obligations, the most modern European codification and one which has benefited from the experiences gathered in other countries.[25] Of even more recent date is the civil code of Québec which entered into force in 1994. Another interesting mixed legal system at the intersection between common law and civil law is just about to modernize its codification substantially.[26] In Germany, ambitious schemes to reform the entire law of obligations have been aborted, but a draft commissioned by the minister of justice and limited to the two most notorious problem areas[27] was published in 1992[28] and appears to have a chance of being implemented in due course.[29] The English Law

---

[24] On which see Reinhard Zimmermann, 'Savigny's Legacy: Legal History, Comparative Law, and the Emergence of a European Legal Science', (1996) 112 *Law Quarterly Review* 582ff.; Albrecht Zeuner, 'Rechtskultur und Spezialisierung', (1997) *Juristenzeitung* 480ff.

[25] See Arthur Hartkamp, 'International Unification and National Codification and Recodification of Civil Law', in Attila Harmathy and Agnes Nemeth (eds.), *Questions of Civil Law Codification* (1990), pp. 67ff.

[26] See Joachim Zekoll, 'Zwischen den Welten: Das Privatrecht von Louisiana als europäisch–amerikanische Mischrechtsordnung', in Zimmermann (n. 20) 11ff.

[27] These are breach of contract and (liberative) prescription.

[28] Bundesminister der Justiz (ed.), *Abschlußbericht der Kommission zur Überarbeitung des Schuldrechts* (1992).

[29] Possibly in the context of implementation of the Directive 1999/44/EC on certain aspects of the sale of consumer goods and associated guarantees (25 May 1999) which has to occur by 1 January 2002. See Jürgen Schmidt-Räntsch,

Commission asked for the preparation of a Contract Code in 1966. The draft code, produced by Harvey McGregor, became known outside England in 1990 on the occasion of a conference in Pavia; and even though the project has been dropped in England, it was published jointly by Giuffré and Sweet and Maxwell in 1993.[30] In many states of Central and Eastern Europe, endeavours to replace the socialist civil codes by modern codifications have made remarkable progress.[31] The significance attached to this issue was reflected by the great interest displayed by the governments of these states in the Colloquium on Codification that was organized by the Council of Europe, in co-operation with the Czech secretary of justice, in September 1994 in Kromĕříž.[32] In the area of international commerce, the success story of the (Vienna) Convention on Contracts for the International Sale of Goods of 1980 springs to mind; it has been adopted by close to fifty states (among them ten of the member states of the European Union[33]) and is

'Gedanken zur Umsetzung der kommenden Kaufrechtsrichtlinie', (1999) 7 *Zeitschrift für Europäisches Privatrecht* 294ff.

[30] Harvey McGregor, *Contract Code: Drawn up on Behalf of the English Law Commission* (1993). Professor Gandolfi, in his foreword, compares the significance of this draft with man's landing in the moon and with the fall of the Iron Curtain.

[31] Thus, for example, Part I of the new Russian Civil Code entered into force on 1 January 1995, Part II on 1 March 1996. See Oleg Sadikov, 'Das neue Zivilgesetzbuch Rußlands', (1996) 4 *Zeitschrift für Europäisches Privatrecht* 258ff.; Sadikov, 'Das zweite Buch des neuen Zivilgesetzbuches Russlands', (1999) 7 *Zeitschrift für Europäisches Privatrecht* 903ff. For an English translation, see Peter B. Maggs and A. N. Zhiltsov, *The Civil Code of the Russian Federation*, Parts I and II (1997).

[32] See the report by Miroslav Liberda in (1995) 3 *Zeitschrift für Europäisches Privatrecht* 672ff.

[33] It has not been implemented by Greece, Portugal, Belgium, the United Kingdom and Luxembourg; concerning Great Britain, see the comments by Barry Nicholas, *The United Kingdom and the Vienna Sales Convention: Another Case of Splendid Isolation?* (1993).

starting to give rise to a considerable amount of case law in the Convention's member states.[34]

Of particular significance for the private law of the European Union has been a resolution of 26 May 1989 by the European Parliament calling upon the member states to begin with the necessary preparations for the drafting of a uniform European code of contract law.[35] This was reemphasized in another resolution of 6 May 1994 which specifically endorsed and supported the work of the Commission on European Contract Law.[36] The Principles of European Contract Law were also warmly welcomed at the symposium 'Towards a European Civil Code' that was organized by the Dutch government early in 1997, at a time when the Netherlands chaired the Council of the European Union.[37]

V OTHER PROJECTS

Another initiative that has to be mentioned in the present context are the Principles of International Commercial Contracts, prepared by the International Institute for the Unification of Private Law in Rome (Unidroit) and published

[34] See Michael R. Will, *International Sales Law Under CISG: The First 284 or so Decisions* (1996); for Germany, see Ulrich Magnus, 'Stand und Entwicklung des UN-Kaufrechts', (1995) 3 *Zeitschrift für Europäisches Privatrecht* 202ff.; Magnus, 'Das UN-Kaufrecht: Fragen und Probleme seiner praktischen Bewährung', (1997) 5 *Zeitschrift für Europäisches Privatrecht* 823ff.; Magnus, 'Wesentliche Fragen des UN-Kaufrechts', (1999) 7 *Zeitschrift für Europäisches Privatrecht* 642ff.

[35] See (1993) 1 *Zeitschrift für Europäisches Privatrecht* 613ff.

[36] See (1995) 3 *Zeitschrift für Europäisches Privatrecht* 669 and the comments by Winfried Tilmann, 'Zweiter Kodifikationsbeschluß des europäischen Parlaments', (1995) 3 *Zeitschrift für Europäisches Privatrecht* 534ff.

[37] See, e.g., the report by Winfried Tilmann, 'Towards a European Civil Code', (1997) 5 *Zeitschrift für Europäisches Privatrecht* 595ff., and the contributions collected in (1997) 5 *European Review of Private Law* 455ff.

late in 1994.[38] Their structure is similar to that of the
Principles: each provision is followed by corresponding comments and illustrations. Comparative notes have, however,
been deliberately excluded. It is unclear how this is supposed
to emphasize the international character of the rules.[39] The
Unidroit project[40] differs from that of the Commission on
European Contract Law mainly in the fact that its objective
is global, rather than merely European. As early as 1971,
a group of three prominent comparative lawyers representing the civil law, common law and socialist legal families
were entrusted with the preparation of the project, until,
almost simultaneously with the Commission on European
Contract Law, a working group of almost twenty members
started with the preparation of a set of Principles. That group
included, among others, members from the United States,

---

[38] Unidroit (ed.), *Principles of International Commercial Contracts* (1994). See
also Michael Joachim Bonell, *An International Restatement of Contract Law*
(2nd edn, 1997). A German translation of the entire book has appeared
under the title *Grundregeln der internationalen Handelsverträge ('Unidroit-
Prinzipien')*; for the text of the articles, see also Schulze and Zimmermann
(n. 2) III.15.

[39] Unidroit, *Principles* (n. 38) viii.

[40] On which see, e.g., Jürgen Basedow, 'Die Unidroit-Prinzipien der inter-
nationalen Handelsverträge und das deutsche Recht', in *Gedächtnisschrift
für Alexander Lüderitz* (2000), pp. 1ff.; Klaus-Peter Berger, 'Die Unidroit-
Prinzipien für internationale Handelsverträge: Indiz für ein autonomes
Wirtschaftsrecht?', (1995) *Zeitschrift für Vergleichende Rechtswissenschaft*
217ff.; Michael Joachim Bonell, 'Die Unidroit-Prinzipien der internationalen
Handelsverträge: Eine neue Lex Mercatoria?', (1996) 37 *Zeitschrift für
Rechtsvergleichung* 152ff.; Arthur Hartkamp, 'The Unidroit Principles for
International Commercial Contracts and the Principles of European Contract
Law', (1994) 2 *European Review of Private Law* 341ff.; Johann Christian
Wichard, 'Die Anwendung der Unidroit-Prinzipien für internationale Handelsverträge durch Schiedsgerichte und staatliche Gerichte', (1996) 60 *RabelsZ*
269ff.; and the contributions by various authors published in (1992) 40 *American Journal of Comparative Law* 617ff. and in (1995) 69 *Tulane Law Review*
1121ff.

Japan, China, Australia, Québec and Ghana. Like the Commission on European Contract Law the Unidroit working group consists predominantly of professors, though some of them simultaneously pursue careers in practice. A certain degree of co-ordination between the two groups was (and continues to be) achieved as a result of the fact that several members belonged (and continue to belong) to both of them. In most areas both sets of Principles follow a very similar approach and come to similar, or even identical, solutions. By the time when Part I of the Principles of European Contract Law was published, the Unidroit Principles were ahead insofar as they already contained rules on formation, validity and interpretation. With the publication of the consolidated version of Parts I and II the Commission on European Contract Law has taken the lead in that it includes rules on the authority of agents. Unidroit is currently dealing with this topic; apart from that, it has an agenda which very largely corresponds to that of the European Contract Law Commission.[41]

Other projects aiming at providing sets of Principles of European Private Law are under way. In Pavia an 'Academy of European Private Lawyers' established itself in 1990 and

---

[41] For further discussion of the Principles of European Contract Law and the Unidroit Principles of International Commercial Contracts, of their legal nature and their relationship with the national legal systems, and of other means of unifying international commercial law, see Klaus Peter Berger, *The Creeping Codification of the Lex Mercatoria* (1999); Berger, 'Einheitliche Rechtsstrukturen durch außergesetzliche Rechtsvereinheitlichung', (1999) *Juristenzeitung* 369ff.; Franco Ferrari, 'Das Verhältnis zwischen den Unidroit-Grundsätzen und den allgemeinen Grundsätzen internationaler Einheitsprivatrechtskonventionen', (1998) *Juristenzeitung* 9ff.; Ralf Michaels, 'Privatautonomie und Privatkodifikation: Zu Anwendbarkeit und Geltung allgemeiner Vertragsrechtsprinzipien', (1998) 67 *RabelsZ* 580ff.; Paul-A. Crépeau and Elise M. Charpentier, *Les Principes d'Unidroit et le Code civil du Québec: valeurs partagées?* (1998); and the contributions to Jürgen Basedow (ed.), *Europäische Vertragsrechtsvereinheitlichung und deutsches Recht* (2000).

is busy, under the direction of Giuseppe Gandolfi, drafting a European Contract Code.[42] The approach and methodology adopted by the Academy appear to be quite different from that of both the Commission on European Contract Law and Unidroit. In particular, the Academy has decided to adopt as models for its work Book IV of the Italian *codice civile* (as taking an intermediate position between the two principal strands which form the continental civil law, i.e., the French and the German) and the McGregor Code.[43] In 1999 an International Working Group on European Trust Law produced a volume entitled *Principles of European Trust Law*, containing a set of principles, a commentary and national reports for Scotland, Germany, Switzerland, Italy, France, Spain, Denmark and the Netherlands.[44] Since 1992 a group of scholars in the area of delict/tort has met on a regular basis to discuss fundamental issues of delictual liability and the future structure and direction of a European law of tort/delict. Several volumes dealing with individual issues of central importance have been published;[45] on this basis a set of European Principles will be elaborated. The most ambitious project, so far, is the Study Group on a European Civil Code which was established in 1998 by Christian von Bar and which aims at identifying fundamental rules covering the law relating to economic assets (or the patrimony)

---

[42] See, e.g., Giuseppe Gandolfi, 'Pour un code européen des contrats', (1992) *Revue internationale de droit comparé* 707ff.

[43] See n. 30.

[44] D. J. Hayton, S. C. J. J. Kortmann and H. L. E. Verhagen, *Principles of European Trust Law* (1999).

[45] Jaap Spier (ed.), *The Limits of Liability* (1996); Spier (ed.), *The Limits of Expanding Liability* (1998); Helmut Koziol, *Unification of Tort Law: Wrongfulness* (1998); for general background, see Ulrich Magnus, 'Elemente eines europäischen Deliktsrechts', (1998) 6 *Zeitschrift für Europäisches Privatrecht* 602ff.; Spier and Olav A. Haazen, 'The European Group on Tort Law ("Tilburg Group") and the European Principles of Tort Law', (1999) 7 *Zeitschrift für Europäisches Privatrecht* 469ff.

at large.[46] Three working groups have been established, one in Osnabrück dealing with non-contractual obligations, one in Hamburg dealing with secured transactions and financial services and one in Tilburg/Utrecht dealing with sales and services. These rules will be presented, eventually, in the form of a Restatement with commentary. The Principles of European Contract Law will form an integral part of this overarching structure.

I should perhaps add that personally I have regarded my work in the (third) Commission on European Contract Law as a particularly stimulating opportunity for furthering the development of a European legal scholarship in the field of private law. This, I think, is of far greater importance today than the implementation of a European code of contract law.[47] Even if such a code should, one day, be implemented,[48]

---

[46] Christian von Bar, 'Die Study Group on a European Civil Code', in *Festschrift für Dieter Henrich* (2000), pp. 1ff.

[47] I have expressed my views, in that regard, in 'Savigny's Legacy: Legal History, Comparative Law, and the Emergence of a European Legal Science', (1996) 112 *Law Quarterly Review* 576ff. and in the Clarendon Lectures for 1999 which will by published by Oxford University Press in 2001 under the title *Roman Law, Contemporary Law, European Law: The Civilian Tradition Today*. See also, e.g., the discussion in Reiner Schulze, 'Allgemeine Rechtsgrundsätze und europäisches Privatrecht', (1993) 1 *Zeitschrift für Europäisches Privatrecht* 442ff.; Christoph Schmid, 'Anfänge einer transnationalen Privatrechtswissenschaft in Europa', (1999) 40 *Zeitschrift für Rechtsvergleichung* 213ff.; Jürgen Basedow, 'Anforderungen an eine europäische Zivilrechtsdogmatik', in Reinhard Zimmermann, Rolf Knütel and Jens Peter Meincke (eds.), *Rechtsgeschichte und Privatrechtsdogmatik* (2000), pp. 79ff.

[48] For forceful arguments in favour of a code on the law of obligations, see Winfried Tilmann, 'Artikel 100 a EGV als Grundlage für ein Europäisches Zivilgesetzbuch', in *Festskrift* (n. 15) 351ff.; Jürgen Basedow, 'Das BGB im künftigen europäischen Privatrecht: Der hybride Kodex', (2000) 200 *Archiv für die Civilistische Praxis* 445ff.; see also Ole Lando, 'The Principles of European Contract Law After Year 2000', in Franz Werro (ed.), *New Perspectives on European Private Law* (1998), pp. 59ff. and the contributions to Dieter Martiny and Norman Witzleb (eds.), *Auf dem Wege zu einem Europäischen*

it will benefit much from the kind of intensive scholarly endeavour that preceded the drafting of the German Civil Code at the end of the nineteenth century. Primarily, therefore, I see the Principles of European Contract Law as an attempt to provide a starting point and conceptual focus for a discussion of problems in contract law transcending the borders of the individual legal systems; and also as a yardstick against which the solutions in the national legal systems may be evaluated. The Principles, in other words, might serve a similar function as did Roman law in those parts of nineteenth-century Germany where a codification of private law (the Prussian code, the Austrian code, the *code civil*, the Saxonian Civil Code, etc.) prevailed: they may constitute a conceptual basis for the comprehension of all particular laws prevailing in Europe.[49]

Zivilgesetzbuch (1999). For a contrary view, e.g., Pierre Legrand, 'Against a European Civil Code', (1997) 60 *Modern Law Review* 44ff.

[49] See, for nineteenth-century Germany, Paul Koschaker, *Europa und das römische Recht* (4th edn, 1966), p. 292; see also Reiner Schulze, 'Vergleichende Gesetzesauslegung und Rechtsangleichung', (1997) *Zeitschrift für Rechtsvergleichung* 193. For first steps in that direction concerning Québec and German law, see Crépeau and Charpentier and the contributions in Basedow (both n. 41).

1

CONTOURS OF A EUROPEAN LAW
OF SET-OFF

I SIX PRELIMINARY POINTS

For the purposes of this chapter, the following legal systems have been taken into account: Austrian law, Dutch law, English law, French law, German law, Greek law, Italian law, Scots law, Spanish law and Swedish law. Belgian, Danish, Finnish, Irish and Portuguese law have been insufficiently accessible to me.[1] Following the approach adopted, for instance, by Zweigert and Kötz,[2] French, English and German law are regarded as the prime exponents of the three major 'legal families' traditionally recognized within Europe.[3] Specific attention will also be paid to Dutch and Italian law in view of the fact that both countries, in the process of recodifying their private law, have drawn on the (continental) comparative experience and can no longer simply be regarded as

---

[1] Danish law, in this area, largely corresponds to Swedish law: see B. Gomard, *Obligationsret*, 3rd part (1993), pp. 177ff. and the overview by Inger Dübeck, *Einführung in das dänische Recht* (1996), pp. 199f.; Belgian law is very similar to French law: see H. de Page, *Traité élémentaire de droit civil Belge*, vol. III (3rd edn, 1967), pp. 613ff. and the overview by J. Herbots, *Contract Law in Belgium* (1995), n. 387.

[2] Konrad Zweigert and Hein Kötz, *Introduction to Comparative Law* (3rd edn, 1998, transl. Tony Weir), pp. 323ff.

[3] On the notion of 'legal families' and its usefulness for comparative studies, see Hein Kötz, 'Abschied von der Rechtskreislehre?', (1998) 6 *Zeitschrift für Europäisches Privatrecht* 493ff.

members of the 'Romanistic' legal family.[4] But, as will become apparent, other legal systems (such as, in the present context, the Nordic ones) are also able to contribute valuable experiences.[5]

The first two propositions are straightforward. (i) All legal systems under consideration recognize that a debtor may, under certain circumstances, defeat his creditor's claim in view of a cross-claim against that creditor. All legal systems, in other words, recognize the institution of set-off (compensation/Aufrechnung/verrekening/kvittning).[6] (ii) The most important effect of set-off in all legal systems consists in a discharge of the obligations of the debtor

---

[4] As far as the *codice civile* is concerned see, e.g., Giorgio Cian, 'Fünfzig Jahre italienischer Codice civile', (1993) 1 *Zeitschrift für Europäisches Privatrecht* 120ff.; concerning the Burgerlijk Wetboek, see Ulrich Drobnig, 'Das neue niederländische Gesetzbuch aus rechtsvergleichender Sicht', (1993) 1 *European Review of Private Law* 171ff. Generally on the idea of codification in contemporary Europe, see above pp. 9ff.

[5] On the fundamental unity of private law in the Nordic countries, see Zweigert and Kötz (n. 2) 276ff.; Gebhard Carsten, 'Europäische Integration und nordische Zusammenarbeit auf dem Gebiet des Zivilrechts', (1993) *Zeitschrift für Europäisches Privatrecht* 335ff.; see also the observations in Simon Whittaker and Reinhard Zimmermann, 'Good Faith in European Contract Law: Surveying the Legal Landscape', in Reinhard Zimmermann and Simon Whittaker (eds.), *Good Faith in European Contract Law* (2000), pp. 55ff.

[6] It should, however, be noted that set-off tends to be recognized only at a fairly mature stage within the development of a legal system. For Roman law, see Heinrich Dernburg, *Geschichte und Theorie der Kompensation* (2nd edn, 1868), pp. 15ff.; W. W. Buckland and Peter Stein, *A Textbook of Roman Law from Augustus to Justinian* (3rd edn, 1963), p. 703; Michael E. Tigar, 'Automatic Extinction of Cross-Demands: Compensatio from Rome to California', (1965) 53 *California Law Review* 226ff. For medieval Germanic law, see Werner Ogris, 'Aufrechnung', in *Handwörterbuch zur deutschen Rechtsgeschichte*, vol. 1 (1971), cols. 254ff. For France, see Dernburg 272ff. For English law, see Roy Goode, *Legal Problems of Credit and Security* (2nd edn, 1988), pp. 132ff.; Rory Derham, *Set-Off* (2nd edn, 1996), pp. 7ff.

and the creditor towards each other, as far as they are coextensive.[7]

Two more preliminary points should be uncontroversial. (iii) All legal systems allow set-off by agreement: two parties may agree to discharge their mutual obligations by setting off one against the other.[8] This follows from the general recognition of freedom of contract. The admissibility of contractual set-off appears to be so self-evident that most codifications do not even mention it.[9] (iv) Set-off must be distinguished from counterclaim ('Widerklage').[10] The latter is a purely

---

[7] France: 'les deux dettes s'éteignent réciproquement' (Art. 1290 *code civil*); England: 'to the extent of his set-off . . . discharged from performance' (*Halsbury's Laws of England*, vol. XLII (4th edn, 1983), n. 410); Germany: 'daß die Forderungen, soweit sie sich decken, als . . . erloschen gelten' (§ 389 BGB); Netherlands: 'gaan beide verbintenissen tot hun gemeenschappelijk beloop teniet' (Art. 6:127 BW).

[8] See the overview provided by Philip R. Wood, *English and International Set-Off* (1989), 24-43ff.; for England, see Derham (n. 6) 540ff.; for Scotland: William W. McBryde, *The Law of Contract in Scotland* (1987), 22-70; for Germany: Joachim Gernhuber, *Die Erfüllung und ihre Surrogate* (1994), pp. 326ff.; for Austria: Silvia Dullinger, *Handbuch der Aufrechnung* (1995), pp. 295ff. There is now a comprehensive monograph by Klaus-Peter Berger, *Der Aufrechnungsvertrag* (1996). Usually the parties resort to set-off by agreement if one or other of the normal requirements for set-off is not met. This is particularly obvious for the French *compensation conventionnelle*, or *facultative*; see François Terré, Philippe Simler and Yves Lequette, *Droit Civil: Les Obligations* (5th edn, 1993), n. 1312. An agreement for a current account implies that the debits and credits will be set off against each other at each balancing of the account; on set-off in current account relationships, see Wood, 3-1ff.; Berger, 173, 285ff.; Art. 6:140 BW; C. J. van Zeben, J. W. du Pon and M. M. Olthoff, *Parlementaire Geschiedenis van het Nieuwe Burgerlijk Wetboek*, Boek 6 (1981), pp. 517ff.; for a comparative evaluation, see Wood, 24-36ff.

[9] But see Art. 1252 *codice civile* (compensazione voluntaria).

[10] For France, see Terré, Simler and Lequette (n. 8) n. 1313; for England, see Sheelagh McCracken, *The Banker's Remedy of Set-Off* (1993), pp. 117ff.; Wood (n. 8) 6-1ff.; Derham (n. 6) 2f.; Gerhard Kegel, *Probleme der Aufrechnung: Gegenseitigkeit und Liquidität rechtsvergleichend dargestellt* (1938), pp. 14ff.; for Germany, see Leo Rosenberg, Karl-Heinz Schwab and Peter Gottwald, *Zivilprozeßrecht* (15th edn, 1993), pp. 552ff.

procedural device which, under certain circumstances, allows the court to consider the claimant's action and an independent cross-action brought by the defendant in the same proceedings. The present paper does not deal with counterclaim but confines itself to set-off.

(v) A note on terminology: six member states of the European Union use a term derived from the Latin 'compensatio'. Austrian law uses it as an alternative to 'Aufrechnung'.[11] And even though 'set-off' is now in common use in Scotland, the traditional Scottish term is 'compensation'.[12] Since it is therefore used, or at least understood, in the three major linguistic families within the EU, the term 'compensation' may well be regarded as the most suitable choice for a set of principles of European law. On the other hand, however, it must also be taken into account that 'compensation' has a different meaning for English lawyers[13] and might therefore be a source of ambiguity or misunderstanding. Thus, somewhat reluctantly, we will continue to use the term 'set-off'. (vi) Set-off has not traditionally been a topic to which a large amount of scholarly attention has been devoted.[14] In some countries there are now signs of a change in attitude.[15] But the comparative literature remains very sparse.[16] At the same time, it

[11] See Helmut Koziol and Rudolf Welser, *Grundriß des bürgerlichen Rechts*, vol. 1 (10th edn, 1995), p. 277.
[12] McBryde (n. 8) 22-48; see also *The Laws of Scotland: Stair Memorial Encyclopedia*, vol. xv (1996), n. 877.
[13] See, e.g., David M. Walker, *The Oxford Companion to Law* (1980), p. 262; Peter Cane, *The Anatomy of Tort Law* (1997), pp. 103ff., 231ff.
[14] This may be due to the fact that 'set-off is a body of law that offers fearsome technicalities but few issues that really stir the blood' (see the quotation in Derham (n. 6) vii).
[15] Particularly in England. See the monographs by Goode, McCracken and Derham (nn. 6, 10) and the handbook by Wood (n. 8). For Germany, see the work by Berger (n. 8); for Austria the work by Dullinger (n. 8).
[16] For significant contributions, see Wilhelm Haudek, 'Kompensation (Aufrechnung)', in *Rechtsvergleichendes Handwörterbuch für das Zivil- und*

should be noted that set-off is of very considerable practical significance, on both a national and an international level.[17] It covers an enormous range of situations, including, perhaps most prominently, banking relationships.[18] The present paper, however, attempts to map out the contours of a general regime of set-off without taking account of specificities arising in the field of banking law.

II PROCEDURAL OR SUBSTANTIVE NATURE OF SET-OFF?

1 A civil law/common law divide?

The first important issue to be determined is whether set-off should be regarded as a purely procedural device or as a matter of substantive law. At first blush, we appear to be dealing with a clear-cut civil law/common law divide with Scotland, in this instance,[19] joining English law. Roy Goode, in particular, has emphasized the purely procedural character of

Handelsrecht des In- und Auslandes (ed. F. Schlegelberger), vol. V (1936), pp. 58ff.; Kegel (n. 10); Heiko Eujen, *Die Aufrechnung im internationalen Verkehr zwischen Deutschland, Frankreich und England* (1975); Wood (n. 8) 24-1ff. Most recently, see the comparative remarks, focusing on Italian law, by Giorgio Cian, 'Hundert Jahre BGB aus italienischer Sicht', (1998) 6 *Zeitschrift für Europäisches Privatrecht* 219ff. and Gerhard Wagner, 'Die Aufrechnung im europäischen Zivilprozeß', (1999) *Praxis des Internationalen Privat- und Verfahrensrechts* 65ff.

[17] '[It] plays a crucial role in international financial and commercial affairs': Wood (n. 8) vii.

[18] The 'Banker's Remedy of Set-Off' (see the title of Sheelagh McCracken's book) was prominent in Roman law already; it was referred to as *agere cum compensatione*. For details see the literature quoted in n. 25.

[19] On the traditionally close relationship between Scots law and continental civil law, see, however, the contributions in David L. Carey Miller and Reinhard Zimmermann (eds.), *The Civilian Tradition and Scots Law: Aberdeen Quincentenary Essays* (1997); on its development as a mixed legal system, see Kenneth Reid and Reinhard Zimmermann, *A History of Private Law in Scotland*, 2 vols. (2000).

set-off.[20] All continental legal systems, on the other hand, agree on the substantive nature of set-off. This difference, according to Professor Goode,[21] is reflected in the fact that the civilian set-off operates retrospectively to extinguish the claim *pro tanto* at the moment the cross-claim becomes due, whereas set-off in English law takes effect on and from the date of judgment. English law, in other words, is based on a two-stage inquiry. The courts first have to determine whether, as a matter of substantive law, the defendant owes to the claimant the sum claimed by the latter. If this has been established, judgment would normally have to be against the defendant. In view of the defendant's claim against the claimant, the court may now dismiss the claim (or grant judgment for a reduced sum).[22] But up to the moment of judgment, the defendant is liable to the claimant for the full amount of the claimant's claim. This has a number of consequences.[23] Most importantly, perhaps, neither the mere assertion of the cross-claim nor its assertion prior to legal proceedings provides justification for withholding payment. As a result, the claimant is not prevented from exercising his extrajudicial rights and remedies for default, such as termination of the contract.

2 *The civilian experience*

Upon closer inspection, however, the differences between the English and continental models of set-off do not appear to

---

[20] Goode (n. 6) 132f., 138ff.; and see the references in McCracken (n. 6) 113ff. But cf. Roy Goode, *Commercial Law* (2nd edn, 1995), p. 671 ('What is not clear is whether set-off is purely procedural, so that it does not relieve the defendant from liability in respect of the plaintiff's claim except at the point of judgment, or whether in certain circumstances it operates as a substantive defence').

[21] Goode (n. 6) 139.   [22] See, e.g., *Halsbury* (n. 7) n. 410.

[23] See Wood (n. 8) 2-192ff.; Goode (n. 6) 144f.

be quite as deeply rooted. In the first place it has to be remembered that the continental model originated in Roman law. Yet one of the most characteristic features of set-off in Roman law was its distinctly procedural flavour.[24] Whether – and, if so, in which manner and under which circumstances – a set-off could be effected depended entirely on the nature of the formula applicable in a given situation. Four different regimes were eventually developed:[25] the one relating to *bonae fidei iudicia*, the next to *actiones stricti iuris* in general, the third to a specific *actio stricti iuris* concerning bankers (*argentarii*) where an automatic set-off was built into the formula and the fourth one operating with regard to debts due to an insolvent estate. With the demise of the classical formulary procedure, we find a trend towards assimilation and generalization which culminated in Justinian's Corpus Juris Civilis.[26] According to Inst. IV, 6, 30, Justinian's streamlined form of set-off operated 'ut actiones ipso iure minuant'.[27] This phrase, which seems to be in strange contrast to the language used in other places of the Corpus Juris,[28] has given rise to intense disputes lasting from the thirteenth to

---

[24] Both Gaius and Justinian deal with set-off as part of their discussion of the law of actions: Gai. IV, 61ff.; Inst. IV, 6, 30. For modern English law see, e.g., Peter Birks (ed.), *English Private Law*, vol. II (2000), where set-off is dealt with in the chapter on civil procedure (19.174ff.).

[25] For details, see Max Kaser, *Das römische Privatrecht: Erster Abschnitt* (2nd edn, 1971), pp. 644ff.; Reinhard Zimmermann, *The Law of Obligations: Roman Foundations of the Civilian Tradition* (1990, paperback edn 1996), pp. 761ff.

[26] See Max Kaser, *Das römische Privatrecht: Zweiter Abschnitt* (2nd edn, 1975), pp. 447f.; Zimmermann (n. 25) 766f.

[27] See also C. 4, 31, 14: 'Compensationes ex omnibus actionibus ipso iure fieri sancimus.'

[28] See C. 4, 31, 14, 1 ('compensationis obici iubemus', 'opponi compensationem'). Whether texts like C. 4, 31, 4, Paul. D. 16, 2, 4 and Paul. D. 16, 2, 21 are interpolated (as is very widely assumed) needs to be examined again. The phrase 'ipso iure' may have been used by the classical jurists.

the twentieth centuries.[29] Two different schools of thought eventually emerged. The one found its clearest expression in Art. 1290 *code civil*: 'La compensation s'opère de plein droit par la seule force de la loi, même à l'insu des débiteurs.'[30] As soon as (and to the extent that) two debts capable of being set off against each other confront each other, both of them are extinguished *ipso iure*.[31] French courts and legal writers have not, however, found it practical to implement this regime in its most literal and uncompromising form. Set-off is held to be effective only if the defendant raises it in court.[32] Strictly speaking, therefore, the automatic discharge of the two debts confronting each other is subject to a *condicio iuris* that the defence of compensation be pleaded in court.[33]

The other school of thought, dating back to the glossator Azo,[34] always insisted on the necessity of a declaration by

---

[29] For details, see Dernburg (n. 6) 281ff.; Fridolin Eisele, *Die Compensation nach römischem und gemeinem Recht* (1876), pp. 211; Tigar, (1965) 53 *California Law Review* 235ff.; Otto Prausnitz, *Die Geschichte der Forderungsverrechnung* (1928), pp. 133ff.; J. H. Loots and P. van Warmelo, 'Compensatio', (1956) 19 *Tydskrif vir Hedendaagse Romeins-Hollandse Reg* 176ff.; Pascal Pichonnaz, 'The Retroactive Effect of Set-Off (Compensatio)', (2000) 68 *Tijdschrift voor rechtsgeschiedenis* 547ff.

[30] Essentially the same regime was adopted in the Netherlands (Art. 1462 old BW), in Spain (Art. 1.202 *código civil*), in Italy (Art. 1286 *codice civile* of 1865) and also in Austria (§ 1438 ABGB).

[31] On the term 'ipso iure' in this context, see Robert Joseph Pothier, *Traité des obligations*, in *Oeuvres*, Paris (1835), § 635: 'Cette interprétation est conforme à l'explication que tous les lexicographes donnent à ces termes, ipso iure. Ipso iure fieri dicitur, dit Brisson, quod ipsa legis potestate et auctoritate, absque magistratus auxilio et sine exceptionis ope fit . . . Verba ipso iure, dit Spigelius, intellegitur sine facto hominis. Ipso iure consistere dicitur, dit Pratejus, quod ex sola legum potestate et auctoritate, sine magistratus opera consistit.'

[32] Terré, Simler and Lequette (n. 8) n. 1311 ('en dépit de la lettre de l'article 1290').

[33] Haudek (n. 16) 64.

[34] '[S]ed ego puto ea[m] ipso iure tunc demum fieri cum a partibus est opposita': *Summa Codicis*, Lib. IV, 'De compensationibus rubrica' (p. 140, left column, in Azo, *Summa Codiciis*, Lugduni, 1552).

the defendant in the course of the legal proceedings brought against him, to set off his claim against that of the claimant. The effect of that declaration, however, is retroactive: the claims are 'deemed to have expired, *pro tanto*, at the moment when they first confronted each other being suitable for set-off'.[35] Down to the end of the nineteenth century, it was maintained by influential authors that the *exceptio compensationis* had to be raised in court.[36] The draftsmen of the BGB eventually decided to give in to a strong tendency to regard an extrajudicial declaration to the other party as sufficient to effect set-off.[37] While, therefore, the substantive character of set-off is undisputed in both French and German law, it is still remarkable that there traditionally used to be (Germany) or still is (France) a procedural side to it.

3 *The English experience*

Secondly, the differences are also reduced in significance if we look at the English experience. Set-off in English law developed slowly. General recognition of set-off was only brought about by two statutes dating from the first half of the eighteenth century.[38] According to s. 13 of the Insolvent Debtors

---

[35] See § 389 BGB.

[36] See Dernburg (n. 6) 529ff.; Bernhard Windscheid and Theodor Kipp, *Lehrbuch des Pandektenrechts* (9th edn, 1906 (reprint 1963)), § 349, 5 (acknowledging, however, that the contrary view was widespread in practice); cf. also Pichonnaz, (2000) 68 *Tijdschrift voor rechtsgeschiedenis* 552ff.

[37] For the background, see Franz von Kübel, *Recht der Schuldverhältnisse*, part 1 of Werner Schubert (ed.), *Die Vorlagen für die erste Kommission zur Ausarbeitung des Entwurfs eines Bürgerlichen Gesetzbuches* (1980), pp. 1075ff.; 'Motive', in Benno Mugdan, *Die gesammten Materialien zum Bürgerlichen Gesetzbuch für das Deutsche Reich*, vol. II (1899), pp. 58f. The same approach has been adopted in Greece (Art. 441 ZGB) and in the Netherlands (Art. 6:127 (1) BW).

[38] For details, see William H. Loyd, 'The Development of Set-Off', (1916) 64 *University of Pennsylvania Law Review* 551ff.; Goode (n. 6) 133ff.; McCracken (n. 10) 53ff.; Derham (n. 6) 9ff.

Relief Act of 1729 (which was confirmed and amended by s. 4 of the Debtors Relief Amendment Act of 1735), where there are mutual debts between the claimant and the defendant, 'one Debt may be set against the other'. These Statutes of Set-Off were designed to avoid circuity of action and multiplicity of suits.[39] At the same time, they aimed at mitigating the rigour of the common law:[40] recognition of set-off, so it was stated, was 'highly just and reasonable at all times'.[41] Prior to the enactment of the statutes, the Court of Chancery had occasionally intervened in order to assist defendants on the basis of a cross-claim against the claimant.[42] But equitable relief was usually either founded upon a custom that the accounts should be balanced, or on an implied agreement to this effect.[43] Apart from that, set-off was recognized in bankruptcy.[44] The Statutes of Set-Off stimulated the Court of Chancery to develop a set of rules which came to be known as equitable set-off and covered a considerably wider range of cases.[45] The resulting

[39] See, e.g., *Hutchison v. Sturges*, (1741) Willes 261, 125 ER 1163, at 1163–4 (per Willes, C. J.) and the references in Derham (n. 6) 9.

[40] Goode (n. 6) 135.   [41] See McCracken (n. 10) 54.

[42] See the references in Loyd, (1916) 64 *University of Pennsylvania Law Review* 547ff.; Goode (n. 6) 134; and Derham (n. 6) 7f., 38. There may be an intellectual link between cross-claim in Chancery and the civilian *reconventio* (counterclaim) procedure; Tigar, (1965) 53 *California Law Review* 249 refers to (Lord Chief Justice) Gilbert, *The History and Practice of the High Court of Chancery* (1758), pp. 45ff., for this proposition. It is not unlikely that proceedings in Chancery may have been inspired, more particularly, by the treatment of cross-demands in canon law. The canonists referred to 'mutuae petitiones' (which, in turn, they took from C. 4, 31, 6): see Tigar, 242ff.

[43] Derham (n. 6) 7.

[44] For the development of insolvency set-off, see Goode (n. 6) 134f.; Derham (n. 6) 158ff.

[45] For details, see Goode (n. 6) 136f.; McCracken (n. 10) 57ff.; Derham (n. 6) 38ff. Civilian ideas may have played a role: Kegel (n. 10) 12; Loyd, (1916) 64 *University of Pennsylvania Law Review* 546ff.; and see the discussion by Joseph Story, *Commentaries on Equity Jurisprudence* vol. II (13th edn, 1886

discrepancy between equitable and statutory set-off has been considerably reduced as a result of the fusion of common law and equitable jurisdiction by the Supreme Court of Judicature Act of 1873. All courts are now empowered to administer both equity and law. Still, modern authors continue to distinguish between statutory and equitable set-off even though it is acknowledged that, as a result of the expansion of the latter, the former has become of significantly less importance.[46]

It is obvious that, like its continental counterpart, set-off originated as a procedural device. Much less obvious is the answer to the question whether it still has to be considered in this light. For even if it has to be pleaded in court, such a plea may still be based on a substantive defence. This is indeed the view increasingly taken by modern English commentators, as far as equitable set-off, or at least certain forms of it, are concerned.[47] The arguments advanced are complex and largely, of course, turn on the correct interpretation of the relevant case law. It is not possible to attempt, within the wider framework of this chapter, to present an independent evaluation of these cases and come to a considered conclusion as to the true nature of set-off in English law. Still, it is significant to note that a strong body of opinion now favours

(reprint 1988)), nn. 1430ff.; William David Evans and Robert Joseph Pothier, *A Treatise on the Law of Obligations*, translated from the French, vol. II (Appendix) (1826), pp. 98ff.; and Tigar, (1965) 53 *California Law Review* 249ff. Roman law was discussed in, *inter alia*, *Whitaker v. Rush*, (1761) Amb., 27 ER 272 and *Freeman v. Lomas*, (1851) 9 Hare 109, 68 ER 435, 437. Lord Mansfield's statement in *Green v. Farmer*, (1768) 4 Burr. 2214, 98 ER 154 ('Natural equity says, that cross-demands should compensate each other, by deducting the lesser sum from the greater; and that the difference is the only sum which can be justly due') is often referred to. Lord Mansfield, however, continues: 'But positive law, for the sake of the forms of proceedings and convenience of trial, has said that each must sue and recover separately.'

[46] Goode (n. 6) 154f.

[47] McCracken (n. 10) 111ff.; Derham (n. 6) 56ff.; Wood (n. 8) 4-1ff.

the substantive nature of equitable set-off.[48] There is, as yet, no agreement, as to what exactly that entails. According to Derham,[49] the creditor as a matter of equity is not entitled to treat the debtor as being indebted to him if there is an entitlement to an equitable set-off. While the cross-demands, as a matter of law, remain in existence between the parties until extinguished by judgment, it is unconscionable, in equity, for the creditor even before then to regard the debtor as being in default under these circumstances. Philip R. Wood goes even further when he asserts that set-off may be exercised either as a self-help remedy or in judicial proceedings and that, for default purposes, it should be retroactive to the time when the debtor's cross-claim accrued.[50]

From the point of view of comparative jurisprudence, the modern approach is attractive for at least two reasons. While it has never been doubted that insolvency set-off aims to do justice between the parties,[51] it recognizes that equitable set-off, too, is based on notions of fairness and natural justice.[52] As a result, all forms of set-off appear to be rooted in a common set of values and can thus be regarded as emanations of one and the same substantive idea rather than of somewhat idiosyncratic procedural technicalities. Such an analysis would, moreover, tie in very well with the underlying rationale traditionally advanced for set-off in continental jurisprudence: that a person who sues another for an amount which he is bound to pay to him is acting in contravention of the precepts of good faith (*dolo petit qui petit quod statim redditurus est*).[53] In the second place, there can be no doubt

---

[48] Derham (n. 6) 56ff.; Wood (n. 8) 4-1ff.   [49] Derham (n. 6) 57.

[50] Wood (n. 8) 4-24ff.   [51] McCracken (n. 10) 48ff.; Goode (n. 6) 135.

[52] See, in particular, McCracken (n. 10) 53ff., 66ff.

[53] Dernburg (n. 6) 361; Windscheid and Kipp (n. 36) § 349, 2; Börries von Feldmann, in *Münchener Kommentar zum Bürgerlichen Gesetzbuch*, vol. II (3rd edn, 1994), § 387, n. 1; Berger (n. 8) 61ff. The 'dolo petit' rule appears in Paul. D. 44, 4, 8 pr.

that both insolvency set-off and set-off by agreement are sub-stantive in nature. This is immediately obvious for the latter form of set-off: the parties agree extrajudicially to set off their mutual claims against each other.[54] But it is also generally acknowledged for insolvency set-off: it operates automati-cally upon the occurrence of a bankruptcy or a winding-up so as to bring about a set-off at that date.[55] Equitable set-off, however, is closely related to both insolvency set-off and contractual set-off and thus it would be awkward to qualify it as a merely procedural shield rather than as a substan-tive defence. It is closely related to *insolvency set-off* in that equitable considerations require the protection of a person who is sued even though he has a claim for the same amount against his creditors. His dilemma is only much more obvi-ous in cases where that creditor has become insolvent. This is the reason why insolvency set-off led the way towards a general recognition of set-off:[56] a substantive legal idea often gains momentum only when it has established itself in a sit-uation of specific distress.[57] Yet, it is still the same idea on account of which the defendant is seen to deserve protection. And equitable set-off is closely related to *contractual set-off* in that (i) before the enactment of the Statutes of Set-Off, equity tended to look for an implied agreement for a set-off,[58] and (ii) even today there is a considerable readiness on the part of the courts to infer such an agreement.[59] Both from a historical point of view and from a comparative perspec-tive there does not appear to be a sharp division but rather a sliding scale between equitable and contractual set-off.

[54] See also Goode (n. 6) 169.
[55] Goode (n. 6) 177; Derham (n. 6) 186ff.; see also McCracken (n. 10) 186ff.
[56] See Goode (n. 6) 134f.; McCracken (n. 10) 48ff.; Derham (n. 6) 158ff.
[57] Kegel (n. 10) 42.
[58] Derham (n. 6) 8 ('in the absence of an insolvency, equity at that time would look for evidence, however slight, of an agreement for a set-off').
[59] Goode (n. 6) 144.

4 *Evaluation*

The last point leads us to a more general comparative evaluation between set-off in England and on the continent. The fragmentation between statutory set-off, equitable set-off and insolvency set-off still today reflects the development of the notion of set-off in English legal history. On the one hand, of course, it was based on the jurisdictional distinction between law and equity which, in the meantime, has become obsolete. On the other hand, it is related to the traditional notion of the independence, in principle, of the mutual promises constituting a contract[60] (which, in turn, derives from the origin of modern English contract law in the action of *assumpsit*). But just as refined rules relating to breach of contract have been developed from this point of departure,[61] neither the notion of independent promises nor the formal distinction between warranties and conditions[62] (which has given way to a substantive inquiry into whether or not there was substantial failure of performance) should today stand in the way of a streamlined and substantive approach towards set-off. Even in England, arguably, a general contract law requires a general and uniform answer to the question of when a debtor may refuse to pay as a result of the fact that the creditor is under an obligation to pay the same, or a greater, sum to him. The progress from a fragmented to a streamlined and uniform approach, of course, implies a shift from procedure to substance. It has occurred in continental jurisprudence without having led to any adverse consequences. A set of European principles should therefore

---

[60] See also Goode (n. 6) 133.

[61] See Reinhard Zimmermann, "'Heard melodies are sweet, but those unheard are sweeter . . .".: Condicio tacita, implied condition und die Fortbildung des europäischen Vertragsrechts', (1993) 193 *Archiv für die Civilistische Praxis* 153ff., for an account of this development and for further references.

[62] Cf. the argument advanced by Goode (n. 6) 143.

opt for set-off as a substantive device. This is all the more desirable since there is, as yet, no uniform law of procedure which could accommodate a procedural conception.[63]

III SET-OFF *IPSO IURE* OR BY DECLARATION?

1 *Introduction*

The second problem to be resolved relates to the operation of (a substantive concept of) set-off. Five different models are distinguishable. Set-off may lead to the two obligations being discharged, *ipso iure*, as soon as they confront each other. This is the rule laid down in Art. 1290 *code civil*. However, as has been pointed out already,[64] French courts require set-off to be pleaded in court. In actual fact, therefore, they apply a second model: discharge *ipso iure* subject to the matter being raised by the defendant in subsequent judicial proceedings. This model has also been adopted in Spanish[65] and, at least at first blush, in Italian law.[66] The position in Scotland is similar but not identical (a third model): compensation must be pleaded in court and sustained by judgment before it has effect. If it is sustained, it works retrospectively.[67] It does not, therefore, operate *ipso iure*.[68]

---

[63] But see, e.g., Jeroen M. J. Chorus, 'Civilian Elements in European Civil Procedures', in Carey Miller and Zimmermann (n. 19) 295ff. (referring, *inter alia*, to a report by the Storme Commission, published in 1994); C. H. van Rhee, 'Civil Procedure: A European Ius Commune', (2000) 8 *European Review of Private Law* 589ff.

[64] See n. 32.

[65] See Art. 543 *in fine*, Ley de Enjuiciamento Civil (Civil Procedure Act).

[66] See Art. 1242 (1) *codice civile*: 'La compensazione estingue i due debiti dal giorno della loro coesistenza. Il giudice non può rilevarla d'ufficio.'

[67] McBryde (n. 12) 22-70; *Laws of Scotland* (n. 12) n. 877.

[68] In spite of James Viscount of Stair, *The Institutions of Scotland*, vol. 1 (4th edn, 1826), Book I, Tit. XVIII, VI ('for thereby two liquid obligations do extinguish each other ipso jure, and not ope exceptionis only').

Whether there is a practical difference between the second and the third model is not immediately clear. The fourth model is the one adopted first in German law: set-off has to be asserted by an extrajudicial, informal and unilateral declaration to the other party, whereupon it works retrospectively.[69] It has been followed in Austrian law (in spite of the fact that § 1438 ABGB would appear to endorse the *ipso iure* effect of set-off),[70] in Greece[71] and in the new Dutch Civil Code.[72] It also appears to enjoy widespread support in Italian law.[73] Finally, one can imagine a (fifth) model, in terms of which a declaration to set off one claim against another does not operate retrospectively but merely has *ex nunc* effect. This is the view to which, according to the prevailing opinion, Swedish law subscribes.[74]

Obviously therefore, set-off should not be allowed to operate *ipso iure* in the strict sense of the word: the obligations are discharged *sine facto hominis* and this state of affairs has to be taken account of *ex officio* in subsequent legal

[69] §§ 388f. BGB.

[70] Koziol and Welser (n. 11) 279, 280f.; Peter Rummel, in Peter Rummel, *Kommentar zum Allgemeinen Bürgerlichen Gesetzbuch* (2nd edn, 1992), § 1438, nn. 11, 14 (prevailing view).

[71] Art. 441 *Astikos Kodikas*; on which see Michael P. Stathopoulos, *Contract Law in Hellas* (1995), n. 241.

[72] Artt. 6:127 (1), 129 BW; on which, see A. S. Hartkamp, *Mr. C. Asser's Handleiding tot de Beoefening van het Nederlands Burgerlijk Recht*, Part I (11th edn, 2000), nn. 530, 538.

[73] See Massimo Bianca, *Diritto civile*, vol. IV (L'obbligazione) (1990), p. 494; Giorgio Cian and Alberto Trabucchi, *Commentario breve al Codice civile* (5th edn, 1997), Art. 1242 (2); P. Perlingueri, *Dei modi di estinzione delle obbligazioni diversi dell'adempimento* (1975), pp. 273ff.; Cian, (1998) 6 *Zeitschrift für Europäisches Privatrecht* 220f.

[74] There are no statutory provisions in Swedish law regulating the requirements and the effect of set-off ('kvittning'). The matter is thus left to custom, courts and legal writers. For details, see Stefan Lindskog, *Kvittning: Om avräkning mellan privaträttsliga fordringar* (1984), pp. 533ff., 526f. English law also merely attributes *ex nunc* effect to set-off: it takes effect on and from the date of judgment.

proceedings. It appears to be the common European experience that this kind of regime would pay insufficient attention to the requirements of legal certainty.

2 *Extrajudicial declaration or defence to be pleaded in court?*

Apart from that, there are two separate issues that may be distinguished. In the first place it has to be determined whether an extrajudicial and informal, unilateral declaration by one party to the other is sufficient or whether an *exceptio compensationis* has to be pleaded in court. The general drift of European legal development appears to be leading towards the former solution. This was the view already of the draftsmen of the German Civil Code who pointed to the Saxonian Civil Code (1863), to the draft code of Bavaria (1860–4), to the Dresden Draft of a General German Law of Obligations (1866) and to developments in Swiss legislation and in German legal practice,[75] and it has recently been confirmed by the draftsmen of the new Dutch Civil Code who have moved away from the French model and have essentially adopted the German one.[76] On a practical level, both solutions very largely coincide[77] and thus the choice is more one of technique than legal policy. In this respect, however, it is obvious that the French solution is merely an attempt to make the best of the practically unsatisfactory, and much criticized,[78] provision of Art. 1290 *code civil*. It is based on the doctrinal anomaly that an automatic discharge

---

[75] Von Kübel (n. 37) 1079, 1081.
[76] See *Parlementaire Geschiedenis* (n. 8) 489f., 494, 499; *Asser*/Hartkamp (n. 72) n. 530. Italian law has experienced a similar shift of approach towards the German model; see n. 71.
[77] For this view, see also Haudek (n. 16) 64; Kegel (n. 10) 9.
[78] See, e.g., Terré, Simler and Lequette (n. 8) n. 1309.

of an obligation may not automatically be taken into account in judicial proceedings involving this obligation. This, in turn, is usually justified by imputing a waiver to a defendant who does not raise the defence of set-off in the course of the legal proceedings initiated against him by the claimant:[79] an artificial construction that tends to contort the concept of a 'waiver'.

Moreover, the French solution which was originally more liberal in recognizing set-off would now appear to be marginally more restrictive as a result of requiring a declaration in court. From the point of view of legal certainty, this is unnecessarily rigorous since, as between the parties, an extrajudicial declaration is quite sufficient. As long as, however, legal certainty prevails, the general policy of the law should be to facilitate the exercise of a right of set-off. After all, it is squarely based upon the general principle of good faith,[80] as recognized in Art. 1:201 PECL[81] and leads to a considerable practical simplification in the implementation of payments. Moreover, if set-off aims to avoid circuity of action and multiplicity of suits,[82] a solution is arguably preferable which, at least occasionally, avoids a lawsuit altogether, rather than making the effect of set-off depend upon legal proceedings having been instituted. In many cases, of course, the same result could be arrived at by relying on set-off by agreement. But a creditor whose debtor has declared set-off does not always agree with the debtor's act in the sense that he can be taken to have concluded a contract with him concerning set-off. Often, he merely acquiesces in the mutual

---

[79] 'Rénonciation': Terré, Simler and Lequette (n. 8) n. 1310.

[80] See above, text before n. 53.

[81] On the questions of whether, and how far, this provision can be regarded as giving expression to a principle inherent in the national private laws of the member states in the European Union, see the case studies, the comparative observations and the final evaluation in Zimmermann and Whittaker (n. 5).

[82] See n. 39.

discharge of the obligations and any attempt to construe an agreement would be purely fictitious.

It is therefore proposed that set-off in European private law should operate on the basis of an informal, unilateral declaration which has to be communicated to the other party. If the matter subsequently comes to court, the judgment has a merely declaratory effect: it does not bring about the set-off but merely confirms that it has been brought about.[83]

3 *Retroactivity or* ex nunc *effect?*

Secondly, the issue of retroactivity. All legal systems of the 'Romanistic' and the 'Germanic' legal families regard the obligations as discharged from the moment when, being suitable for set-off, they first confronted each other.[84] They do this either because they subscribe to the *ipso iure* operation of set-off or because they attribute *ex tunc* effect to the declaration of set-off. There are subtle differences between these two ways of looking at the matter.[85] *Ipso iure compensatur*: this would appear to entail that examination of the requirements of set-off has to be thrown back to the moment in the past when the obligations have become discharged. A legal system operating with the notion of a retroactive declaration, on the other hand, would normally attribute retroactivity only to the effect of set-off. The substantive requirements of set-off have to be met at the time when set-off is declared.[86] This difference of approach has consequences in cases where

---

[83] As to the merely declaratory nature of the judgment, French and German law are not, of course, in disagreement. A different view had been adopted by a number of German pandectists: see, e.g., Windscheid and Kipp (n. 36) § 349, 4. Contra: von Kübel (n. 37) 1080ff.

[84] See above pp. 25f.   [85] For what follows, see Eujen (n. 16) 65f.

[86] Helmut Heinrichs, in *Palandt, Bürgerliches Gesetzbuch* (58th edn, 1999), § 387, n. 3; Gernhuber (n. 8) 310. For Austria, see Rummel/Rummel (n. 70) § 1438, n. 10.

set-off was possible at some time in the past but where one of its substantive requirements has, in the meantime, fallen away. Contrary to French law, German law would not, in principle, regard set-off as possible in this situation.[87]

By and large, however, both approaches lead to the same practical results. Thus, for instance, it is generally accepted that interest no longer accrues (and where it has been paid it may be reclaimed by means of the *condictio indebiti*),[88] that neither party can be held to have been in *mora debitoris* and that conventional penalties have not become exactable.[89] Also, a claim against which the defence of prescription may be raised can still be used for purposes of set-off, if prescription had not yet occurred when set-off could first have been declared. This consequence is natural enough for a legal system subscribing to the *ipso iure* effect of set-off[90] but it does not fit in well with the notion of set-off which is retroactively effective.[91] For at the time when set-off was

---

[87] There are, however, many important exceptions to this principle; see §§ 390 (2), 392, 406 BGB and Gernhuber (n. 8) 286ff. The difference mentioned in the text becomes relevant, for instance, where one of the parties assigns his claim to a third party after set-off has become possible but before one of its requirements has fallen away again. See Eujen (n. 16) 65f.

[88] But see Art. 6:129 (2) BW with *Parlementaire Geschiedenis* (n. 8) 497.

[89] See Haudek (n. 16) 63f.; for Germany: Karl-Heinz Gursky, in *J. von Staudingers Kommentar zum Bürgerlichen Gesetzbuch* (13th edn, 1995), § 389, nn. 18ff.; Gernhuber (n. 8) 309ff. For Austria, see Rummel/Rummel (n. 70), § 1438, n. 14; for the Netherlands: Asser/Hartkamp (n. 72) n. 538 and also Art. 6:134 BW; for Italy: Cian and Trabucchi (n. 73) Art. 1242 (2).

[90] Boris Starck, Henri Roland and Laurent Boyer, *Droit Civil: Les Obligations*, vol. II (5th edn, 1997), n. 2103. For Italy, see Art. 1242 (2) *codice civile*.

[91] Hence the special rules of §§ 390, 2 BGB, Art. 443 *Astikos Kodikas* and Art. 6:131 (1) BW (on which see *Parlementaire Geschiedenis* (n. 8) 503). For Scotland, see David Johnston, *Prescription and Limitation* (1999), 4.101 (1); for England, see Wood (n. 8) 13-18ff.; for Austria, see Koziol and Welser (n. 11) 281, but also the objections raised by Rummel/Rummel (n. 70) § 1438, n. 15 and Dullinger (n. 8) 165ff. In German law, too, the rule of § 390, 2 BGB has been criticized as being in conflict with the general policy of the law of prescription by Frank Peters and Reinhard Zimmermann, 'Verjährungsfristen', in

declared, one of its substantive requirements (that the claim of the person declaring set-off must be enforceable)[92] was no longer met. This draws our attention to the fact that neither *ipso iure* set-off nor retroactivity are carried through in all their consequences. To the contrary: they have to suffer a whole range of exceptions.[93] A conspicuous example, regarding French law,[94] concerns the situation where a debtor has paid his debt even though it had already been discharged by way of set-off. Here one should have expected the debtor to be granted the *condictio indebiti*: he has, after all, paid a debt that had already been discharged. According to the *code civil*, however, this is only the case if he had 'une juste cause d'ignorer la créance qui devait compenser sa dette'.[95] In all other situations, 'l'effet de plein droit est totalement écarté'.[96] In Germany, the question has for a long time been disputed;[97] the prevailing view today is that a

---

Bundesminister der Justiz (ed.), *Gutachten und Vorschläge zur Überarbeitung des Schuldrechts*, vol. 1 (1981), p. 266; Peter Bydlinski, 'Die Aufrechung mit verjährten Forderungen: Wirklich kein Änderungsbedarf?', (1996) 196 *Archiv für die Civilistische Praxis* 293ff. Swedish law, strangely, also has a rule which mirrors § 390, 2 BGB: § 10 preskriptionslag. It does not correspond to the general *ex nunc* effect of set-off in Swedish law and is therefore, understandably, the subject of criticism; see Lindskog (n. 74) 115ff.

[92] See IV.3 in this chapter.

[93] See also *Parlementaire Geschiedenis* (n. 8) 494 ('Welk stelsel men ook kiest, er zullen derhalve steeds correcties met betrekking tot de rechtsgevolgen daarvan moeten worden aangebracht'). Concerning the system of a retroactive declaration as it prevails in Austria and Germany, see the analysis by Dullinger (n. 8) 158ff.

[94] For exceptions to the German rule of retroactivity of the effects only, not of the substantive requirements of set-off, see n. 87.

[95] Art. 1299 *code civil*.

[96] Terré, Simler and Lequette (n. 8) n. 1310. Cf. also Haudek (n. 16) 63.

[97] Largely as a result of the fact that the *condictio indebiti* had been granted under the *ius commune*; see Ulp. D. 12, 6, 30; Ulp. D. 16, 2, 10, 1 ('Si quis igitur compensare potens solverit, condicere poterit quasi indebito soluto'); Dernburg (n. 6) 587ff.; Windscheid and Kipp (n. 36) § 349, 3. See also the critical discussion of the question in von Kübel (n. 37) 1083f.

person who has paid without realizing that he could have declared set-off cannot avail himself of an unjustified enrichment claim.[98]

These inconsistencies raise the question of whether it is sound, in principle, to attribute *ex tunc* effect to the declaration of set-off. The only policy arguments raised in favour of retroactivity are (i) that it is typically in accordance with the presumed intention of the parties,[99] and (ii) that protection must be granted to parties who rely on a position in which they may give notice of set-off.[100] Retroactivity, so it is argued, would therefore lead to results which are in conformity with equity and good faith.[101] The first of these arguments is based on speculation. There is no evidence as to what people generally think once they realize that they are in a position both of creditor and debtor towards each other.[102] The second argument, which is related to the first one, is even less convincing. As long as a person is unaware of the fact that he may easily effect payment or discharge his obligation by giving notice of set-off there can be no reliance that might require protection. Any advantage arising to him

---

[98] *Staudinger*/Gursky (n. 89) § 389, n. 4; Gernhuber (n. 8) 288f. The same view is taken for Austrian law by Rummel/Rummel (n. 70) § 1438, n. 15 (who, however, records a number of dissenting authors); and for Italian law by Cian and Trabucchi (n. 73) Art. 1242 (1). See also the discussion by Dullinger (n. 8) 162ff.

[99] See, e.g., Gernhuber (n. 8) 309.

[100] See, e.g., *Palandt*/Heinrichs (n. 86) § 389, n. 2.

[101] See, e.g., Protokolle, in Mugdan (n. 37) 562.

[102] The operation of current account ('Kontokorrent') may even be taken as an indication that set-off is not supposed, by the commercial community, to operate retrospectively, since interest is taken into account as it has become due for each of the mutual obligations up to the moment when the balance is drawn; see Bydlinski, (1996) 196 *Archiv für die Civilistische Praxis* 287f. If it were true that whoever is in a position to give notice of set-off no longer regards himself as debtor and thus relies on not having to make payment, this argument would favour set-off *ipso iure* rather than a retroactive one: Dullinger (n. 8) 180f.

under the regime of retroactivity would be a windfall. Once he does realize that he may effect set-off, the policy of the legal system should be to encourage him to do so as soon as possible. The state of pendency[103] existing before set-off has been declared is undesirable from the point of view of clarity and legal certainty. As long as the law does not require more than an informal declaration to the other party, it hardly asks too much of a debtor who wants to be sure that he no longer has to pay interest or of a creditor whose claim is about to prescribe. Arguably, therefore, reliance on the mere possibility of declaring set-off does not deserve to be protected. The law, after all, not only puts up certain substantive prerequisites for set-off but also requires set-off to be declared; and it does so for good reason.[104] Much of what is said by the proponents of retroactivity appears to be inspired by an unfounded belief that this notion is intrinsically related to the 'essence' of set-off.[105] Historically, we are probably dealing here with an unreflected continuation of a thinking pattern of the *ius commune*.[106] And while a true 're-statement' of private law in Central and Southern Europe[107]

---

[103] See von Kübel (n. 37) 1081.

[104] The reason for requiring a declaration as opposed to accepting set-off *ipso iure* is to promote legal certainty; see III.1 *in fine* and *Parlementaire Geschiedenis* (n. 8) 494. Legal certainty is gravely jeopardized, however, if the law first regards two obligations as existing, in order to declare subsequently that they must not be taken to have existed, after all. The result is that certain legal consequences concerning these obligations (like *mora debitoris*) first arise and later have to be taken not to have arisen.

[105] See the references in Gernhuber (n. 8) 229. That there is no real justification in modern contract law for maintaining the retroactive effect of set-off is also emphasized by Pichonnaz, (2000) 68 *Tijdschrift voor rechtsgeschiedenis* 560ff.

[106] See Pichonnaz, (2000) 68 *Tijdschrift voor rechtsgeschiedenis* 552ff.

[107] Along the lines of the American Restatements; on which see *Juristenzeitung* 1995, 478; Shael Herman, 'Schicksal und Zukunft der Kodifikationsidee in Amerika', in Reinhard Zimmermann (ed.), *Amerikanische Rechtskultur und europäisches Privatrecht* (1995), pp. 71ff.; Thomas Schindler, 'Die

might well have to perpetuate these thinking patterns, the Principles of European Private Law have a greater room for manoeuvre as a result of the fact that those legal systems that have not been encumbered by the heritage of Justinian's dark pronouncements[108] (i.e., Swedish law and English law[109]) merely attribute *ex nunc* effect to set-off. It is proposed to follow their lead in this respect and to adopt a rule according to which the notice of set-off leads to a discharge *pro tanto* of the obligations confronting each other.

What would be the consequences arising under such a regime? Interest (on both obligations) would run until set-off has been declared. It is therefore advantageous to the party paying the higher rate of interest to declare set-off. This he will normally do as soon as he becomes aware of this possibility. And as long as he is unaware of it, he must, in any event, expect to pay whatever statutory or conventional interest may be applicable.[110] Concerning liability for *mora debitoris* the position would be as follows. If B under a contract of sale has to pay A a sum of 100,000 on 10 October and fails to pay on that date, he would normally have failed to perform without excuse under Art. 8.108 PECL. A has the option of claiming performance, of claiming damages, or of terminating the contract. If B fails to declare a set-off or if it is only subsequently that he becomes aware of the fact that he has a claim against A for the same amount, this does not condone his inactivity on 10 October. Whether conventional penalties have become due from a party who has not exercised his right to give notice of set-off depends on the

Restatements und ihre Bedeutung für das amerikanische Privatrecht', (1998) 6 *Zeitschrift für Europäisches Privatrecht* 277ff.

[108] See p. 24.   [109] See pp. 23, 33.

[110] It is remarkable, in this context, that Art. 6:129 (3) BW now restricts the retroactive effect of set-off, in that interest that has been paid may not be reclaimed. For the convincing arguments in favour of this rule, see *Parlementaire Geschiedenis* (n. 8) 497.

interpretation of the relevant clause. Normally, the penalty will have to be paid. Particularly difficult restitution problems do not arise. If payment is made after set-off has been declared it may be reclaimed since it is *indebitum solutum*. If it was made before the declaration of set-off, it has had the effect of discharging the obligation and thereby removing the mutuality requirement for set-off.

These results, to my mind, cannot be regarded as inequitable.[111] On the contrary: since they reflect the situation as it would have had to be evaluated if both obligations had been *paid* at the moment when notice of set-off was given, they tie in well with the normal rules relating to the discharge of an obligation.[112] In any event, they do not justify a set of rules that is (i) based on a somewhat artificial fiction (both obligations 'must be taken to have been discharged at the moment')[113] and therefore difficult to explain doctrinally,[114] (ii) detrimental to legal certainty,[115] (iii) not practicable without recognizing a number of exceptions,[116]

---

[111] For an excellent, and detailed, argument along these lines, see Bydlinski, (1996) 196 *Archiv für die Civilistische Praxis* 281ff.; and Dullinger (n. 8) 174ff., 182ff.

[112] See the example given by Bydlinski, (1996) 196 *Archiv für die Civilistische Praxis* 286f.

[113] See § 389 BGB.

[114] For a discussion of what happens, conceptually, at the moment when two claims confront each other being suitable for compensation ('Aufrechnungslage' – are the two obligations still entirely independent or are they already, in some way or other, related to each other?), see Kegel (n. 10) 6ff.; Gernhuber (n. 8) 229ff.; *Staudinger/*Gursky (n. 89) Vorbem. zu §§ 387ff., nn. 13ff. This was, of course, also a topic which was hotly debated in the pre-codification *ius commune*; see, e.g., Windscheid and Kipp (n. 36) § 349, 1–4; von Kübel (n. 37) 1075ff., 1080f.; Dullinger (n. 8) 151ff.

[115] It was already acknowledged by the draftsmen of the BGB that the introduction of a notice requirement without retroactive effect would lead to 'legal clarity and simplicity'. A few lines later they referred to 'a principle which is admittedly fascinating in view of its clarity and simplicity': 'Motive', in Mugdan (n. 37) 60.

[116] See the discussion earlier in this section.

(iv) fraught with difficult problems of calculation as, for instance, in cases of a claim for damages on account of the loss of negotiable instruments which are subject to fluctuating market rates[117] and (v) more likely to lead to windfall gains than to the protection of reasonable reliance.

4 *Insolvency set-off*

Most legal systems have special rules dealing with insolvency set-off.[118] Generally speaking, these rules attest to a very widespread feeling among all legal systems that the commencement of insolvency proceedings should not deprive a creditor of his right to effect set-off. Even English law, insofar, attributes 'automatic' effect to set-off; insolvency set-off was in fact the first type of set-off that was formally recognized by legislation.[119] The policy ground usually given for this preferential treatment is the perceived injustice that a person should have to pay the full amount of his liability to a bankrupt and at the same time be confined, as far as his own claim is concerned, to a proportional share in the

[117] For details, see *Staudinger*/Gursky (n. 89) § 389, nn. 31ff.; and see Art. 6:129 (3) BW (sanctioning another exception to the principle of retroactivity!); for comment, see *Parlementaire Geschiedenis* (n. 8) 497f. and *Asser*/ Hartkamp (n. 72) 539.

[118] For France, see Art. 33 (1) loi du 25 janvier relative au redressement et à la liquidation judiciaire, as modified by the loi du 10 juin 1994, on which see Georges Ripert and René Roblot, *Traité de droit commercial*, vol. II (15th edn by Philippe Delebecque and Michel Germain, 1996), nn. 3039f.; for England, see s. 323 Insolvency Act (1986), on which see Goode (n. 6) 176ff. and the discussion by Wood (n. 8) 7-1ff. and Derham (n. 6) 149ff.; for Germany, see §§ 94ff. Insolvenzordnung; for Italy, see Art. 56 I legge fallimentare, on which see Bianca (n. 73) 511ff. and Perlingueri (n. 73) 260ff.; for Austria, see §§ 19f. Ausgleichsordnung and §§ 19f. Konkursordnung, on which see Rummel/Rummel (n. 70) § 1439, n. 9 and Dullinger (n. 8) 307ff.; for Sweden, see chapter 5, §§ 15–17 konkurslag (1987); for Scotland, see McBryde (n. 12) 22-75ff. For a comparative evaluation, see Wood (n. 8) 24-49.

[119] See the references in n. 38.

insolvent estate. This argument does not seem to be particularly strong. For it should be kept in mind that the effect of set-off is to prefer one creditor over the general body of creditors, and that it therefore operates against the policy favouring equal treatment of creditors.[120] 'It is debatable', as Derham points out,[121] 'whether the justice in favour of setting off cross-demands is always so great that it should allow assets available for distribution amongst the general body of creditors to be depleted in favour of a single creditor in possession of the right, with the consequent reduction in the dividend payable generally.' None the less, in view of the unanimity among European legal systems on the point, it may be advisable to retain some measure of protection for a creditor who, at the time of commencement of the insolvency proceedings, was in a position to give notice of set-off. This could be done by requiring the administrator of the bankrupt's estate to deduct from his own claim on behalf of the bankrupt's estate whatever the bankrupt himself owed to that particular creditor. He would thus only be allowed to claim 'cum deductione'.[122] Such a rule cannot, however, be part of a set of principles of private law; it would have to feature in a European insolvency regime.

IV THE REQUIREMENTS FOR SET-OFF

1 *Mutuality*

We now have to turn our attention to the requirements under which set-off may be declared. There is fairly widespread agreement, in principle, among the legal systems under consideration but a few differences in detail have to be

---

[120] Derham (n. 6) 153.   [121] Derham (n. 6) 154.
[122] Like the Roman *bonorum emptor*; see Kaser I (n. 25) 645f.; Zimmermann (n. 25) 765.

considered. In the first place, there has to be *concursus debiti et crediti* (mutuality, réciprocité, Wechselseitigkeit)[123] in the sense that the creditor of the one claim is the debtor under the other, and vice versa.[124] In England, the underlying idea is often expressed by stating that the claims must exist between the same parties and in the same right.[125] Thus, there can be no set-off between a debt due by a person in his own right and one due to him as trustee, tutor, administrator or executor.[126] The Dutch BW has specifically added a provision according to which the right of set-off does not exist with reference to a debt and a claim falling into estates which are distinct from each other.[127] This clarification is arguably unnecessary in a code. Details as to what exactly *concursus debiti et crediti* implies also need not be set out. The details follow from general principle and depend upon the way in which the national legal systems deal with issues like trusteeship and agency.[128]

Two problems, however, deserve to be mentioned. (i) Where a debt has been secured by way of suretyship it is widely regarded as inequitable if the creditor were able to recover from the surety in cases where the main debtor may declare set-off.[129] French law, of course, does not have a

---

[123] On the German terminology (normally the term 'Gegenseitigkeit' is used), see Dieter Medicus, *Schuldrecht I: Allgemeiner Teil* (10th edn, 1998), n. 263.

[124] See Art. 1289 *code civil* and Terré, Simler and Lequette (n. 8) 1297; Wood (n. 8) 14-1ff.; Derham (n. 6) 319ff.; § 387 BGB and Gernhuber (n. 8) 233ff.; Art. 1241 *codice civile* and Bianca (n. 73) 481ff.; Art. 1195 *código civil*; Art. 6:127 (2) BW and *Asser*/Hartkamp (n. 72) n. 533; §§ 1438, 1441 ABGB and Koziol and Welser (n. 11) 278; Dullinger (n. 8) 5ff.; McBryde (n. 12) 22-60ff.; Art. 440 *Astikos Kodikas*; Lindskog (n. 74) 43; Haudek (n. 16) 59f.; Wood (n. 8) 24-155ff.

[125] See, e.g., Goode (n. 6) 154. [126] McBryde (n. 12) 22-60.

[127] Art. 6:127 (3) BW (on which, see *Parlementaire Geschiedenis* (n. 8) 491).

[128] For a detailed comparative discussion, see Kegel (n. 10) 51ff.

[129] The same applies in cases of real securities of an accessory nature, like pledges or hypothecs. See, for example, Art. 1247 (2) *codice civile*, Art. 6:139 BW and

problem with this situation: since set-off operates *ipso iure*, the surety can simply draw attention to the fact that the main debt has been discharged and that consequently he is no longer liable.[130] Under the regime for set-off proposed in the present essay protection should be granted to a surety against a claim by the creditor in situations where the creditor can satisfy himself by declaring set-off against a claim of the main debtor, and perhaps also where the main debtor may declare set-off against the claim of the creditor.[131] But this must be left to a set of principles dealing with suretyship.

(ii) All legal systems concur in granting some measure of protection to a debtor whose creditor has assigned the claim to a third party. If the debtor could have discharged his obligation towards the assignor by declaring set-off, he may still do so

§§ 1137, 1211 BGB. Real security, however, does not fall within the compass of the present inquiry.

[130] This follows from the accessory nature of the surety's obligation; on the accessoriness of suretyship in general, see Zimmermann (n. 25) 121ff., 142ff.; Mathias Habersack, 'Die Akzessorietät: Strukturprinzip der europäischen Zivilrechte und eines künftigen europäischen Grundpfandrechts', (1997) *Juristenzeitung* 801ff. For France, see Art. 1294 (1) *code civil* ('La caution peut opposer la compensation de ce que le créancier droit au débiteur principal'). For Spain, see Art. 1197 *código civil*; for Italy see Art. 1247 *codice civile*.

[131] Cf. § 770 II BGB (which, however, applies only to the first of the two situations mentioned). For details, see Reinhard Zimmermann, 'Die Einrede der Aufrechenbarkeit nach § 770 Abs. 2 BGB', (1979) *Juristische Rundschau* 495ff. Art. 6:139 (1) BW corresponds to § 770 II BGB (see *Parlementaire Geschiedenis* (n. 8) 515f.). In Austria the same approach is supported by a number of authors, but there are others who argue that the surety may declare set-off by relying on the main debtor's claim against the creditor; see Rummel/Rummel (n. 70) § 1442, n. 20 and the discussion by Dullinger (n. 8) 20ff. The latter approach is the one endorsed by Art. 447 *Astikos Kodikas*. According to English law, the surety may rely on the principal debtor's set-off, as far as insolvency set-off and set-off agreements are concerned. The position concerning statutory and equitable set-off is uncertain. For details, see Derham (n. 6) 639ff. He argues that 'the surety can defend himself on the basis of any defence of set-off available to the debtor, provided that the debtor is a party to the action'. For a comparative analysis, see Kegel (n. 10) 132ff.

if he is sued by the assignee, provided his own claim already existed and had become due[132] at the time when the assignment became effective.[133] If the two obligations arise from the same legal relationship, the debtor may even rely on his right to set-off without the latter restriction.[134] In some legal systems the pertinent rules are, it is submitted rightly, seen to belong to the law relating to the assignment of claims,[135] since they constitute an integral part of a broader inquiry: how the legal system has to protect a debtor when the creditor assigns his claim to a third party.[136] None of the legal systems under consideration requires the debtor's consent, though some of them insist upon a formal notification.[137] Thus, he will usually be faced with a *fait accompli*: he knows that he now has to pay to his new creditor but he has lost the chance to discharge his obligation by declaring set-off to the old: hence, his need to be protected.[138]

---

[132] According to some legal systems it does not matter whether the debtor's claim was due at the time when the assignment was effected, as long as it was not to become due later than the claim against which it was to be set off.

[133] Or (where that is not implicit, see n. 137) when the debtor got to know about the assignment.

[134] For a clear statement to this effect, see Art. 6:130 (1) BW, on which see *Parlementaire Geschiedenis* (n. 8) 499ff. and *Asser/Hartkamp* (n. 72) nn. 541ff. For similar rules, see Art. 1295 *code civil* and Eujen (n. 16) 35f.; Derham (n. 6) 567ff.; see also Art. 1248 *codice civile*, Art. 1198 *código civil*, § 406 BGB, §§ 448, 463 *Astikos Kodikas*, § 1442 ABGB, §§ 18, 28 lag om skuldebrev. See also Hein Kötz, *European Contract Law* (1997, transl. Tony Weir), p. 430 and, for a detailed comparative discussion, Kegel (n. 10) 138ff.; Wood (n. 8) 24-170ff.

[135] See §§ 406 BGB and 463 *Astikos Kodikas*.

[136] See Kötz (n. 134) 281ff.; see also Zimmermann (n. 25) 66.

[137] For a comparative analysis, see Hein Kötz, 'Rights of Third Parties: Third Party Beneficiaries and Assignment', in *International Encyclopedia of Comparative Law*, vol. VII, chapter 13 (1992), nn. 86ff. German law, on the other hand, requires merely an agreement between assignor and assignee.

[138] The same applies in cases of an attachment of the claim against the person who wishes to declare set-off and also where a limited real right has been created. See, for example, Art. 6:130 (2) BW, §§ 392, 1070 I, 1275 BGB.

2 *Obligations of the same kind*

Secondly, both obligations must be of the same kind:[139] a money claim can be set off only against a money claim, a debt for the delivery of grain only against a claim for the delivery of grain of the same kind. English law confines set-off to money debts.[140] This is explicable in view of the exceptional character of specific performance. Moreover, it reflects economic realities in that, in other countries too, compensation usually relates to money debts. The prime example of non-monetary obligations, to which set-off may be relevant today, are securities, whether certificated or dematerialized. Whether claims are of the same kind depends on their state at the time that notice of set-off is given. The most important practical problem, in the context of the present requirement for set-off, relates to foreign currency debts. A straightforward solution was the one traditionally adopted in English law where foreign currency debts were always converted to pounds sterling at the rate of exchange of the date when they fell due. In the 1975 case of *Miliangos v. George Frank (Textiles) Ltd*,[141] however, it was held that an English court may give judgment for a sum of

---

[139] § 387 BGB ('ihrem Gegenstande nach gleichartig'); for details, see Gernhuber (n. 8) 236ff.; Art. 6:127 (2) BW ('een prestatie...die beantwoordt aan zijn schuld'); for details, see *Asser*/Hartkamp (n. 72) n. 534; § 1438 ABGB; for details, see Rummel/Rummel (n. 70) § 1440, n. 1 and Dullinger (n. 8) 77ff.; Art. 440 *Astikos Kodikas*; Art. 1234 (1) *codice civile*; Art. 1196 (2) *código civil*; Lindskog (n. 74) 43; McBryde (n. 12) 22-53f. Art. 1291 (1) *code civil* lays down the same principle but adds: 'Les prestations en grains ou denrées non contestées, et dont le prix est réglé par les mercuriales, peuvent se compenser avec des sommes liquides et exigibles.' According to Terré, Simler and Lequette (n. 8) n. 1298, '[c]ette innovation des rédacteurs du code civil, dont le bien fondé et l'opportunité sont loin d'être évidents, ne paraît pas avoir connu beaucoup d'applications'. For a general comparative survey, see also Wood (n. 8) 24-145C ff.

[140] Goode (n. 6) 153, 157f.; Wood (n. 8) 9-1ff.; Eujen (n. 16) 52.

[141] [1976] AC 443 (HL).

money expressed in a foreign currency and that conversion will normally take place at the date when the court authorizes enforcement of the judgment in pounds sterling.[142] This applies to statutory set-off; the position with regard to equitable set-off still appears to be unclear.[143] According to the prevailing opinion in German law, debts in foreign and domestic currency are never 'of the same kind'. Set-off can consequently be effected only if the parties have so agreed.[144] There are good reasons for regarding this view as outdated.[145] French legal writers incline towards accepting set-off concerning debts in different currencies except where they are not convertible.[146] The Principles should take their lead from Art. 8 (6) of the EU Regulation on the Introduction of the Euro[147] which came into force on 1 January 1999. In terms of this regulation, the euro has become the uniform denomination for those countries that have joined the monetary union. For a transitional period (until 31 December 2001) the former national currencies will be regarded as sub-units of the euro. As a result, set-off is no longer prevented, within the euro-zone, as a result of the fact that the obligations are expressed in different currencies. This should also be the rule with respect to other currencies. It is in line with the modern view increasingly adopted in the national legal systems[148] since it facilitates set-off without

---

[142] Derham (n. 6) 130f.

[143] Derham (n. 6) 131f. See also the detailed discussion by Wood (n. 8) 11-1ff. on foreign currency debts in the context of set-off in general. Scots law follows *Miliangos*; see *Commerzbank Aktiengesellschaft v. Large*, 1977 SC 375.

[144] See, e.g., *Münchener Kommentar*/von Feldmann (n. 53) § 387, n. 16; Staudinger/Gursky (n. 89) § 387, n. 67.

[145] Gernhuber (n. 8) 238ff. (conversion at the date of set-off).

[146] Terré, Simler and Lequette (n. 8) n. 1298; see also Eujen (n. 16) 37. For the Netherlands, see *Asser*/Hartkamp (n. 72) n. 534. For a comparative evaluation, see Wood (n. 8) 24-34.

[147] No. 974/98 of 3 May 1998 OJEC 1998, 139 (1).

[148] Cf., e.g., Artt. 1278f. *codice civile*; Rummel/Rummel (n. 70) § 1440, n. 2.

unduly prejudicing the reasonable interests of the creditor of the principal claim.[149]

3 Cross-claim due, party declaring set-off may perform

Discussion of the next requirement first of all calls for a terminological clarification. The claim brought against the party declaring set-off will henceforth be referred to as the principal claim, whilst the claim of the party declaring set-off will be termed the cross-claim. This, I think, is a fair reflection of the terminology prevailing in most European legal systems. Since set-off amounts to a form of enforcement of the cross-claim, the cross-claim has to be enforceable (exigible, durchsetzbar, afdwingbaar). Thus, it has to be due, the other party must not be able to raise a defence, and we must not be dealing with a *naturalis obligatio*.[150] The principal claim, on the other hand, does not necessarily have to be due; it is quite sufficient that the person declaring set-off may effect performance.[151] For as soon as a debtor may thrust his payment upon his creditor (which may be long before the claim falls due) there is no reason not to allow him to declare set-off. Before the debtor of the principal claim may effect performance, however, he may not

---

[149] On the legal nature of a foreign currency debt, see Karsten Schmidt, in *Staudinger, Kommentar zum Bürgerlichen Gesetzbuch* (12th edn, 1983), § 244, nn. 11ff.; Helmut Grothe, *Fremdwährungsverbindlichkeiten* (1999), pp. 558ff.; Dullinger (n. 8) 78ff.

[150] Terré, Simler and Lequette (n. 8) n. 1300; Derham (n. 6) 27f.; §§ 387, 390 (1) BGB and Gernhuber (n. 8) 247ff.; Art. 6:127 (2) BW and *Asser*/Hartkamp (n. 72) n. 536; Art. 1243 (1) *codice civile* and Bianca (n. 73) 485f.; Art. 1196 (3 and 4) *código civil*; Art. 440 *Astikos Kodikas*; Lindskog (n. 74) 43; Koziol and Welser (n. 11) 279; Dullinger (n. 8) 78ff.

[151] § 387 BGB and Gernhuber (n. 8) 252ff.; Art. 6:127 (2) BW and *Parlementaire Geschiedenis* (n. 8) 492; Rummel/Rummel (n. 70) § 1439, n. 7; Stathopoulos (n. 71) 164 (against the wording of Art. 440 *Astikos Kodikas*); Lindskog (n. 74) 43.

declare set-off. These rules appear to flow naturally from the way in which set-off is proposed to operate. If some national legal systems, at the moment, decide differently, this is attributable to the different construction of set-off chosen by these systems. Thus, according to English law, the principal claim also has to be enforceable. This is a natural consequence of the – traditionally – procedural character of set-off in that legal system: if the claimant were to sue on a claim which is not enforceable the defendant would not even have to plead set-off in order to secure a judgment in his favour.[152] And if Art. 1291 (1) *code civil* also requires both claims to be 'exigible',[153] this follows from the *ipso iure* effect of compensation: none of the claims can be labelled principal claim or cross-claim. French courts, however, often reach the same result as German law by means of *compensation facultative*:[154] the party exposed to a claim which has not yet become due may renounce the legal protection granted to him.[155]

4 Liquidity

There is an obvious danger that a defendant may protract legal proceedings by invoking set-off on account of cross-claims which cannot easily be proved, the existence of which is as yet uncertain, etc. This danger was already recognized by Justinian; he ordered judges to take account of the plea of set-off only 'si causa ex qua compensatur liquida sit et non multis ambagibus innodata, sed possit iudici facilem

---

[152] Eujen (n. 16) 63.
[153] Cf. also Art. 1243 (1) *codice civile* and Bianca (n. 73) 485f.; Art. 1196 (3) *código civil*.
[154] See Eujen (n. 16) 63.
[155] On *compensation facultative*, see Terré, Simler and Lequette (n. 8) n. 1312; Kegel (n. 10) 10; Eujen (n. 16) 45f.

exitum sui praestare'.[156] French law has elevated this crite-rion ('liquidité') to a fifth substantive requirement of set-off which, moreover, does not apply only to the cross-claim but also to the principal claim.[157] This must be seen against the background of the *ipso iure* effect of set-off in French law: unless the principal claim and the cross-claim are easily as-certainable it would be impossible to say whether, and to what extent, they have been discharged. But the requirement of 'liquidité' also gives rise to a number of problems. The status of a claim may change and a claim which is likely to succeed today may be entirely unlikely to succeed tomorrow (as, for instance, when the creditor has lost some crucial doc-uments proving his claim).[158] If a legal system determines the issue of 'liquidité' at the moment when the two claims first confronted each other, the procedural considerations justi-fying the requirement would be disregarded: for if a lawsuit were to arise later, its speedy progress would now be en-cumbered by sorting out the details of an (unascertained) cross-claim.[159] If, on the other hand, 'liquidité' is required at the moment when legal proceedings commence, we are faced with an awkward state of pendency: who knows whether, at some stage in the future, a lawsuit may still be filed con-cerning the one or other claim and how difficult it may, by then, have become to prove the latter and to determine its extent?[160] It is small wonder that the practical significance of the requirement of 'liquidité' has been watered down consid-erably in French legal practice. On the one hand, the judge

---

[156] C. 4, 31, 14, 1; cf. also Inst. 4, 6, 30 and Kaser I (n. 25) 448.

[157] Art. 1291 and see Terré, Simler and Lequette (n. 8) n. 1299; Kegel (n. 10) 160ff.; Wagner, (1999) *Praxis des Internationalen Privat- und Verfahrens-rechts* 72. Cf. also Art. 1243 *codice civile* (on the interpretation of which, see Perlingueri (n. 73) 294); Art. 1196 (4) *código civil*, and (somewhat differently) Art. 1244 *Astikos Kodikas*.

[158] Kegel (n. 10) 166.   [159] Kegel (n. 10) 166.

[160] Kegel (n. 10) 167.

is granted some leeway in determining whether the claim is sufficiently certain in order to be treated as 'liquide' and can thus be taken into account for purposes of set-off.[161] On the other hand, and more importantly, the device of *compensation judiciaire* may be resorted to, provided the defendant asserts his cross-claim by way of a cross-action (*demande reconventionelle*). The legal nature of *compensation judiciaire* is disputed[162] but since the judge may decide to deal with both actions at one and the same time, and to give judgment for the balance, it has at least the practical effect of set-off.[163] Where both claims arise from the same legal relationship this is the way the judge has to proceed.[164]

Even in France, therefore, the emphasis has shifted from substantive law to procedure. The path towards an *entirely* procedural solution had been mapped out, many centuries before, by Justinian. Using his constitution in C. 4, 31, 14 as a basis, the glossators placed the matter into the hands of the judge (*officium judicis*).[165] Dernburg in his great monograph[166] and Windscheid in his influential textbook[167] subscribed to the same view: set-off is not prevented on account of the fact that the cross-claim still needs to be ascertained, by way of calculation or proof. But the judge may (and has to) refuse to consider the issue of set-off in the present legal proceedings if its determination would unduly

---

[161] Eujen (n. 16) 38.

[162] On *compensation judiciaire*, see Starck, Roland and Boyer (n. 90) n. 2095; Terré, Simler and Lequette (n. 8) 1313; Eujen (n. 16) 38ff.; Kegel (n. 10) 10f.; Bianca (n. 73) n. 257; Wagner, (1999) *Praxis des Internationalen Privat- und Verfahrensrechts* 69.

[163] According to Terré, Simler and Lequette, the obligations are, however, not to be taken to be discharged *ipso iure* but only from the date of judgment.

[164] According to Terré, Simler and Lequette, we are dealing with a privileged form of set-off which therefore operates *ipso iure*.

[165] See the quotation provided by Kegel (n. 10) 162: 'liquidi ad non liquidum an compensatio fiat, vel non fiat, officio judicis definitur'.

[166] Dernburg (n. 6) 554ff.   [167] Windscheid and Kipp (n. 36) § 350, 5.

protract these proceedings. An exception was recognized in cases in which principal claim and cross-claim arise from the same legal relationship. The draftsmen of the BGB followed suit and did not, therefore, make liquidity of the cross-claim a requirement for set-off.[168] They could refer to two provisions of the Civil Procedure Act (which have been preserved, essentially unchanged, until today) according to which the court may decide to deal separately with principal claim and cross-claim (as long as both of them do not arise from the same legal relationship) and that a provisional judgment may be given, under these circumstances, concerning the claim.[169]

It may have become obvious that the French and German approaches do not differ much in their practical results: there is a fairly wide judicial discretion as to whether the cross-claim may be set off against the principal claim except in cases where both claims arise from the same legal relationship.[170] The German solution does not appear to be particularly elegant in that a claimant who wishes to enforce his (provisional) judgment runs the risk that such a step may later turn out not to have been based on a valid title, after all: with the consequence that he will have to render restitution and to pay damages.[171] The French solution, on the other hand, overshoots the mark in two respects and suffers from a fundamental weakness on a conceptual level. (i) There is no reason to require the *principal* claim to be ascertained.[172]

---

[168] Von Kübel (n. 37) 1092. The same view is usually today advocated (in spite of § 1439 ABGB) for Austrian law: see Rummel/Rummel (n. 70) § 1439, n. 6; Koziol and Welser (n. 11) 279; Dullinger (n. 8) 90ff. For a comparative evaluation, see Kegel (n. 10) 158ff.; Eujen (n. 16) 27f.

[169] See §§ 145 III, 302 ZPO.

[170] See the comparative evaluation by Eujen (n. 16) 63f.

[171] § 302 III, IV ZPO; and see the criticism in *Parlementaire Geschiedenis* (n. 8) 509f.

[172] *Parlementaire Geschiedenis* (n. 8) 490.

This applies *a fortiori* in a system where set-off would not operate *ipso iure*. (ii) Not always does it constitute an act of chicanery if the defendant pleads set-off on the basis of an unascertained cross-claim: it may be quite possible to establish all details concerning the cross-claim within the period which legal proceedings involving the principal claim will take anyway; it may be certain that the cross-claim exceeds the amount of the principal claim, etc.[173] Thus, a substantive requirement of liquidity, without any discretion on the part of the judge, would too much inhibit the possibility of set-off as a convenient means of discharging two obligations at one and the same time. If, however, such discretion is granted to the judge, then (iii) it appears awkward to establish a requirement for set-off on the level of substantive law which is, in practice, undermined procedurally.[174]

It may therefore be preferable to adopt a third approach which can, essentially, be regarded as a compromise between the first two. If the cross-claim cannot readily be ascertained, the judge is empowered to adjudicate upon the principal claim without taking account of the set-off declared by the defendant, provided the principal claim is otherwise ready for adjudication.[175] Thus, the judge is given discretion. He will have to take account of all the circumstances of the case, such as the probable duration of the proceedings concerning both principal claim and cross-claim, or the effect of a delay on the claimant. But it may be possible to guide him in the exercise of this discretion by distinguishing two

---

[173] *Parlementaire Geschiedenis* (n. 8) 490f. Cf. also the idea underlying Art. 1243 (2), first alternative, *codice civile*.

[174] Thus, it was pointed out by Meijers that Art. 1463 (old) BW was usually circumvented ('ontgaan') by a procedure similar to the French *compensation judiciaire* ('conventie en reconventie'): *Parlementaire Geschiedenis* (n. 8) 490.

[175] This is the approach adopted in Dutch law; see Art. 6:136 BW; *Parlementaire Geschiedenis* (n. 8) 509f.; *Asser*/Hartkamp (n. 72) nn. 550f. Meijers had originally proposed a solution along the lines of German law.

cases. (i) If the principal claim and the cross-claim arise from the same legal relationship, the judge will not normally confine his attention to the principal claim but will deal also with the cross-claim and consider the issue of set-off. (ii) If the principal claim and the cross-claim do not arise from the same legal relationship, the decision will normally go the other way: commercial predictability and fairness demand that, when a party has an ascertained claim, he should not be held up in pursuing this claim. If the judge decides to adjudicate upon the principal claim, his judgment is not merely of a provisional nature. His decision rests solely on the merits of the claimant's claim which he regards as being unaffected by the declaration of set-off. As a result, the declaration of set-off must be regarded as ineffective, set-off as not having occurred. The defendant will therefore have to pursue his claim by means of an independent suit.[176]

V SITUATIONS WHERE SET-OFF IS EXCLUDED

Every legal system recognizes situations where set-off is excluded. Occasionally, this results from the application of more general principles of law ('estoppel');[177] in other cases we are dealing with peculiarities based on national traditions

---

[176] This solution should also be acceptable to English law where as far as statutory set-off is concerned, both claims are traditionally required to be liquidated or ascertainable with certainty. As in German law, the matter is considered only in the course of legal proceedings. As in French and German law, the matter is considered in a different light where the claims have arisen from the same legal relationship. Some doubt has been expressed as to how stringently the liquidity rule will continue to be applied in other cases. For details of what constitutes a liquidated claim, see Wood (n. 8) 2-68ff.; for a comparative discussion, see Kegel (n. 10) 170ff.; Eujen (n. 16) 53, 63f. For Scotland, see McBryde (n. 12) 22-56ff.

[177] See Eujen (n. 16) 54.

and concerns (such as the German rule of § 395 BGB which is based entirely on reasons of administrative expediency).[178] But we also find a number of rules which appear to embody evaluations which are found, in some or other form, in all, or most, European legal systems. Firstly, it is recognized everywhere that the right of set-off may be excluded by contract.[179] This follows from the general principle of freedom of contract. Of course, the general limitations of private autonomy must be observed (e.g., the rules dealing with unfair standard terms in consumer contracts). Secondly, the view is widely held that set-off should not be allowed to deprive a person of claims (such as those for maintenance or wages) which provide him with a minimum level of subsistence.[180] The simplest, most appropriate and most

---

[178] Against a claim by a local authority, by a state or by the Federal Republic, set-off is permissible only if the performance is due to the same fund, or 'statio fisci', from which the claim of the party declaring set-off is to be paid. For details, see Gernhuber (n. 8) 273f.; for Austria: § 1441 ABGB; for Sweden: Lindskog (n. 74) 373f. (applying this rule also for the benefit of certain private enterprises). In Germany, an exception is recognized concerning tax claims: cf. § 226 AO and *Staudinger*/Gursky (n. 89) § 395, n. 8: set-off may be declared against tax claims, as long as the cross-claim is liquidated. The restriction of § 395 BGB does not apply. In other countries, set-off against tax claims is excluded; for France, see Terré, Simler and Lequette (n. 8) n. 1302 *in fine*; for special rules in England, see Wood (n. 8) 12-172; Derham (n. 6) 418ff.; in the Netherlands *Asser*/Hartkamp (n. 72) n. 553; in Italy Cian and Trabucchi (n. 73) Art. 1246, VI, n. 1.

[179] Starck, Roland and Boyer (n. 90) n. 347; Derham (n. 6) 140ff.; Gernhuber (n. 8) 274f.; Bianca (n. 73) n. 251; *Asser*/Hartkamp (n. 72) n. 531; Koziol and Welser (n. 11) 280; Lindskog (n. 74) 303f.; McBryde (n. 12) 22-74; Eujen (n. 16) 64f.

[180] Cf. Art. 1293, no. 3 *code civil* and Terré, Simler and Lequette (n. 8) n. 1302; § 394 BGB and Gernhuber (n. 8) 261ff.; Art. 1246 (3) *codice civile* and Bianca (n. 73) n. 251; Art. 6:135 (a) BW and *Asser*/Hartkamp (n. 72) n. 552; Art. 1200 (2) *código civil*; Koziol and Welser (n. 11) 280 and Dullinger (n. 8) 121ff.; Art. 451 *Astikos Kodikas*; Lindskog (n. 74) 247ff., 283; concerning English law, see Wood (n. 8) 12-104ff.; Eujen (n. 16) 53; for a comparative evaluation, see Haudek (n. 16) 61.

comprehensive way of dealing with this issue is to prohibit set-off to the extent that the principal claim is not capable of attachment.[181] Whether, and to what extent, the principal claim is capable of attachment is decided by the law applicable to that issue.

Thirdly, all continental legal systems have preserved a provision which dates back to the Codex Iustiniani: 'Possessionem autem alienam perperam occupantibus compensatio non datur.'[182] The French code contains a fairly literal version of this rule: set-off may not take place as far as the claim for restitution of an object is concerned of which the owner was unlawfully deprived.[183] The German BGB has generalized the underlying idea:[184] set-off is not permissible against a claim arising from a wilful delict. The same rule has now been enacted in the Netherlands,[185] in view of the serious criticism levelled against its French-inspired predecessor.[186] But what exactly is the underlying idea? Two propositions have been advanced. (i) The rule is designed to ensure that the creditor receives what is due to him within a reasonable time and without having to argue about cross-claims by the tortfeasor.[187] (ii) The rule aims at keeping self-help under

---

[181] See, most recently, Art. 6:135 (a) BW and *Parlementaire Geschiedenis* (n. 8) 508.

[182] C. 4, 31, 14, 2: on which see Dernburg (n. 6) 511ff.

[183] Art. 1293, no. 1 *code civil* and Terré, Simler and Lequette (n. 8) 1302; Art. 1246 (1) *codice civile*; § 1440 ABGB.

[184] § 393 BGB, von Kübel (n. 37) 1094f. and Gernhuber (n. 8) 259ff.; along the same or very similar lines Greece (Art. 450 (1) *Astikos Kodikas*), Spain (D. Ignacio Casso y Romero, *Diccionario de derecho privado*, vol. 1 (3rd edn, 1967), p. 1015); Sweden (Lindskog (n. 74) 258ff.) and the Netherlands (Art. 6:135 (b) BW). For a comparative evaluation, see Haudek (n. 16) 62. For certain traces, or 'latent expressions', of the rule in English law, see Wood (n. 8) 12-127ff.

[185] See n. 184.   [186] See *Parlementaire Geschiedenis* (n. 8) 508.

[187] See BGH, *Neue Juristische Wochenschrift* 1987, 2997 (1998); *Münchener Kommentar*/von Feldmann (n. 53) § 393, n. 1.

control; for a creditor who is unable, for some or other reason, to collect what is due to him, might otherwise be tempted to seek satisfaction by wilfully inflicting injuries on his debtor and then giving notice of set-off.[188] It has correctly been pointed out[189] that the first of these propositions barely does more than repeat the content of the rule. It does not say why proceedings have to be sped up in this specific case and not in others. The second proposition is more convincing, even though the usual textbook example of a disappointed creditor boxing the ears of his debtor may not appear to be practically relevant. More realistic is the situation where the creditor is in a position of bailee vis-à-vis some or other object belonging to his debtor and proceeds wrongfully to sell that object in order to satisfy himself. Thus, a rule along the lines of § 393 BGB might be advisable, in spite of the fact that it has given rise, in its practical application, to a number of problems.[190]

Fourthly, in some national legal systems it is regarded as desirable to prohibit contributories to a company from setting off the company's debt to them against their liability for unpaid calls.[191] Such a rule serves to safeguard the interest of the company's creditors in the undiminished capital fund of the company. It will, however, have to be implemented as part and parcel of a regulation of company law rather than the general rules on set-off.

---

[188] Gernhuber (n. 8) 259f.; *Staudinger*/Gursky (n. 89) § 393, n. 1.

[189] Gernhuber (n. 8) 259.

[190] Does it apply to intentional breaches of contract (for details, see *Staudinger*/Gursky (n. 89) § 393, nn. 7f.)? What is the position if both the principal claim and the cross-claim arise from a wilful delict (Gernhuber (n. 8) 260f.)?

[191] There are a number of differences in detail; see, for England, Wood (n. 8) 12-130ff.; Derham (n. 6) 250ff.; for Germany, Gernhuber (n. 8) 270ff.; for Austria, Rummel/Rummel (n. 70) § 1440, n. 28; for France, Eujen (n. 16) 43 and 64. The matter is widely held to be one of company law.

VI MISCELLANEOUS PROBLEMS

Finally, there are two miscellaneous matters which are dealt with in a number of legal systems. (i) Set-off is not excluded by the fact that performance of the two obligations has to occur at different places. Thus, it may happen that the creditor of the principal claim suffers damages as a result of not receiving performance or not being able to effect performance at the right place. It appears reasonable to grant him a claim to recover such damages.[192] (ii) If either of the parties has several claims suitable for set-off, the party giving notice of set-off may determine which of these claims are to be set off against each other. If no such specification is given, or if the other party objects without undue delay, the general rules relating to the appropriation of performance[193] apply *mutatis mutandis*.[194]

VII SUMMARY

To sum up: the Principles of European Contract Law should deal with set-off as a matter of substantive law (II). Set-off should operate on the basis of an extrajudicial, informal and unilateral declaration which has to be communicated to the other party (III.1–2). Such a declaration should not

[192] Art. 1296 *code civil*; § 391 BGB; Art. 1245 *codice civile*; Art. 6:138 BW; Art. 1199 *código civil*; Art. 446 *Astikos Kodikas*. And see *Parlementaire Geschiedenis* (n. 8) 514f.; Dullinger (n. 8) 80ff.; Wood (n. 8) 24-31ff.

[193] See Art. 7:109 PECL.

[194] For Germany, see § 396 BGB; for the Netherlands, see Art. 6:137 BW; for Greece, see Art. 452 *Astikos Kodikas*; for Austria, see Rummel/Rummel (n. 70) § 1438, n. 17. And see von Kübel (n. 37) 1093f.; *Parlementaire Geschiedenis* (n. 8) 512ff.; Wood (n. 8) 24-33. In legal systems where set-off operates *ipso iure*, the first part of this proposition does not, of course, apply and the rules relating to the appropriation of performance apply *mutatis mutandis*; for France, see Art. 1297 *code civil*, for Italy, see Art. 1249 *codice civile*; for Spain, see Art. 1199 *código civil*.

have retrospective effect (III.3). The operation of set-off depends upon five requirements. There has to be *concursus debiti et crediti* (IV.1) and both obligations must be of the same kind (IV.2). The cross-claim has to be due (IV.3) and the party declaring set-off must be entitled to effect performance (IV.3). A debtor may not normally set off a claim which is unascertained as to its existence or to its amount. He may only do so if the set-off does not prejudice the interests of the other party. Where the claims of both parties arise from the same legal relationship, it is presumed that the interests of the other party will not be prejudiced (IV.4). Set-off may be excluded by agreement. It cannot be effected against a claim to the extent that that claim is not capable of attachment, and against a claim arising from a wilful delict (V). There have to be rules dealing (i) with the problem of set-off concerning two obligations which have to be performed at different places and (ii) with the situation where one of the parties has two or more claims against the other party or has to perform two or more obligations towards the other party (VI).

2

LIBERATIVE PRESCRIPTION I:
THE CORE REGIME

I POLICY CONSIDERATIONS

An obligation is a legal tie which binds a debtor to the necessity of making some performance.[1] If such performance is not forthcoming, the creditor may bring an action. But he may not wait indefinitely before he chooses to enforce his right. All legal systems today recognize certain temporal limitations, be it under the name of (negative, or extinctive) prescription, or limitation of actions.[2] But they have not always done so. In classical Roman law most actions were not subject to any limitation period.[3] In England the first Statute of Limitations dates from the early seventeenth century.[4] In pre-reception Germany the view prevailed that something that has been wrong for hundred years cannot be right even for an hour.[5] And the South

---

[1] This is the famous definition contained in Inst. See III, 13 pr., as translated by Peter Birks and Grant McLeod, *Justinian's Institutes* (1987).

[2] Concerning terminology, see pp. 69ff., 75.

[3] See Max Kaser, *Das römische Privatrecht: Zweiter Abschnitt* (2nd edn, 1975), p. 71; Reinhard Zimmermann, *The Law of Obligations: Roman Foundations of the Civilian Tradition* (1990, paperback edn 1996), pp. 769f.; E. Kaufmann, in *Handwörterbuch zur Deutschen Rechtsgeschichte*, vol. V (1998), cols. 734ff.; David Johnston, *Prescription and Limitation* (1999), 1.13. For a more detailed discussion of the development of prescription of actions in Roman law, see Mario Amelotti, *La prescrizione delle azioni in diritto romano* (1958).

[4] Andrew McGee, *Limitation Periods* (3rd edn, 1998), p. 2.

[5] Eduard Graf and Mathias Dietherr, *Deutsche Rechtssprichwörter* (2nd edn, 1869), p. 95.

African Xhosa have a proverb according to which 'debts never rot'.

This obvious reluctance in pre-modern societies to impose limitation periods is readily understandable in view of the fact that any such measure effectively amounts to an act of expropriation:[6] a claim is an asset within the property of the creditor which largely loses its value if it can no longer be pursued in court. What, then, are the reasons that have prompted the introduction of limitation periods? The English limitations legislation is, essentially, based on the considerations[7] (i) that, as the years pass by, it becomes more and more difficult for the debtor to defend himself against his creditor's claim; (ii) that the lapse of time engenders the reasonable expectation that an incident which might have given rise to a claim may be treated as closed, and that potential debtors may adjust their behaviour accordingly; and (iii) that it is in the public interest that legal disputes are resolved swiftly so as not to create a source of uncertainty, unfairness and increased cost of litigation.

The same reasons have been advanced in continental legal systems. Loss of right as a result of lapse of time is a means to an end, not an end in itself, as the draftsmen of the German Civil Code recognized.[8] Protection must be granted

---

[6] See also Christian von Bar, *The Common European Law of Torts*, vol. II (2000), n. 554. In this context it may be interesting to observe that acts of expropriation were also not recognized as such in classical Roman law; see Max Kaser, *Das römische Privatrecht: Erster Abschnitt* (2nd edn, 1971), pp. 404f. But see Martin Pennitz, *Der 'Enteignungsfall' im römischen Recht der Republik und des Prinzipats* (1991).

[7] See the succinct analysis in *Consultation Paper* No. 151, entitled 'Limitation of Actions', by the English Law Commission (1998), pp. 11ff.; cf. also N. H. Andrews, 'Civil Procedure', in Peter Birks (ed.), *English Private Law*, vol. II (2000), 19.94.

[8] 'Motive', in Benno Mugdan, *Die gesammten Materialien zum Bürgerlichen Gesetzbuch für das Deutsche Reich*, vol. I (1899), p. 512; see also Johnston (n. 3), 1.31, drawing attention to a variety of authors in the civilian tradition

to a debtor who, in view of the 'obfuscating power of time',[9] finds it increasingly difficult to defend a claim (i); lapse of time suggests a certain indifference on the part of the creditor towards his claim which, in turn, engenders a reasonable reliance in the debtor that no claim will be brought against him (ii); and prescription prevents long-drawn-out litigation about claims which have become stale (iii).[10] 'Interest rei publicae ut sit finis litium' was described, in this context, as a 'favourite and universal maxim' in an English case;[11] 'ne autem lites immortales essent, dum litigantes mortales sunt', as the matter had been put, 'with singular felicity',[12] by a Dutch writer about a century earlier.[13] Friedrich Carl von

who regarded prescription as a matter of utility rather than equity. Even if it is not just, it satisfies practical demands.

[9] Bernhard Windscheid and Theodor Kipp, *Lehrbuch des Pandektenrechts* (9th edn, 1906), § 105 (at 544).

[10] See, for a detailed analysis, Karl Spiro, *Die Begrenzung privater Rechte durch Verjährungs-, Verwirkungs- und Fatalfristen*, vol. 1 (1975), §§ 3ff.; see also Frank Peters and Reinhard Zimmermann, 'Verjährungsfristen. Der Einfluß von Fristen auf Schuldverhältnisse. Möglichkeiten der Vereinheitlichung von Verjährungsfristen', in Bundesminister der Justiz (ed.), *Gutachten und Vorschläge zur Überarbeitung des Schuldrechts*, vol. 1 (1981), pp. 104, 112f., 189f., 288ff.; Bundesminister der Justiz (ed.), *Abschlußbericht der Kommission zur Überarbeitung des Schuldrechts* (1992), pp. 34f.; Frank Peters, in Staudinger, *Kommentar zum Bürgerlichen Gesetzbuch* (13th edn, 1995), Vorbem. zu §§ 194ff., nn. 5ff.; Matthias Unterrieder, *Die regelmäßige Verjährung: Die §§ 195 bis 202 BGB und ihre Reform* (1998), pp. 14ff.; Hartmut Oetker, *Die Verjährung* (1994), pp. 33ff.; Helmut Heinrichs, 'Überlegungen zum Verjährungsrecht, seine Mängel, seine Rechtfertigung und seine Reform', in *Karlsruher Forum* (1991), pp. 6f.; A. S. Hartkamp, *Mr. C. Asser's Handleiding tot de Beoefening van het Nederlands Burgerlijk Recht, Verbintenissenrecht*, Deel I (10th edn, 1996), n. 653; M. M. Loubser, *Extinctive Prescription* (1996), pp. 22ff.; Johnston (n. 3), 1.40ff., 1.58ff.

[11] *Cholmondeley v. Clinton*, (1820) 2 Jac & W 139, 37 ER 527 (577).

[12] Joseph Story, *Commentaries on the Conflict of Laws* (8th edn, 1883), n. 576.

[13] Johannes Voet, *Commentarius ad Pandectas* (Halae, 1778), Lib. II, Tit. I, 53. Voet's great commentary on the Digest first appeared in two volumes, in 1698 and 1704.

Savigny counted the prescription of claims among the most important and beneficial of legal institutions;[14] Joseph Story thought that it was based on 'the noblest policy'.[15] Prescription thus aims, in a very special sense, at legal certainty.

II LEGAL LITERATURE AND LAW REFORM

Obviously, therefore, we are dealing with an institution that constitutes an indispensable feature of a modern legal system. Moreover, it is of enormous practical importance.[16] At the same time, however, surprisingly little academic attention has traditionally been devoted to it.[17] For in spite of having been graced by the attention of some of the greatest legal minds of the nineteenth century,[18] the topic of prescription, or limitation, has until recently very widely been regarded as dull and unrewarding.[19] This may be due to the fact that, both in England and on the continent, prescription, or limitation,

[14] Carl von Savigny, *System des heutigen Römischen Rechts*, vol. v (1841), p. 272. Along the same lines, see P. A. Fenet, *Recueil complet des travaux préparatoires du Code civil*, vol. xv (1836) 573 ('Of all the institutions of private law, prescription is the one that is most necessary for the social order'); I am grateful to Professor Denis Tallon for drawing my attention to this. Most recently, see N. H. Andrews, 'Reform of Limitation of Actions: The Quest for Sound Legal Policy', (1998) 57 *Cambridge Law Journal* 590 ('truly the gateway to justice'). On the other hand, it is occasionally emphasized that the defence of prescription does not rest on strong grounds for substantive justice, or morality; see, e.g., von Bar II (n. 6), n. 545 (the 'morally weakest defence').

[15] Story, *Commentaries* (n. 12), n. 576.

[16] See, for instance, Peters and Zimmermann (n. 10) 103ff.

[17] This applies at least as far as prescription as a general topic of academic discussion and inquiry is concerned. Henner Haug, *Die Neuregelung des Verjährungsrechts* (1999), p. 11, on the other hand, correctly points out that it is hardly possible to keep track of the literature devoted to specific aspects of prescription.

[18] See, e.g., nn. 14, 15.

[19] See Reinhard Zimmermann, 'Die Verjährung', (1984) *Juristische Schulung* 409; Loubser (n. 10) 1; McGee (n. 4) 2f.

is entirely a creation of statutory law; and that the relevant provisions still reflect the somewhat haphazard history of the subject. The first comprehensive modern treatise, based on Swiss law but also taking account of other continental codifications, appeared in 1975.[20] Since then, academic interest has picked up considerably, notably in Germany. In England, too, a number of treatises devoted to limitation periods have been published in recent years.[21] 'Extinctive prescription' was one of the topics discussed at the XIVth Congress of the International Academy of Comparative Law in August 1994;[22] since then, important monographs have appeared, *inter alia*, in South Africa[23] and Scotland.[24]

A not inconsiderable amount of legal literature has also been generated by attempts to reform or harmonize the law of prescription/limitation.[25] For, on the one hand, in a number of countries the relevant body of law is viewed with great concern. In Germany, the rules relating to prescription are

[20] This is the standard treatise by Spiro, quoted n. 10.
[21] See the references in McGee (n. 4) 3 and Andrews, (1998) 57 *Cambridge Law Journal* 589f.
[22] Documented in Ewoud H. Hondius (ed.), *Extinctive Prescription: On the Limitation of Actions* (1995).
[23] The work by Loubser, quoted n. 10.
[24] The work by Johnston, quoted n. 3. For the Netherlands, see M. W. E. Koopmann, *Bevrijdende verjaring* (1993).
[25] See, for Germany, Helmut Heinrichs, 'Reform des Verjährungsrechts', (1982) *Neue Juristische Wochenschrift* 2021ff.; Heinrichs (n. 10) 3ff.; Wolfgang Grunsky, 'Vorschläge zu einer Reform des Schuldrechts', (1982) 182 *Archiv für die Civilistische Praxis* 453ff.; Karl Spiro, 'Zur Reform der Verjährungsbestimmungen', in *Festschrift für Wolfram Müller-Freienfels* (1986), pp. 617ff.; Dieter Rabe, 'Vorschläge zur Überarbeitung des Schuldrechts: Verjährung', (1992) *Neue Juristische Wochenschrift* 2395ff.; for Belgium, see M. E. Storme, 'Perspectieven voor de bevrijdende verjaring in het vermogensrecht met ontwerpbepalingen voor een hervorming', (1994) *Tijdschrift voor Privaatrecht* 1977ff. For a comparative discussion, focusing on English, Dutch and Greek law, and the German reform proposals, see Gerhard Dannemann, Fotios Karatzenis and Geoffrey V. Thomas, 'Reform des Verjährungsrechts aus rechtsvergleichender Sicht', (1991) 55 *RabelsZ* 697ff.

widely regarded as one of the least satisfactory features of the BGB;[26] in England, the law of limitation of actions is considered to be incoherent, unnecessarily complex, outdated, uncertain, unfair and inefficient.[27] But these are not the only countries in which a pressing need for legislative reform has been recognized.[28] Reform proposals have been submitted by a special commission charged with the revision of the law of obligations in Germany[29] and by the Law Commission in England.[30] Other countries have overhauled their law of prescription in the process of recodification, most notably the Netherlands[31] and Québec.[32] The most recent piece of reform legislation, however, is the one enacted in Belgium.[33]

---

[26] For all details, see Peters and Zimmermann (n. 10) 186ff.; for a discussion in English, see Reinhard Zimmermann, 'Extinctive Prescription in German Law', in Erik Jayme (ed.), *German National Reports in Civil Law Matters for the XIVth Congress of Comparative Law in Athens* (1994), pp. 153ff.

[27] *Law Commission Consultation Paper* (n. 7) 241ff.

[28] See, e.g., Ewoud Hondius, 'General Report', in Hondius (n. 22), pp. 24f. ('At present, the law relating to extinctive prescription is in turmoil'). Regarding France, see Alain Bénabent, 'Le chaos du droit de la prescription extinctive', in *Mélanges dédiés à Louis Boyer* (1996), pp. 123ff.

[29] See *Abschlußbericht* (n. 10). This commission was established early in 1984 and it was instructed to revise the law of (liberative) prescription, the law relating to breach of contract and warranty claims. Concerning the law of prescription, the commission took as its starting point a report and reform proposal submitted, at the request of the minister of justice, in 1981 by Frank Peters and Reinhard Zimmermann (see above n. 10). For further literature, see Zimmermann (n. 26) 155.

[30] See *Law Commission Consultation Paper* (n. 7); on which, see Andrews, (1998) 57 *Cambridge Law Journal* 589ff.

[31] See, in particular, the monograph by Koopmann (n. 24); Asser/Hartkamp (n. 10), nn. 648 ff.; Dannemann, Karatzenis and Thomas, (1991) 55 *RabelsZ* 697ff.

[32] See Patrice Deslauriers, 'Québec', in Hondius (n. 22), pp. 287ff.

[33] Wet van 10 juni 1998 tot wijziging van sommige bepalingen betreffende de verjaring. Artt. 2262, 2262bis and 2263 Belgian *code civil* were inserted or amended by this statute. See Ignace Claeys, 'De nieuwe verjaringswet: een inleidende verkenning', (1998–9) *Rechtskundig Weekblad* 377ff. for details,

On the other hand, it is widely acknowledged that the adoption of a uniform regime governing limitation periods, particularly in international sales law, would facilitate the development of international trade. For this reason a convention was drafted by the United Nations Commission on International Trade Law (Uncitral) in the early 1970s; it was approved in June 1974, amended by a Protocol adopted in 1980 and entered into force on 1 August 1988.[34] However, it has, so far, been conspicuously less successful than the Convention on the International Sale of Goods, since it has been ratified by only seventeen states, none of them belonging to the European Union.[35]

as well as the contributions to Hubert Bocken et al. (eds.), *De herziening van de bevrijdende verjaring door de Wet van 10 juni 1998: De gelijkheid hersteld?* (1999).

[34] It can be consulted at www.un.or.at/uncitral/english/texts/sales/limitcon.htm. The German version may be found in Reiner Schulze and Reinhard Zimmermann (eds.), *Basistexte zum europäischen Privatrecht* (2000), II.10. For a commentary, see (1979) 10 *Uncitral Yearbook* 145ff.; see also, e.g., Karl Spiro, 'Befristung und Verjährung der Ansprüche aus dem Wiener Kaufrechtsübereinkommen', in Hans Hoyer and Willibald Posch (eds.), *Das einheitliche Wiener Kaufrecht* (1992), pp. 195ff.; Ulrich Magnus, 'Aktuelle Fragen des UN-Kaufrechts', (1993) 1 *Zeitschrift für Europäisches Privatrecht* 90ff.; Magnus, 'Stand und Entwicklung des UN-Kaufrechts', (1995) 3 *Zeitschrift für Europäisches Privatrecht* 214f.; K. Boele-Woelki, 'De verjaring van vorderingen uit internationale koopovereenkomsten', in *Europees Privaatrecht* (1996), pp. 99ff.

[35] As per 1 February 1999 the convention had entered into force, in its amended version, in Argentina, Belarus, Cuba, Czech Republic, Egypt, Guinea, Hungary, Mexico, Moldova, Poland, Romania, Slovakia, Slovenia, Uganda, United States of America, Uruguay and Zambia. See Schulze and Zimmermann (n. 34) II.10 for details. For the reason why the Convention has been ratified, so far, mainly by third-world and ex-socialist countries (conspicuous exception: the United States, where the Convention entered into force in December 1994), see Frank Diedrich, 'Lückenfüllung im Internationalen Einheitsrecht', (1995) *Recht der Internationalen Wirtschaft* 362: the export-oriented nations in Western Europe regard the four-year period of Art. 8 as too long. See also the interesting background information on the origin of this provision provided by Boele-Woelki (n. 34) 120f.

III PRESCRIPTION OF CLAIMS AND LIMITATION OF ACTIONS

Hitherto two different terms have been employed for the legal institution under consideration: (negative/extinctive) prescription and limitation of actions. The former is used in the legal systems belonging to the Romanistic legal family and is derived from the Roman *longi temporis praescriptio*.[36] The bracketed qualification[37] is intended to make clear that we are not dealing here with acquisitive (or positive) prescription: the acquisition of title to property as a result of lapse of time. This was the historical root of the notion of *longi temporis praescriptio*[38] which was extended only in the post-classical period to the limitation of actions.[39] Under the older *ius commune* the Roman term was still used in a broad sense to cover what was usually referred to as 'acquisitive' and 'extinctive' prescription.[40] The natural law codifications proceeded from this basis[41] as do Scots[42] and South African law.[43] Predominantly, however, the combination of both

[36] The German (and Austrian) term is 'Verjährung', the Dutch one 'verjaring'.

[37] The term 'negative prescription' is used in Scotland. See Johnston (n. 3) 1.13.

[38] See Kaser I (n. 6) 424ff.; Johnston (n. 3) 1.15; Dieter Nörr, *Die Entstehung der longi temporis praescriptio* (1969).

[39] Kaser II (n. 3) 71f., 285ff.; Amelotti (n. 3) 211ff.; Johnston (n. 3) 1.116ff.; cf. also Peters and Zimmermann (n. 10) 112f.

[40] See the references in Zimmermann (n. 3) 768, n. 141. For a discussion of the development, see Helmut Coing, *Europäisches Privatrecht*, vol. I (1985), pp. 183ff.; Coing, *Europäisches Privatrecht*, vol. II (1989), pp. 280ff.; Oetker (n. 10) 20ff.; Johnston (n. 3) 1.31ff.

[41] §§ 1478ff. ABGB; Artt. 2219ff. *code civil*. In both countries, however, this approach is criticized today and both institutions are usually discussed separately, the one in the context of the law of obligations, the other of the law of property. See Helmut Koziol and Rudolf Welser, *Grundriß des bürgerlichen Rechts*, vol. I (10th edn, 1995), pp. 184ff.; vol. II (10th edn, 1996), 86ff.; Murad Ferid and Hans-Jürgen Sonnenberger, *Das französische Zivilrecht*, vol. I/1 (2nd edn, 1994), 1 C 191.

[42] Prescription and Limitation (Scotland) Act 1973.

[43] Prescription Act 68/1969; and see Loubser (n. 10) 21f.

legal institutions under one and the same doctrinal umbrella is no longer regarded as helpful today since they are largely governed by different rules. The modern approach gained ground in nineteenth-century scholarship[44] and found its way into the twentieth-century codifications.[45] In England, interestingly, prescription is a term that has retained its original, acquisitive flavour.[46]

The functional equivalent to 'extinctive' prescription in English law is 'limitation of actions'. As the term suggests, the English institution is procedural in nature: limitation does not affect the right (i.e., the substantive 'cause of action') but merely the ability to pursue that right in court.[47] This approach is by no means alien to the civilian tradition. Up to the nineteenth century, *longi temporis praescriptio* was usually related to the right to sue and was thus seen to bar the action.[48] In Germany, the notion of 'Klageverjährung' gave way to that of a prescription affecting

---

[44] Savigny (n. 14) 266 referred to acquisitive and extinctive prescription as 'artificial terms' which are 'totally reprehensible'; cf. also, e.g., Windscheid and Kipp (n. 9) § 105, nn. 1a and 6; Coing II (n. 40) 281f.

[45] Thus, prescription of claims is dealt with in §§ 194ff. BGB (general part), usucaption ('Ersitzung') in §§ 937ff. BGB (law of property). The *codice civile* deals with usucaption ('usucapione') in Artt. 1158ff. (law of property) and with prescription ('prescrizione') in Artt. 2934ff. (as part of book 6, devoted to protection of rights). For the Dutch BW, see Artt. 3:99ff. and 3:306ff. (both in book 3 dealing with patrimonial law in general, the former (still called 'verkrijgende verjaring') in title 4 (acquisition and loss of property), the latter ('bevrijdende verjaring') in title 11 (rights of action)).

[46] Andrew McGee, 'England', in Hondius (n. 22), p. 135: 'for a Common Lawyer the term "extinctive prescription" has an odd ring. "Prescription" is a term usually used in the common law to denote the process by which limited rights of use over another's land (such as easements) may be acquired.'

[47] Characteristically, therefore, limitation is discussed in the chapter devoted to civil procedure in Birks (n. 7).

[48] See, for example, §§ 150, 151, 155 of the Saxonian Civil Code; Savigny (n. 14) 265ff.; Alois Brinz, *Lehrbuch der Pandekten*, vol. 1 (3rd edn, 1884), § 114; Coing I (n. 40) 187; see also *Staudinger*/Peters (n. 10) § 194, n. 2. On the Roman notion of 'actio', see Kaser I (n. 6) 223ff.

the substantive claim, i.e., barring the right rather than the remedy ('Anspruchsverjährung'), only as a result of Bernhard Windscheid's famous monograph on the action of Roman private law from the point of view of contemporary law.[49] A number of continental legal systems have followed suit.[50] But there are also other views. According to the French *code civil* '[t]outes les *actions . . .* sont prescrites'[51] and Art. 2223 *code civil* enjoins judges not to supply 'd'office le moyen résultant de la prescription'. This is clearly a procedural approach. On the other hand, however, prescription is described as 'un moyen . . . de se libérer' in Art. 2219 and as a means of extinguishing an obligation in Art. 1234.[52] Understandably, in view of these somewhat contradictory pronouncements, academic opinion has vacillated: the *théorie classique*, prevailing in the nineteenth century, took a procedural perspective

[49] Windscheid, *Die Actio des römischen Civilrechts vom Standpunkte des heutigen Rechts* (1856); Windscheid and Kipp (n. 9) §§ 43, 106. 'Anspruch' was the term coined by Windscheid in order to remould the German *actio* into a term of substantive rather than procedural law. It has become one of the central conceptual pillars of modern private law doctrine in Germany; see, e.g., Reinhard Zimmermann, 'An Introduction to German Legal Culture', in Werner F. Ebke and Matthew W. Finkin, *Introduction to German Law* (1996), p. 31, with references.

[50] See, for the Netherlands, Art. 3:306 BW, referring to 'verjaring van een rechtsvordering'; significantly, Koopmann uses the term 'Anspruchsverjährung'. See also Spiro (n. 10) § 241 who regards this as the approach generally followed in continental legal systems. According to Loubser (n. 10) 13, 'denial of the ability to enforce a substantive right by legal process is an integral part of such a right'. The qualification of prescription/limitation as substantive or procedural used to be of considerable practical importance for private international law (is prescription/limitation governed by the *lex causae contractus* or the *lex fori*?). However, England and Scotland now also apply the *lex causae* (Foreign Limitation Periods Act of 1984, in force since October 1985). For details, see Boele-Woelki (n. 34) 100ff.

[51] Art. 2262 *code civil* (emphasis added).

[52] See also Art. 2934 (1) *codice civile*: 'Ogni diritto si estingue per prescrizione'; Art. 2938 *codice civile*: 'Il giudice non può relevare d'ufficio la prescrizione non opposta.'

whereas in the course of the twentieth century prescription came to be seen, predominantly, as an institution of substantive law, extinguishing the right rather than merely barring the action.[53] As a result of parliamentary endorsement of the procedural perspective in the course of the reform of the *code de procédure civile* in 1975 (the draftsmen still following Pothier in this respect!), opinion has started to vacillate again;[54] still, however, prevailing doctrine today subscribes to the principle that the obligation itself is extinguished.[55]

But even if a legal system regards prescription as a matter of substantive law, it may take what is often dubbed a 'weak' or a 'strong' approach. Once the period of prescription has run out, the claim may be held to have ceased to exist (strong effect);[56] or the debtor may merely be granted a right to refuse performance (i.e., a defence on the level of substantive law; weak effect).[57] Thus, if the debtor has paid

[53] See Ferid and Sonnenberger (n. 41) 1 C 245.

[54] Ferid and Sonnenberger (n. 41) 1 C 245f.; François Terré, Philippe Simler and Yves Lequette, *Droit Civil: Les Obligations* (7th edn, 1999), n. 1403.

[55] Gabriel Marty, Pierre Raynand and Philippe Jestaz, *Les Obligations*, vol. II (2nd edn, 1989), nn. 341f. French law also recognizes a number of cases where expiration of very short periods of prescription merely leads to a presumption that payment has been made ('prescription présomptive'): Artt. 2271ff. *code civil*; Terré, Simler and Lequette (n. 54) n. 1376; Ferid and Sonnenberger (n. 41) 1 C 250; Unterrieder (n. 10) 84ff.; cf. also Artt. 2954ff. *codice civile*. Such a presumption provides only an imperfect protection against unjustified claims and therefore always requires, in addition, a proper prescription regime. If the general period is brief, an additional presumptive prescription would render the law in this area unnecessarily complex. For criticism, see Spiro (n. 10) § 254; Peters and Zimmermann (n. 10) 263f.; Loubser (n. 10) 9f.

[56] According to ss. 8A, 6, 7 Prescription and Limitation (Scotland) Act 1973 prescription has the effect of extinguishing the obligation in question; see also Johnston (n. 3) 4.101. The same position applies in South Africa: s. 10 (1) Prescription Act 68 of 1969; and see Loubser (n. 10) 15ff. Also according to Art. 2934 (1) *codice civile*, prescription extinguishes the obligation; and see § 1449 ABGB; Art. 1234 *code civil*.

[57] See § 222 1 BGB and *Staudinger*/Peters (n. 10) § 222, nn. 34ff.; cf. also Art. 272 1 *Astikos Kodikas* and, for Dutch law, *Asser*/Hartkamp (n. 10) n. 655. This

in spite of prescription having occurred, he has paid with legal ground according to the latter approach and should be unable to recover;[58] whereas he should be able to recover as having paid without legal ground according to the former approach.[59] This consequence, however, is not normally drawn by legal systems subscribing to the strong effect of prescription.[60] Nor do all of them, as might have been thought logical, regard prescription as a matter which must be taken into account by the court *ex officio*.[61] Effectively, therefore, it is the weak effect of prescription that has been gaining ground internationally. This is not surprising in view of the fact that it would appear to be most appropriate in view of the aims pursued by the law of prescription.[62] For there is no reason for a legal system to foist its protection upon a debtor who is willing to pay[63] and who can thus be taken to acknowledge that he is under an obligation to do so; and the public interest ('ut sit finis litium'[64]) is not adversely affected if a debtor is allowed to pay even after the period

---

approach is supported by Spiro (n. 10) §§ 226ff., 241, 244; Loubser (n. 10) 14f.; *Abschlußbericht* (n. 10) 100f.

[58] § 222 II BGB; Art. 63 II OR; Peters and Zimmermann (n. 10) 136; Koziol and Welser (n. 41) 189; Spiro (n. 10) § 233; Loubser (n. 10) 16; Art. 26 Uncitral Convention (n. 34).

[59] Whether payment has been made with or without legal ground is the key issue for the application of the modern civilian version of the *condictio indebiti*; for details, see Reinhard Zimmermann, 'Unjustified Enrichment: The Modern Civilian Approach', (1995) 15 *Oxford Journal of Legal Studies* 403ff.

[60] See, e.g., Art. 2940 *codice civile*; s. 10 (3) (South African) Prescription Act 68 of 1969.

[61] § 1501 ABGB; Art. 2938 *codice civile*; s. 17 (1) (South African) Prescription Act 68 of 1969; see also von Bar II (n. 6) n. 545.

[62] See also the analysis by Spiro (n. 10) §§ 241, 244; Loubser (n. 10) 14ff.; Oetker (n. 10) 60ff.

[63] The arguments advanced in the course of preparing the BGB are still valid today; for a summary see Peters and Zimmermann (n. 10) 136.

[64] See pp. 63f.

of prescription has run out.[65] While any prescription regime will inevitably result in creditors being unable to pursue even entirely valid claims, the law should not endorse this consequence where it is unnecessary in terms of the underlying policy objectives.

It is noticeable that legal systems attributing a strong effect to prescription come very close, as far as practical results are concerned, to those subscribing to the weak approach. The same is true if one compares legal systems adopting a substantive with those adopting a procedural approach.[66] Thus, under the common law, since prescription bars the remedy and not the right, it is a matter of course that the debt can still be paid and that any such payment cannot later be recovered.[67] All in all, the discussion is less concerned with practical results than with the true construction, or theory, of prescription. On that level, however, it may be maintained that the weak substantive approach is able to explain the practical results more satisfactorily;[68] and that,

[65] To the contrary, it may be argued that to allow the debtor to reclaim what he has given would be detrimental to the public peace: after the debtor has paid the matter must be regarded as settled.

[66] See, as far as French and German law are concerned, Ferid and Sonnenberger (n. 41) 1 C 197, 1 C 246; concerning German and English law see, e.g., *Law Commission Consultation Paper* (n. 7) 234 (10.144). But see also the remarks by Spiro (n. 10) § 241.

[67] French law reaches the same result; see Ferid and Sonnenberger (n. 41) 1 C 248.

[68] See also Loubser (n. 10) 15ff. What remains of the obligation after prescription has occurred is often described as 'naturalis obligatio', both in legal systems which, in principle, proceed from the assumption that the obligation is extinguished and in those which hold that the obligation continues to exist: see, e.g., Philippe Malaurie and Laurent Aynès, *Les Obligations* (10th edn, 1999/2000), n. 1097; *Staudinger*/Peters (n. 10) § 222, n. 34; *Asser*/Hartkamp (n. 10) n. 657; Spiro (n. 10) § 244. But it has also, correctly, been noted that the use of such terminology is not very helpful in view of the fact that we are not dealing with a 'naturalis obligatio' in the historical sense of the word: after all, the creditor's claim is perfectly enforceable (as long as prescription is not invoked).

moreover, the procedural flavour inherent in the notion of a defence (though one on the basis of substantive law) provides a bridge between a purely procedural and a purely substantive concept of prescription.[69] Notice must also be taken of the decision in the Rome Convention on the Law Applicable to Contractual Obligations in favour of a substantive characterization of limitation/prescription.[70] And finally, it would appear that in a code of contract law the notion of a 'remedy' (as employed in chapter 9 of the *Principles of European Contract Law*) can hardly be taken to be a purely procedural one and that the right to withhold performance under Art. 9:201 presumably constitutes a defence like the defence of prescription in the jurisdictions endorsing a 'weak' prescription regime. As a result, then, it may be desirable to abandon the current terminology. 'Extinctive prescription' is inappropriate in view of the fact that prescription does not extinguish the right. 'Limitation of actions' should be avoided because of its purely procedural frame of reference. 'Limitation of claims' would be one possibility, 'liberative prescription' the other. Of these two the latter is more specific and descriptive, and hence preferable.

---

[69] The truth of the matter is, as Kurt Lipstein has pointed out, that prescription/limitation in every European system contains substantive as well as procedural elements: 'Qualification', in *International Encyclopedia of Comparative Law*, vol. III, chapter 5 (2000), n. 29; cf. also *Staudinger*/Peters (n. 10) § 194, n. 4. It may be pointed out, in this context, that the Uncitral Convention attempts, as it were, to sit on the fence; it 'avoids choosing between whether it deals with the institution of prescription as it is known in certain legal systems or of limitation as it is known in others': Hans Smit, 'The Convention on the Limitation Period in the International Sale of Goods: Uncitral's First-Born', (1975) 23 *American Journal of Comparative Law* 339; cf. also Boele-Woelki (n. 34) 112ff. Thus, it merely uses the term 'limitation'; on the other hand, it uses the notion of 'claims' which can no longer be exercised.

[70] Art. 10 (1) (d).

IV STRIKING THE BALANCE

1 *Principal components of a prescription regime*

One of the most characteristic features of any prescription regime is the close interrelation between its individual components.[71] The principal components are: the period of prescription; when the period begins to run; under which circumstances prescription is suspended; in which cases the period begins to run afresh; and whether the parties, by agreement, may facilitate or render more difficult the prescription of a claim. Thus, for instance, a uniform period of prescription may be more acceptable if the parties are able to extend or shorten it to suit the requirements of a specific type of claim. A great degree of uniformity may therefore be balanced by making the prescription regime non-mandatory. Or, if the period of prescription is very long, the rules about suspension, or renewal, will not be practically very relevant. They become crucially important, however, in case of short prescription periods. Or, perhaps, most importantly: a period of one year may be a relatively short period; and it may be too short, at least from the point of view of the creditor, if it runs from an objective date (such as delivery) and without any regard as to whether the creditor knew about his claim or could have known about it. By the same token, even a one-year period may be perfectly adequate if the prescription regime does take account of these subjective factors. Generally speaking it may be said that a debtor-friendly (i.e., a short) period of prescription requires the rules concerning commencement, suspension and renewal to be tilted in favour of the creditor to achieve an acceptable balance. Thus, it is always dangerous to look at any one individual facet of a prescription regime in isolation.

---

[71] See also Spiro (n. 10) §§ 256ff.

2 *Balancing the interests*

In addition, it must always be kept in mind that the prescription regime as a composite whole reflects a balancing of conflicting interests.[72] Here we may turn to the policy considerations mentioned above.[73] They require the law to recognize the institution of liberative prescription. Considerations (i) and (ii) focus on protection of the debtor and militate in favour of a strict regime whereas (iii) is more ambiguous. For the public interest is not served if creditors do not have a reasonable chance to pursue well-founded claims. A prescription regime which bites too hard would ultimately lead to the fundamental inconsistency that the legal system takes away with the one hand what it gives with the other. It would grant legal rights without practical value. Moreover, it would induce creditors to pursue their rights prematurely and would thus engender rather than prevent unnecessary lawsuits.[74] If the law of prescription enables the debtor summarily to defend himself against a claim brought against him by invoking prescription, it does so because the claim may well be unfounded and because it may have become impossible for him to establish that fact: policy consideration (i) above. For a certain period, however (e.g., for as long as one usually keeps receipts for payments made), it is not normally difficult for a debtor to show that the claim brought against him is unfounded (e.g., because he has already paid). Were he allowed to resort to the defence of prescription when the law could reasonably expect him to raise whatever other defence may be available to him, his protection would, as it

---

[72] See also Oetker (n. 10) 55; and Andrews, (1998) 57 *Cambridge Law Journal* 595, who emphasizes that a satisfactory law of limitation must involve the balancing of competing considerations.

[73] See pp. 63f.

[74] See also *Law Commission Consultation Paper* (n. 7) 14.

were, overshoot the mark. For by resorting to the defence of prescription, the debtor would be able to defeat claims which are, very often, well-founded.

That well-founded claims may be defeated is, of course, the necessary price a legal system has to pay if it wishes to provide the debtor with an easy means to defeat unfounded ones.[75] A very delicate line therefore has to be drawn as to when that price (to be paid by the creditor!) is justified by a preponderance of benefits for the debtor. But since it is the creditor who has to pay the price, policy consideration (ii) comes into play again. A creditor, in a way, is acting against the precepts of good faith if he sits on his rights without exercising them[76] and only pounces upon his debtor at some later stage. His behaviour has engendered a reasonable reliance in the debtor that he may treat the matter as closed. But the creditor's behaviour can be held against him only if he has had a chance to pursue his claim. It would be manifestly unjust to hold a creditor accountable for not bringing an action against his debtor if he either was unable or could not reasonably be expected to do so.[77] This would seem to

---

[75] Attention very widely tends to focus on the fact that prescription rules may have the effect of depriving a creditor of a well-founded claim. Much less attention tends to be paid to the many cases in which prescription rules prevent unjustified claims from being successfully pursued: Peters and Zimmermann (n. 10) 104.

[76] Inherent in prescription is thus an element of 'Verwirkung'; on which see, in general, *Staudinger*/Peters (n. 10) § 194, nn. 17ff.; Günter H. Roth, in *Münchener Kommentar zum Bürgerlichen Gesetzbuch*, vol. II (3rd edn, 1994), nn. 360ff.; and see the references in Simon Whittaker and Reinhard Zimmermann, 'Good Faith in European Contract Law: Surveying the Landscape', in Reinhard Zimmermann and Simon Whittaker (eds.), *Good Faith in European Contract Law* (2000), pp. 25, 31f., as well as case study 22 in the same volume (at 515ff.).

[77] As to the required balance which needs to be struck see also Spiro (n. 10) § 258. That the commencement of the period of prescription is the most crucial point in determining the reasonableness of a prescription regime has also been noted by others; see, e.g., Matthias E. Storme, 'Constitutional Review of

be a strong argument in favour of a regime which, while taking account of the creditor's position in determining when the period of prescription begins to run and under which circumstances it may be suspended (broadly speaking, the creditor must have a fair opportunity of pursuing his claim), would revolve around a comparatively short prescription period.[78]

V THE ARGUMENT FOR UNIFORMITY

1 *Public policy*

The first of these two considerations obviously applies to all kinds of claims: with whichever claim we are dealing, the creditor must have a fair chance of pursuing it. The rules about commencement and extension may thus be of general application. Arguably, therefore, the period can also be of general application. For if the rules concerning commencement and suspension ensure that a claim does not prescribe in a situation where the creditor could not have known about

---

Disproportionately Different Periods of Limitation of Actions (Prescription)', (1997) 5 *European Review of Private Law* 84. Commencement of prescription is also the key issue inspiring Neil Andrews' comments in (1998) 57 *Cambridge Law Journal* 589ff.

[78] See, in this context, two decisions of the Belgian Constitutional Court (Arbitragehof) of 21 March 1995 and 20 September 1996, in the latter of which a prescription rule was struck down as unconstitutional. An important element in the reasoning of the court was the fact that the short period of prescription applicable in the case had started to run long before the damages had become apparent. For discussion, see Storme, (1997) 5 *European Review of Private Law* 82ff.; Claeys, (1998–9) *Rechtskundig Weekblad* 381 (who concludes that all short prescription periods might eventually be regarded as unconstitutional as long as they begin to run before the injured person could become aware of the damage caused). There has also been some doubt about the constitutionality in Irish law of a limitation regime which has the effect of depriving a person of a property right even when he was ignorant of the fact that he had such a right in the first place; see the references in von Bar II (n. 6) n. 554.

it, where it was impossible for him to pursue it, or where it would otherwise be unreasonable to expect him to do so, even a two-year period would give him enough time, no matter whether his claim is based on contract, tort/delict or unjustified enrichment. On the other hand, even a much longer period may sometimes be insufficient if it were to be counted from an objective date and without adequate grounds for extension.

A prescription regime which is as simple, straightforward and uniform as possible would also be desirable from the perspective of public policy.[79] Liberative prescription is intended, *inter alia*, to prevent unnecessarily costly and long-drawn-out lawsuits ('ut sit finis litium'). It would therefore be intolerable if the prescription rules themselves could easily give rise to litigation – litigation which merely concerns the question whether or not prescription has occurred in a particular case. Before this question was decided by the final court of appeal, even more years would have passed and it would now be all the more difficult to litigate about the merits of the case, which would, however, be necessary if it were ultimately held that prescription had not in fact occurred. The German law reports are full of litigation of this kind; it is typical of an extremely differentiated system of liberative prescription.[80] Wherever we have a rule laying down a period of prescription for a specific type of claim, it is necessary to define that type of claim. The concepts used in any such definition, however, are open to interpretation, even if they

---

[79] See Peters and Zimmermann (n. 10) 289. Andrews, (1998) 57 *Cambridge Law Journal* 596, on the other hand, regards strict uniformity of limitation periods as undesirable.

[80] For a detailed discussion, see Peters and Zimmermann (n. 10) 186ff.; see also the overview in English in the volume edited by Jayme (n. 26) 154ff. Similar criticisms have been made in England: *Law Commission Consultation Paper* (n. 7) 244; for France, see Bénabent (n. 28) 123ff.

are as specific as '[claims concerning] work on buildings'[81] or payment for a 'service rendered for the trade conducted by the debtor'.[82] At the same time, any type of claim described in one prescription rule will border on other rules providing for different periods of prescription. Every creditor against whom the shorter of the two periods has expired will thus be tempted to argue that his claim falls under the provision with the longer period, and the courts will then have to determine where exactly the line between these two provisions must be drawn. If, moreover, for some or other reason one of these different prescription rules is regarded as inadequate, or as less adequate than the other, there is the added danger that courts and legal writers may be tempted to distort the concepts used in these rules[83] and to redefine the borderline between contracts of service (*locatio conductio operarum*) and contracts for work (*locatio conductio operis*),[84] or between contract and delict[85] *sub specie praescriptionis* rather than from a general perspective.

2 *Criteria for differentiation?*

Moreover, there do not appear to be any general criteria which would be both sufficiently clear and convincing to provide a basis for a differentiated prescription regime, at

---

[81] § 638 BGB; see Zimmermann (n. 26) 168.

[82] § 196 I no. 1, 11 BGB; see Zimmermann (n. 26) 161 and Peters and Zimmermann (n. 10) 176f.

[83] On the explosive potential inherent in a differentiated prescription regime, see the discussion by Peters and Zimmermann (n. 10) 196ff., with examples. See also Claeys, (1998–9) *Rechtskundig Weekblad* 379, with the observation that '[i]n de rechtspraak was de vindingrijkheid dan ook groot om te ontsnappen aan de korte verjaring'. And see Andrews, (1998) 57 *Cambridge Law Journal* 605 (the tail – limitation rules – must no longer wag the dog – the substantive principles of liability in contract and tort).

[84] See Zimmermann (n. 26) 172.

[85] See the example discussed in Zimmermann (n. 26) 170.

least not within the law of obligations.[86] Of course, one might want to subject claims arising from everyday trans-actions, or claims of a petty nature, to shorter periods of prescription than complex or extraordinary claims. But it is impossible to draw a plausible borderline and to define this borderline in precise statutory terms. Another poten-tial point of reference might be the professional position of debtor and/or creditor.[87] But any regulation based on it would either be very casuistic and in permanent danger of becoming outdated,[88] or too abstract and general (and thus open to conflicting interpretation). Moreover, any such dif-ferentiation would only appear to make sense as far as the right to performance and possibly also a claim for damages for breach of contract are concerned. It is much less convinc-ing for claims arising *ex lege*: claims, in other words, with the handling of which even a professional person often has little experience. At the same time, however, such claims aris-ing *ex lege* always provide a possible alternative to a claim for specific performance; for non-performance by the debtor may be based on the conviction that the contract is invalid.

The most common criterion employed in the context of dif-ferentiated periods of prescription is the (legal) nature of the claim.[89] But this criterion, too, does not ultimately appear

---

[86] Peters and Zimmermann (n. 10) 290ff.

[87] See, most recently, the proposal by Andrews, (1998) 57 *Cambridge Law Jour-nal* 600ff. (arguing for a different starting date concerning claims of 'those engaged in trade and business'. The concerns underlying this proposal can, however, be accommodated by the way in which the discoverability test is applied. What is reasonably discoverable depends, of course, not least of all on the experience and professional status of the claimant).

[88] See, for example, the regulation in § 196 BGB (discussed in Zimmermann (n. 26) 159ff.).

[89] See, e.g., the draft of the commission charged with the reform of the German law of obligations, drawing a distinction between claims arising *ex con-tractu* and those arising *ex lege*. For trenchant criticism of this dichotomous structure of the law of prescription, see Haug (n. 17) 20ff. For equally forceful

to be suitable. Whether or not prescription has occurred is a question which often has to be determined at a time when the legal position between the parties is unclear. It may be doubtful whether a contract is valid. The creditor, therefore, does not know whether he has a claim for specific performance, or for damages, or a claim based on unjustified enrichment or perhaps even *negotiorum gestio*. Or a contract lies on the borderline between sale and lease, or sale and contract for work, or contract for work and contract of service. Or the creditor's claim for damages may be based on contract or tort/delict (or *culpa in contrahendo*, wherever that may fit in[90]). What the older codifications tended to overlook is that hardly any claim within the field of the law of obligations can be dealt with in isolation. This interconnectedness is of particular relevance with regard to the law of liberative prescription – with the result, *inter alia*, that differentiated periods of prescription tend to lead to inconsistencies in result and evaluation.[91]

criticism concerning a similar approach adopted by the new Belgian law, see Claeys, (1998–9) *Rechtskundig Weekblad* 391ff.; Bart Claessens and Delphine Counye, 'De repercussies van de Wet van 10 juni 1998 op de structuur van het gemeenrechtelijke verjaringsregime', in Bocken et al. (n. 33) 82f.; cf. also Andrews, (1998) 57 *Cambridge Law Journal* 605ff.

[90] It is governed by the rules relating to contracts in German law (see Zimmermann and Whittaker (n. 76) 172f.) and forms part of the law of delict in France (see, e.g., Stephan Lorenz, 'Die culpa in contrahendo im französischen Recht', (1994) 2 *Zeitschrift für Europäisches Privatrecht* 218ff.). The development in Germany has been most recently outlined by Tomasz Giaro, 'Culpa in contrahendo: Eine Geschichte der Wiederentdeckungen', in Ulrich Falk and Heinz Mohnhaupt (eds.), *Das Bürgerliche Gesetzbuch und seine Richter* (2000), pp. 113ff. Cf. also Ole Lando and Hugh Beale (eds.), *Principles of European Contract Law* (2000), Artt. 2:301f., and comparative notes at 189ff.; Spiro (n. 10) § 298.

[91] For the following paragraph, see Peters and Zimmermann (n. 10) 292. For similar criticism concerning English law, see *Law Commission Consultation Paper* (n. 7) 242f. The Belgian Constitutional Court has even held, in two startling pronouncements from 1995 and 1996, that such inconsistencies, based upon widely diverging periods of prescription, may constitute an act of

Thus, for instance, restitution claims arising as a result of the invalidity of a contract should not prescribe after a longer period than contractual claims for specific performance: the obfuscating power of time hits the debtor as hard in the one case as in the other. At the same time, it would be inadvisable to differentiate between contractual restitution claims and those based on unjustified enrichment,[92] or between the different types of unjustified enrichment claims. Unjustified enrichment, however, is frequently an alternative to *negotiorum gestio*. There is also so often a concurrence between claims based upon unjustified enrichment and delict that they should be subject to the same prescription regime. Delictual claims, in turn, are so closely related to *culpa in contrahendo* or to contractual claims for consequential loss that no distinction should be drawn here either; and claims in damages for non-performance should not, at any rate, be subject to a longer period of prescription than the claim for specific performance in view of the aggravated problems of proof. In this way nearly all important types of claims are interconnected with each other. This is, incidentally, also the reason why the prescription rules should not be tailored specifically to contractual claims (as might be expected in a set of Principles of European Contract Law). If prescription rules are to conform to the general policy objectives mentioned above, they cannot attempt to provide the best possible regime for each individual type of claim but must be applicable as broadly

unconstitutional discrimination. For comment, see Storme, (1997) 5 *European Review of Private Law* 82ff.; Claeys, (1998–9) *Rechtskundig Weekblad* 379ff. For details, see Hubert Bocken, 'Gelijkheid in aanspreeklikheid – De rechtspraak van het Arbitragehof en de ontwikkeling van het aansprakelijkheidsrecht', in Bocken et al. (n. 33) pp. 3ff.

[92] The BGB provides two different sets of rules in this context; for discussion, see Reinhard Zimmermann, 'Restitution After Termination for Breach of Contract in German Law', (1997) *Restitution Law Review* 13ff. Other countries (as, for instance, Italy) recognize only one restitution regime.

as possible.[93] In particular, they have to take account of the need for clarity, certainty and predictability which is jeopardized by any unnecessary complexity.[94] Thus, it is distinctly better to have a regime that does not suit all claims equally well than one that makes it difficult for debtors as well as creditors to assess their position and adjust their behaviour accordingly.[95]

VI THE DEVELOPMENT OF THE LAW OF LIBERATIVE PRESCRIPTION: INTERNATIONAL TRENDS

If we look at the development of the law of liberative prescription, at new enactments and proposed drafts,[96] we find a number of trends that have arisen over the past hundred years which appear to fall in line with the above considerations.[97]

---

[93] This is one reason why the Uncitral Convention (n. 34) should be treated with caution: it merely deals with claims arising from a contract for the international sale of goods.

[94] Peters and Zimmermann (n. 10) 288f.; Loubser (n. 10) 24; Johnston (n. 3) 1.63; Andrews, (1998) 57 *Cambridge Law Journal* 591.

[95] See also Spiro (n. 10) § 259; Hondius (n. 22) 16 ('Legal certainty requires the law to provide for as few exceptions as possible'). On the notion of legal certainty, in this context, see also Oetker (n. 10) 36ff.

[96] For a comparative overview of the relevant provisions in England, the Netherlands and Greece, see Dannemann, Karatzenis and Thomas, (1991) 55 *RabelsZ* 697ff. Comparative remarks concerning England, France, Austria, Czechoslovakia, Sweden, Turkey and Greece may be found in *Karlsruher Forum* (1991), pp. 30ff. For the prescription of claims arising from delict/tort, see the comprehensive comparative overview (concerning the member states of the European Union) by von Bar II (n. 6) n. 547.

[97] The present chapter will confine its attention to claims arising within the law of obligations. This is the field covered by many modern prescription regimes, either expressly or effectively: see Art. 127 OR; § 1451 read in conjunction with § 1458f. ABGB. According to Artt. 3:306ff. BW, prescription refers to 'rechtsvorderingen'; on which concept, see *Asser*/Hartkamp (n. 10) nn. 638ff.; for Belgium, see Claeys, (1998–9) *Rechtskundig Weekblad* 386ff.; for South Africa, see Loubser (n. 10) 26ff. For general discussion see Spiro (n. 10)

1 *Shorter prescription periods*

In the first place, there is a clear tendency towards shorter periods of prescription.[98] The German Civil Code (1900) still retained the thirty-year period of post-classical Roman vintage as the 'regular' period of prescription.[99] But it is generally recognized today that the ever-increasing 'acceleration of history' has rendered this period entirely unsuitable to modern circumstances.[100] It effectively constitutes an exemption from prescription. Even the BGB,[101] therefore, subjected a whole variety of practically very important claims to shorter periods of prescription;[102] and since 1900, the German Parliament has laid down further exceptions to the regular period in countless statutes outside the framework of the BGB.[103] Significantly, however, it has not only been

[98] §§ 334ff. The German notion of 'Anspruchsverjährung' covers much wider ground than the law of obligations; for criticism, see Peters and Zimmermann (n. 10) 186, 287f. The law of obligations is a sufficiently broad and distinct area to warrant a special set of rules. Of course, there is a very close relationship to the law of property. But there we are often dealing with the protection of absolute rights (such as the right of ownership). If they were subject to prescription, this would entail a considerable, and arguably unjustifiable, qualification of the absolute right. Thus, it may be maintained that claims arising from absolute rights should perish only with the absolute right itself. At any rate, there will have to be careful co-ordination with the law of usucaption. See also Hondius (n. 22) 7f.

[99] § 195 BGB. On the historical background, see the references in nn. 38f.

[100] See also the *Law Commission Consultation Paper* (n. 7) 243, criticizing the traditional six-year (!) period for having originated at a time 'when documents sent by horse or ship where the sole means of communication other than face to face contact'. But cf. also Spiro (n. 25) p. 630 (who draws attention to factors rendering claims today less precarious than in former times).

[101] But the trend towards shorter periods started much earlier. Generally one may say that the history of the prescription periods is the history of these periods gradually becoming shorter. For nineteenth-century German law, see Peters and Zimmermann (n. 10) 115f.

[102] For an overview, see Peters and Zimmermann (n. 10) 108ff., 115ff.

[103] For details, see Peters and Zimmermann (n. 10) 149ff.; see also the overview in *Staudinger*/Peters (n. 10) § 195, nn. 52ff.

Parliament that has severely reduced the field of application of § 195 BGB:[104] the courts, too, have done their utmost to reinforce this tendency.[105] The Swiss Code of Obligations (as revised in 1911) has a general prescription period of ten years;[106] at the same time, its range of application is even more narrowly circumscribed by shorter periods than in Germany.[107] A similar regime (general prescription period of ten years with exceptional, shorter periods for a range of important claims) prevails under the Italian *codice civile* (1942).[108] Somewhat more conservative is the new Dutch Civil Code. Its prescription provisions, contained in Book 3 of the BW, came into force in 1992 but they are based on a draft by Professor E. M. Meijers which was published in 1954.[109] Meijers had considered introducing a general ten-year period but, in the end, decided not to break with tradition quite so dramatically. Thus, he introduced a twenty-year period.[110] But this is only nominally the general period; effectively it is the five-year period prescribed in Artt. 3:307 (performance of a contractual obligation), 3:308 (payments of interest, life rents, dividends, etc.), 3:309 (unjustified enrichment), 3:310 (damages) and 3:311 BW (right of action to

---

[104] The same trend may be observed in France; see Monique Bandrac, 'France', in Hondius (n. 22) 151ff.

[105] For details, see Zimmermann (n. 26) 157 ff.; Peters and Zimmermann (n. 10) 191f. and the references cited there. The general prescription period in the Greek code (1940) is twenty years (Art. 249 *Astikos Kodikas*); for many practically very important claims, however, the code lays down much shorter periods. Cf. also Artt. 309, 310, 482, 498 of the Portuguese *código civil* (1960).

[106] Art. 127 OR.

[107] See the discussion in Peters and Zimmermann (n. 10) 268f.; for all details, see Spiro (n. 10) §§ 263ff.

[108] Artt. 2946ff. *codice civile*.

[109] *Ontwerp voor een nieuw burgerlijk wetboek*, E. M. Meijers, Toelichting, Eerste Gedeelte (Boek 1–4) (1954), 301ff.

[110] See Art. 3:306 BW. The new Belgian law has a general prescription period of ten years (§ 2262bis (1) Belgian *code civil*).

set aside a contract for failure to perform or a right of action to correct such a failure). The South African Prescription Act 68 of 1969 lays down a general prescription period of three years,[111] the Prescription and Limitation (Scotland) Act of 1973 subjects the vast majority of claims within the law of obligations to a five-year period,[112] the Uncitral Convention of 1974 (which, however, deals only with claims arising from an international sale of goods!) contains a four-year period.[113] The Civil Code of the German Democratic Republic (1976) did not have a general prescription period; effectively, however, personal claims were subject to a period of either two or four years.[114] The English Limitation Act 1980 recognizes a period of six years for actions both on tort and on 'simple contract'.[115] There is no provision that would 'naturally apply'[116] to claims under the law of restitution but they are usually held to be covered by s. 5 (six years for an action founded on simple contract).[117] Belgium, after the reform legislation of 10 June 1998, has a general prescription period for all personal claims of ten years (Art. 2262bis § 1). The most radical proposal (two years) was advanced by Peters and Zimmermann (1981);[118] the German commission charged with reforming the law of obligations eventually recommended three years for the majority of cases.[119] In the new Russian Civil Code,[120] we find a general prescription period

---

[111] Section 11 (d).   [112] Section 6 (with schedule 1).   [113] Art. 8.

[114] § 474 I nos. 2 and 3 ZGB (GDR).

[115] Sections 2 and 5.   [116] *Law Commission Consultation Paper* (n. 7) 243.

[117] See the references in *Law Commission Consultation Paper* (n. 7) 86ff.

[118] Peters and Zimmermann (n. 10) 296ff.   [119] §§ 195 I, 199 I, 201 BGB-KE.

[120] Part I entered into force on 1 January 1995, Part II on 1 March 1996. See, in this regard, Oleg Sadikov, 'Das neue Zivilgesetzbuch Rußlands', (1996) 4 *Zeitschrift für Europäisches Privatrecht* 258ff.; Sadikov, 'Das zweite Buch des neuen Zivilgesetzbuches Rußlands', (1999) 7 *Zeitschrift für Europäisches Privatrecht* 903ff. I have relied on the English translation by Peter B. Maggs

of three years (Art. 196), and exceptional periods of one year (liability for defects in contracts for work (exception: building contracts) and transportation contracts (Artt. 725 I, 797 III)) and ten years (Art. 181: claims arising from invalidity of contract). Québec (1994) now has a general three-year period for 'actions to enforce a personal right';[121] and the English Law Commission (1998) recommends a uniform limitation period of three years.[122]

2 Uniform prescription periods

Secondly, there is an equally clear tendency towards uniformity.[123] In Germany, the extraordinary degree of differentiation between the various periods prescribed in the code as well as by countless statutes outside the code has contributed, at least as much as the unsuitable length of a number of those periods, to a minefield of problems within the law of liberative prescription – and further afield.[124] Only somewhat less complex is the regulation in the Swiss code: ten years for specific performance of a contractual obligation and damages for non-performance[125] (though there is much criticism as to the latter proposition[126]), five years for

and A. N. Zhiltsov, *The Civil Code of the Russian Federation*, Parts I and II (1997). On the legal situation prior to new code's coming into force, see Peters and Zimmermann (n. 10) 278f.

[121] Art. 2925 *code civil du Québec.*

[122] *Law Commission Consultation Paper* (n. 7) 281ff., 403f., 408ff.

[123] See also Hondius (n. 22) 17.

[124] There is usually a great degree of differentiation in the prescription regimes of EU member states which are still based on pre-1900 codes and statutes. This is true, for instance, for France and Austria (for criticism, see Koziol and Welser I (n. 41) 185).

[125] Art. 127 OR; and see Werner Schwander, *Die Verjährung außervertraglicher und vertraglicher Schadensersatzforderungen* (1963), pp. 83ff., 135ff.

[126] See Schwander (n. 125) 135ff.

a number of specifically enumerated claims concerning, *inter alia*, payment for the delivery of certain goods and the rendering of certain services,[127] one year for delictual claims[128] (and possibly also damages for non-performance?[129]) as well as for unjustified enrichment claims,[130] one year or five years for warranty claims, depending on whether they are based on a contract of sale or contract for work and on whether the defect concerns a movable object or a piece of property, and in some cases even six months.[131] The Italian code, too, has a long list of individual types of claims, to which it applies periods of five, three and two years, one year and six months.[132] The Dutch code effectively establishes five years as the general prescription period for the law of obligations but does so in a number of specific provisions concerning individual types of claims.[133] The Scottish Act is similar in that it also provides a broad field of application for its five-year period but does so by way of a somewhat cumbersome enumeration of the relevant claims.[134] A three-year period applies to personal injuries actions and to actions for defamation.[135] The traditional six-year period in England today applies only to a minority of tort actions;[136] actions for personal injuries (three years), negligent latent damage (three years), product liability (three years) and defamation and malicious falsehood (one year) are subject to separate rules[137] – a state of affairs that has recently been criticized by the Law Commission. The German Democratic Republic

---

[127] Art. 128 OR.   [128] Art. 60 OR.   [129] See Spiro (n. 10) §§ 295ff.
[130] Art. 67 OR (this rule has been much criticized; but see Spiro (n. 10) §§ 291, 300ff.).
[131] Artt. 210 I, 219 III, 371 II, 315 OR.   [132] Artt. 2947ff. *codice civile*.
[133] Artt. 3:307ff. BW; see pp. 87f.
[134] Prescription and Limitation (Scotland) Act 1973, s. 6 with schedule 1.
[135] Sections 17, 18 and 18 A.
[136] *Law Commission Consultation Paper* (n. 7) 241.
[137] Limitation Act 1980, ss. 4 A, 11, 11 A, 12, 14 A.

had periods of six months, two, four and ten years;[138] the new Russian Civil Code has periods of one, three and ten years.[139] The German Reform Commission recommends periods of three, five and ten years (essentially: three years for contractual and delictual claims; five years in disputes concerning defective buildings and the delivery of defective materials to be used for the erection of a building; ten years for unjustified enrichment).[140] The new Belgian law has five years for claims arising from extra-contractual liability and ten years for all other personal claims.[141] The most streamlined sets of rules (apart, of course, from the Uncitral Convention relating to the international sale of goods) are those proposed by Peters and Zimmermann (two years, applicable across the board, except for two situations where periods of one and five years are recommended)[142] and the English Law Commission (core regime of three years applicable, effectively, across the board),[143] and those enacted in South Africa (three years)[144] and Québec (three years, except with

---

[138] §§ 474, 480 ZGB (GDR).

[139] See above, text to n. 120. The general prescription period of three years has been welcomed by Mario Pellegrino, 'Übergang zur Marktwirtschaft und allgemeines Vertragsrecht im neuen russischen Zivilgesetzbuch', (1998) *Recht der Internationalen Wirtschaft* 506.

[140] §§ 195, 198, 199, 201 BGB-KE.

[141] Art. 2262bis (1) and (2) Belgian *code civil*; for criticism concerning their differentiation, see Claeys, (1998–9) *Rechtskundig Weekblad* 391ff. and Claessens and De Counye (n. 89). For penetrating criticism concerning the differentiation, for purposes of the law of prescription, between claims arising from contractual and delictual liability, see Claeys, (1998–9) *Rechtskundig Weekblad* 391ff. and Andrews, (1998) 57 *Cambridge Law Journal* 605ff.

[142] § 195 BGB-PZ; for motivation, see Peters and Zimmermann (n. 10) 292ff.

[143] *Law Commission Consultation Paper* (n. 7) 400ff. (general prescription period of three years).

[144] Prescription Act 68 of 1969, s. 11 (d); there are a few exceptional situations (most of them relating to debts owed to the state and placing the latter in a privileged position; on the reason for retaining these special periods, see

regard to actions for defamation, which are subject to a prescription period of one year).[145] A period of three years also appears to be emerging as a uniform limitation period in European Union legislation.[146]

3 *The discoverability criterion*

In the third place, and closely related to the general tendency towards shorter periods of prescription, the idea has been gaining ground that prescription should not run unless the creditor knew (or ought reasonably to have known) about his claim.[147] More precisely, there has been a trend towards (i) applying this subjective criterion to a growing range of claims while (ii) reducing its inherent potential to delay the commencement of prescription by moving from actual knowledge towards a test of discoverability. The German Civil Code recognizes the subjective criterion only with regard to delictual claims: the injured party has to have had knowledge of the injury and of the identity of the person bound to make compensation (§ 852 I BGB).[148] While this rule is regarded widely as one of the more successful components of the German law relating to prescription, the requirement of 'knowledge' has caused certain difficulties and has been considerably watered down in practice.[149] Nevertheless, the

J. C. de Wet – the father of the South African act – *Opuscula Miscellanea* (1980), p. 111).

[145] Artt. 2925, 2929 *code civil du Québec.*

[146] Christian von Bar, *The Common European Law of Torts*, vol. 1 (1998), n. 395.

[147] For delict/tort, see the comparative overview by von Bar II (n. 6) nn. 554ff.

[148] The position in Greek law, insofar as discussed in the text, is identical to that in German law: Art. 937 *Astikos Kodikas.*

[149] For details, see Peters and Zimmermann (n. 10) 178; Zimmermann (n. 26) 174; Haug (n. 17) 144f.; Heinz Thomas in Palandt, *Bürgerliches Gesetzbuch* (59th edn, 2000), § 852, nn. 4ff.

scope of application of § 852 I BGB has been extended both by the legislature and by the courts.[150] The courts have even, for some time, toyed with the idea of extending the subjective criterion to damages claims based on latent defects;[151] ultimately, however, they dropped it as being too blatantly *contra legem*.[152]

The Swiss code also requires knowledge but does not confine this criterion to the law of delict: it also applies to actions based on unjustified enrichment.[153] The Dutch code requires knowledge in the case of unjustified enrichment claims, claims for the recovery of damages (based on delict and on non-performance[154]), and claims 'to set aside a contract for failure to perform it or to correct such a failure'.[155] According to the English Limitation Act, knowledge is relevant as far as actions for personal injuries or death, for latent damage in the tort of negligence, and products liability are concerned.[156] The Scottish Act applies a discoverability test to latent damage and personal injuries and a knowledge test to actions for defamation.[157] Québec also requires knowledge in the case of defamation and for actions based on the invalidity of a contract[158] but has a discoverability

---

[150] For details, see Peters and Zimmermann (n. 10) 184; Zimmermann (n. 26) 174; *Palandt*/Thomas (n. 149) § 852, n. 1. In particular, most instances of strict liability are subject to the three-year period running from knowledge.

[151] Cf. BGH, (1973) *Neue Juristische Wochenschrift* 843 (at 845); BGH, (1978) *Neue Juristische Wochenschrift* 2241.

[152] BGHZ 77, 215ff.; for further literature, see the references in Zimmermann (n. 26) 170.

[153] Artt. 60 I, 67 I OR. Similarly § 475 no. 2 ZGB (GDR).

[154] *Asser*/Hartkamp (n. 10) n. 674.   [155] Artt. 3:309, 310, 311 BW.

[156] See Limitation Act 1980, ss. 11, 11 A, 12, 14, 14 A. See also von Bar II (n. 6) n. 559.

[157] Prescription and Limitation (Scotland) Act 1973, ss. 11(3), 17, 18 and 18 A; see also Johnston (n. 3) 4.17ff.

[158] Artt. 2927, 2929 *code civil du Québec*.

test for actions arising 'from moral, corporal or material damage'.[159] According to the Russian Civil Code, the general prescription period in terms of Art. 196 starts to run when the creditor knew or should have known of the existence of the claim.[160] The most far-reaching proposals are those of Peters and Zimmermann (with regard to all claims covered by the regular prescription period,[161] prescription does not run for as long as the creditor, without being grossly negligent, is unaware of the identity of his debtor and of the object and the legal basis of his claim[162]) and by the English Law Commission (prescription begins to run from when the claimant knows, or ought reasonably to know, that he has a cause of action).[163] This approach was implemented in South Africa some time ago: prescription does not begin to run until the creditor acquires knowledge of the identity of the debtor and of the facts from which the debt arises, or could have acquired such knowledge by exercising reasonable care.[164] Originally, i.e. as from 1969, this provision was confined to non-contractual debts.[165] Following a recommendation by the South African

---

[159] Art. 2926 *code civil du Québec*; on which provision, see Deslauriers (n. 32) 299f.

[160] Art. 2001 Russian Civil Code. Exceptions appear in Artt. 181, 200 II, 725, 797 III Russian Civil Code.

[161] See n. 118.   [162] § 199 BGB-PZ.

[163] *Law Commission Consultation Paper* (n. 7) 250ff. For details of what exactly the claimant ought to know, see p. 266. For criticism of these proposals, see Andrews, (1998) 57 *Cambridge Law Journal* 589ff.

[164] Section 12 (3) Prescription Act 68 of 1969. Where the debtor wilfully prevents the creditor from acquiring such knowledge, the prescription period does not commence to run while the creditor is ignorant of the debt. For commentary on the knowledge requirement, see Loubser (n. 10) 100ff. It should be noted that, technically, this approach is implemented by means of a legal fiction. For according to s. 12 (1) prescription commences to run when the debt is due. Section 12 (3) deems a debt not to be due until the creditor has knowledge of the identity of the debtor and of the fact from which the debt arises.

[165] On the concept of 'debt' in South African law, see Loubser (n. 10) 26ff.

Law Commission, it was amended in 1984 so as to refer also to debts arising from contract. The German Reform Commission, however, has shrunk back from accepting a uniform approach along these lines and proposes, essentially, to perpetuate the regime contained in the BGB (knowledge rather than discoverability; applicability confined to delictual claims).[166] Art. 10 of the Product Liability Directive of the European Union, on the other hand, provides that the three-year period has to begin to run from the day 'on which the plaintiff became aware, or should reasonably have become aware', of the damage, the defect and the identity of the producer. Generally speaking, discoverability may be regarded as the emerging general standard in European Community legislation, as far as prescription is concerned.[167]

Of considerable interest, in the present context, is also the emergence of the principle of discoverability in Canadian case law.[168] The most authoritative statement is that of the Supreme Court of Canada where it was held that 'a cause of action arises for purposes of a limitation period when the material facts on which it is based have been discovered or ought to have been discovered by the plaintiff by the exercise of reasonable diligence'.[169] In Belgium, two decisions by the Constitutional Court[170] are regarded by one commentator as 'the deathblow' for all rules providing for short prescription periods, 'unless prescription runs only from the moment of which the damage manifests itself'.[171]

---

[166] §§ 199, 201 BGB-KE.

[167] See von Bar I (n. 146) n. 395.

[168] See the discussion by Nathalie Des Rosiers, 'Canada', in Hondius (n. 22), pp. 101ff., who describes this as '[w]ithout question, the major development in the area of extinctive prescription in Canadian common law'.

[169] *Central Trustco v. Rafuse*, [1986] 2 SCR 147; 31 DLR (4th) 481.

[170] On which, see nn. 78–91.

[171] Storme, (1997) 5 *European Review of Private Law* 88; see also Claeys, (1998–9) *Rechtskundig Weekblad* 381. The new Belgian law of 10 June 1998

VII THE CORE REGIME

This overview confirms the policy-based considerations: there should be one period of prescription which should apply as widely as possible; this uniform period would have to be relatively short (somewhere between two and six years); and whether or not the period runs should depend on a test of discoverability. Taking account of the more recent proposals and enactments, three years would appear to be widely regarded as the most suitable general prescription period.[172] Leaving aside, for the moment, the question of claims established by legal proceedings,[173] it does not seem necessary to lay down any longer or shorter prescription periods for specific types of claims; not, at least, if we confine our attention to the law of obligations. For it is noticeable that special periods enacted or proposed within any one legal system are not normally deemed necessary in others. This observation lends support to the view that, while a regime tailored for specific types of claims may be more suitable for these claims in isolation, a uniform regime can provide, at least, a *satisfactory* solution while procuring all the additional advantages associated with uniformity. This applies, for instance, to the six-year period in respect of a debt arising from a bill of exchange or other negotiable instrument or from a notarial contract provided in the South African Act,[174] or to the twelve-year period for an action upon a speciality of the

---

requires knowledge, as far as the five-year period for delictual claims is concerned: Art. 2262bis Belgian *code civil*; for discussion, see Claeys, (1998–9) *Rechtskundig Weekblad* 394ff.

[172] See also Andrews, (1998) 57 *Cambridge Law Journal* 592, at 597 who regards a three-year period as appropriate because it is 'long enough to allow the parties a good opportunity to collect their wits, review their finances, assess their chances and negotiate a settlement'.

[173] On which, see pp. 112ff.

[174] Section 11 (c) Prescription Act 68 of 1969.

English Act,[175] or to the special treatment provided for actions for defamation in England, Québec and Scotland (but, while in England and Québec the special period is one year, in Scotland it is three years!).[176] The German Reform Commission wants to subject unjustified enrichment claims to a ten-year period of prescription and claims arising in connection with defective buildings to a five-year period.[177] This is necessary only in view of the fact that the commission does not accept a discoverability test for the commencement of prescription. As soon as a person reasonably ought to know that he can reclaim what he has given without legal ground, or that he can sue the contractor for damages arising from a defect in his new house, a three-year period is quite adequate. In Switzerland even a one-year period is regarded as sufficient in the former case.[178]

This example demonstrates that there is a fundamental choice to be made. If discoverability applies across the board, a uniform three-year period is acceptable. If, however, the uncertainty necessarily associated with a discoverability criterion is regarded as sufficiently serious to tie

---

[175] Limitation Act 1980, s. 8; but see *Law Commission Consultation Paper* (n. 7) 325f.

[176] Limitation Act 1980, s. 4 A; Art. 2929 *code civil du Québec*; Prescription and Limitation (Scotland) Act 1973, s. 18 A. Andrews, (1998) 57 *Cambridge Law Journal* 596, argues in favour of retaining an exceptional shorter period for defamation. See also the two exceptions provided in the Peters and Zimmermann proposals, concerning claims for the return of property which has been handed over to another person (five years) and certain claims arising after the expiry of a contract of lease, or of a similar contract involving the return of a piece of property (one year). These exceptions are not found in other legal systems and have also not been supported by the German Reform Commission.

[177] §§ 198, 195 II and III BGB-KE. According to the Russian Civil Code, on the other hand, an exceptional period of *three* years applies in the case of defective buildings (Art. 725 I) (as opposed to the one-year period in the case of other defective performances of work).

[178] Art. 67 OR; for comment, see Spiro (n. 10) §§ 300ff.

commencement of the period, as far as possible, to objective criteria only (such as due date, delivery, completion (of a building), breach of duty), the consequence is necessarily a differentiated system of prescription periods.[179] For the objective criteria most suited to individual types of claims will differ. Moreover, there is a very wide consensus that not all types of claims should be subjected to an objective regime: the prescription of delictual claims must depend on knowledge (or the reasonable possibility of acquiring knowledge).[180] It is, however, precisely with regard to delictual claims (and, more specifically, those arising from personal injury) that the knowledge/discoverability criterion is, practically, most important.[181] The other type of situation where a creditor will often be unaware of his claim is breach of contract. Delict and breach of contract are (or can be) closely related; the one claim is often an alternative for the other.[182] If it is unfair in the one case to deprive a creditor of his claim before he knew or reasonably could have known of it, it is equally unfair in the other. This is the very consideration that prompted the amendment of the South African Prescription

---

[179] This is the approach preferred by the German Reform Commission; the reasons are set out in *Abschlußbericht* (n. 10) 54ff. See also see Haug (n. 17) 44, 88ff., 150ff. (who regards the uncertainties connected with a subjective criterion as being intolerable); Unterrieder (n. 10) 271ff. For a principled and policy-based argument favouring retention of a differentiated system (though quite a different one from that proposed by the German Reform Commission), see Andrews, (1998) 57 *Cambridge Law Journal* 589ff. The point of departure, however, is the same: the starting date for prescription should not always be discoverability but one that is conceptually more precise and that gives rise to less evidential difficulty (i.e., for English law, accrual of the cause of action).

[180] This is even accepted by the legal systems, or law reform bodies, most sceptical towards the knowledge or discoverability criterion, particularly the German Reform Commission. See also the comparative analysis by von Bar II (n. 6) nn. 554ff.

[181] This is confirmed by Loubser (n. 10) 105ff.

[182] A prominent example is medical negligence.

Act in 1984.[183] Once, therefore, a legal system is prepared
to swallow the subjective criterion with regard to damages
claims, it might as well, in view of the interconnectedness of
claims within the law of obligations,[184] accept it across the
board. The price to be paid in terms of legal uncertainty is
not considerable. For, to mention some prominent types of
claims, the parties to a contract will normally know when
their transaction has been concluded and when they are entitled to demand its (specific) performance. Also, they will
usually be aware whether it has been avoided with the result that they may claim restitution of any benefit conferred,
particularly under a system that makes avoidance for error,
or *metus*, or *dolus* dependent on notice to the other party.[185]
And, as far as restitution for wrongs is concerned, it is too
close to delict to justify a different treatment.

VIII THE LONG-STOP PERIOD

Two additional points, however, still remain to be considered. The first is very widely recognized. If we have a core
regime of a short period of prescription which decisively
hinges on (reasonable) discoverability, it may happen that
prescription is postponed for twenty or thirty years, or even
longer. But prescription should not be deferred indefinitely;
at some stage, the parties must be able to treat the incident as indubitably closed. This is why even the BGB in its
§ 852 provides for a long-stop period of thirty years (from
the moment when the wrongful act was committed) beyond
which no claim can be brought, regardless of the creditor's

---

[183] Loubser (n. 10) 102; see the text after n. 165. The new Belgian act, which
perpetuates this distinction, is subject to severe criticism; see the references in
n. 141. See also the critical remarks (concerning Swiss law) by Spiro (n. 10)
§ 295f.; and see Peters and Zimmermann (n. 10) 223f.
[184] See the text above nn. 89–95.   [185] Art. 4:112 PECL.

knowledge.[186] It is an approach which is increasingly gaining support[187] and it indeed appears necessary as a counterbalance to the discoverability principle. The question is how long the period[188] should be. Once again, we observe an international trend – though not an entirely unequivocal one – towards a shorter period. The Swiss code has ten years in the two situations where it requires knowledge,[189] the Dutch code[190] and the Scottish Act[191] have long-stops of twenty years, East Germany had ten years[192] and the English Act recognizes two exceptional long-stops of ten and fifteen years.[193] Peters and Zimmermann recommend a general long-stop of ten years.[194] The German Reform Commission, once again, is more cautious: they propose a period of thirty years for personal injury claims and ten years for other

[186] The Greek rule is the same except that the long-stop is twenty years (Art. 937 (1) *Astikos Kodikas*).

[187] See, for example, M. E. Storme, 'Belgium', in Hondius (n. 22), p. 58, who regards this as the only balanced solution; *Law Commission Consultation Paper* (n. 7) 284ff. (with references); Des Rosiers (n. 168) 106f.; see also the approach adopted in the Product Liability Directive, Artt. 10f. (three and ten years) and Art. 17 of the Convention on Civil Liability for Damage Resulting from Activities Dangerous to the Environment (three and thirty years). On the other hand, neither the South African Prescription Act nor the *code civil du Québec* recognizes a long-stop; for discussion, see Loubser (n. 10) 37; Deslauriers (n. 32) 300.

[188] On its legal nature, see pp. 104, 106ff.; for the time being, I will use the term 'long-stop'.

[189] Art. 60 1, 67 1 OR. For comparative discussion (as per 1975), see Spiro (n. 10) § 42).

[190] Artt. 3:309, 310, 311 BW.

[191] The 'long negative prescription' of s. 7 of the Prescription and Limitation (Scotland) Act 1973 (on which see Johnston (n. 3) 7.01ff.) effectively acts as a long-stop: *Law Commission Consultation Paper* (n. 7) 185. It commences when the relevant obligation becomes enforceable.

[192] § 475 no. 2 ZGB (GDR).

[193] Sections 11 A and 14 A Limitation Act 1980, relating to actions for latent damage (in the tort of negligence) and product liability.

[194] § 208 BGB-PZ.

delictual claims.[195] The English Law Commission presents a solution based on a ten-year long-stop applicable to all actions other than those for personal injury for which thirty years are recommended.[196] The new Belgian law has a long-stop of twenty years (applicable to all delictual claims for damages).[197]

Once again, therefore, there appear to be two options: differentiation or uniformity. The main objection against a comparatively short long-stop period is that it may be considered inadequate for personal injury claims. This is obvious from both the German and the English reform proposals; but the concern is also shared by other systems. Most situations which have been specified as being particularly problematic (sexual abuse of children, asbestosis, environmental damages)[198] fall into the category of personal injury claims. The reasons for treating them differently are that there is often a long latency period[199] and that life, health and bodily integrity (and possibly also freedom)[200] are particularly valuable objects of legal protection:[201] personal injuries are generally regarded as more serious than property damage or economic harm.[202] For the latter, even a short long-stop of ten years is very widely regarded as sufficient. There should also be no objection to subjecting other types

---

[195] §§ 199, 201 BGB-KE.

[196] *Law Commission Consultation Paper* (n. 7) 284ff.

[197] Art. 2262bis § 1 al. 2 Belgian *code civil*. For details, see Claeys, (1998–9) *Rechtskundig Weekblad* 388ff.

[198] See, for example, Hondius (n. 22) 9ff.

[199] See, e.g., *Law Commission Consultation Paper* (n. 7) 290.

[200] Which is included in the proposal by the German commission on the ground that unlawful deprivation of liberty may lead to psychological damage which manifests itself only much later: *Abschlußbericht* (n. 10) 76.

[201] *Abschlußbericht* (n. 10) 75.

[202] For criticism of the differentiation between 'personal injury claims' and other claims, see Haug (n. 17) 39ff. and the references cited there; von Bar II (n. 6) n. 548 is also sceptical.

of claims (specific performance, unjustified enrichment, etc.) to a ten-year long-stop.[203]

Alternatively, one might try to find a compromise solution which accommodates both personal injury and other claims while not providing a perfect solution to either of them.[204] The arguments in favour of this option[205] may be listed as follows: (i) even a thirty-year period will not provide a perfect solution for personal injury claims since there will still be cases in which the creditor did not know about his claim.[206] (ii) It is easy to imagine that an incident causes both personal injury and damage to property. A defective machine explodes and damages the purchaser's health and property. Or asbestos is used in the process of renovating a house; after some years, the owner contracts asbestos-related cancer and has to undergo expensive treatment; at the same time the

---

[203] See the proposals by the English Law Commission and Peters and Zimmermann; the German Reform Commission even proposes a prescription period of three years (to be counted from due date, not from discoverability!) for contractual claims and ten years (also to be counted from due date, not from discoverability) for unjustified enrichment claims.

[204] This is the solution adopted, most recently, in Belgium (though only for delictual claims); see n. 197.

[205] Apart from the one based on general policy mentioned pp. 8of. See also the arguments advanced by Spiro (n. 10) § 42 in support of the ten-year period of Art. 60 I OR, covering all delictual claims.

[206] See, e.g., the two English cases (one involving mesothelioma, the other asbestosis) mentioned in the *Law Commission Consultation Paper* (n. 7) 291. The Dutch Hoge Raad has decided in two recent pronouncements that the twenty-year long-stop laid down in Art. 3:310 BW can be set aside under exceptional circumstances: HR 28 April 2000, *Nederlandse Jurisprudentie* 430/431. Both cases concerned a special type of cancer caused by exposure to asbestos; the incubation period is normally between twenty and forty years. The court based its ruling on Art. 6:2 BW (according to which any rule of law, general usage or legal act is not applicable as far as it is, under the circumstances, inappropriate according to the precepts of good faith ('redelijkheid en billijkheid')). My thanks to Advocate General Jaap Spier and Professor Ewoud Hondius for referring me to these decisions.

house has to be pulled down. If it is possible, after all those years, to prove who was responsible for using asbestos, and that the presence of asbestos in the house has caused the owner's disease, it is hard to see why the owner should be able to pursue the claims arising from infringement of his health but not those based on damage to his property: if the one is established, so is the other. (iii) It is as difficult for the debtor to defend himself after twenty or thirty years in a personal injury action as it is in an action concerning damage to property. The obfuscating power of time does not distinguish between different types of claims. Witnesses die, the debtor's memory fades, vital documents are lost, etc. Once again, it must be remembered that we usually see only the hardship involved for a creditor who is barred by prescription although he has been able, even after the lapse of many years, to establish his claim; and that we tend to forget about the many cases in which a prescription regime prevents unjustified claims from being (successfully) pursued. (iv) Defective products are an important source of personal injury claims. Here we have a general long-stop (for personal injuries and damage to property) in our national legal systems as a result of the Product Liability Directive; and it was the relatively short period of ten years which was regarded as sufficient in this situation.[207]

On balance, therefore, it appears to be preferable to fix one long-stop period applicable for all claims. But how long should it be? The twenty-year period of the new Belgian act has to be evaluated against the background of a normal prescription period of five years for delictual claims and ten years for all other personal claims. It appears to be too long

[207] Art. 11 of the Directive concerning Liability for Defective Products. The period starts to run as soon as the producer has brought the defective product into circulation.

in relation to a general period of three years. The ten-year period of the Product Liability Directive, on the other hand, would not sufficiently express the compromise character of the solution required. Fifteen (or twelve) years (i.e., not more than four or five times the normal period) would seem to be more appropriate. It is readily acknowledged that this may cause hardship in a number of cases. But, as was pointed out already, even the traditional period of thirty years may cause hardship; and at a time characterized by vastly increased mobility and rapid change in the general conditions of life it appears quite incongruous to attempt to unravel incidents that have happened thirty years ago and thus to cling to a period that still dates from the time before the Industrial Revolution.

IX IMPLEMENTING THE CORE REGIME

The second point is this: it has been emphasized that prescription should not run while the creditor is unaware of his claim and cannot reasonably become aware of it. It still has to be decided how that policy should be implemented. At first blush it might appear natural to link the discoverability criterion to the commencement of prescription.[208] But there is an alternative: prescription is suspended as long as the creditor is unaware of his claim and cannot reasonably become aware of it. If one were to adopt this alternative approach, what would be the date of commencement of prescription?

---

[208] This is the approach adopted, for instance, in § 852 1 BGB; Artt. 60 1, 67 1 OR; Artt. 3:309, 310, 311 BW; Art. 2926 *code civil du Québec*; Art. 2262bis (2) Belgian *code civil* (on which see Claeys, (1998–9) *Rechtskundig Weekblad* 394ff.); and proposed by the English Law Commission (see *Consultation Paper* (n. 7) 250ff.).

1 *Commencement of prescription*

The English Limitation Act refers to the date of accrual of the cause of action.[209] But this is the language of the law of procedure, which is not appropriate with regard to a substantive prescription regime. Could one say accrual of the claim?[210] That would be a somewhat unusual phrase; moreover, it would also not be unambiguous. Thus, South African courts have been in doubt as to whether it refers to the date when performance by the debtor becomes due or whether accrual can actually occur before that date.[211] A second possible option would be to choose the very first moment in the life of a claim. This is the approach adopted by § 198 BGB: prescription begins to run from the moment when the claim comes into being. It is, however, very widely agreed that this is not what is meant and that § 198 BGB has to be taken to refer to the date when the claim becomes due.[212] This is indeed appropriate in view of the fact that prescription should run only against a creditor who has the possibility of interrupting, or at least suspending, it by enforcing his claim in court. Due date (which may be defined as the time when a party has to effect performance)[213] is a concept

---

[209] See, for instance, Limitation Act 1980, ss. 2 and 5. This is the moment 'when a potential plaintiff first has a right to succeed in an action against a potential defendant' (*Preston and Newsom on Limitation of Actions* (4th edn, ed. John Weeks, 1989), p. 8; see also Dannemann, Karatzenis and Thomas, (1991) 55 *RabelsZ* 702).

[210] This is done in Artt. 9 1, 10, of the Uncitral Convention.

[211] See Loubser (n. 10) 48f., 52.

[212] See Peters and Zimmermann (n. 10) 172ff.; *Staudinger*/Peters (n. 10) § 198, nn. 1ff. But cf. Unterrieder (n. 10) 299ff.

[213] This is the phrase used in Art. 7:102 PECL. Art. 7:102 provides a regulation only for contractual claims. Concerning claims *ex lege*, the general rule would appear to be that the debtor has to effect performance once all requirements for the creditor's claim have been met.

which is widely known and relevant in many other situations; and it is also used very widely, internationally, in the present context.[214] There are a number of reasons for relying on it also in the present set of principles and for thus relegating discoverability[215] to a ground for extension (in the form of suspension of prescription).[216]

2 *Maximum period of extension of prescription*

(i) Even if discoverability were to determine the commencement of prescription, it would also have to be required that the obligation has come into existence and that performance is due. This is either regarded as implicit in the notion of knowledge or discoverability,[217] or ensured by means of a somewhat artificial fiction.[218] (ii) That prescription should not run against a creditor who cannot reasonably become aware of his claim is one specific emanation of a much wider

---

[214] Prescription starts to run when the creditor's claim becomes enforceable, according to § 1478 ABGB; Art. 130 I OR; Art. 2935 *codice civile*; s. 12 South African Prescription Act 68 of 1969; Claeys, (1998–9) *Rechtskundig Weekblad* 394 and Claessens and De Counye (n. 89) 84, concerning Belgian law; for Scotland, see Johnston (n. 3) 4.06ff.; § 196 BGB-KE; Peters and Zimmermann (n. 10) 302; Koopmann (n. 24) 45ff.; Loubser (n. 10) 48ff.; Spiro (n. 10) § 26. According to Art. 251 *Astikos Kodikas*, the claim must have come into being and have become enforceable.

[215] For the elements on which discoverability should focus, see pp. 148f.

[216] Practically, this means that normally prescription does not start to run until the moment of reasonable discoverability; it is, in other words, a case of an 'initial suspension'. The notion of a suspension affecting a period of prescription from the very moment when it would, but for the impediment suspending it, have started to run (and thus, effectively, suspending the commencement of prescription) is familiar in a number of countries; see § 204 BGB ('Anlaufhemmung') and Peters and Zimmermann (n. 10) 128; Art. 256 *Astikos Kodikas*; for Italy, see Art. 2941 (1) *codice civile*.

[217] See, for example, Arndt Teichmann, in Othmar Jauernig, *Bürgerliches Gesetzbuch* (9th edn, 1999), § 852, n. 6.

[218] This is the technique employed by the South African Prescription Act 68 of 1969: s. 12 (3).

idea: a claim must not prescribe if it is impossible for the creditor to pursue it (*agere non valenti non currit praescriptio*).[219] This is why prescription does not run in cases of *vis maior*,[220] and why completion is delayed if the creditor is legally incompetent and does not have a legal representative,[221] or if an estate is without a representative or heir.[222] All these impediments are taken into account by extending the period of prescription. Thus, it would appear to be systematically more satisfactory to deal with the discoverability issue under the heading of extension of prescription.

(iii) If a creditor brings an action against his debtor, he has to establish the requirements on which his claim is based. That his claim has not prescribed is not one of those requirements. Prescription is a defence.[223] If it is invoked by the debtor, it is he who has to establish the requirements of that defence. The central requirement, of course, is that the period of prescription applicable to this claim has elapsed. That depends on the date of commencement. If that were the date of discoverability, the debtor would, in many cases, face an unreasonably difficult task. For whether the damage to the creditor's house, the injury to his body, the consequences flowing from defective delivery, etc., were reasonably discoverable, or whether the creditor perhaps even had positive knowledge, are matters within the creditor's sphere and largely removed from the debtor's range of perception.[224]

---

[219] See pp. 132f.   [220] See pp. 129ff.   [221] See pp. 134ff.

[222] See p. 141.   [223] See pp. 72ff.

[224] Peters and Zimmermann (n. 10) 248, 306. Cf. also Loubser (n. 10) 112; *Law Commission Consultation Paper* (n. 7) 398 ('The date of discoverability is concerned with the knowledge of the plaintiff rather than the defendant . . . In consequence it will commonly be more difficult and expensive for the defendant to provide evidence of the knowledge of the plaintiff at a particular date, than for the plaintiff to provide such evidence'); contra: Claeys, (1998–9) *Rechtskundig Weekblad* 396, according to whom, under Belgian law, the debtor has to prove knowledge on the part of the creditor (Claeys, however,

Also, by and large, and considering the full range of possible claims, the creditor will normally know about his claim at the time the latter falls due; at least he can reasonably be expected to know about it. That, exceptionally, he did not do so, is a matter to be raised, and established to the satisfaction of the court, by the creditor. This would come out more clearly if discoverability were not to be made a requirement for commencement of prescription but if the fact that the creditor could not reasonably be aware of his claim were to give rise to an extension of prescription: that prescription is suspended or otherwise extended must, according to general principle, normally be proved by the creditor.

(iv) This way of proceeding would also considerably simplify the structure of the proposed prescription regime, for we would then not need a separate long-stop period running from a date different to that of the 'normal' period of prescription and subject to specific regulation concerning extension, renewal etc. The three-year period could simply be regarded as the one and only general period of prescription with due date as the general date of commencement; in addition, it could simply be laid down that prescription is not to be extended for more than fifteen[225] years. This latter rule, while not necessarily applying to all grounds for suspension (in particular, suspension in case of legal proceedings), would certainly cover suspension in case of ignorance

also refers to the contrary view adopted in France). Generally on onus of proof concerning prescription requirements, see also Spiro (n. 10) §§ 359f., who states that the creditor will have to prove the special circumstances based on his person or his specific situation which he adduces in order to invoke suspension of prescription. Also, according to Spiro, the creditor will have to establish why he may have been unable to pursue his claim once it came into existence. Somewhat inconsequentially, however, he then asserts that knowledge, on the part of the creditor, will 'probably' have to be proved by the debtor.

[225] See p. 104.

and also a number or other grounds for extension.[226] The long-stop is thus turned into a maximum period of extension. This scheme would, once again, promote certainty and uniformity.

3 *Claims for damages*

There is only one situation which requires special consideration. Due date is clearly inappropriate as a point of reference for any long-stop (whether enacted by way of a separate period or by way of placing a ceiling upon extensions of the 'regular' period) concerning claims for damages.[227] For it is specifically the 'latent damages' problem that can lead to a long delay of prescription. A claim for damages in delict is generally due as soon as it comes into being. But it comes into being only when all requirements of the rule imposing liability have been met. One of them will often be the occurrence of damages;[228] and damages will sometimes only occur many years after the act giving rise to liability (infringement of somebody else's personal integrity or property etc.) was committed. If a legal system accommodates the reasonable interests of the creditor by suspending prescription as long as the damage is not discoverable, it cannot sensibly operate with a long-stop period running from the moment when the damage occurs. This would be a long-stop that does not bite: occurrence of the damage (a moment which may be

---

[226] See pp. 147f. On the terminology adopted here (suspension and delay of completion of prescription as the two ways of extending prescription), see p. 139.

[227] As far as both delictual and contractual damages are concerned; see, for the Dutch provision of Art. 3:310, *Asser*/Hartkamp (n. 10) n. 674.

[228] But this can be subject to dispute and may sometimes depend on the way in which the liability rule is drafted; see, for example, *Staudinger*/Peters (n. 10) § 198, nn. 21ff.; Loubser (n. 10) 79ff.

very difficult to determine, particularly in cases of patrimonial loss)[229] and discoverability are often closely related. A long-stop counting from the act giving rise to liability would, therefore, clearly be desirable.[230] It counterbalances both the emphasis on the creditor's interest and the uncertainty inherent in the discoverability criterion. If, however, the long-stop counts from the act giving rise to liability rather than due date, the same regime can quite safely be applied to the normal, three-year period of prescription. For the suspension rule outlined above, focusing on the moment of discoverability, ensures that prescription does not run before the damage has occurred.

Prescription should, therefore, begin to run when all the other requirements for a claim for damages have been met, i.e., at the moment when the unlawful act has been committed (or at the moment when the breach of contract has occurred).

One can, therefore, envisage a general rule to the effect that prescription begins to run from the time when the debtor has to effect performance or, in the case of a claim for damages, from the date of the act which gives rise to the claim. In the case of delict/tort, this would be the moment when the unlawful act was committed; prescription of a claim for damages for non-performance runs from the date of non-performance,[231] prescription of a claim for *culpa in*

---

[229] See the example discussed by *Staudinger*/Peters (n. 10) n. 22. Also see von Bar II (n. 6) n. 551.

[230] The comparative evidence, in this regard, is quite clear; see, for example, § 852 I BGB; Art. 60 I OR; Art. 3:310 BW; *Law Commission Consultation Paper* (n. 7) 288f.; for the new Belgian law, see Art. 2262bis Belgian *code civil* and Claeys, (1998–9) *Rechtskundig Weekblad* 394; cf. also Art. 2947 *codice civile* ('dal giorno in cui il fatto si è verificato'; this relates to the five-year prescription period for claims in delict); Art. 10(1) Unidroit Convention (relating, of course, only to breach of contract).

[231] See Artt. 8:101, 8:108, 9:501ff. PECL.

contrahendo from the moment when the other party breaks off negotiations contrary to good faith and fair dealing.[232] This solution has the additional advantage of avoiding any doctrinal dispute as to whether (and under which circumstances) a claim for damages can be taken to exist, under general principles, only when damages have occurred.[233]

---

[232] See Art. 2:301 (2) PECL.

[233] See, as far as the discussion in German law is concerned, the references in *Staudinger*/Peters (n. 10) § 198, nn. 17ff.; Ursula Stein, in *Münchener Kommentar* (n. 76) § 852, n. 63. For comparative observations, see Spiro (n. 10) § 42.

3

LIBERATIVE PRESCRIPTION II:
ADDITIONAL ISSUES

I PRESCRIPTION OF A CLAIM ESTABLISHED BY LEGAL PROCEEDINGS

In most codifications and reform proposals we find a special rule concerning prescription of a claim established by legal proceedings. The period provided in these rules is normally a long one: thirty years according to § 218 I BGB, § 205 I BGB-KE[1] and s. 11 (a) (ii) (South African) Prescription Act 89 of 1969; twenty years according to Art. 268 *Astikos Kodikas*, Art. 3:324 BW and s. 7 read in conjunction with schedule 1, (2) (a) Prescription and Limitation (Scotland) Act 1973; and ten years according to Art. 137 II OR, Art. 2953 *codice civile*, § 480 I ZGB (GDR), § 197 BGB-PZ, Art. 2924 *code civil du Québec* and according to the new Belgian law.[2] Only the (English) Limitation Act 1980 recognizes a shorter period (six years, according to s. 24 of the act) and the Law Commission in their consultation paper even recommend applying the 'core regime' (i.e., essentially, a three-year period).[3] The Uncitral Convention on Limitation

---

[1] The same rule applies in Austrian law; see Helmut Koziol and Rudolf Welser, *Grundriß des bürgerlichen Rechts*, vol. 1 (10th edn, 1995), 187.

[2] For the latter, see Bart Claessens and Delphine Counye, 'De repercussies van de Wet van 10 juni 1998 op de structuur van het gemeenrechtelijke verjaringsregime', in Hubert Bocken et al. (eds.), *De herziening van de bevrijdende verjaring door de Wet van 10 juni 1998* (1999), 80.

[3] *Consultation Paper* No. 151 ('Limitation of Actions') by the English Law Commission (1998), 370.

does not deal with the matter.[4] Obviously, in a number of systems (particularly in Germany, Switzerland, Italy and the Netherlands), the period chosen for the prescription of claims established by legal proceedings is the general prescription period; but in other systems (notably South Africa and the two German reform drafts) the long period has been enacted, or proposed, as an exception to much shorter general prescription periods.

The specific thrust of the respective provisions in the former legal systems is to cut off any doctrinal discussion as to the effect of the judgment on the original claim (does it continue to exist, or is it substituted by a new claim?[5]): the general prescription period applies even if a shorter period would have applied to the original claim on which the creditor has brought his action.[6] But there are also good policy reasons to subject claims established by a judgment to a fairly long prescription period. We merely have to look back at the basic policy considerations underlying the law of prescription.[7] A claim established by judgment is as firmly and securely established as is possible and is thus affected by the 'obfuscating power of time' to a very much lesser extent than other claims.[8] Moreover, the creditor has made it abundantly clear that he is serious about pursuing his claim; the

---

[4] Art. 5 (d) Uncitral Convention; and see the commentary in (1979) 10 *Uncitral Yearbook* 153.

[5] For the pre-codification *ius commune*, see Bernhard Windscheid and Theodor Kipp, *Lehrbuch des Pandektenrechts* (9th edn, 1906), § 129, n. 3; for echoes of this debate in South Africa and Scotland, see Max Loubser, *Extinctive Prescription* (1996), 39; David Johnston, *Prescription and Limitation* (1999), 6.43ff.; and see Karl Spiro, *Die Begrenzung privater Rechte durch Verjährungs-, Verwirkungs- und Fatalfristen*, vol. 1 (1975), § 162.

[6] See the wording of § 218 1 BGB which clearly brings out this point. Before the enactment of the BGB the question was disputed; see 'Motive', in Benno Mugdan, *Die gesammten Materialien zum Bürgerlichen Gesetzbuch für das Deutsche Reich*, vol. 1 (1899), 538 with references to pre-1900 legislation.

[7] See pp. 63f. [8] See also 'Motive' (n. 6) 538; Spiro (n. 5) § 162.

debtor cannot, therefore, be under any illusion that he might not, one day, have to pay. And, thirdly, the legal dispute between the parties has now been resolved. It does not create a source of uncertainty or a danger to the public interest. To the contrary: it would create unnecessary costs, and thus be more injurious to the public interest, if a short prescription period were to force the creditor in regular intervals to attempt an act of execution which, in view of the debtor's financial position, he knows to be futile.[9] The law of prescription here, as always, should prevent, not encourage or even engender, litigation.

As always, of course, there is something arbitrary in fixing a specific period. But ten years would appear to be a reasonable choice in view of the fact that (i) it is the period most frequently found, or proposed, in modern legislation, and (ii) it strikes a reasonable balance between the two extremes of thirty years (German law) and six (or even three) years (English law and Law Commission proposal, respectively). Admittedly, the introduction of a special period for claims established by judgment would be in conflict with the general quest for uniformity. But we are dealing here with a clearly distinguishable type of claim that does not interfere with any others. The general reasons militating against a differentiated regime do not apply in this specific situation.

German law recognizes one exception to the long prescription period for claims established by judgment: it applies a short period of four years when the claim in question relates to periodic payments falling due only in the future.[10]

---

[9] See, e.g., Bundesminister der Justiz (ed.), *Abschlußbericht der Kommission zur Überarbeitung des Schuldrechts* (1992), 79.

[10] § 218 II BGB; for Austria, see Koziol and Welser (n. 1) 187.

The German Commission proposes to retain this rule.[11] It is a rule intended to protect the debtor: it might be unduly burdensome for him if he would have to be prepared for thirty years (from due date) to prove that he had paid.[12] But, on the one hand, it must be remembered that the period proposed here is ten, not thirty years. On the other hand, it may be argued that a rule like § 218 II BGB pays insufficient attention to the reasonable interests of the creditor. Not rarely does it happen that a person liable to pay maintenance makes off and remains untraceable for a long time. The creditor is normally unable, under these circumstances, to effect a renewal of prescription by means of an act of execution. German courts have thus allowed him once again to bring an action against his debtor (which may be served upon him by public notification):[13] a highly unsatisfactory emergency solution in view of the fact that the matter is *res judicata* and should not normally, for a second time, be the object of litigation. That a maintenance debtor may have to keep, for a long time, his receipts for payments made on a claim established by judgment does not distinguish him from other debtors under a claim established by judgment.

---

[11] § 205 III BGB-KE. The Dutch code has a rule according to which 'payments to be made annually or more frequently pursuant to a decision are prescribed in five years': Art. 3:324 (3) BW. See also Spiro (n. 5) § 164 with references to Swiss case law and literature. Spiro regards a rule like the one contained in § 218 II BGB as following from general principles. This does not appear to be correct: if a claim for maintenance has been established, the mere fact that individual amounts fall due only at a later stage does not change the fact that the claim has been established by judgment.

[12] Frank Peters and Reinhard Zimmermann, 'Verjährungsfristen', in Bundesminister der Justiz (ed.), *Gutachten und Vorschläge zur Überarbeitung des Schuldrechts*, vol. I (1981), 125.

[13] See Börries von Feldmann, in *Münchener Kommentar zum Bürgerlichen Gesetzbuch*, vol. I (3rd edn, 1993), § 219, n. 11 with references to German case law.

It is the consequence of the long prescription period for this type of claim.[14]

The ten-year period proposed is a normal prescription period which is subject to the general rules. The one issue that merits special consideration is when it starts to run. The choice would seem to be between the date of judgment and the date when that judgment becomes final (i.e., when an appeal is not, or no longer, possible). The second of these alternatives is the one more often found in existing legislation;[15] it commends itself for reasons which will become apparent when we look at the closely related question of the effect of legal proceedings upon a period of prescription.[16] A declaratory judgment is sufficient for the application of the ten-year period, as long as it establishes the claim and not merely one of its prerequisites.[17]

It cannot be specified exactly which other instrument obtained by the creditor can have the effect of triggering the ten-year period. The relevant criterion will have to be whether

---

[14] See Peters and Zimmermann (n. 12) 263, 320.
[15] Date of judgment: Switzerland (Spiro (n. 5) § 162); the Netherlands (Art. 3:324 (1) BW). Date when judgment becomes final: Germany (§ 218 I BGB); Greece (Art. 268 *Astikos Kodikas*); Italy (Art. 2953 *codice civile*); § 197 I BGB-PZ; § 205 I BGB-KE. According to s. 24(1) of the English Limitation Act 1980 (cf. also *Law Commission Consultation Paper* (n. 3) 370), the limitation period applicable to actions on a judgment starts to run from the date on which the judgment becomes enforceable. This appears to be too restrictive since it excludes declaratory judgments which, though not enforceable, still establish the claim sufficiently firmly to warrant application of the special regime for claims established by judgment; see Spiro (n. 5) § 133; Frank Peters, in J. von Staudinger, *Kommentar zum Bürgerlichen Gesetzbuch* (13th edn, 1995), §§ 164–240, § 218, n. 5. This point has also been recognized in South African case law (see Loubser (n. 5) 135) in spite of s. 15(4) Prescription Act 68 of 1969.
[16] See pp. 117ff.
[17] If a judgment establishes a duty, on the part of the debtor, to make periodic payments in the future, prescription concerning each of these payments, in accordance with general principles, starts to run only when it falls due.

it is regarded as enforceable as if it were a judgment.[18] A court-approved settlement of the claim between the parties presents an obvious example. Arbitral awards present another.

II THE EFFECT OF JUDICIAL PROCEEDINGS ON THE PERIOD OF PRESCRIPTION

1 *The options*

If the creditor institutes an action on his claim, he does what the law of prescription expects him to do, both in the public interest and in the interest of his debtor: he takes the initiative to bring about an authoritative decision on the dispute. It would be manifestly unfair if prescription continued to run whilst judicial proceedings are pending.[19] The debtor is now able to raise whatever other defence he may have; he can be under no illusion that his creditor may wish to treat the incident as closed; and the proceedings prevent the claim from becoming stale.[20] In this situation a legal system can do one of three things. It can determine that the period of prescription ceases to run (i); that it is 'interrupted', with the effect that it starts to run afresh, once the act of interruption has taken place, or ended (ii); or that it is suspended as long as legal proceedings are pending (iii). (i) is the consequence following most naturally from a concept of a limitation of *actions* and is thus applicable in England;[21] however, it is

---

[18] For Germany, see §§ 218–220 BGB; § 197 BGB-PZ; § 205 BGB-KE.

[19] Cf., e.g., Spiro (n. 5) § 128 and *Abschlußbericht* (n. 9) 84 (the creditor has to be protected against the possibility that his claim prescribes in the course of the legal proceedings aimed at its enforcement).

[20] See the policy considerations pp. 63f.

[21] Andrew McGee, *Limitation Periods* (3rd edn, 1998), paras. 2.001ff.; *Law Commission Consultation Paper* (n. 3) 164. However, it may be equally possible for a legal system endorsing the concept of a limitation of *actions* to

also the approach adopted by the Uncitral Convention.[22] It does not commend itself for present purposes for either it leaves open the question of what happens when the legal proceedings have ended without a decision on the merits of the claim,[23] or it has to deal with this question by way of a somewhat artificial fiction.[24]

attribute no effect at all to the initiation of legal proceedings on the running of the period. This appears to be the US approach: Hans Smit, 'The Convention on the Limitation Period in the International Sale of Goods: Uncitral's First-Born', (1975) 23 *American Journal of Comparative Law* 342. The action, after all, has been brought in time (i.e., before the period of limitation has run out) and the substantive right remains unaffected. The main effect of holding that the period continues to run is that it precludes a claimant from indefinitely suspending it by bringing successive actions (Smit 342). Also, in the situation where the action is dismissed because of an abuse of process (see *Grovit v. Doctor*, [1997] 1 WLR 640 (HL)) the claimant may now be barred from bringing another action because the limitation period has run out. The statement both in McGee and the *Law Commission Consultation Paper*, quoted above, is incidentally in strange contrast to a statement by the House of Lords in *Birkett v. James*, [1978] AC 287 (HL), where it was held that an action will not normally be dismissed for want of prosecution where it appears that the claimant could simply issue a new writ and commence legal proceedings again. According to McGee (n. 21) 22.036, this 'will almost always be the position where the primary limitation period has not expired'. This appears to indicate that, in England also, the limitation period continues to run.

[22] Art. 13.

[23] If, on the other hand, the limitation period is held to continue to run its course (with the consequences sketched above n. 21), this can easily lead to situations of hardship. Due to differences in civil procedure, court structure and legal profession, this may not be as obvious in English or US law as it is in at least some continental countries. Thus, in Germany it can easily happen that the action is brought before a court which does not have jurisdiction to hear the case (local court, as opposed to regional court, etc.). The action is then dismissed as being inadmissible rather than unfounded and the claimant will have to bring his action before the proper court.

[24] Art. 17 (1) Uncitral Convention ('the limitation period shall be deemed to have continued to run' where such legal proceedings have ended without a decision binding on the merits of the claim). But in terms of Art. 17 (2), the creditor is entitled to an extra period of one year if, at the time such legal proceedings ended, the limitation period has expired or has less than one year

2 *Interruption of prescription*

(ii) is the solution traditionally adopted in Roman law-based legal systems; we find it, for example, in Art. 2244 *code civil*, § 1497 ABGB, § 209 BGB, Art. 138 OR, Art. 261 *Astikos Kodikas*, Art. 2943 *codice civile*, Art. 3:316 BW, s. 15 (South African) Prescription Act 68 of 1969, Art. 2892 *code civil du Québec* and also in Scots law.[25] There is, however, something odd in the idea that the bringing of an action should interrupt rather than merely suspend prescription.[26] For by instituting his action the claimant sets in motion the court proceedings which last until a decision is given or until the case has been otherwise disposed of. Thus, we are not, as in other cases of interruption, dealing with a momentary event which could not sensibly extend the original prescription period, but with a continuing process.[27] At the end of this process, there is normally clarity about the merits of the claim. And if there is not, there is no reason to have the entire period of prescription run afresh. Those legal systems subscribing to this approach either tend to specify how long the 'interruption' lasts,[28] or they regard every act by any of the parties to the proceedings, and by the court, as a new cause of interruption.[29] Both constructions

---

to run. For criticism, see Smit, (1975) 23 *American Journal of Comparative Law* 342ff.

[25] As to the latter, see Prescription and Limitation (Scotland) Act 1973, ss. 6, 7 and 9, and Johnston (n. 5) 5.04ff.

[26] Peters and Zimmermann (n. 12) 260ff.; *Abschlußbericht* (n. 9) 84f.; Johnston (n. 5) 5.43.

[27] For the difference between interruption and suspension, see Spiro (n. 5) §§ 127, 160.

[28] See, e.g., § 211 BGB, Art. 261 *Astikos Kodikas*, Art. 2945 *codice civile*, Art. 2896 *code civil du Québec*. According to § 1497 ABGB, interruption lasts as long as the judicial proceedings are 'properly continued'.

[29] Art. 138 OR (cf. also Spiro (n. 5) §§ 147ff.); for Scots law, see Johnston (n. 5) 5.40.

are unsatisfactory. In particular, they lead to unnecessary complexities as well as undesirable practical consequences in cases where the proceedings have ended without a decision on the merits of the claim. Even an action that is dismissed without consideration about the merits of the claim (because it has been brought before a court lacking jurisdiction or because it is procedurally defective in other ways) has to have some effect on the running of the period of prescription because: (a) the creditor cannot always avoid the defect; (b) it would be impracticable to investigate in every individual case whether he can be blamed for proceeding as he did; and (c) he has, after all, demonstrated his determination to pursue his claim.[30] Legal systems subscribing to

---

[30] See Spiro (n. 5) § 139; Peters and Zimmermann (n. 12) 262, 309. According to § 1497, 2 ABGB, only an action that meets all procedural requirements has the effect of interrupting prescription. In nineteenth-century German law, even procedurally defective actions were regarded as sufficient, though not an action that was dismissed for lack of jurisdiction of the court. The position in French law is exactly the other way round (Art. 2246 *code civil*). According to Art. 2943 (3) *codice civile*, interruption is effective even if the judge to whom the action is submitted lacks jurisdiction; the same applies to an action which is otherwise defective as long as it can be regarded as an act placing the debtor in default. According to § 212 I, II BGB, if the proceedings end with a decision not turning on the merits of the claim, commencement of the proceedings is not to be treated as an interruption; however, the creditor is given the opportunity to retain the effects of interruption by instituting another action within six months after the end of the first proceedings: prescription is then deemed to have been interrupted by the first action. Thus, we are dealing here with a double fiction. The same regime applies if the claimant subsequently withdraws the action he has brought. Cf. also Art. 263 *Astikos Kodikas*, Art. 3:316 (2) BW. As in Germany, Greece and the Netherlands, an action that is subsequently withdrawn is usually treated in the same way as a procedurally defective action; see Spiro (n. 5) § 142 with references. Swiss law attributes the effect of interruption only to actions which result in a decision on the merits of the case (see Spiro (n. 5) §§ 139ff. for a detailed discussion; procedurally defective actions effectively lead only to a suspension of the claim in that, according to Art. 139 OR, the creditor is granted a minimum period of six months for reattempting to interrupt prescription after his first action

option (ii) can come to only one of two conclusions in these cases: prescription is interrupted (this would go too far); or it is not interrupted, after all (this does not only entail a clumsy fiction but is also practically unsatisfactory for the reasons just mentioned).

3 *Suspension of prescription*

The preferable solution, and one providing a *via media* between the first two solutions, is (iii): prescription is suspended while the legal proceedings last. If these proceedings lead to a judgment on the merits of the claim, there are two possibilities. Either the claimant succeeds, in which case his claim is now established by legal proceedings and thus subject to the prescription period for claims based on a judgment.[31] Or the action is dismissed and it is now authoritatively settled that there is no claim that could be subject to prescription. Where the proceedings end without a decision on the merits of the claim (because the action is procedurally defective, or because it has subsequently been withdrawn), the creditor merely has what remains of the old period of prescription to renew his action. This is exactly what is required. In particular, no certainty as to the substance of the claim has been

has been dismissed) and gets into difficulties where the claimant withdraws the action he has brought (the question is consequently disputed; see the discussion by Spiro (n. 5) §§ 139ff. If the action which is now withdrawn would have led to a decision on the merits of the case, it would have interrupted prescription; otherwise it would not have done so. But it is both awkward and inefficient to investigate the – by now purely hypothetical – question of whether an action would have led to a decision on the merits of the case merely in order to sort out prescription matters). These problems are largely obviated by 'downgrading' the effects of judicial proceedings from interruption to suspension.

[31] See pp. 112ff.

achieved which might justify the setting in motion of a new period of prescription under headings (i) and (iii) of our policy considerations.[32]

Special attention may have to be paid to the claimant whose action is dismissed, for procedural reasons, at a time when only very little of the old period of prescription is left. Here it is often regarded as reasonable to fix a minimum period which he should have at his disposal after suspension has ended. The period regarded as appropriate is sixty days in Switzerland,[33] three months in Québec,[34] six months in Germany,[35] in Greece[36] and in the Netherlands,[37] and one year according to the Uncitral Convention.[38] The German Reform Commission, however, does not recommend any extra time since, convincingly, they see no reason to place the

---

[32] See pp. 63f.; and see the arguments advanced by Peters and Zimmermann (n. 12) 262. Some codes specifically deal with the case that the legal proceedings remain in abeyance because the claimant fails to pursue them further; see § 211 II BGB ('interruption ends with the last step in the proceedings taken by the parties or the Court'); Art. 261 *Astikos Kodikas*; Art. 2945 (3) *codice civile* ('the interruption is unaffected, and the new prescription period begins to run from the date which caused the interruption'); in Swiss law, the problem is taken care of by Art. 139 I OR; see also the comparative discussion by Spiro (n. 5) § 147. However, a regulation of this situation appears to be dispensable since, if the claimant fails to take any steps to advance the proceedings, it may normally be expected of the defendant to take whatever steps are necessary to have the action dismissed. See Peters and Zimmermann (n. 12) 261, 325 and also Spiro (n. 5) § 147 (n. 16); contra: *Abschlußbericht* (n. 9) 86. Details, of course, depend on the law of civil procedure applicable to the suit. For the consequences of procedural delays according to English law, see McGee (n. 21) 22.001ff. and *Grovit v. Doctor*, [1997] 1 WLR 640 (HL) ('for a claimant to commence and to continue litigation which he had no intention to bring to a conclusion [can] amount to an abuse of process' with the result that the action may be dismissed).

[33] Art. 139 OR.   [34] Art. 2895 *code civil du Québec*.

[35] § 212 II BGB; cf. also § 206 II BGB-PZ.

[36] Art. 263 (2) *Astikos Kodikas*.   [37] Art. 3:316 (2) BW.

[38] Art. 17 (2) Uncitral Convention.

creditor in a better position than if he had not brought an action in the first place.[39]

When does prescription cease to run in case of legal proceedings? This depends on what is regarded, under the applicable law, as an appropriate act to commence a lawsuit.[40] Suspension lasts until a decision has been passed which is final – i.e., against which an appeal is not permissible[41] – or until the case has been otherwise disposed of. Conveniently then, if the judgment has been in favour of the claimant, prescription of his claim based upon the judgment should also start only at that moment and not already when judgment is given.[42] The latter approach[43] would appear to be related to the view, rejected above, that every event within the legal proceedings, including the judgment itself, constitutes a cause of interruption.

Normally, the claimant will bring an action with the aim of obtaining a title to start execution. However, an application for a declaratory judgment establishing the claim is sufficient for the purposes of suspending prescription:[44] just as the declaratory judgment itself is sufficient to warrant application of the special regime discussed above, sub I.

---

[39] *Abschlußbericht* (n. 9) 86.

[40] See the comparative observations in (1979) 10 *Uncitral Yearbook* 159. According to English law, the claimant has to issue proceedings against the defendant; see the discussion in *Law Commission Consultation Paper* (n. 3) 391f. In Germany, the statement of claim must have been served (§ 253 ZPO; *Staudinger*/Peters (n. 15) § 209, nn. 36ff.).

[41] See § 211 I BGB, § 206 I BGB-PZ, § 209 I BGB-KE, Art. 2945 *codice civile*, Art. 2896 *code civil du Québec*.

[42] See above, p. 116.

[43] As adopted, particularly, in Switzerland: see Spiro (n. 5) § 162; but cf. also Art. 3:324 BW.

[44] § 209 BGB; § 205 BGB-PZ; § 208 BGB-KE; Spiro (n. 5) § 133; Loubser (n. 5) 135; comparative: Spiro (n. 5) § 133.

The rules applicable to judicial proceedings also apply to other proceedings, as long as these proceedings aim at procuring an instrument which is enforceable. Details depend on the applicable law.[45]

III RENEWAL OF PRESCRIPTION

1 *Terminology I*

Civilian legal systems traditionally distinguish between 'interruption' and 'suspension' of prescription. If prescription is interrupted, the time which has elapsed before the interrupting event is not taken into account; prescription begins to run afresh. Suspension of prescription, on the other hand, has the effect that the period during which prescription is suspended is not counted in calculating the period of prescription; when the cause of suspension ends, it is therefore the old prescription period that continues to run its course (unless the period of prescription had not even started to run in which case it starts to run only after the cause of suspension has ended).[46] In spite of its near universal acceptance, the term

---

[45] It is widely recognized that prescription is suspended or interrupted while arbitration proceedings are pending: § 220 BGB; Art. 135 II OR; Art. 269 *Astikos Kodikas*; Art. 2943 (4) *codice civile*; Johnston (n. 5) 5.07f.; Loubser (n. 5) 125; Art. 14 Uncitral Convention; § 217 BGB-KE. Concerning commencement of suspension in this case, see §§ 220 II BGB and 217 BGB-KE. The principle has to be that the creditor has to have done everything in his power to start arbitration proceedings.

[46] For statutory definitions of interruption and suspension along these lines, see, e.g., §§ 205, 217 BGB; Artt. 257, 270 *Astikos Kodikas*; §§ 1494ff. ABGB; generally, see Windscheid and Kipp (n. 5) § 108f.; Spiro (n. 5) §§ 69ff., 127ff.; Peters and Zimmermann (n. 12) 124ff. English law, traditionally, subscribes to the principle that once time has started to run it cannot be suspended. It recognizes only certain situations in which the commencement of a limitation period may be delayed or where the period may start again (i.e., where

'interruption'[47] (based on the *interruptio temporis* of the Roman sources[48]) is awkward and perhaps even slightly misleading; it should be replaced by the more descriptive term 'renewal'.[49]

Obviously, renewal is the more radical interference with prescription. It is justified only in two cases: acknowledgement of the claim by the debtor and acts of execution effected by, or at the application of, the creditor.

2 *Acts of execution*

If the creditor has obtained a judgment that has become enforceable, or any instrument which is enforceable under the law under which it was made, his claim based on such a judgment, or other instrument, is also subject to prescription, though the period applicable is the long one discussed above, sub 1. As a result, his claim can, once again, be threatened by prescription. The only way for the creditor to prevent this from happening (apart from extracting an acknowledgement from the debtor) is to attempt an act of execution. Such an act of execution will normally be of a momentary character and cannot, therefore, if it is to have any beneficial effect for the creditor, merely constitute a ground for suspension (or delay of completion) of prescription. Also, the creditor

'the clock is reset'). The latter alternative corresponds to what is called 'interruption' in the civilian tradition and what will be referred to as 'renewal' in the present essay. That 'interruption' sometimes takes the protection of a claimant too far comes out clearly in *Sheldon v. RHM Outhwaite (Underwriting Agencies) Ltd.* [1996] AC 102, a case of subsequent concealment, where suspension would have been the most logical result. See, e.g., the *Law Commission Consultation Paper* (n. 3) 149ff.; and see the remarks p. 129, n. 69.

[47] French: 'interruption'; Italian: 'interruzione'; German: 'Unterbrechung'; Dutch: 'stuiting'.

[48] See Windscheid and Kipp (n. 5) § 108, n. 1 a.

[49] Peters and Zimmermann (n. 12) 310; accepted by *Abschlußbericht* (n. 9) 81.

has formally made clear that he insists on his claim. His act of execution therefore has to have the effect of a renewal of prescription.[50]

Normally, the attempt of execution will be effected at the application of the creditor by a court or public official. It is then sufficient for renewal of prescription that the creditor has made the application, as long as the application is not invalid or is not withdrawn before the act of execution has been attempted.[51]

3 Acknowledgement

If the debtor acknowledges the claim against him, he does not require the protection granted to him by the defence of prescription. Protection must, in turn, be granted to the creditor who may rely on his debtor's declaration and refrain from instituting an action against him. The creditor's earlier silence no longer carries the same weight, particularly not as far as the debtor's expectation of being able to treat the incident as closed is concerned.[52] Also, the debtor's acknowledgement removes, to a considerable extent, uncertainty surrounding the claim. It is therefore generally recognized that such an acknowledgement has to affect the running of the period of prescription.[53] The only sensible way

---

[50] See § 209 II no. 5 BGB; § 197 II BGB-PZ; § 207 BGB-KE; Art. 135 II OR; Art. 264 *Astikos Kodikas*; Art. 2943 *codice civile*; Art. 2244 *code civil*; Johnston (n. 5) 5.55; implicitly also Art. 3:316 BW and many other laws. See generally Spiro (n. 5) § 134; *Abschlußbericht* (n. 9) 80ff.

[51] On acts of execution which are invalid for lack of one of their general requirements, and withdrawal of the application for execution, see § 216 BGB; § 207 II BGB-KE; generally, see Spiro (n. 5) §§ 134, 139ff.

[52] Spiro (n. 5) § 150; *Abschlußbericht* (n. 9) 81.

[53] The question was disputed under the *ius commune*; see the references in Peters and Zimmermann (n. 12) 130. For critical comment today, see *Staudinger*/Peters (n. 15) § 208, nn. 3f.

in which the law can take account of the matter is by way of a renewal of prescription. This, too, appears to be generally accepted.[54]

English law and the Uncitral Convention[55] require the acknowledgement to be in writing. The argument for recognizing only written acknowledgements is that they promote legal certainty.[56] Most European codifications, however, and also the laws of Québec and South Africa regard as sufficient an informal acknowledgement, which may be either express or implied.[57] Of course, it may sometimes be difficult to interpret the debtor's conduct but these difficulties can be resolved, as with all declarations or other conduct which may have legal relevance, by having recourse to the general rules of interpretation.[58] Moreover, even a written statement by the debtor will often be open to various interpretations. The general trend in contract law has certainly been towards informality[59] and though we are not dealing here with a contractual declaration[60] there is no reason to regard an acknowledgement as sufficiently serious, or special,

---

[54] Art. 2248 *code civil*; § 1497 ABGB; § 208 BGB; Art. 260 *Astikos Kodikas*; Art. 135 I OR; Art. 2944 *codice civile*; Art. 3:318 BW; s. 14 (1) (South African) Prescription Act 68 of 1969; Johnston (n. 5) 5.66ff.; Art. 20 Uncitral Convention; English Limitation Act 1980, ss. 29ff. (though not for all claims); § 198 BGB-PZ; § 206 BGB-KE; Art. 2898 *code civil du Québec*; *Law Commission Consultation Paper* (n. 3) 308ff. (recommending an extension of the present regime to all claims).

[55] See the references in n. 54. The *Law Commission Consultation Paper* (n. 3) 317f. recommends retention of this requirement.

[56] *Law Commission Consultation Paper* (n. 3) 317.

[57] See, specifically, § 1497 ABGB and s. 14 (1) (South African) Prescription Act 68 of 1969.

[58] For details, see Spiro (n. 5) §§ 154f.; for the German case law, see *Staudinger*/Peters (n. 15) § 208, nn. 10ff.

[59] See generally Reinhard Zimmermann, *The Law of Obligations: Roman Foundations of the Civilian Tradition* (1990, paperback edn 1996), pp. 85ff.

[60] The legal nature of an acknowledgement is explored by Spiro (n. 5) §§ 151ff.; *Staudinger*/Peters (n. 15) § 208, nn. 5ff.

or inherently precarious, to warrant the introduction of a form requirement. In none of the countries just mentioned has the position been regarded as unsatisfactory[61] and the German reform proposals, for example, do not even contemplate a change in this regard.

Legal certainty is safeguarded sufficiently if the law requires, as indeed it widely does,[62] acknowledgement of the claim vis-à-vis the creditor. The latter cannot reasonably rely on an acknowledgement of which he merely hears through a third party; it is often based on considerations arising from the relationship between debtor and third party and is not sufficient evidence of any clear appreciation, on the part of the debtor, of being bound towards the creditor.[63]

Obvious examples of legal acts implying an acknowledgement are part payment, payment of interest and the giving of security.[64] The Uncitral Convention recognizes an exception from the form requirement in cases of payment of interest or part payment 'if it can reasonably be inferred from such payment or performance that the debtor acknowledges that obligation';[65] English and Scots law put part payment on a par with an acknowledgement in writing.[66]

---

[61] For Germany, see Peters and Zimmermann (n. 12) 254.

[62] § 208 BGB; § 198 BGB-PZ; § 206 BGB-KE. The same is recognized, though not specifically stated in the codes and statutes, in Switzerland (Spiro (n. 5) § 153), the Netherlands (A. S. Hartkamp, *Mr. C. Asser's Handleiding tot de Beoefening van het Nederlands Burgerlijk Recht, Verbintenissenrecht*, Deel I (10th edn, 1996), n. 680) and South Africa (Loubser (n. 5) 139). English law, Scots law and the Uncitral Convention also require acknowledgement 'to the creditor'.

[63] For a detailed analysis along these lines, see Spiro (n. 5) § 153.

[64] § 208 BGB; Art. 135 I OR; *Asser*/Hartkamp (n. 62) n. 680; Loubser (n. 5) 125, 139; § 198 BGB-PZ; § 206 BGB-KE; Patrice Deslauriers, 'Québec', in Ewoud Hondius (ed.), *Extinctive Prescription* (1995), p. 302.

[65] Art. 20 II.

[66] *Law Commission Consultation Paper* (n. 3) 308ff.; Johnston (n. 5) 5.68ff.

IV SUSPENSION IN CASES OF AN IMPEDIMENT BEYOND THE CREDITOR'S CONTROL

Two particularly important grounds for suspension of prescription have already been discussed: prescription is suspended as long as the creditor does not know, and could not reasonably know, of his claim;[67] and it is suspended while judicial or arbitration proceedings on the claim are pending.[68] A number of legal systems also suspend prescription in cases where it is factually impossible for the creditor to exercise his right.[69] Even though the range of situations considered under this heading is no longer as strictly confined as among nineteenth-century pandectist scholars – incursion of enemies and schism (the latter concerning only claims of the Church)[70] – it is also not extended as liberally

---

[67] See pp. 104 and 106ff.   [68] See pp. 117ff.

[69] English law does not, not even in the case of *Prideaux v. Webber*, (1661) 1 Lev 31, 83 ER 282 (concerning suspension of the King's law during the period of the Commonwealth): see McGee (n. 21) 2.010. It must be remembered, however, that even in contract law the doctrine of frustration started to gain ground only in the second half of the nineteenth century (see *Taylor v. Caldwell*, (1863) 3 B & S 826, 122 ER 300 concerning what a German lawyer would refer to as supervening impossibility). Moreover, it must also be kept in mind that under the Limitation Act 1980 the courts are given discretion to disapply the limitation period in certain situations. For adverse comment, see *Law Commission Consultation Paper* (n. 3) 319ff.; N. H. Andrews, 'Reform of Limitation of Actions: The Quest for Sound Legal Policy', (1998) 57 *Cambridge Law Journal* 607f. (who uses strong language: 'scandalous and disastrous').

[70] Windscheid and Kipp (n. 5) § 109, 3. However, this restrictive approach applied only to long prescription periods, particularly the regular period of thirty years. Prescription periods of one year, and less, were regarded as *tempus utile* where only those days were counted during which the person affected by it was able to do what was required of him: see Windscheid and Kipp (n. 5) § 104. The enactment of § 203 BGB, therefore, can be seen as a compromise solution in order to streamline the law of prescription: the distinction between *tempus utile* and other periods was abandoned.

as under the Prussian code.[71] According to § 203 II BGB, the creditor must not have been prevented from exercising his right as a result of *vis maior* ('höhere Gewalt'), and § 203 I BGB even specifies 'cessation of the administration of justice' as an example.[72] The operative words in the South African Prescription Act are 'prevented by superior force';[73] the Uncitral Convention takes account of 'a circumstance which is beyond the control of the creditor and which he could neither avoid or overcome'.[74] Peters and Zimmermann propose a more liberal rule ('prevented from pursuing his right through no fault of his own'),[75] a suggestion which has been supported by Spiro[76] but rejected by the German Reform Commission.[77] The *code civil du Québec* includes every case of 'impossibilité en fait d'agir'.[78]

In spite of the fact that a number of legal systems do not have any equivalent rule at all[79] or only one which covers a very special situation[80] (and presumably have to take

---

[71] §§ 516ff. I 9 PrALR; for other pre-1900 legislation, see Peters and Zimmermann (n. 12) 127.

[72] Art. 255, I *Astikos Kodikas* is virtually identical.   [73] Section 13 (1) (a).

[74] Art. 21. The Convention avoids the terms 'force majeure' or 'impossibility' in view of the fact that 'they have different connotations in different legal systems'. For comment, see (1979) 10 *Uncitral Yearbook* 164 and Smit, (1975) 23 *American Journal of Comparative Law* 345.

[75] § 201 BGB-PZ; and see the comments on pp. 252, 308.

[76] Karl Spiro, 'Zur Reform der Verjährungsbestimmungen', in *Festschrift für Wolfram Müller-Freienfels* (1986), p. 624.

[77] *Abschlußbericht* (n. 9) 89. The commission proposes, essentially, to retain the present rule.

[78] Art. 2904. The Swiss code has a rule (Art. 134 VI OR) according to which prescription is suspended as long as a claim cannot be asserted before a Swiss court. The interpretation of this rule is disputed: see Spiro (n. 5) § 72; Peters and Zimmermann (n. 12) 271.

[79] For the Netherlands, see *Asser*/Hartkamp (n. 62) n. 684.

[80] Art. 2942 *codice civile*: claims against members of the armed forces, and related persons, in times of war.

recourse to the *exceptio doli* or comparable devices in appropriate cases[81]), it is submitted that the general policy of
the rule is sound. The creditor must have a fair chance of
pursuing his claim; otherwise prescription would hit him
unduly harshly. He can hardly be said to be acting against
the precepts of good faith[82] if he *does not* pursue a claim
which he *cannot* pursue.[83] Also, it must be remembered
that, while the short general period of prescription proposed in the previous chapter accommodates the reasonable interests of the debtor, the rules concerning commencement and suspension of prescription have to be tilted in
favour of the creditor.[84] Moreover, it would seem incongruous to protect a creditor who does not know about his
claim and not the one who is unable to pursue it.[85] At the
same time, it may be possible to limit the impact of a suspension rule concerning cases of factual impossibility not
only by choosing a restrictive formula for defining its range
of application:[86] for there is no compelling reason to extend the period of prescription if the impediment preventing the bringing of an action has ceased to exist well before
the end of the prescription period. This is why the Uncitral
Convention determines that the prescription period 'shall be
extended so as not to expire before the expiration of one year
from the date on which the relevant circumstance ceased

---

[81] See Spiro (n. 76) 624.   [82] See p. 78.

[83] Inherent in prescription is thus always an element of 'Verwirkung'; on which
see, in the present context, *Staudinger*/Peters, Vorbem. zu §§ 194ff. nn. 17ff.;
and see pp. 78 and 156f.

[84] See p. 76.

[85] This would appear to be the consequence of the recommendations of the
English Law Commission.

[86] Such as: 'prevented from enforcing his claim by an impediment which is beyond
his control and which he could not reasonably have been expected to avoid or
overcome'. It would tie in with Art. 8:108 PECL and comes close to Art. 21
Uncitral Convention.

to exist'.[87] Effectively, therefore, the creditor is granted a minimum period of one year during which he must be able to pursue his claim. But this solution also goes beyond what is necessary to protect the reasonable interest of the creditor. On the one hand, one year appears to be somewhat long.[88] On the other hand, it would be quite sufficient to extend the period of prescription by the amount of time for which the creditor was prevented, within the last six months of the prescription period, from pursuing his claim.[89]

The suspension ground just discussed is an emanation of the general principle 'agere non valenti non currit praescriptio': prescription does not run against a person who is unable to bring an action. It was coined or, at any rate,

---

[87] Art. 21. See also the comment in (1979) 10 *Uncitral Yearbook* 164. And see s. 13 (1) (i) (South African) Prescription Act 68 of 1969 and the explanation by Loubser (n. 5) 117.

[88] Most impediments covered by this rule will last for only a short while. It appears to be disproportionate to grant the creditor a full period of one year after the impediment has fallen away. But see also s. 13 (1) (i) South African Prescription Act 68/1969.

[89] The rule might read as follows: 'Prescription is suspended as long as the creditor is prevented from initiating his claim by an impediment which is beyond his control and which he could not reasonably have been expected to avoid or overcome. This applies only if the impediment arises, or subsists, within the last six months of the prescription period.' In other words: when the impediment arises, the period of prescription stops running (as long as the impediment arises, or subsists, within the last six months of the prescription period). Whatever is left of the original period of prescription is available to the creditor from the moment when the impediment falls away (i.e., when suspension ends), no matter whether this also happened within the last six months of the original prescription period, or thereafter. This is not the mechanism adopted in German and Greek law (§ 203 BGB, § 212 BGB-KE; Art. 255, 1 *Astikos Kodikas*) where the period of prescription is suspended for only as long as the creditor is prevented by an impediment happening within the last six months of the period from pursuing his claim. Thus, the maximum period for which prescription may be suspended is six months (see *Staudinger*/Peters (n. 15) § 203, n. 2).

authoritatively established by Bartolus[90] and reasserted itself even where a code decided to turn its face against it.[91] Thus, the draftsmen of the *code civil* did not suspend prescription where the creditor is prevented from exercising his right and, moreover, made it very clear that the suspension grounds provided in the code were to be taken as conclusive.[92] None the less, the courts have drawn upon the old maxim of the Roman–canon common law (which was supposed to have been abolished) in order to establish suspension of prescription in cases of 'impossibilité absolue d'agir'.[93] The French experience may thus be taken to support our assertion that the general policy of the rule discussed in this section is sound.

[90] For details, see Karl Spiro, 'Zur neueren Geschichte des Satzes "Agere non valenti non currit praescriptio"', in *Festschrift für Hans Lewald* (1953), pp. 585ff., 588; see also Detlef Liebs, *Lateinische Rechtsregeln und Rechtssprichwörter* (6th edn, 1998), p. 32.

[91] According to Spiro (n. 90) 593f., the natural law codifications refrained from laying down the general principle since (i) its application in practice had previously, under the *usus modernus pandectarum*, turned out to be too uncertain and (ii) it appeared unnecessary in view of the fact that the prescription periods tended to be very long anyway. Instead, the draftsmen of the codes adopted only some of the more specific grounds for suspension, partly based on this general principle. Pandectist scholars tended to brush aside the principle (see, e.g., Windscheid and Kipp (n. 5) § 109, n. 2) as not having been recognized in the Roman sources.

[92] Art. 2251 *code civil*.

[93] See Murad Ferid and Hans-Jürgen Sonnenberger, *Das französische Zivilrecht*, vol. I/1 (2nd edn, 1994), 1 C 224 (who comment that the courts have decided essentially *contra legem*; the same view is expressed by François Terré, Philippe Simler and Yves Lequette, *Droit Civil: Les Obligations* (7th edn, 1999), n. 1396). Generally on the phenomenon of legal continuity, based on Roman law, in spite of codification, see Reinhard Zimmermann, 'Civil Code and Civil Law', (1994/5) 1 *Columbia Journal of European Law* 89ff. Concerning France and the Netherlands, see Hendrik Kooiker, *Lex Scripta Abrogata: De derde renaissance van het Romeinse recht* (1996), and the comments by Reinhard Zimmermann, 'Heutiges Recht, römisches Recht, heutiges römisches Recht', in Reinhard Zimmermann, Rolf Knütel and Jens Peter Meincke (eds.), *Rechtsgeschichte und Privatrechtsdogmatik* (2000), 2ff.

V EXTENSION IN CASES OF INCAPACITY

1 *The basic options*

'Agere non valenti non currit praescriptio' also requires prescription not to run against a creditor who is subject to an incapacity. The paradigmatic example is the minor.[94] He is unable to pursue his claim in court. Some legal systems, therefore, have indeed established a general rule to the effect that prescription does not run against him; France and England provide the most prominent examples.[95] Arguably, however, it overshoots the mark. For a minor normally has a representative adult (such as a parent or guardian) capable of bringing proceedings on his behalf. Thus, it may be contended that the minor requires protection only in cases where, for some or other reason, he is without such a representative. This is the solution favoured, e.g., in German, Austrian, Greek and Italian law.[96]

The choice between these two approaches is not an easy one. On balance, however, commercial certainty would appear to be too gravely jeopardized if whoever is exposed to a claim by a minor would have to wait at least until the minor has reached the age of majority plus three years.[97] This is particularly obvious where we are dealing with claims other than those for personal injuries, such as contractual claims. If the adult representative fails to act

---

[94] The following remarks apply, *mutatis mutandis*, to persons who lack the capacity to enter legal relations because they are of unsound mind.

[95] Art. 2252 first part *code civil* ('La prescription ne court pas contre les mineurs non émancipés et les majeurs en tutelle'); English Limitation Act 1980, s. 28. For Scotland, see Prescription and Limitation (Scotland) Act 1973, s. 6 (4) (b) and Johnston (n. 5) 6.130ff.

[96] See § 206 BGB; § 1494 ABGB; Art. 258 (2) *Astikos Kodikas*; Art. 2942 *codice civile*.

[97] The problems are illustrated by the case of *Headford v. Bristol and District Health Authority*, [1995] PIQR 180 (Court of Appeal).

in the appropriate manner, this is a risk that falls within the sphere of the minor for whom the representative acts. Moreover, the minor can be protected at least to the extent that prescription of his claims *against the representative adult* is suspended until he reaches the age of majority.[98] Such a right of action against the parent may be 'a poor substitute'[99] for the child's own claim against the third party. But the interest of the minor cannot in this respect prevail against those of the third party, since the legal system may reasonably proceed from the assumption that the parent or guardian will normally look after the interests of the minor. In view of these considerations, it is interesting to note a general and long-standing shift within the continental legal development from taking account of the incapacity as such towards balancing the interests of the minor against the interests of his debtor,[100] a shift which is in line with the more general trend towards shortening the periods of prescription as far as reasonably possible. Significantly, also, neither in France nor in England is the general rule about when prescription does not run against persons subject to an incapacity carried through without exception,[101] and the

---

[98] This is indeed what § 1495 ABGB; § 204 BGB; Art. 2941 (2–4) *codice civile*; and Art. 256 *Astikos Kodikas* provide. For similar rules, see Art. 134 I and II OR and Art. 3:321 (1) (b) BW. Generally, see Spiro (n. 5) §§ 75f.

[99] See Twentieth Report of the (English) Law Reform Committee, as quoted in *Law Commission Consultation Paper* (n. 3) 298.

[100] See 'Motive' (n. 6) 528; Peters and Zimmermann (n. 12) 128. In Switzerland and in the Netherlands this has even led to a situation where the code does not contain any provision suspending the prescription of a minor's claims (except insofar as they are directed against the representative). In Switzerland, courts and legal writers, therefore, in order to grant protection to a minor who lacks a representative, had to have recourse to general principles (abuse of right, *boni mores*); for details, see Spiro (n. 5) §§ 95ff., 106.

[101] Art. 2252, second part *code civil* (on which see Ferid and Sonnenberger (n. 93) I C 223); and see the complex regulation in Limitation Act 1980, ss. 28, 28 A, and the discussion in *Law Commission Consultation Paper* (n. 3) 142ff.

English Law Commission has recently left open the question whether it should be retained.[102]

2 *Details of implementation*

To summarize, and specify: (i) if a person subject to an incapacity is without a representative, prescription for or against him does not occur before one year has passed after either the disability or the lack of representation has been removed. Two additional notes are apposite. (a) Protection of the person subject to an incapacity appears to be necessary only if the lack of representation existed within the last year of the prescription period, as long as the law makes sure that a reasonable period is available after either the incapacity or the lack of representation has been removed.[103] Strictly speaking, therefore, lack of representation does not suspend the running of the prescription period but merely delays completion of prescription. (b) The rule works both ways, i.e., it also affects claims *against* the person under disability.[104] Though not impossible, it is not at all easy for the creditor of a person under disability who lacks a representative to pursue his claim.[105] Thus, it appears to be equitable to grant

---

[102] *Law Commission Consultation Paper* (n. 3) 297ff.

[103] This is (with one exception: a period not of one year but only of six months) the regime applicable according to § 206 BGB and supported both by Peters and Zimmermann (n. 12) § 203 BGB-PZ and by the German Reform Commission; see § 214 BGB-KE. Cf. also Art. 258 II *Astikos Kodikas*. The Italian rule is different in that prescription is suspended for the period during which the person subject to an incapacity lacks a representative and for six months following the appointment of such a representative or the termination of the disability: Art. 2942 *codice civile*.

[104] This is contrary to § 206 BGB (and also Art. 2942 *codice civile*) but reform has been advocated by Peters and Zimmermann (n. 12) 251f., 321 and the German Reform Commission; see *Abschlußbericht* (n. 9) 90f.

[105] In Germany, for example, he has to get a special representative appointed in terms of § 57 of the Code of Civil Procedure. This is often difficult in view of

him the same protection that is granted to the person under disability himself.

(ii) Prescription of claims between a person subject to an incapacity and his representative does not occur before one year has passed after either the incapacity has been removed or a new representative has been appointed. If, as far as third parties are concerned, the minor has to bear the consequences of his representative's failure to act, he must at least be able to sue his representative for damages. This he can do only if he has attained the age of majority. Once again, however, it is unnecessary to suspend prescription.[106] It is sufficient that a reasonable period is available to the creditor for bringing his action after he has reached the age of majority. Once again, also, it is equitable to make the rule work both ways.

(iii) In some countries, sexual abuse of children has given rise to litigation.[107] Where the person abusing the child is an unrelated stranger, the law may arguably rely on the representative adult to take whatever action is appropriate. Where the person abusing the child is the parent himself, suspension of all claims between child and parent during minority would

the fact that it may be doubtful whether the debtor lacks capacity to contract. Also, before the action is brought, nobody is available to whom the creditor may turn to attempt to achieve a settlement out of court. Thus, a rule like § 206 BGB at present engenders rather than prevents lawsuits: Peters and Zimmermann (n. 12) 252.

[106] However, this is the regime normally adopted: see § 1495 ABGB; § 204 BGB; Art. 134 I and II OR; Art. 2941 (2–4) *codice civile*; § 202 BGB-PZ; § 213 BGB-KE. But cf. Art. 3:321 (1) (b) BW and *Staudinger*/Peters (n. 15) § 204, n. 3.

[107] See Ewoud Hondius, 'General Report', in Hondius (n. 64) 9f.; *Law Commission Consultation Paper* (n. 3) 294f. For the Netherlands, see HR 23 October 1998 and 25 June 1999, (2000) *Nederlandse Jurisprudentie* 15/16 (extending the five-year period of Art. 3:310 (1) in situations where the injured party was prevented from instituting his claim because of circumstances attributable to the debtor, particularly psychological superiority; this extension is based on good faith and equity). I am grateful to Professors Arthur Hartkamp and Ewoud Hondius for bringing these decisions to my attention.

help, at least to a certain extent. However, the minor will often have repressed the traumatic childhood experience and may need considerable time to break down the psychological barriers preventing him from acknowledging what has happened. Thus, it may be more appropriate in these cases to suspend, rather than to delay completion of prescription. Moreover, there have been cases where the child is abused by another family member with whom the parent connives or whom he does not want to sue for other reasons. Here it would seem to be necessary to introduce a rule suspending prescription – either of the claims against the third parties or at least against the parent.

3 *Terminology II*

At this stage, another brief note on terminology may be in order. The period of prescription, as has been mentioned earlier,[108] may be renewed ('interrupted') or suspended. Suspension extends a given period of prescription: the period during which prescription is suspended is not counted in calculating the period of prescription.[109] But there is also another device that has the effect of extending the period of prescription: delay of completion of prescription. Here the period of prescription runs its course but it is completed only after the expiry of a certain extra period. While suspension of prescription is a device well known in European civil codes,[110] delay of completion is of more recent vintage (we find it first in §§ 512ff. I 9 of the Prussian code of 1794) but has increasingly gained ground internationally as a milder form of interference with prescription. The

---

[108] See pp. 124f.   [109] See p. 124.
[110] See, e.g., Artt. 2251ff. *code civil*; §§ 1494ff. ABGB; §§ 202ff. BGB; Artt. 255ff. *Astikos Kodikas*; Artt. 2941f. *codice civile*.

German term is 'Ablaufhemmung';[111] the Dutch equivalent
is 'verlenging van de verjaring', a concept which in the new
BW has completely replaced the traditional concept of suspension ('schorsing').[112] The systematic exposition proposed
in the present chapter is therefore as follows: the period of
prescription may be (i) renewed or (ii) extended. An extension may occur either by way of (a) suspension or (b) delay
of completion of prescription.

VI CLOSE PERSONAL TIES AS GROUNDS FOR EXTENSION?

Claims between children and their representatives are merely
one particularly important group of claims covered by § 204
BGB and the equivalent rules in other countries. The same
rule is often applied to claims between spouses: prescription
is suspended as long as the marriage persists.[113] The common denominator is the family tie which constitutes, in the
old-fashioned language of the draftsmen of the BGB, 'a relationship of piety requiring utmost care and protection'.[114]
Prescription of claims between spouses is also suspended in
France,[115] Switzerland,[116] Italy,[117] the Netherlands,[118] South
Africa[119] and Québec[120] but not in England or Scotland. In

---

[111] See 'Motive' (n. 6) 528; Spiro (n. 5) §§ 87ff.
[112] See Artt. 3:320f. BW; *Asser*/Hartkamp (n. 62) n. 682; M. W. E. Koopmann,
Bevrijdende verjaring (1993), pp. 83ff.
[113] § 204 BGB.
[114] 'Rücksicht auf das der Schonung dringend bedürftige Pietätsverhältniß, das
zwischen diesen Personen besteht': 'Motive' (n. 6) 531.
[115] Art. 2253 *code civil*.   [116] Art. 134 III OR.
[117] Art. 2941 (1) *codice civile*.   [118] Art. 3:321 (1) (a) BW.
[119] Section 13 (1) (c) Prescription Act 68 of 1969.
[120] Art. 2906 *code civil du Québec*. Cf. also, e.g., § 1495 ABGB; Art. 256 *Astikos
Kodikas*; and, generally, Spiro (n. 5) § 74. However, prescription is not always
suspended as long as the marriage persists; cf., e.g., Art. 2906 *code civil*

spite of the preponderance of opinion in favour of the rule, it hardly appears defensible today.[121] It leads to problems being swept under the carpet rather than solved. The death of one of the spouses should not enable the other to surprise disagreeable heirs by presenting claims which would normally have prescribed many years ago. Nor should divorce provide the trigger for settling old scores. Marriage would then have had the effect of removing protection against stale claims: a result which may well be regarded as discriminatory.[122] If, on the other hand, one were to regard the rationale underlying § 204 BGB (and equivalent rules in other legal systems) as sound, it is difficult to see why the rule should not be generalized so as to cover other, closely related persons living in a common household.[123] However, delimitation of its range of application would then become an intricate exercise which would inevitably jeopardize legal certainty.[124] The only special rule that is required is the one concerning claims between persons subject to an incapacity and their representatives[125] and it is based on a different rationale: not on the close personal ties existing between these persons but because it is

    du Québec ('La prescription ne court point entre les époux pendant la vie commune').

[121] For what follows, see the spirited attack in *Staudinger*/Peters (n. 15) § 204, n. 2.

[122] *Staudinger*/Peters (n. 15) § 204, n. 2 (who argues that Art. 6 of the Basic Law may be infringed).

[123] This was indeed proposed by Peters and Zimmermann (n. 12) 249f., 316, 321, approved by Spiro (n. 76) 624, but rejected by the German Reform Commission; see *Abschlußbericht* (n. 9) 90. Generally, see Karl Spiro, 'Verjährung und Hausgemeinschaft', in *Festschrift für Friedrich Wilhelm Bosch* (1976), pp. 975ff. The Swiss code contains a rule according to which prescription of the claims of an employee, who lives in a common household with his employer, against that employer is suspended as long as the employment relationship lasts; for details, see Spiro (n. 5) § 77.

[124] See *Abschlußbericht* (n. 9) 90.   [125] See pp. 135, 136.

impossible for the person subject to an incapacity to act on his own.

VII PRESCRIPTION OF CLAIMS BY OR AGAINST AN ESTATE

Another situation, in some respects, is very similar to the one where a person subject to an incapacity is without a representative. When a person has died it can happen, at least under some succession regimes prevailing in Europe, that his estate is temporarily without a personal representative, or heir, who may be sued by creditors of the estate and who can pursue the claims belonging to the estate. The draftsmen of the BGB regarded it as equitable to provide for a delay of completion of prescription on the model established for persons subject to an incapacity.[126] The situations are very similar and so is the underlying rationale: 'agere non valenti non currit praescriptio'. The rule has not given rise to any problems and its wisdom has never been questioned.[127] Few other legal systems, however, contain a similar rule[128] and some even specifically state that prescription is not suspended.[129]

---

[126] Prescription of a claim belonging to the creditor's estate or directed against the debtor's estate does not occur before six months have passed after the claim can be enforced by or against an heir, or by or against a representative of the estate. See § 207 BGB and 'Motive' (n. 6) 530. Unlike § 206 BGB (see n. 107), § 207 BGB works both ways.

[127] Its retention is advocated by Peters and Zimmermann (n. 12) § 204 BGB-PZ and by the German Reform Commission; see *Abschlußbericht* (n. 9) 91.

[128] But see Art. 259 *Astikos Kodikas* and s. 13 (1) (h) (South African) Prescription Act 68 of 1969. In Switzerland, the general provision of Art. 134 VI OR (concerning claims which the creditor is unable to pursue before a Swiss court) appears to be applied in appropriate cases; see Spiro (n. 5) § 72 (pp. 158f.).

[129] Art. 2258 (2) *code civil* ('[La prescription] court contre une succession vacante, quoique non pourvue de curateur').

VIII EXTENSION AS A RESULT OF NEGOTIATIONS

Another ground for suspension has gained considerable support in Germany in recent years: negotiations pending among the parties about the claim, or about circumstances from which a claim might arise. In 1977, Parliament introduced a rule into the code relating to negotiations about compensation to be rendered and suspending prescription of claims in delict.[130] It is based on the consideration that negotiations to reach a settlement out of court deserve to be encouraged. Thus, they should not have to be carried out under the pressure of an impending prescription of the claim. Nor should negotiations be allowed to constitute a trap for the creditor. A debtor who starts negotiating about a claim and who thus prevents the creditor from bringing an action should not later be allowed to refuse to satisfy the claim by invoking the time that has elapsed during those negotiations.[131] Ultimately, therefore, § 852 II BGB has to be regarded as a special manifestation of the principle of good faith as contained in § 242 BGB.[132] It is widely recognized that it is much too narrowly confined. The rule has been applied, *per analogiam*, to certain

---

[130] § 852 II BGB. A number of provisions in special statutes refer to this rule; cf. §§ 14 StVG (Road Traffic Act), 39 LuftVG (Air Traffic Law), 11 HaftpflG (Legal Liability Law), 32 AtomG (Atomic Energy Law), 3 n. 3 PflVersG (Compulsory Insurance Law). Two other rules contained in the BGB are based on similar considerations: § 651 g II 2 (concerning claims arising from deficient package tours) and § 639 II BGB (concerning claims based on defects under a contract of *locatio conductio operis*). Somewhat irritatingly, however, all these provisions diverge as regards the details of implementing this policy.

[131] Peters and Zimmermann (n. 12) 250; *Abschlußbericht* (n. 9) 91.

[132] Under this doctrinal umbrella the rule was recognized by the courts before its enactment. § 852 II BGB has, therefore, not reformed but merely clarified the law. See Ursula Stein, in *Münchener Kommentar zum Bürgerlichen Gesetzbuch*, vol. V (3rd edn, 1997), § 852, n. 67; Karl Schäfer, in J. von Staudinger, *Kommentar zum Bürgerlichen Gesetzbuch* (12th edn, 1986), §§ 833–53, § 852, nn. 116ff.

contractual damages claims;[133] in other cases, the courts still have to fall back directly on § 242 BGB[134] (the appropriate doctrinal pigeonhole being 'unzulässige Rechtsausübung' (inadmissible exercise of a right)).[135] Both German reform proposals therefore recommend a generalized rule along the lines of § 852 II BGB.[136]

At the same time, however, it must be noted that hardly any other legal system appears to have a provision of this kind. But only very few of them are happy to allow the debtor 'to negotiate himself into prescription'.[137] Most of them, in some way or other, want to help the creditor. As far as Switzerland is concerned, Spiro takes prescription to be suspended during negotiations even without a statutory basis.[138] In other countries we find a very extended interpretation of the notions of acknowledgement and waiver; yet others rely on equitable doctrines like promissory *estoppel* or personal bar, or they resort to the general notion of good faith, to the doctrine of abuse of right or to the *exceptio doli*.[139]

---

[133] BGHZ 93, 64 (68f.); and see the references in *Münchener Kommentar*/Stein (n. 132) § 852, n. 67.

[134] See the references in *Münchener Kommentar*/von Feldmann (n. 13) § 194, n. 16; *Münchener Kommentar*/Stein (n. 132) § 852, n. 67; and *Abschlußbericht* (n. 9) 92.

[135] Generally on the meaning and application of good faith in German law, see Simon Whittaker and Reinhard Zimmermann, 'Good Faith in European Contract Law: Surveying the Legal Landscape', in Reinhard Zimmermann and Simon Whittaker (eds.), *Good Faith in European Contract Law* (2000), pp. 18ff. and (concerning prescription) case study 20, German report (pp. 493f.).

[136] § 200 BGB-PZ; § 216 BGB-KE. See also Frank Peters, 'Vergleichsverhandlungen und Verjährung', (1982) *Neue Juristische Wochenschrift* 1857ff. The German Federal Supreme Court regards § 852 II BGB as 'an expression of a general legal principle' (BGHZ 93, 64 (69)).

[137] See the Norwegian report to case study 20 (Prescription I) in Zimmermann and Whittaker (n. 135) 504.

[138] Spiro (n. 5) § 108.

[139] For details, see the country reports for Greece, Austria, France, Belgium, Spain, Italy, the Netherlands, England, Ireland, Scotland and the Nordic

The one argument against a rule suspending prescription in case of negotiations is that it would lead to uncertainty. At what precise moment does suspension start and when does it end?[140] But the alternative, at least for most legal systems,[141] is to grant protection by means of much more general, and even vaguer, doctrines or by a somewhat contorted construction of the parties' actions. The German Federal Supreme Court must be right when it states that application of § 852 II BGB is preferable in comparison with § 242 BGB: the former rule, at least, makes clear within which period after negotiations have ended the creditor has to bring an action.[142] A generalized rule on the model of § 852 II BGB would therefore contribute to, rather than detract from, legal certainty.[143]

countries to case 20, as well as the comparative observations at the end of case 21, in Zimmermann and Whittaker (n. 135) 493ff., 530f. In those legal systems which allow the parties to contract out of the prescription regime and to agree, for example, to suspend prescription while they negotiate (as is the position in English law; see p. 163), the problem is of less practical relevance than in others.

[140] See Twenty-First Report of the (English) Law Reform Committee, as quoted in *Preston and Newsom on Limitation of Actions* (4th edn, 1989) by John Weeks, 146 (nn. 2.60f. of the Report).

[141] And, presumably, also under the Principles of European Contract Law in view of Art. 1:201 (1): 'Each party must act in accordance with good faith and fair dealing.'

[142] BGHZ 93, 64 (69). It is generally recognized in German law that the term 'negotiation' has to be interpreted widely: any exchange of opinion is covered which may reasonably lead the creditor to believe that his claim has not been finally rejected by the other party; see, e.g., *Münchener Kommentar*/Stein (n. 132) § 852, n. 68; generally Spiro (n. 5) § 108.

[143] Once again, it appears to be sufficient to delay completion of prescription rather than to suspend it. Once negotiations have failed, the creditor does not need more than a reasonable minimum period to make up his mind whether to pursue his claim in court. Thus, the rule could read as follows: 'If the parties negotiate about the claim, or about circumstances from which a claim might arise, prescription does not occur before one year has passed after one of the parties has refused to continue negotiations.' Such a minimum period would probably also have to be available if negotiations were regarded as a ground for suspension, in cases where they start only shortly before completion of

In addition, it may appear expedient to introduce a form requirement: suspension begins if one of the parties requests negotiations in writing, and it ends if one of them refuses, in writing, to continue to negotiate.[144] The German Reform Commission, however, has argued against such an approach: it is contrary to general usage and would, moreover, place the party that is less skilful and less experienced at a disadvantage.[145] Also, it is probably too restrictive and would thus, once again, leave too much scope for general good faith considerations.

IX FRAUS OMNIA CORRUMPIT?

In a number of countries we find a general rule in terms of which prescription is suspended if the debtor fraudulently (or deliberately) conceals the existence of the claim.[146] Such

prescription; see § 216 I 2 BGB-KE ('Pending negotiations about the claim, or about circumstances from which a claim might arise, prescription is suspended until one of the parties refuses to continue negotiations. However, prescription does not occur before two months have passed after the end of the suspension').

[144] This is the proposal by Peters and Zimmermann (n. 12) 320f.

[145] *Abschlußbericht* (n. 9) 94.

[146] Art. 2941 (8) *codice civile*. For similar rules, see Art. 255, 2 *Astikos Kodikas* (debtor 'fraudulently dissuading' his creditor from pursuing his claim); Art. 3:321 (1) (f) BW ('between the creditor and a debtor who deliberately hides the existence of the debt or its exigibility'); s. 32 (1) (b) Limitation Act 1980 (postponement where 'any fact relevant to the claimant's right of action has been deliberately concealed from him by the defendant'); s. 6 (4) (a) (i) Prescription and Limitation (Scotland) Act (suspension for any period 'during which by reason of fraud on the part of the debtor ... the creditor was induced to refrain from making a relevant claim in relation to the obligation'); and see s. 12 (2) (South African) Prescription Act 68 of 1969 ('If the debtor wilfully prevents the creditor from coming to know of the existence of the debt'). Most other codes (e.g., the ones in France, Austria, Germany, Switzerland and Québec) do not contain this kind of rule. The German code, however, exempts the creditor from the short prescription periods (six months, one year, five years) for claims based on defective buildings and defective goods

a rule, however, appears to be unnecessary in view of the fact that prescription is suspended anyway, as long as the creditor does not know about his claim.[147] Of practical relevance is only the question whether fraud (as opposed to mere ignorance) should override the long-stop (i.e., within the present framework, whether there has to be an exception to the maximum period of extension).[148] But even in this respect a special rule would do more harm than good.[149] For whether the debtor, under certain circumstances, may be barred from raising the defence of prescription is a question of a general and complex nature that defies any reduction to a simple and straightforward formula. A legal system that recognizes an overriding duty of good faith will not in principle deny such a possibility.[150] Raising a defence of prescription is a legal act which is, like any other legal act, subject to the requirements of good faith. Of course, it must be taken into account that prescription rules are geared, specifically, towards bringing about a state of legal certainty (even at the expense of individual justice) and therefore must not be interfered with lightly. Moreover, even here the lapse of time cannot be considered entirely irrelevant since it becomes increasingly odious and difficult to argue about whether there has been fraudulent concealment or not. Still, however, the good faith issue can arise. But if it does, it does not do so only

---

sold in cases of fraud: §§ 477 I, 638 I BGB. For comparative observations, see also Spiro (n. 5) 82.

[147] See also the comment in the *Law Commission Consultation Paper* (n. 3) 304: 'Indeed it is a further advantage of the general discoverability test that it largely obviates the need for "exceptions" in the case of mistake, fraud and deliberate concealment.'

[148] See the discussion in *Law Commission Consultation Paper* (n. 3) 304ff.

[149] This is also the conclusion by Claeys, (1998–9) *Rechtskundig Weekblad* 397ff., who discusses the question extensively from the point of view of Belgian law.

[150] See pp. 155f.

in a clearly definable category of cases *sub voce* fraudulent concealment of the claim. Force and fear can be equally relevant.[151] And even in cases where there has been neither fraud, nor force, nor fear, a debtor may in certain situations be barred from invoking prescription: particularly where he has promised not to do so.[152] Thus, it is preferable to leave the matter to the application of the general provision in Art. 1:201 PECL.

X SOME DETAILS CONCERNING EXTENSION AND COMMENCEMENT

1 *Range of application of maximum period for suspension*

A number of details concerning extension and commencement of prescription remain to be considered very briefly. We have a general period of prescription of three years which can be extended by means of suspension, or delay of completion. But we also have a long-stop period of fifteen years which, at any rate, applies to suspension in case of ignorance.[153] If we keep in mind the special need for legal certainty in this field of law,[154] the long-stop should apply as broadly as possible. Only reasons inherent in the nature of things should override this final date. Such reasons are apparent in only two situations. The most obvious of them is suspension in case of legal proceedings.[155] One cannot expect more of the creditor than to attempt to establish his claim by judicial proceedings. How long the legal proceedings take

---

[151] See the discussion in Spiro (n. 5) § 82.
[152] See case studies 20 and 21 in Zimmermann and Whittaker (n. 135) 493ff., 508ff.
[153] See pp. 99ff., 106ff.   [154] See pp. 65, 85.   [155] See pp. 117ff.

is very largely a matter he cannot control. Everything is now under way to remove the existing uncertainty and it would clearly be inequitable if the creditor were trapped by prescription in this situation. The other situation is delay of completion of prescription between a person subject to an incapacity and his representative;[156] after all, the claim may arise when the minor is only one or two years old; yet, before he attains the age of majority, more than fifteen years will have passed. Of course, even outside this narrow group of situations there may be exceptional circumstances which may prompt a judge to reject the defence of prescription as being against good faith. But these rare cases defy general definition.

2 *What must the debtor's ignorance relate to?*

Practically the most important ground for extending the period of prescription is lack of knowledge on the part of the creditor.[157] What, precisely, must his (lack of) knowledge relate to? It seems to be widely agreed that the facts giving rise to his claim and the identity of his debtor are the two key issues.[158] In addition, a significance test is sometimes laid down or recommended. Thus, in England, the rules on personal injury provide that the three-year period will not start to run until the claimant knows that

---

[156] See pp. 135ff.   [157] See pp. 106ff.

[158] See s. 12(3) (South African) Prescription Act 68 of 1969; § 199 BGB-PZ (in addition, knowledge about the legal basis of the claim is required; for the reasons see Peters and Zimmermann (n. 12) 247f.); *Law Commission Consultation Paper* (n. 3) 261f. In a number of legal systems the knowledge requirement relates only to specific types of claims, most often delictual ones. Here the codes tend to require knowledge of the damage and the identity of the debtor: see, e.g., § 852 I BGB; Art. 60 OR; Art. 3:310 BW; §§ 199, 201 BGB-KE; and see Spiro (n. 5) § 85.

his injury is significant.[159] The Law Commission recommends that discoverability should focus on the three elements: (a) that the claimant has a cause of action (b) against the defendant which is (c) significant.[160] What this test wants to prevent is that an apparently trivial injury should trigger the prescription period for unexpected, serious consequences arising from the injury at a later stage. Even though this test does not appear in statutory form in any of the civil law jurisdictions, the underlying concern has been accommodated, at least in Germany, by the way in which the courts have interpreted the knowledge requirement concerning claims for damages.[161] Of course, the significance test introduces an element of uncertainty, but the German experience seems to suggest that this is unavoidable.

3 Suspension of prescription 'on legal grounds'?

Obviously, the parties are free to determine at what time the debtor has to render performance. If they agree, when they conclude their contract, that the debtor may perform at a later date than he would normally have to (see Art. 7:102 (1) PECL) they effectively postpone the due date.[162] Prescription, according to the general principle stated above,[163] begins to run only at that later date. If the parties subsequently,

---

[159] Limitation Act 1980, s. 14 (1); similarly for latent damage: Limitation Act 1980, s. 14 A (7).

[160] *Law Commission Consultation Paper* (n. 3) 262ff. (with an overview of similar recommendations of other law reform bodies in the common law world).

[161] See, e.g., the discussion and references in *Münchener Kommentar*/Stein (n. 132) § 852, n. 22.

[162] For subtle doctrinal distinctions, in this respect, see *Münchener Kommentar*/von Feldmann (n. 13) § 202, n. 4.

[163] See pp. 105f.

i.e., after prescription has already stated to run, agree on a postponement of the time when the debtor has to effect performance, such an agreement usually entails an acknowledgement of the claim on the part of the debtor.[164] The consequence is a renewal of prescription.[165] Where the parties merely agree that the creditor may bring his action at a later date (*pactum de non petendo*)[166] and where the debtor cannot, therefore, normally be taken to acknowledge the claim, we have an agreement suspending prescription which is effective according to what will be said below.[167] As a result, a rule along the lines of § 202 BGB[168] appears to be unnecessary.[169]

4 *Duties to refrain from doing something*

Prescription relates to rights to demand payment or any other performance. This also covers cases where the debtor is under a duty to refrain from doing something. When does prescription begin to run in these cases? The due date cannot be the appropriate moment since the creditor's claim is due

---

[164] Peters and Zimmermann (n. 12) 253.   [165] See pp. 126ff.

[166] For details, see *Staudinger*/Peters (n. 15) § 202, nn. 14ff.

[167] See pp. 162ff.

[168] 'Prescription is suspended for as long as the performance is deferred or the debtor is temporarily entitled on any other ground to refuse to make performance.' The second subsection provides for a number of very important exceptions to this rule in practice.

[169] Peters and Zimmermann (n. 12) 253f. (who point out that the complex regulation contained in § 202 BGB is not only unnecessary but has also given rise to problems). The details were much disputed at the time when the rule was drafted (see Peters and Zimmermann (n. 12) 125f.). Other codifications do not usually regulate the problem. The German Commission recommends a rule suspending prescription as long as the debtor, on account of an agreement with the creditor, is temporarily entitled to refuse performance: § 211 BGB-KE and *Abschlußbericht* (n. 9) 88. For comparative discussion, see Spiro (n. 5) § 30.

even before the debtor has infringed his duty.[170] Yet, before such an infringement has occurred, the creditor does not normally have any reason to sue his debtor so as to stop prescription from running. Hence the need for a special rule focusing on contravention.[171] However, two different situations have to be distinguished. Where a debtor is under a duty to refrain from acting in a particular way at a particular moment, no prescription problems can arise: until the debtor infringes that duty, prescription cannot start; if he has infringed it, compliance has become impossible and the creditor can claim only damages. Thus, the only situation that has to be taken care of is the one where the debtor's duty extends over some period of time, i.e., the situation of a continuing duty to refrain from doing something. Here it appears to be appropriate not to let prescription commence, once and for all, with the first act of contravention but with each new act of contravention.[172]

---

[170] See, e.g., *Abschlußbericht* (n. 9) 57f.

[171] See § 198, 2 BGB and the discussion by Peters and Zimmermann (n. 12) 303f.; *Staudinger*/Peters (n. 15) § 198, nn. 33ff. Other codifications do not usually have a specific rule but argue from general principles; see, e.g., Spiro (n. 5) §§ 48f.; Asser/Hartkamp (n. 62) n. 664.

[172] See, for details, Peters and Zimmermann (n. 12) 304; *Abschlußbericht* (n. 9) 58; *Staudinger*/Peters (n. 15) § 198, nn. 33ff. The following example may illustrate the point. A is a former employee of B, an insurance company in Hamburg. He is under a duty not to sell any insurance policies on his own account for the next three years in Hamburg. On 10 March, he sells some policies in a small suburb still belonging to the state of Hamburg. On 10 October, however, he sets up his own insurance agency right in the centre of Hamburg. Concerning the infringement on 10 March, prescription begins to run on that day; concerning the one on 10 October, a new period begins to run on 10 October. This is justified in view of the fact that B may have refrained from taking steps which would have had the effect of extending or even renewing prescription, not because he wanted to condone any infringement of A's duty, but merely because the first infringement was not sufficiently serious to warrant the cost and trouble of taking such steps.

5 *Claims concerning payments for services rendered and goods delivered*

According to § 201 BGB, the prescription period for a whole range of claims concerning payment for services rendered and goods delivered[173] begins to run only from the end of the year in which they have become enforceable. This is a peculiarity of German law that does not appear to have found much favour in other jurisdictions.[174] The draftsmen of this provision wanted to spare the merchants and manufacturers covered by it the inconvenience of having to bear in mind as many different prescription periods running against their claims for payment as they had delivered goods or performed services within any one year.[175] The provision would enable them to check their files only once a year for items still to be collected. These advantages, however, are outweighed by the disadvantages associated with any differentiation in prescription matters.[176] The rule of § 201 BGB is unsatisfactory in a number of respects[177] and any attempt to isolate the

---

[173] They are clumsily enumerated in §§ 196f. BGB; for an overview in English, see Reinhard Zimmermann, 'Extinctive Prescription in German Law', in Erik Jayme (ed.), *German National Reports in Civil Law Matters for the XIVth Congress of Comparative Law in Athens 1994* (1994), pp. 159ff. The draftsmen of the BGB referred to 'Geschäfte des täglichen Verkehrs' (transactions of daily life).

[174] But see Art. 253 *Astikos Kodikas*.

[175] 'Motive' (n. 6) 522f. But this rationale becomes somewhat questionable if one takes account of the many 'irregular' claims falling under §§ 196f. BGB (see Zimmermann (n. 173) 159ff.).

[176] See pp. 79ff.

[177] Thus, it has the consequence that the prescription period for claims of the same kind may differ for up to one year. For criticism, see Peters and Zimmermann (n. 12) 247; Spiro (n. 5) § 125. The rule, however, is defended by the German Reform Commission (n. 9) 58f. One of the principal arguments of the commission for retaining it is that small and medium-sized enterprises in Germany have become accustomed to it. This argument, of course, does not apply on a European level.

relevant claims in a different way would run the danger either of leading to equally inconvenient problems of delimitation or of including a large number of claims to which the rationale underlying the provision would not apply.[178]

6 *Presentation of an invoice*

The German Reform Commission proposes to regulate the situation where the debtor has to effect performance only after the presentation of an invoice: prescription begins to run when creditor can present the invoice.[179] This proposal is based on the desire to preempt disputes about whether the debtor *has to effect performance* only after presentation of the invoice;[180] and on the fear that, if presentation of the invoice does indeed affect the due date, the creditor may be tempted to manipulate prescription in his favour.[181] There is, however, no comparative evidence supporting the desirability of, or perhaps even the need for, a reform along these lines. It will have to be determined by the general rules of interpretation whether the due date is postponed until presentation of the invoice; occasionally, this is provided by statute.

7 *Notice of termination*

In some countries we find a rule dealing with the situation where a person may not demand performance until

---

[178] The latter objection may be raised against the generalized proposal submitted by the German Reform Commission: § 196 II 1 BGB-KE (all contractual remuneration claims; the rule proposed by the commission would, therefore, also cover all occasional sales by private persons).

[179] § 196 II 2 BGB-KE.

[180] For discussion, see *Staudinger*/Peters (n. 15) § 198, nn. 7ff.

[181] *Abschlußbericht* (n. 9) 59f.

he has given notice of termination to the other party:[182] prescription begins to run from the moment when notice can first be given.[183] It is based on a similar fear that the commencement of prescription might otherwise be manipulated in these cases. This fear, however, hardly appears to be justified, for creditors do not normally make their business decisions dependent on how to obtain the benefit of a long prescription period.[184] Moreover, it is difficult to see why comparable cases are not treated alike;[185] indeed, the very fact that they are not, and apparently without any adverse consequences, confirms the view that a regulation is dispensable.

XI EFFECTS OF PRESCRIPTION

1 *Introduction*

The most important effect of prescription has already been discussed: after expiry of the period of prescription the debtor is entitled to refuse performance.[186] He has a defence which he has to invoke if prescription of the claim is to be taken into consideration. The claim as such is not extinguished. Consequently, whatever has been performed in

---

[182] A common example would be a loan repayable upon notice given by the creditor (see § 609 BGB).

[183] See § 199 BGB; Art. 130 II OR; Art. 252 *Astikos Kodikas*. For comparative discussion, see Spiro (n. 5) § 35; Loubser (n. 5) 54ff.

[184] For criticism, see Peters and Zimmermann (n. 12) 245f.; *Abschlußbericht* (n. 9) 65; *Staudinger*/Peters (n. 15) § 199, n. 1. The rule is defended by Spiro (n. 5) § 33 (who, however, also refers to prominent critics like Savigny, Dernburg, Unger and Vangerow).

[185] § 200 BGB deals with the situation where a claim comes into existence only once the creditor has availed himself of a right of rescission. But it does not, for example, cover the case where the creditor has to exercise a right of withdrawal from the contract.

[186] See pp. 72ff.

order to discharge that claim may not be reclaimed merely because the period of prescription had expired.[187] In civilian terminology, performance has not been made 'without legal ground' in this situation. This applies, as some codifications specifically clarify, whether the debtor knew that he could have raised the defence of prescription or not.[188] Five further matters deserve attention.

2 Waiver

As has been pointed out already, raising the defence of prescription can, under certain circumstances, be inadmissible because it constitutes an infringement of the precepts of good faith.[189] This is the case, for instance, where the debtor has prevented the creditor from pursuing his claim in good time, particularly where he has waived his right to raise the defence of prescription. The question is of considerable practical relevance for those legal systems which prohibit agreements rendering prescription more difficult: since they consequently also usually regard a unilateral waiver as invalid, they can help the creditor only by taking recourse to the general good faith provision.[190] In view of the more

---

[187] It may be reclaimed for other reasons, for example, if the debtor has performed under the reservation that the claim had not prescribed or if the creditor had fraudulently induced him to believe that the claim had not prescribed.

[188] § 222 II BGB; § 221 II BGB-KE; Art. 26 Unidroit Convention; and see Spiro (n. 5) § 233. See also p. 73.

[189] See pp. 146f.

[190] For the effect of good faith on the application of the prescription regime and, particularly, on the way in which a waiver is taken into consideration which the debtor has declared before prescription has run out, see Spiro (n. 5) § 343; *Staudinger*/Peters (n. 15) § 222, nn. 17ff., 20ff.; and the country reports for Germany, Greece, Austria, France, Belgium, Spain, Italy, the Netherlands, England, Ireland, Scotland, Denmark, Sweden and Finland to case study 21 (Prescription I) in Zimmermann and Whittaker (n. 135) 508ff. Cf. also Matthias E. Storme, 'Belgium', in Hondius (n. 64) 44, at 70f.

liberal regime advocated here[191] the problem is largely obviated: a waiver is no longer objectionable merely on account of the fact that the parties would not have been allowed to render prescription more difficult. Moreover, it is reasonable to assume that there will usually have been a tacit agreement. Nevertheless, the problem can still arise, particularly in cases where the debtor waives his right to invoke prescription shortly before the end of the maximum periods of fifteen or thirty years envisaged in chapter 2, sub IX.2 and the present chapter, sub XII.2. Here the debtor will be barred from invoking the defence of prescription for the period that he has delayed enforcement of the claim (Art. 1:201 PECL).

After prescription has occurred, the debtor is entitled to waive his right of invoking the defence of prescription, either by way of agreement with his creditor or unilaterally:[192] after all, the claim still exists and the waiver merely has the effect of removing the possibility of preventing it from being enforced.

3 'Verwirkung'

The principles of good faith and fair dealing may not only prevent the debtor from invoking the defence of prescription; they may also prevent the creditor from bringing a claim even before the period of prescription has run out. This may be the case if he has engendered reasonable reliance on the part of the debtor that he would no longer pursue his claim.[193]

---

[191] See pp. 162ff.

[192] See Art. 2220 *code civil*; Art. 276 *Astikos Kodikas*; Art. 2937 *codice civile*; *Staudinger*/Peters (n. 15) § 222, nn. 28ff.; Art. 322 (2) BW; *Asser*/Hartkamp (n. 62) nn. 659ff.; Koopmann (n. 112) 95ff.; Spiro (n. 5) § 343; Loubser (n. 5) 150ff.

[193] All legal systems possess mechanisms for the protection of the reasonable reliance of a debtor in situations where the creditor has failed to bring a claim

However, under a prescription regime with a short regular prescription period (like the one proposed here), this situation will be practically much less relevant than it is in legal systems with a very long period.

4 Ancillary claims

Prescription occurs 'ut sit finis litium'. The law wants to prevent litigation about stale claims, both in the public interest and in order to protect the debtor.[194] This policy would be undermined if the creditor could still sue his debtor for interest that may have become due on a claim for which the period of prescription has run out; for the debtor, in order to defend himself, might then be forced to go into the merits of the principal claim itself. The same considerations apply to other claims of an ancillary nature, such as those for emoluments and costs.[195] Hence the need for a rule that such claims prescribe with the principal claim,

for some time. At the same time, however, it is generally agreed that sitting on one's right as such, i.e., mere inactivity on the part of the creditor, does not lead to a loss of right. In German law, the doctrine of 'Verwirkung' has been developed to deal with this situation; it is a specific emanation of the principle of good faith. See, e.g., Max Vollkommer, in Jauernig, *Bürgerliches Gesetzbuch* (8th edn, 1997), § 242, nn. 53ff.; Gerhard Kegel, 'Verwirkung, Vertrag und Vertrauen', in *Festschrift für Klemens Pleyer* (1986), pp. 513ff.; Filippo Ranieri, 'Bonne foi et exercice du droit dans la tradition du civil law', (1998) *Revue internationale de droit comparé* 1066ff. The notion of 'Verwirkung' has been received in a number of countries; for Spain, see Antoni Vaquer Aloy, 'Importing Foreign Doctrines: Yet Another Approach to the Unification of European Private Law? Incorporation of the Verwirkung Doctrine into Spanish Case Law', (2000) 8 *Zeitschrift für Europäisches Privatrecht* 301ff. For a comparative analysis, see case study 22 in Zimmermann and Whittaker (n. 135) 515ff. (with country reports for Germany, Greece, Austria, France, Belgium, Spain, Italy, the Netherlands, England, Ireland, Scotland, Denmark, Norway, Sweden and Finland).

[194] See pp. 63f.
[195] For details, see *Staudinger*/Peters (n. 15) § 224, nn. 5ff.

even if the prescription period applicable to them has not yet expired.[196]

5 *Real securities*

Somewhat different considerations apply when it comes to determining the effect of prescription on real security[197] provided by the debtor or a third party. Here, too, the policy of the prescription rules is arguably compromised if the creditor may sell what has been given to him by way of pledge[198] even though the claim which the pledge was intended to secure has prescribed. For where the pledge was given by the debtor himself, he will now have to raise the question whether that claim was, or still is, well-founded; and, where a third party has given the pledge, the debtor will now have to fear the third party's right of recourse.[199] On the other hand, however, it may also be argued that this risk was inherent in the transaction from the beginning and could be taken into consideration by the debtor.[200] Moreover, legal certainty would also be adversely affected if the creditor were not allowed to retain what he had received by way of security: 'quieta non movere' not only requires that the debtor may not reclaim

---

[196] § 224 BGB; Art. 133 OR; Art. 274 *Astikos Kodikas*; Johnston (n. 5) 4.101 (3); s. 10 (2) (South African) Prescription Act 68 of 1969; § 211 BGB-PZ; § 224 BGB-KE; Art. 27 Uncitral Convention (confined to interest); cf. also Art. 3:312 BW; Spiro (n. 5) §§ 59, 236 (who asserts that this is 'generally recognized today'). For the *ius commune*, see Peters and Zimmermann (n. 12) 140.

[197] The effect of prescription of the main claim on the claim against a surety is traditionally a matter of suretyship law: see § 768 BGB; Art. 502 OR; Art. 7:852 BW.

[198] The following discussion focuses on security rights in movables; the conclusions reached, however, apply with even greater force to security rights over immovables.

[199] See Peters and Zimmermann (n. 12) 264f. See also *Asser*/Hartkamp (n. 62) n. 658 ('aangezien de schuldenaar anders aan de verjaring weinig zou hebben').

[200] *Abschlußbericht* (n. 9) 106.

what he has given in order to discharge a claim that has prescribed, but also that he may not reclaim an object given as
security at a time when the claim had not prescribed. The
creditor obtains possession of the object for the purpose, as
the draftsmen of the BGB saw it, 'to obtain satisfaction from
that object in all circumstances up to the value of the object
pledged'.[201] These considerations have prompted the draftsmen of the Dutch code to differentiate between possessory
and non-possessory securities.[202] However, discrimination of
the non-possessory security, under the auspices of the law of
prescription, appears to be problematic in view both of its
overwhelming practical importance, and of the considerable
differences in legal regulations existing in Europe today.[203]
Some countries have effective mechanisms substituting for
the transfer of possession;[204] and these non-possessory
security rights clearly have to be treated, as far as the prescription rule under consideration is concerned, like the traditional pledge. Both in Switzerland[205] and in Germany[206]
it has been found desirable, or necessary, to subject even
the transfer of ownership by way of security to the same
regime.[207] Thus, if a distinction is to be drawn it should be,

[201] See the reference in Peters and Zimmermann (n. 12) 137.

[202] Art. 323 (1) and (2) BW; Koopmann (n. 112) 14. See also *Asser*/Hartkamp
(n. 62) n. 658 arguing that possession of the pledge on the part of the creditor
creates a presumption that the debt has not been discharged.

[203] See Ulrich Drobnig, 'Security Rights in Movables', in Arthur Hartkamp,
Martijn Hesselink et al. (eds.), *Towards a European Civil Code* (2nd edn,
1998), pp. 511ff.

[204] See Drobnig (n. 203) 517.

[205] Spiro (n. 5) 223 (on the basis of Art. 140 OR which was originally intended
to cover the pledge with possession).

[206] § 223 II BGB. For England, see Preston and Newsom (n. 140) 12 ('A security
may be enforceable even if given for a statute-barred debt and if the creditor
has any lien or charge for his debt he can enforce the lien or charge after the
debt is barred').

[207] This regime has not given rise to problems; see *Abschlußbericht* (n. 9) 105.

rather, between accessory and non-accessory securities.[208] On the other hand, however, it may be premature to attempt to deal with the matter before a set of European principles on security rights has been drafted.

6 Set-off

A claim that has prescribed can no longer be enforced. But it may still provide a valid basis for a right of set-off. A number of codifications contain rules to the effect that the right of set-off is not excluded by the prescription of the cross-claim, provided it could have been set off against the principal claim at a time when it had not prescribed.[209] The policy of these rules is to preserve a right of set-off that has once accrued, even though set-off has not been declared at that stage.[210] It does not, however, fit in well with the policy considerations underlying the law of prescription.[211] The 'obfuscating power of time'[212] affects the creditor's claim in the same way, no matter whether it is pursued by way of action or used in

[208] This is the proposal submitted by Peters and Zimmermann (n. 12) 310. For a discussion of the principle of accessoriness, in the context of the development of European private law, see Mathias Habersack, 'Die Akzessorietät: Strukturprinzip der europäischen Zivilrechte und eines künftigen europäischen Grundpfandrechts', (1997) *Juristenzeitung* 857ff. (862ff.).

[209] See § 390, 2 BGB; Art. 443 *Astikos Kodikas*; Art. 120 III OR and Spiro (n. 5) § 216; Art. 131 (1) BW; Koziol and Welser (n. 1) 281; Johnston (n. 5) 4.101; Art. 25 (2) Uncitral Convention.

[210] The rule tries to take account of the retroactive effect of the declaration of set-off; see pp. 36ff. Obviously, it is unnecessary in a legal system (like the French one) where set-off operates *ipso iure*. But cf. for Italy Art. 1242 *codice civile* which specifically spells out that set-off is excluded only if prescription was completed on the date on which the debts began to coexist.

[211] See Peters and Zimmermann (n. 12) 266; Peter Bydlinski, 'Die Aufrechnung mit verjährten Forderungen: Wirklich kein Änderungsbedarf?', (1996) *Archiv für die Civilistische Praxis* 293ff.

[212] See p. 64, n. 9.

order to give notice of set-off. In both cases the debtor needs protection; in both cases, too, it would run counter to the public interest if a stale claim could become the object of litigation. Set-off, according to what has been set out above,[213] should no longer have *ex tunc* effect. This simplifies matters, for we merely have to look at the moment when set-off is declared. Obviously, considering the policy of the law of prescription, it cannot be declared where the debtor (of the cross-claim) has previously invoked prescription. But since he has no reason to invoke prescription unless the creditor asserts a claim against him (whether by way of bringing an action or by declaring set-off), he will have to be granted a reasonable period, after he has received notice of set-off, to raise the defence of prescription. If he fails to do so, the set-off is effective: after all, the claim continues to exist in spite of the prescription period having run out.

7 *Defences*

Prescription of defences raises difficult problems doctrinally. Under the *ius commune*, defences were widely regarded as not being subject to prescription: 'quae ad agendum sunt temporalia, ad excipiendum sunt perpetua'. This principle is still accepted in a number of jurisdictions.[214] Most legal systems, however, do not have a general rule. But a number of them have specific provisions in terms of which defences may, under certain circumstances, survive prescription of the claim on which they are based. Whether these provisions are

---

[213] See pp. 39ff.
[214] See, for France, Ferid and Sonnenberger (n. 93) 1 C 249; for Belgium, Storme (n. 190); for Greece, Art. 273 *Astikos Kodikas*; for South Africa Loubser (n. 5) 7f. The position is essentially the same in English law as a result of the fact that only the remedy and not the right is barred.

expressions of, or exceptions to, a general rule is disputed.[215] The matter appears to be relevant in practice only as far as rights to withhold performance (like the one provided in Art. 9:201 PECL) are concerned.[216] According to the prevailing opinion in Germany, such rights can still be used as a shield, even if the claim on which they are based can no longer be used as a sword.[217] This appears to be right since a regime under which one party to a contract would still be able to enforce performance whereas the other would effectively have lost its claim would be unacceptably hard for the latter.[218]

XII AGREEMENTS CONCERNING PRESCRIPTION

1 *Agreements rendering prescription more difficult*

There is a considerable divergence of views as to whether it is possible for parties to contract out of the prescription

---

[215] See Spiro (n. 5) § 215; Peters and Zimmermann (n. 12) 266. Sometimes a distinction is drawn between 'independent' defences and defences based upon a claim; 'independent' defences are not subject to prescription, others are: see *Münchener Kommentar*/von Feldmann (n. 13) § 194, n. 23. The distinction goes back to pandectist scholarship (see Windscheid and Kipp (n. 5) § 112), but it has always been regarded as problematic (see Windscheid and Kipp (n. 5) § 112, n. 8).

[216] See Peters and Zimmermann (n. 12) 266.

[217] See *Staudinger*/Peters (n. 15) § 222, n. 37; Art. 6:56 BW. Cf. also § 212 BGB-PZ and § 222 BGB-KE and, generally on prescription defences (and the effect of prescription of claims on defences), Spiro (n. 5) §§ 215f., 540.

[218] A has sold a car to B. The car has to be delivered on 10 October 1996, the purchase price has to be paid on 10 December of the same year. The prescription period for both claims is three years. After three years B has still not received the car. If he sues A for the car after 10 October, A can raise the defence of prescription. If A, in turn, sues B for the purchase price on 10 November, B may exercise his right to withhold performance in terms of Art. 9:201 PECL; it remains unaffected by the prescription of his own claim against A. After 10 December, B can raise the defence of prescription against A's claim.

regime by lengthening or shortening the prescription period, by providing for different starting dates, by introducing additional, or opting out of existing, grounds for suspension, etc. Swiss, Greek and Italian law are particularly strict in this regard: they prohibit agreements either way.[219] The Uncitral Convention, too, regards its prescription regime as mandatory.[220] A number of legal systems allow the parties to facilitate prescription, especially by providing for a period that is shorter than the statutory one, while they refuse to recognize agreements rendering prescription more difficult, especially by extending the statutory period.[221] In these countries, the prescription regime is thus of a unilaterally mandatory character. Finally, the German Reform Commission and the English Law Commission recommend recognition, in principle, of agreements both ways.[222] This seems to tie in with the legal position prevailing in England today.[223]

The prohibition of agreements rendering prescription more difficult is often justified with reference to the public

---

[219] Art. 129 OR; Art. 275 *Astikos Kodikas*; Art. 2936 *codice civile* ('È nullo ogni patto diretto a modificare la disciplina legal della prescrizione'). Cf. also, most recently, Art. 2884 *code civil du Québec* (on which, see Deslauriers (n. 64) 314).

[220] Art. 22 ('The limitation period cannot be modified or affected by any declaration or agreement between the parties.' There are two exceptions, the one permitting the debtor at any time during the running of the period to extend it by a declaration in writing to the creditor; the other sanctioning, under certain circumstances, a clause in the contract of sale, in terms of which arbitral proceedings are to be commenced within a shorter period of limitation than that prescribed by the Convention).

[221] § 1502 ABGB and Koziol and Welser (n. 1) 189; § 225 BGB; for the Netherlands, see *Asser*/Hartkamp (n. 62) n. 678; for France, see Ferid and Sonnenberger (n. 93) 1 C 254ff.

[222] § 220 BGB-KE (and see *Abschlußbericht* (n. 9) 97ff.); *Law Commission Consultation Paper* (n. 3) 389ff. For criticism, see Andrews, (1998) 57 *Cambridge Law Journal* 602f., 610.

[223] See *Law Commission Consultation Paper* (n. 3) 389; Gerhard Dannemann, Fotios Karatzenis and Geoffrey V. Thomas, 'Reform des Verjährungsrechts aus rechtsvergleichender Sicht', (1991) 55 *RabelsZ* 705.

interest which the prescription of claims is intended to serve.[224] It must, however, be remembered that the prescription of claims predominantly serves to protect the debtor;[225] and that, where he renounces such protection, the exercise of his private autonomy may well be seen to prevail over the public interest. Also, the general prescription periods applying in countries objecting to agreements rendering prescription more difficult are comparatively long (ten, twenty or thirty years) so that a further lengthening may indeed be problematic – much more problematic, at any rate, than where we have a short general prescription period. Widely, therefore, agreements lengthening the period are specifically admitted, where the period is, exceptionally, a short one.[226] Contractual warranties concerning latent defects in buildings or goods are thus permitted even if they have, as they often do, the effect of lengthening the period of prescription.[227] Equally, it tends to be accepted that the prohibition does not affect agreements which indirectly render prescription more difficult, such as agreements postponing the due date of a claim, or *pacta de non petendo*.[228] However, it is not easy to see why the parties should not be able to postpone the commencement of prescription as such if they *can* postpone the due date for the claim. Moreover, these subtle distinctions provide ample opportunity for effectively circumventing the

---

[224] See, e.g., *Münchener Kommentar*/von Feldmann (n. 13) § 225, n. 1; and see the references in Peters and Zimmermann (n. 12) 141. But cf. also Spiro (n. 5) § 343 read with § 15; *Staudinger*/Peters (n. 15) § 225, n. 3.

[225] See pp. 63f.

[226] For Germany, see §§ 477 (1) 2, 480 (1) 2, 490 (1) 2, 638 (2) BGB, §§ 414 (1) 2, 423, 439 HGB; for Switzerland, see Spiro (n. 5) § 345.

[227] See, e.g., Harm Peter Westermann, in *Münchener Kommentar zum Bürgerlichen Gesetzbuch*, vol. III (3rd edn, 1995), § 477, nn. 21ff.; Spiro (n. 5) § 346.

[228] For details, see *Staudinger*/Peters (n. 15) § 225, nn. 7ff.; Spiro (n. 5) § 344.

prohibition.[229] These problems would be obviated by abandoning the prohibition.

This appears all the more desirable under a system such as the one proposed in this and the previous chapter. Party autonomy provides the necessary counterbalance to (i) the short general prescription period of three years and (ii) the uniformity of the regime in general.[230] Neither the three-year period nor a number of the other rules fit all types of claims and all imaginable situations equally well. The parties must be free to devise a more appropriate regime, as long as they observe the general limitations placed on freedom of contract. Thus, for instance, the draftsmen of the Uncitral Convention obviously regard four years as the most appropriate period for claims arising from an international sale of goods[231] and there is no reason why the parties to a contract of sale should not be allowed to adopt this period for their contract. The Dutch code specifies a period of five years for claims for damages.[232] Again, it can hardly be regarded as objectionable if two parties want their damages claims to be subject to a five- rather than a three-year period. And more generally it must be kept in mind that the system proposed in this essay rests on a delicate act of balancing of interests,[233] and that a reasonable balance can conceivably be achieved in quite a different way.[234] The parties to a contract may quite reasonably regard suspension of prescription in case of ignorance as a source of uncertainty and they may wish to counterbalance the exclusion of this rule by providing for a longer period.

[229] *Staudinger*/Peters (n. 15) § 225, n. 2, pointedly maintains that the parties do not meet insurmountable obstacles if they wish to extend the period of prescription.

[230] See pp. 79ff., 89ff.   [231] Art. 8 Uncitral Convention.

[232] Art. 3:310 BW.   [233] See pp. 87, 93.

[234] As is demonstrated, for example, by Andrews, (1998) 57 *Cambridge Law Journal* 593ff.

2 *Restrictions*

Two provisos have to be made, however. (i) Standard contract terms interfering with the prescription regime must be scrutinized particularly carefully.[235] The Unfair Contract Terms Directive provides the necessary tool.[236] (ii) Public interest does not require a prescription regime to be mandatory: party autonomy may, to a large extent, prevail. The public interest is not adversely affected if a claim prescribes in seven rather than three years – not sufficiently adversely affected, at any rate, to override the decision of a debtor to waive his protection by agreement with his creditor. The debtor should not, however, be able to agree upon a period of, say, fifty years since that would effectively exclude the claims against him from prescription. This is why the German Commission proposes a limit of thirty years (calculated from the statutory date of commencement of prescription).[237] The Law Commission's *Consultation Paper* suggests that the long-stop period as well as the date triggering it might become mandatory.[238] If it is taken into account that a thirty-year period, at present, is still applicable for a variety of claims in some of the member states of the EU, the borderline for party autonomy should certainly not be fixed below this level.

3 *Agreements facilitating prescription*

What has been said above applies with even greater force to agreements facilitating prescription, especially by shortening the period. They are much more widely recognized

---

[235] For the reasons, see *Staudinger*/Peters (n. 15) § 225, n. 21.
[236] See *Abschlußbericht* (n. 9) 100. Cf. also Art. 4:110 PECL.
[237] § 220, 3 BGB-KE.
[238] *Law Commission Consultation Paper* (n. 3) 390.

even today;[239] moreover, they do not conflict with the public interest-based policy underlying the law of prescription.[240]

XIII SUMMARY

In summary, a set of European principles governing liberative prescription could look as follows. (i) The right to demand payment or any other performance ('claim') is subject to prescription. (ii) The general period of prescription is three years. (iii) The period of prescription for a claim established by judgment is ten years. The same applies to a claim established by an arbitral award or other instrument which is enforceable as if it were a judgment. (iv) Prescription begins to run from the time when the debtor has to effect performance or, in the case of a claim for damages, from the date of the act which gives rise to the claim. The period of prescription for a claim established by legal proceedings begins to run from the moment when the judgment becomes final, though not before the debtor has to effect performance. Where the debtor is under a continuing duty to refrain from doing something, prescription begins to run with each act of non-compliance. (v) If the debtor acknowledges the claim, vis-à-vis the creditor, by part payment, payment of interest, giving of security, or in any other manner, prescription begins to run again.[241] The ten-year period of prescription for a claim established by

---

[239] See p. 163.

[240] They promote these policy considerations even more effectively than the normal regime; see, e.g., Zimmermann (n. 173) 188; *Asser*/Hartkamp (n. 62) n. 678. Even agreements such as these are regarded as undesirable by Spiro (n. 5) §§ 347ff. (who, however, also points out that the parties are free to limit their claims in other ways; considerable problems of delimitation can ensue).

[241] The period of prescription will have to be the general period of prescription; in cases of prescription of a claim established by legal proceedings, this should not, however, operate to the prejudice of the ten-year period.

legal proceedings begins to run again with each reasonable attempt of execution undertaken by, or at the application of, the creditor. (vi) Prescription is suspended as long as the creditor does not know, and cannot reasonably know, of the facts giving rise to his claim, of the identity of his debtor and that his claim is not insignificant. (vii) Prescription is suspended from the moment when judicial proceedings on the claim are begun. Suspension lasts until a decision has been passed which is final, or until the case has been otherwise disposed of. The same applies, *mutatis mutandis*, to arbitration proceedings and to all other proceedings initiated with the aim of obtaining an instrument which is enforceable as if it were a judgment. (viii) Prescription is suspended as long as the creditor is prevented from enforcing his claim by an impediment which is beyond his control and which he could not reasonably have been expected to avoid or overcome. This applies only if the impediment arises, or subsists, within the last six months of the prescription period. (ix) If the parties negotiate about the claim, or about circumstances from which a claim might arise, prescription does not occur before one year has passed since the last communication made in the negotiations. (x) If a person subject to an incapacity is without a representative, prescription for or against him does not occur before one year has passed after either the incapacity or the lack of representation has been removed. Prescription of claims between a person subject to an incapacity and his representative does not occur before one year has passed after the incapacity has been removed. (xi) Where the creditor or debtor has died, prescription of a claim by the creditor's estate or against the debtor's estate does not occur before one year has passed after the claim can be enforced by or against an heir, or by or against a representative of the estate. (xii) Prescription cannot be extended, on account of the grounds of extension previously mentioned, to more than fifteen years. This does not apply to suspension of prescription on account of judicial or other proceedings and to delay of completion in cases of incapacity. (xiii) After expiry of the period of prescription the debtor is entitled to refuse performance. Whatever has been performed in order to discharge a claim may not be reclaimed merely because the period of prescription had expired. (xiv) The period of prescription for claims for interest, and other claims of an ancillary nature, expires not later than the period for the principal claim. (xv) A claim in relation to which the period of prescription has expired may none the less be set off, unless the debtor has invoked prescription previously or does so within two months of receiving notice of set-off. (xvi) Prescription may be facilitated, especially by shortening the period of prescription, by agreement between the parties. The parties may also agree to render prescription more difficult, especially by extending the period of prescription, up to a maximum of thirty years.

INDEX

Index

Index

Index

HOLYROOD
AND
CANONGATE

A Thousand Years of History

E. PATRICIA DENNISON

Birlinn

First published in 2005 by
Birlinn Limited

West Newington House

10 Newington Road

Edinburgh

EH9 1QS

www.birlinn.co.uk

19-Jul-2006

£9.99

ISBN10: 1 84158 404 5

ISBN13: 978 1 84158 404 1

British Library Cataloguing-in-Publication Data
A catalogue record for this book is available
from the British Library

The Publisher acknowledges subsidy from the Russell Trust and
the Scotland Inheritance Trust towards the publication of this volume

Typesetting and prepress origination by Brinnoven, Livingston
Printed and bound by GraphyCems, Spain

CONTENTS

ACKNOWLEDGEMENTS

Firstly, I would like to give my thanks to the many people of Canongate who shared with me their experiences of life in the old burgh. I have been helped with reminiscences, in particular, by Reverend Charlie Robertson, minister of the parish church, Miss Jennifer Calcott, daughter of the governor of Queensberry Hospital, and Mrs Anne Reid, who trained as a social worker in the Canongate area. Mr John Young and Mr Donald Macleod, both brought up as Canongate boys, gave me a great insight into the sometimes harsh, but full life that Canongate offered young people in the first half of the twentieth century. Lt.-Col. Ian Ballantyne, Mr Morris Rourke and residents of Whitefoord House have also kindly given me an understanding of a bygone Canongate and access to their records.

Mr A. Knowles of Scottish and Newcastle Breweries and Mr George Insill have very kindly allowed me an insight into the brewing process. Dr Neil MacGillivray gave me access to his Ph.D. thesis, 'Food, Poverty and Epidemic Disease, Edinburgh: 1840–1850', for which I thank him. I am particularly grateful also to Mrs Annie Lyell, Dr Winifred Coutts and Dr Jill Turnbull for their practical assistance.

I am grateful to the staff at Birlinn for their assistance during the publication process. The staff of National Archives of Scotland; the National Library of Scotland at both George IV Bridge and Causewayside; the Edinburgh Room, Central Library, Edinburgh City Libraries; the University of Edinburgh Library; Huntly House Museum; the People's Story Museum; the Royal Commission on Ancient and Historical Monuments of Scotland; Edinburgh City Archives, the Scottish Life Archive, National Museums of Scotland; and the Archive and Business Record Centre, University of Glasgow, have been generous with their time and eased the research process. I am particularly grateful for the help of Mr Jimmy Hogg at the Central Library, Edinburgh.

Finally, I mostly wish to thank my husband, Michael, for his practical assistance, our exchange of ideas, and for his tolerance of my preoccupation with Holyrood and Canongate.

E. Patricia Dennison
Edinburgh, September 2005

Picture Acknowledgements

Illustrations are reproduced by the kind permission of the following:

The Trustees of the National Library of Scotland, 8, 11, 36, 37, 40, 41, 46, 57, 65, 69, 73, 76, 109, 113, 116, 138, 142; SUAT, 15, 16, 17, 26,; Aberdeen Art Gallery & Museums Collections, 18; Edinburgh City Libraries 24, 42, 139, 140, 166 , 170, 172, 173; Rev. C. Robertson, 38, 43, 83, 88, 101, 111; The National Gallery of Scotland, 48, 98; The National Museum of Scotland, 59, 115, 163; The Royal Commission for Ancient and Historical Monuments, 80, 114, 154, 158,165; Miss J.Calcott, 96, 176; The Cavaye collection of Thomas Begbie prints, City of Edinburgh Museums and Galleries, 124, 146, 148, 151; Scottish Brewery Archive, Glasgow University Archive Services, 132, 133; The Hurd Rolland Partnership, 163, 169; The City of Edinburgh Council, 174; Whitefoord House Veterans Residence, 177; Incorporation of Wrights and Masons in the collection of the Edinburgh Trades Maiden Fund; 48.

Every effort has been made to trace copyright holders and we apologise in advance for any unintentional omissions, which we would be pleased to correct in any subsequent edition of the book.

GLOSSARY

Almshouse	House for support and lodging of the poor; sometimes a hospital.
Aquamanile	Pottery or metal jug, in shape of an animal, used to hold water for washing hands between courses of a meal.
Backlands	Area of a burgage plot (*see* below) behind the frontage sometimes accessed through a close. Originally intended for growing produce and keeping animals; site of wells and midden heaps. Eventually housed working premises of craftsmen and poorer members of burgh society.
Bailies	Burgh office-bearers who performed routine administration.
Baxters	Bakers
Booths	Small open-fronted stalls, sometimes free-standing, but often appended to the fronts of houses lining the street, where merchants and craftsmen sold their goods.
Bronze Age	Prehistoric period between the Neolithic and the Iron Age (*see* below) or around 2000 BC–AD 500. Named because of the introduction of bronze-working.
Burgage plot	Division of land, often of regular size and forming a long rig, allocated to a burgess. Once built on, it contained the house on the frontage (*see* Frontage) and a backland (*see* Backlands). In time, with pressure for space, the plots were often subdivided

	(*see* Repletion) Plots were bounded by ditches, wattle fences or stone walls.
Burgess	Person who enjoyed the privileges and responsibilities of the freedom of the burgh.
Close	*See* Vennel.
Cordiners	Leather workers.
Cutler	Person who makes or sells knives.
Daills	Boards.
Feu-ferme	Payment of burgh dues to the crown by pre-agreed annual sum
Fleshers	Butchers.
Frontage	Part of a burgage plot (*see* above) nearest the street. Usually occupied by a frontage building.
Hammermen	Metalworkers and associated craftsmen.
Heid-dykes	Small continuous fencing at tail end of tofts, often containing back yetts (*see* below), giving access to burgh common land and the countryside.
Hinterland	Rural area around a burgh, to which the burgh looked for economic and agricultural support; hinterland likewise dependent on burgh market.
Indwellers	Unprivileged, non-burgess dwellers in a town.
Iron Age	Final prehistoric period in Britain, named because of the introduction of iron-working. Running from around 500 BC–AD 500, although the latter half is often termed the Roman Iron Age.
Liners	Burgh officers with responsibility to measure burgage plots and supervise building matters.
Litster	Dyer.
Mantua	Woman's loose outer garment.
Merk	13s 4d, two-thirds of Scots pound.
Midden	Dumping ground for refuse.
Mortcloth	Funeral pall.
Palisading	Timber fencing.

Plot	*See* Burgage plot.
Ports	Gates.
Repletion	*See* Burgage plot.
Sasine	Act of giving legal possession of property.
Solar	Medieval chamber, usually on an upper floor.
Stent	Assessment; rent; tax.
Syboe	Young onion; shallot; spring onion.
Toft	Burgage plot.
Tolbooth	Meeting place of the burgh council, collection point for market tolls and often the town jail.
Tolls	Payments for use of burgh market.
Topography	Physical characteristics of land.
Tron	Public weigh-beam.
Unfree persons	Those not holding the rights and privileges of burgess-ship.
Vennel	Alley; narrow back lane.
Wynd	Narrow alley.
Yett	Gate.

ABBREVIATIONS

APS	*The Acts of the Parliaments of Scotland*
BOEC	*Book of the Old Edinburgh Club*
CSP Scot	*Calendar of State Papers relating to Scotland and Mary, Queen of Scots*
ECA	Edinburgh City Archives
Edin. Recs.	*Extracts from the Records of the Burgh of Edinburgh*
NAS	National Archives of Scotland
NLS	National Library of Scotland
PSAS	*Proceedings of the Society of Antiquaries of Scotland*
RCAHMS	Royal Commission on the Ancient and Historical Monuments of Scotland
RMS	*Registrum Magni Sigilii Regum Scotorum*
RRS	*Regesta Regum Scottorum*
SBRS	Scottish Burgh Record Society
SHS	Scottish History Society
SRS	Scottish Record Society
TA	*The Accounts of the Lord High Treasurer of Scotland*

LIST OF ILLUSTRATIONS

Colour Plate Section

1

BEFORE HOLYROOD

The site where the abbey of Holyrood and its burgh of Canongate would develop was a dramatic one. Overshadowed to the south by the heights of Salisbury Crags and Arthur's Seat, and to the north by Calton Hill, the setting was one that would mean that the lives of the people here, throughout their history, would be dominated by geography and geology. To the west was another imposing outcrop, a massive volcanic plug, with the spine of a tail-like ridge of protected sedimentary rock running eastwards for about a mile. At the foot of that ridge would later stand the abbey and its burgh.

But it was not only these rocky protuberances that would dominate the lives of those who came to live here. There was another feature that would mould the settlement and the livelihoods of the inhabitants

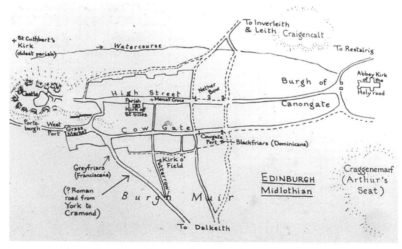

Site of early settlement (by courtesy of GWS Barrow)

for centuries – water. The site was bordered both to the north and to the south by water-logged land, the areas near to the modern thoroughfares now called Calton Road and Holyrood Road being, in effect, small rivers or burns. Even into the late fifteenth and early sixteenth centuries these routeways were both called 'Strand', indicating their proximity to water. What is not clear is whether, on reaching the hollow at the foot of the present Canongate, these two small rivers met and formed a lagoon-like effect, leaving access to where the abbey would be founded by merely a narrow pass on raised ground – almost a causeway. There was certainly a 'loch' that had to be cleared in the early sixteenth century to make way for James IV's (1488–1513) new south gardens in Holyrood and there was a pond and a bog just to the north-west until the eighteenth century at least. Archaeological evidence confirms that the south-east end of Canongate was once water-logged and formed part of a loch at the foot of the Crags.

There were water-courses to the west also. To the north of where the Old Town of Edinburgh now stands was a steep incline to a rivulet, dammed in the late fifteenth century to become the Nor' Loch; it would not be built upon until the nineteenth century. To the south lay the Cowgate valley, deeper then than it now appears and part of it covered by the 'Cowgate loch', which was drained at the end of the fifteenth century.

Could such an inhospitable environment attract settlers? It is known that Din Eidyn, the volcanic rock on which Edinburgh Castle now stands, supported human occupation a thousand years before the first Roman invasions, by which time it lay within the territory of the Votadini. Around 600 it was the centre of the Gododdin court of the north British kings. From this time, there was probably continuously a fortified stronghold on the rocky crag. Simeon of Durham, writing in c.1112, whilst assessing the possessions of the bishopric of Lindisfarne in 854, included in his compilation the church and town of 'Edwinesburch', which implies that there was an already established settlement on the site of Edinburgh. By the reign of Malcolm III (1058–93) it is known that Edinburgh was a royal residence. Clearly, Edinburgh was a well-established township that could support the presence of a royal court.

But what of the site that would become Canongate?

It has been known for some time that there was Iron Age occupation on the rocky crags now called Arthur's Seat. Was it possible that the marshy lands and lochs at the foot of the Crags could have served as hunting grounds for food supplies for early peoples such as these? Excavations in Edinburgh and the area around – Lothian – have already suggested that it was possible that there had been settlement in the Canongate area from very early times. Archaeological excavations have discovered Bronze Age flint tools, which suggest that, at the very least, this marshy plain was once used as a hunting and fishing ground by prehistoric man. But, even more importantly, the discovery of metallurgical activities near the abbey, roof tiles and a ditch dating from before 1128 tells us that people were living on this rather inhospitable site before Holyrood Abbey and Canongate existed.

This can be reinforced by documentary evidence. In 1128, King David I (1124–53) established an abbey dedicated to the Holy Rood on the – probably very marshy – site at the foot of the long ridge leading from the volcanic plug. What is made very clear in the charter founding this abbey is that there was already a church built on the site. This implies that there was a nearby resident workforce. If this was a pastoral, rather than a monastic, church there were probably also lay people nearby to whom the church ministered. How many were settled here and how they lived we do not know. What is important is that we know that people were living on this site before the foundation of Holyrood Abbey and its burgh of Canongate.[1]

When David I, acting in the name of Christ and in honour of the Holy Rood and of St Mary the Virgin and of all the saints, established the abbey, he granted it to the Augustinian canons resident at that time in windy quarters at Edinburgh Castle. The Augustinian order of regular canons was under the rule of St Augustine of Hippo who died in 430. This order took some time to be fully recognised, but by 1125 there were over thirty monasteries in England and Wales, but only one in Scotland – and that was at Scone. Augustinian priories were intended, amongst other things, to function as support for lay communities. It seems probable that David I planned that the abbey would serve the community that was already living in the area. His choice of an Augustinian foundation may have been a reflection of an already existing situation, perhaps an ecclesiastical site serviced by a priesthood, with a related lay settlement; this was certainly the case in Dunfermline, when David I's mother, Queen Margaret, founded the Benedictine monastery there soon after 1069.

One of the legends associated with the site is that in 1128 on the feast of the Holy Cross, King David was out hunting below Arthur's Seat. Temporarily separated from his followers, the king was confronted by a large white stag, which unhorsed and threatened to kill him. A vision of the Holy Cross, however, encouraged and reassured the king and the stag took flight, or the king defended himself with the Holy Cross and the stag ran off in fear. In thanksgiving for this deliverance David I established an abbey dedicated to the Holy Rood. This is, in fact, a late medieval adaptation of a well-known legend told of St Hubert. There is nothing whatsoever to link King David I with this apochryphal tale. But whether or not the founding of the abbey was the result of a vision, from early times a stag's head and a cross have been the arms of the burgh of Canongate.

An alternative, and maybe more plausible, explanation for King David's founding of the new abbey is that his mother, Queen Margaret, had reputedly brought with her to Scotland a gold cross which contained within it part of the True Cross; the cross was placed for safekeeping with the Augustinian canons, then living in Edinburgh Castle; and it was in honour of this cross that the new foundation was made and the abbey of Holyrood was founded.

Whatever was truth, half-truth or legend, the founding of the abbey was the prelude to the existence of the burgh of Canongate. For, in support of his new foundation, David I granted that the abbey should have a burgh. And so the burgh of Canongate came into existence – a small burgh, but one that would play a significant role in Scotland's history.

2

LIFE IN MEDIEVAL CANONGATE

With the founding of the Augustinian abbey of Holyrood a new burgh came into existence. This would later be called 'Canongate', meaning the 'gait', 'road' or 'walk' of the canons. A burgh was a legal entity, with specific privileges and responsibilities for the freemen, or burgesses, of the town. The early settlers formed the nucleus of this burgess class and the non-privileged members of the society were called indwellers. Scots and foreigners – Flemish and English – would all be deliberately attracted to the new burgh by a process called *kirseth* – a period of time, usually a year and a day, during which the new burgess was permitted to build his home free of all burghal dues or taxes. In exchange, these incomers brought skills as craftsmen and merchants.

The New Burgh of Canongate

There were two interesting factors about the site of this new burgh. It sat right beside the abbey and it was to be confined on the west by the already existing burgh of Edinburgh, founded by David I some time around 1124–27. Such physical closeness of two independent burghs was unique in Scotland.

There were two other intriguing features in Canongate's charter of erection. Firstly, the foundation of an associated burgh for the abbey was a privilege bestowed on only one other religious house in the twelfth century – that of Arbroath. So, Canongate and the abbey were highly privileged and an integral part of David I's policy of founding burghs, usually royal burghs dependent on the king as burgh superior. Both Berwick and Roxburgh, and possibly also Dunfermline, Stirling, Perth and Edinburgh, were granted burghal status even before David I became king of Scots in 1124. His reign saw the bestowing of status of 'burgh' on more – probably some thirteen or fourteen – small townships and urban settlements, including that of Canongate.[1]

Secondly, Scottish burghs were essentially established for mercantile reasons. Trade was their lifeblood; all burghs were granted the right to hold a market. But Canongate was specifically given the right to use the market of Edinburgh, a privilege unknown in any other burgh, and one that would permit Canongate to share in Edinburgh's market catchment area – an issue that would lead to a great deal of later dissension. These trading rights, in time, brought several advantages, but perhaps of most significance to burgesses was the freedom from payment of toll, or dues, to the owner of a market, so enabling a burgess from Canongate to travel at will around the whole kingdom buying and selling.[2]

When establishing the burgh, David I also endowed the abbots of Holyrood with an extensive area, or regality, which included the barony of Broughton, the lands of Pleasance and adjacent areas, and part of Leith. This also gave Canongate a port. Those living in the regality were obliged to attend the Canongate market (initially in Edinburgh), pay the market dues or tolls and obey its rulings. In time, however, the burgesses of Canongate came to hold their own markets in their own burgh.

But it was not only the burgesses who benefited financially. Through their economic activities, the burgesses of Canongate supported the Abbey of Holyrood financially. The tolls that were paid by outsiders to attend the burgh market, even if originally paid in kind, could be changed to cash and supplied the burgh superior, the Abbot of Holyrood, with a regular income. Burgh rents were a further source of revenue that benefited the abbey. All burgesses had the duty to watch and ward, or protect, their burgh, ensuring not only the security of the town, but also the safety of an excellent source of income to the burgh superior.

The granting of burgh status gave other fundamental rights to its privileged inhabitants.[3] Most striking was the relative freedom of a burgess: while recognising the authority of the burgh and its superior, other feudal ties were severed. The harshest punishment under burgh law was banishment from the community, for this meant loss of all personal rights and privileges. And a burgess had the right to be tried in the court of his own burgh. Allied to this personal freedom went the right to burgage tenure, the right to hold a burgage plot in the burgh and build on it.[4]

Another feature of the infant burgh was that a new urban parish appears to have been carved for it out of the existing parish at Edinburgh. Canongate was detached from the *parochia* of St Cuthbert under the castle of Edinburgh, the mother church of the shire of Edinburgh, which itself had been annexed to Holyrood at its foundation, and the burgesses of Canongate were from then on to worship in the parochial aisle within the nave of the abbey, served by a canon of the abbey. This was to be their parish church.

So, here was a new Augustinian foundation and a new burgh, both with considerable privileges, as well as responsibilities. Their task was now to display these privileges and responsibilities and make their imprint on the townscape.

Town Planning

We do not know how exactly the first burgesses delineated and protected their township. Ditching was an obvious first step; and the pre-burghal settlement had already used such a protection. By the time records are extant, ditches are also associated with walling, which might vary from something as slight as wooden palisading that was regularly blown down in high winds, as at Linlithgow, to stone walling as at Perth. Stone walls were rare in Scotland in the Middle Ages; and there are no examples of the great fortifications of the type associated with York, Carlisle or Carcassone. It seems safe to assume that Canongate never had strong stone walls. Even as late as 1513, there was complaint that the burgesses neglected to 'fosse, bulwarke, toure, turate and itherwise strengthen' their town, other than having insignificant 'civil' walls. Instead, the town depended on its ditch, which as late as June 1492 was referred to as *capitalis fossa* (the main or great ditch), although this implied that lesser ditches also existed, probably as dividing lines between individual properties. There are numerous references in the burgh's records to walls in the town, with various names, such as 'yard dykes', 'dykes of the orchards', and 'heid dykes'. The heid dykes stood at the end of the burgage plots, beside the town ditch.[5]

All these references suggest that Canongate was delineated to the

Timothy Pont's *c.*1590 view of Canongate, as detailed by Hondius

north and the south by ditching and small walling. There was, of course, no need for delineation to the west and east of the burgh. To the east stood the abbey and to the west the bigger, and more bullish, burgh of Edinburgh. The walls to the north and south were really little more than fencing or walling at the end of burgage plots, or tofts, many of which probably had small gates piercing them, giving the burgesses access to the burgh's two back lanes, the Strands, and beyond to the common lands. In effect, this was not a defensive barrier, but a psychological one. It was intended to demarcate those within the burgh from those without.[6]

Although Canongate set itself apart from those beyond its bounds, it also needed close contact with outsiders. Town gates, or ports, were the official entrances and exits to the burgh. The main port of entry was the Water Gate or Watergate. This stood to the north-east of the town, giving access to the important route to the port of Leith and took its name from a large pond for watering horses. There was probably a port near to the abbey, leading south past the foot of Salisbury Crags, but this is not clearly defined in the documents. To the east, there was no access, other than by a small gate to the church of Holyrood and the parish aisle where the townspeople worshipped. Edinburgh stood to the west; there was no need for Canongate to build a port here, for looming over the little burgh was the imposing east port of Edinburgh – the Netherbow.

The Water Gate [From *Old and New Edinburgh*]

The main purpose of ports was to control entry and exit from the town. They were shut at curfew, usually dusk, and opened at dawn. During this time, no one was permitted to come and go by the small gates in the 'heid dykes'. The ports were also closed at times of crisis – if plague or other disease threatened, or if the town was likely to come under attack. The assault of Richard II's (1377–99) troops in 1380, resulting in the burning of the town, was sure evidence that the gates and walls did not offer much defence. But the official town ports also provided another important function: they permitted access – controlled access. Through the ports came the people of the countryside to visit the town's market; and here the dues to attend the market might be collected, as well as at the tolbooth.

Having demarcated itself from the surrounding countryside, the burgh also needed to lay out the town itself. In burghs there was a quite deliberate planning of streets and burgage plots, often respecting natural features such as rivers, marshes and hills. St Andrews, which was founded between 1124 and 1144 by Robert, bishop of St Andrews,

The Netherbow Port seen from Canongate
[From *Old and New Edinburgh*]

was laid out by Mainard the Fleming, who had probably planned Berwick-on-Tweed. Glasgow, founded between 1175 and 1178 by the Bishop of Glasgow, was planned by Ranulf of Haddington, probably after laying out Haddington. They worked to precise plans and were probably specifically invited to the new burghs to perform these tasks. With documentary, archaeological and cartographic information, we now know that a high degree of precision went not only into the initial dividing up of the available street frontage, but also into the subsequent maintenance of these delineations by the appropriate town officers, the liners, who were appointed by the burgess community. The identity of the first town planner of Canongate is unknown; but it is likely that he was a canon or someone closely associated with the abbey.[7]

The topography of Canongate was such that there could be only

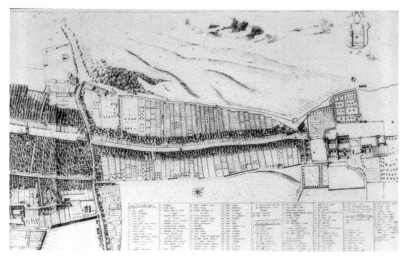

The lay-out of burgage plots, as depicted by Gordon of Rothiemay, *c.*1647

one main street – the High Street. Running at right angles to this, in a herring-bone pattern, were the burgage plots on which the burgesses were to build their homes. Initially, the plots were divided from each other by small ditches, but by the end of the Middle Ages the majority of these had been replaced with small walls. At the rear of the plots were the two back lanes, the Strands, one to the north and one to the south. The natural water features beside these two Strands meant that there was a narrowing of the town as it approached the east end, pinched as it was between the two water courses. As a result, the burgage plots at the east end of the town were not as long as those at the west.

It is safe to assume that once the formal laying out of the burgh had commenced, burgage plots would have been set down as close as possible to the abbey, as this was initially the focal point and protective element for the new burgh. One property in the 1480s, on the south side of and fronting Canongate High Street, lay immediately to the west of 'Abbey Cloise'; but to its south it was bordered by a garden of the monastery. Two tenements were sited between the 'abbay yet' and a waste land and certain houses belonging to the abbey in 1498. A further tenement is recorded as 'lying near the gate of the monastery of Holyrood', with a 'common wynd' on the west, the garden of the monastery on the south and the highway on the north. Thus, properties at the east end of the town had a close physical and psychological connection with the abbey precincts. As time went on, burgage plots were laid down westwards until they were contiguous with those of Edinburgh, running back from its own High Street. Had there not been the Netherbow Port making its great statement about Edinburgh's status, the two High Streets with their herring-bone burgage plots leading off might have appeared as one long street of a mile's length.[8]

In spite of the fact that Canongate stretched from the abbey gates to Edinburgh's Netherbow Port, a distance of some 600 yards, it was still a very small town. Population figures for most towns in the Middle Ages are difficult to determine. The vast majority would house only a few hundred people. Dunfermline had a population of only about 1,100 in 1500 and Glasgow, it has been argued, had 1,500 people in 1450. The first remotely accurate assessments for most towns came as late as the seventeenth century; of 44 burghs paying tax in 1639, it is estimated that 33 still had a population of 2,000 or less. So, it is safe to assume that Canongate housed, at most, only a very few hundred people in the Middle Ages. All would have known each other.

Canongate Homes

The burgesses usually built their homes at the front of the plot. Originally these were simple buildings, some of them being only single rooms. Twelfth- and thirteenth-century dwellings were basically huts made of stakes and interwoven wattle with free-standing posts to support the walling. These supporting posts could become precariously inefficient and unstable in wet weather. Roofs were normally thatched with cut heather or turves of growing plants that offered water-resistance; doors were often only straw mats or wattle; and there is no evidence of windows in these simple, early houses. Floors were sand, clay or silt, probably scattered with litter such as heather, bracken or cereal straw, for warmth and comfort. Most homes, however, did have a hearth for warmth and cooking, set directly on to the floor as a clay-lined hollow or a stone slab. The smoke would percolate out of the house by a small hole in the roof, inevitably making the interior very dark, fuggy and smoky.

From the late thirteenth century most town dwellings showed a growing sophistication. Instead of walls supported by free-standing posts, stakes were set into ground sills of wood, which, in turn, were often superseded by stone foundations for ground sills – a much more secure system of holding up the walls. Exterior walls were reinforced with heavy clay, dung, mud or peat cladding to exclude cold and draughts. And when archaeological evidence shows interior partition walls there is sure indication of different functional areas, the larger being for living or working quarters and the smaller for storage or animal shelter.

The majority of houses were built of wood throughout the Middle Ages. Much of the material for their construction was felled in the forests of the nearby Boroughmuir. By the end of the medieval period a number of houses were constructed of stone at ground level, with upper storeys of timber. Larger wooden houses were sometimes roofed not with thatch, but with tiles or slates, each tile or slate overlapping another and being fixed to the wooden sarking by nails at the top corners. The tiles surmounting the ridge were often gaily decorated and finished in a yellow, green or brown glaze. Many of the properties must have been prestigious, with a number of chambers, ranging from 'upper halls' to vaults and cellars.

The first firm documentary evidence for stone dwelling houses in Scotland comes as late as the fourteenth century – three in Ayr, one in Edinburgh and one in Aberdeen. An earlier reference to a burgh house with a solar in what is now Abbey Street, St Andrews, in a document of the 1240s, strongly suggests a stone building, at least on the first floor, even though the upper floors may have been of timber. In 1487, Robert Lauder, bailie of Canongate, gave permission for a house or houses to be built of stone taken from a garden dyke to the west, so it is known that stone houses existed in Canongate.[9] Archaeological evidence also indicates the presence of stone houses in the Middle Ages. It is possible that one dates to the thirteenth century. If so, it would be one of the earliest medieval stone houses in Scotland. Given the prestigiousness of Holyrood Abbey this is not surprising; and it is safe to assume that the property was associated with the abbey.

But the majority of the townspeople did not live in housing like this. Life for them was much simpler. There was no pressure for space in the burgh: gardens, orchards and barns were abundant; and many people often tended their own livestock in their backlands. A large number of the tofts ran without subdivisions from frontage to heid dyke. On the other hand, there are references to burgage plots being parcelled into smaller units, a process called repletion. The sasine records speak of 'inner lands' of tenements and 'myddil mansiones' – here are indications of the origins of the narrow closes, typical of much of early modern Canongate and Edinburgh. And for all these properties in the rear of backlands, it was essential to have 'free ische and entrie' – uncluttered, unbarred exit to the street and entry to the backlands.[10]

The rear of many burgage plots housed middens, wells, workshops, gardens and animals. A number of the properties had their own personal wells, but a significant proportion also housed kilns and 'steipstanes' (hollowed stone troughs for steeping malt or flax). This indicates an element of industrial activity. Skinners, tanners, masons, brewers, shoemakers and cutlers all held property in Canongate. Some would have plied their craft in their own backlands, possibly using the sources of water at the foot of their burgage plots. But the frontages of the burgage plots also offered commercial opportunities – brew houses, taverns and booths lined the street.[11]

For the majority of the townspeople, life would have been very simple. From knowledge of other medieval burghs, it is clear that the interiors of most houses would have had few luxuries. Beds were usually of the box-bed variety and in the poorest homes bedding would have been straw. By the fifteenth and sixteenth centuries better-quality homes had sheets, blankets, bolsters and coverlets. In the most prestigious dwellings, feather bolsters and feather beds, sometimes draped with curtains, were in use. Straw was the traditional medieval floor covering – it was cheap and could be replaced easily. Only in the most luxuriously appointed homes would there have been carpets.[12]

Tables might be one of two types. The compter was a reckoning table, marked out in squares, although it is possible, according to medieval paintings, that the table might be covered with a squared tablecloth. The more common form of table was the trestle table – a board with trestles to support it. This had the great advantage of being removable at the end of a meal, so releasing precious space in cramped living conditions. Chairs would have been found in only the wealthiest of houses; the form, or bench, was the usual type of seating.

Medieval wooden barrel and plates

Storage was also essential. Barrels stored salted meat and fish and dried goods, particularly in the winter seasons when fresh meat was not readily available; and some homes might even have a meat 'army' (cupboard, armoury) and bread 'army' to keep food clean. Wooden kists were the normal form of general storage – they could also be used as seating – and in well-appointed homes there might even be a 'towel burd' (cupboard) for bed linen, table cloths and serviettes. The stone houses lining the Canongate would have been luxuriously appointed with such amenities. The utensils used in the majority of homes were simple. Plates and dishes were usually made of wood or pewter. Jugs and drinking vessels were made of pottery while cooking utensils, such as goose pans, fish pans, kale pans, girdles, spits and ladles, were made of iron. Only in the wealthiest of households would items such as silver spoons, mirrors, clocks or books be found.

All homes needed lighting at night. The most usual forms were candles, supported by brass candelabra in the wealthiest homes, or lamps which burned oil, probably from flax imported from abroad or

Medieval pottery

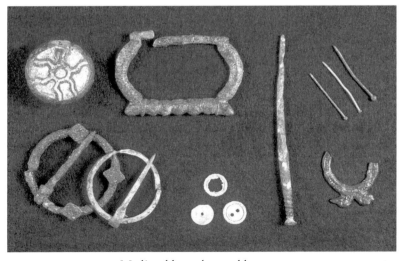

Medieval brooches and buttons

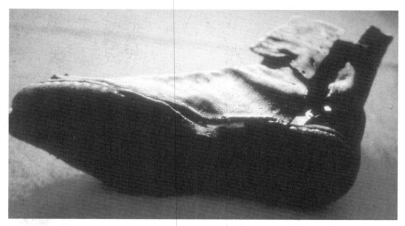

Medieval leather shoe

grown in the backlands of the tofts, in the poorer dwellings. Heating in the colder months was essential. The most common fuel was coal, although peat and wood were also used.

Clothing would vary greatly according to wealth. It is known that velvets, silks and cloth of gold were imported. The really fortunate burgesses might dress in gold rings adorned with rubies, sapphires, garnets and the like, silver crosses and belts and strings of pearls, but this was not typical of the average person in Canongate. The most common materials used for clothing were coarse cloth, of wool, canvas or fustian, a type of rough linen. Lace tags, buckles and brooches decorated these simple materials. Jackets and shoes were made of leather, and were often mended and reused. The majority of medieval town dwellers probably dressed themselves in domestically produced cloth. From documentary records it is known that most town dwellers possessed spinning wheels and carding combs, as well as shuttles and ancillary equipment for weaving. Needles and thimbles have been found on many urban sites that have been excavated.

Also produced at home was much of the food eaten by the ordinary townspeople. Cereals, mainly wheat and barley and oats, with some rye, were the staple of the diet. These were usually grown in the town's crofts, or arable lands. Exactly where Canongate's crofts were is not clear. The land immediately adjacent to the burgh was possibly too

Medieval people at work

water-logged for cultivation. The burgesses probably had cultivated crofts in the Pleasance and the regality of Broughton, granted to the abbey at its foundation. After a bad harvest, grain could be imported from nearby areas such as the fertile lands of East Lothian or from overseas, in particular the Baltic region, via the town's port at Leith. Oatcakes were common, and these were supplemented by bread. For home consumption, the grain was ground on domestic handmills but, if for sale, the townspeople had to take their grain to the abbey's own mill, the Canon Mill, situated to the north of the burgh, at what is now called Canonmills. This mill was driven by a lade diverted from what was then called 'the great river of the Water of Leith'. For this, the burgesses had to pay dues. Similarly, bread might be baked at home for personal consumption in a private oven. Many of these were sited in the backlands, rather than within the homes, because of the risk of fire. The sale of this bread was forbidden, as production of bread for profit was the prerogative of the baxter, or baker, craft.

Archaeological evidence has shown that beef, pig, horse, sheep, deer and goat were all butchered and eaten in towns, with spiced meat being eaten in winter. Chickens and geese were reared in the backlands and small wild birds were trapped for the table. Some properties also had dovecots in their gardens, for the supply of pigeons or doves as a delicacy.[13] Fish and shellfish were readily available at the market, as were any dairy products and eggs not produced at home. Most vegetables, such as leeks, fat hen (a 'weedy' plant – *chenopodium album*), syboes, cabbage and kale, were probably grown in the backlands, with mushrooms and other fungi being gathered outside the town. More exotic produce, such as apples, onions and spices, was imported. To supplement this, wild berries were collected. Archaeological evidence in other towns points to the consumption of brambles, blaeberries, raspberries, wild cherries, rowans and elderberries.

Water was readily available in the two Strands. The monks of Holyrood had probably taken advantage of the excellent springs in the area for their brewing from the time of their arrival in Canongate. But with the growth of domestic industry water tended to become polluted, so the usual drink for most, including children, was ale, brewed in the town. The wealthier classes favoured imported wine.

This was a relatively balanced diet, if somewhat limited and variable according to the seasons – as long as famine did not hit. As early as 1154, the *Chronicle of Holyrood* bemoaned 'a very great famine and pestilence amongst animals'; and in 1256, according to the *Chronicle of Lanercost*, famine fell upon the country due to 'a great corruption of the air and inundation of rain'. Such disasters were to hit the country, and Canongate, throughout the medieval period and would get worse in the sixteenth and seventeenth centuries.

Work filled most of the daylight hours, but there were a few opportunities for relaxation. Labour was interspersed to some extent with pastimes – foot and hand ball, dicing with gaming pieces and ceramic and stone counters, pennystanes, and chess, as well as drinking, story-telling and gossiping. In winter the townspeople sledged and skated. The wealthier members of society might also enjoy archery, hawking and hunting; and those who were close to the king might even partake of a little jousting in the royal grounds or hunt in the deer park at Holyrood. Children had little toys, such as pottery or carved dolls and animals; and all ages could enjoy the visits of travelling jesters, tumblers, pipers, drummers, minstrels and actors. Canongate, like many towns in Scotland, also enjoyed the revels at Maytime and the Robin Hood festivities (*see* Chapter 3). But medieval life was hard.

The Town: Market and Trading

It was not only wine that was imported via Leith to the Canongate market. Merchants brought in exotic fruits and vegetables and these were put up for sale at the town's market. Produce that could not be grown in the backlands or burgh crofts could be purchased, as could imports from the surrounding hinterland and from further afield, such as butter from Orkney. At its foundation, Canongate was given the right to buy and sell at the market of Edinburgh. This meant that the burgesses of Canongate could use Edinburgh's market without payment of toll and possibly also share in the profits of the market.[14] It is very likely that this was resented by the Edinburgh merchants. At some point, however, and exactly when is unclear, the burgesses of Canongate began to hold their own markets in their own burgh. By 1471, the records indicate that there was a tolbooth and a market cross is documented by 1572.[15] But this does not mean that they did not exist earlier and a market may have functioned in Canongate even before the building of a tolbooth. Even though Canongate was a separate burgh with its own tolbooth and market cross, it is clear that Edinburgh continued to think that it could dominate its little neighbour. As late as 1506 the authorities in Edinburgh gained the support of the king that no goods should be bought or sold at Leith or Canongate unless checked by the custumars of Edinburgh, with due customs, or duties, paid to them. The Edinburgh records give clear examples of its perceived problems with indwellers or unfreemen trading from Canongate and felt it within their remit to stop such malpractice in defence of their own liberties. On 3 April 1588 the Edinburgh Council minuted that a fish market had been set up in Canongate. Far from feeling that this would deter Canongate burgesses from benefiting from the profits of Edinburgh's fish market, it was deemed that a Canongate market would threaten Edinburgh's freedom to hold such a market and a magistrate was dispatched to Canongate to close it down. This action came at a time when Edinburgh was in the process of upgrading their High Street by removing all fourteen markets sited there to less prestigious streets such as Cowgate, Grassmarket and nearby wynds. But just outside Edinburgh's Netherbow Port, Canongate's continued to function. This did not suit the larger burgh.

Market days must have been noisy, dirty and thronged with people from the town and countryside. The sale of meat caused much of the dirt and noise. The most effective, and simplest, way of carting meat to the market was to bring it in on the hoof. The bellowing animals were then slaughtered on the public thoroughfare. The resulting squalor probably seems unacceptable to modern eyes, but little was wasted from the carcasses or left to lie around the streets. Animal skins were tanned and used by the leather workers, or cordiners. Most of the carcass would become meat and be eaten and even intestines and stomach linings were converted to sausage- and haggis-type foods and tripe. Bones could be transformed into useful objects such as pins, needles, combs and cutlery; and horse jaw bones made excellent medieval skates. Fats were rendered down for candles and soap. Any rejected bones or gristle would be removed rapidly by scavenging dogs. The potential filth in the street was also added to by the practice of fishmongers gutting their catch at the market and rejecting unusable bits and pieces onto the ground.

In amongst this seeming chaos the traders called out their wares to those passing by. Goods were placed for sale on open, wooden surfaces wheeled into the market place rather like flat wheelbarrows. Canongate did not have an open area on its High Street that might function as a market square, so the whole length of the street became, in effect, a market, with the transportable 'counters' strategically placed. The street was also lined with temporary wooden structures, or booths, abutting the front of the houses lining the High Street.

These also served as retail outlets or workshops for the town's craftsmen and merchants. The area around the tolbooth and the market cross was the most desirable and the best stance for selling food or craftsmen's products.

Care of the Sick

The dirt that accumulated in unswept streets, with animal and human waste pitched out and rotting on the roadway, meant infection was rife. Houses with only straw as carpeting could have the flooring replaced regularly but it often became sodden and foul; cleanliness within the average home was primitive. Kitchen and eating utensils were probably inadequately cleaned; and storage in wooden barrels and use of wooden plates meant that, when cracked, they could become dangerously unhygienic. Forks were not used – only spoons and knives – and eating with dirty fingers brought obvious contamination. In the backlands, agricultural, residential and industrial activities intermingled and brought potential disease. Too often, wells were placed close to midden pits. Lined only with wattle, seepage was inevitable.

But archaeological evidence, in Canongate and other burghs, suggests that, although there was a certain inevitable squalor, attempts were made to introduce an element of cleanliness. In wealthier homes, washing, both of utensils and of one's person, was more common. Aquamaniles on the table for the washing of hands between courses is a physical reminder of this. Even in poorer homes, however, all was not mindless squalor. In Perth, interior floors were sometimes raised above adjacent middens and paths to assist drainage within the homes; wattle rafts were placed on pathways and in latrine areas, to compensate for sogginess; and some homes even had the luxury of indoor latrines with toilet seats, with moss being used as toilet paper. Culverting and drains to remove effluence have been found in many towns, in the streets and also in the backlands. There are references in the records to private people digging drains to empty water closets and remove other waste water. As long as these drains did not breach another's land or the common highway this was acceptable. If, however, permission had not been granted to dig in the street the authorities insisted on the closing up of these sewers, as not in the common good.

The authorities in all towns in the Middle Ages seem to have had an uphill struggle to maintain a measure of cleanliness and remove public filth. Acts were passed to keep the public wells and water untainted; gutters were built on the streets to remove accumulated water; midden pits were removed from the highway and placed elsewhere in the backlands or, in the case of riverside or coastal towns, the river or the sea. Sometimes the authorities insisted that the culprits should remove their own filth; and it is possible that occasionally an official cleaner was appointed, similar to the rakers of London who were supplied with a cart and a horse. Clearly, town councils were aware of the need for cleanliness, but whether it was achieved is another matter. The numbers of times that the same rulings had to be passed would suggest that they were largely ignored.

Inevitably, in these conditions and in an age of primitive medical knowledge and no antibiotics, many succumbed to ill-health and disease. Certain diseases were rife in the medieval town. Some were endemic and chronic. Leprosy was common throughout western Europe. Knowledge of the disease was such that the need for isolation was understood and many towns had their own leper house safely outwith their boundaries. Where the lepers of Canongate were exiled to is unclear. Edinburgh had a leper house to its north-east, near to Trinity College.[16] Lepers from Canongate may have been accepted there but this is uncertain – they would certainly not have been permitted to remain in the town. Within the issue of leprosy is the root of many of the medieval problems of dealing with health. Decisions were often left to the burgh authorities – probably well-intentioned, but usually non-medical, men. They had the power to adjudicate on a number of physical matters – whether an heiress was a virgin; or whether a bad case of acne was in fact the dreaded leprosy. If these amateurs so decided, the victim entered a living death. If, as seems likely, the custom of the Scandinavian countries was followed, the victim was laid on a table before an altar of the parish church, covered with a mort-cloth, and was declared dead to the living world. From then on they were to live apart with the lepers, who might approach the healthy only in representative small numbers to collect food supplies, waving their clappers and bells and keeping down-wind of their more fortunate brethren. They, leprous or not, were condemned for life to live apart from husband, wife, parents or children.

Trinity Church

In spite of the horrors of leprosy, the greatest fear was of plague or 'pest'. The fourteenth-century cartulary of the monastery of Kelso includes a translation in the Scots dialect of Sir John de Mandeville's Latin account of plague as 'Ane Tretyse Agayne the Pestilens'. This underlines the terror that 'pest' brought. In fact, plague was several diseases, the bubonic form being the most common. But 'pest' in the records, because of lack of medical knowledge, may have concealed other diseases, such as typhus, which hit communities when resistance was low, as often happened after famine. Bubonic plague itself is fairly easily identified in medieval urban documents, as it hit in sudden, virulent epidemics and exhibited itself by swellings – *buboes* – on the body. Bubonic plague was kept active by rats and other rodents, particularly the imported black rat, *rattus rattus*, which preferred indoor to outside living, unlike the native rat of Scotland. Predominantly wooden housing, which was easily gnawed, inadequate sanitation, soggy, soiled straw on the floors and relatively poor standards of cleanliness encouraged the vermin. If they also carried infected fleas, such as *xenopsylla cheopis*, which bit and attached themselves to human beings, the disease was transferred. Pneumonic plague was also prevalent in Scotland, both as a secondary infection to bubonic plague and as a primary disease. It could be transported by Flugge droplets – moisture on the breath – for two metres by talking and up to three to four metres by sneezing or coughing. The cold and rain that Canongate experienced, along with many other towns along the Forth and Tay valleys, tended to encourage pneumonic plague. Plague first hit Scotland seriously in 1349–50, returning at regular intervals until the last great epidemic, in the 1640s.

Towards the end of the medieval period, increasing migration from the countryside and trade with foreign parts brought contact with new types of bacteria and viruses, many perhaps concealed in the records as 'pest'. One disease that was to afflict Scotland in the closing years of the fifteenth century was syphilis. Whether this was a totally new disease or merely a variant of earlier venereal diseases is still under debate. Equally, it is possible that the syphilis that caused such distress at this period had been in existence before but was not readily distinguished from leprosy. But, whatever the case, this strain, or awareness of it, hit the country in epidemic proportions. 'Gore' or 'grangore' – as syphilis was called at the time – was causing concern in Aberdeen in April 1497; by September it had arrived in Edinburgh, probably by sea. It came with such virulence that James IV ordered that all those suffering from the infection in the capital were to be banished to the island of Inchkeith in the Forth. This control was inadequate and by the next year Linlithgow, Stirling and Glasgow had succumbed.[17]

These were merely the more dramatic of medieval diseases. Many succumbed to the debilitating effect of illnesses suffered also in the twentieth century. Cholera, tuberculosis, smallpox, amoebic dysentry, osteoporosis, spina bifida and related problems such as hydrocephale, and arthritic conditions were all prevalent. So were *caries,* gingivitis and other dental problems. Added to this, medieval people were host to a number of parasites. Fleas and ticks were irritants. More debilitating and nauseous were fluke-worm, ringworm and parasitic worms, often passed on from animals. Two of these worms were *trichuris* and *ascaris,* which developed in the small intestine and then travelled throughout the body, burying into the liver, heart, lungs and trachea. Apart from the immediate discomfort and inconvenience any parasitic infection reduced resistance to other illnesses.

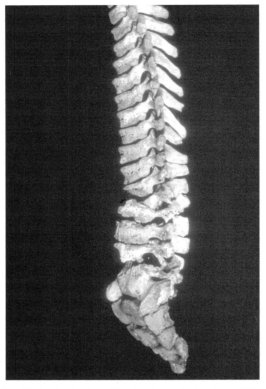

The spine of a child who had suffered tuberculosis; the child was probably
paralysed from the waist down as a result of damage to the spinal cord

In such conditions, life was tough. Perhaps the most vulnerable
groups were the unborn and infants. From conception, existence
was precarious. There is not the evidence for Canongate, but there
is no reason to believe that conditions were any better here than
in Linlithgow. Excavations there of foetal and prenatal skeletons
suggest that some foetal babies were as young as five to seven months,
intrauterine. Even if by some amazing chance they were born alive,
they could not have lived long without modern medical techniques.
It is unclear whether the number of skeletons of the perinatal group,
that is from seven months intrauterine to two months after birth,
represents stillbirths or live, but it serves to show how fragile life was

at this stage. A very high proportion died before the age of eighteen, the vast majority in infancy. Studies of the enamel on teeth suggests that youngsters were not weaned until nearly two years old – so infants were losing the immunities in the mother's milk at the very stage that they were becoming actively mobile and could investigate midden heaps and the like. It is thought that the high mortality rate was most likely attributable to respiratory infections and gastroenteritis in an age when no antibiotics were available.

So what could medieval townspeople do to counteract these diseases and ill-health?

Care of the sick was largely a matter of self-help. Herbs were grown and collected for their medicinal and restorative properties. *Hyoscyamus niger* (henbane) and *atropa belladonna* (deadly nightshade) could, in the first case, act as a sleep inducer and, if taken in greater quantities, result in hallucinations and narcosis, and the second worked as a muscle relaxant, if care was taken not to overdose. Poppies and their seeds were the essential source of opium. Many other plants, from hemp, flax and witch hazel to mushrooms, could provide relief from pain or discomfort. Imported fruits, such as figs, could act as purgatives, but these were available only to the wealthy. Leeching was also practised, although this may not always have been available to all the townspeople of Canongate, as often the services of a professional leecher were necessary and this could prove costly. Although there was an increasing interest in medicine in the fifteenth century, particularly in the reigns of James III (1460–88) and James IV, with Scottish texts becoming more readily accessible and continental medical textbooks being translated, it is doubtful whether the increasing knowledge reached the ordinary townsfolk.

Provision for the care of the sick was minimal, other than by self-help. Hospitals, or almshouses, might house a few fortunate inmates, but they were not open to all. An almshouse founded in Peebles in 1464 sums up the medieval attitude: its purpose was 'for tyl harbry in it pur foulk for saull heile' (for to harbour in it poor folk for soul health). Spiritual healing was as important, if not more so, as physical, medical attention.

Life was short and brutal for most. The harshness of life is evidenced in skeletal remains. Men's height averaged about five feet five inches to five feet seven inches (1.65–1.70 m) and women's between five feet one inch and five feet three inches (1.55–1.6 m). Women's stature is closer to the modern norm and may be a reflection that the female children may not have been as susceptible to illness as male children. Where women did suffer was in the child-bearing years when, with multiple and difficult births and related obstetric problems, a female was at her most vulnerable. Indeed, one sample survey in Aberdeen suggests that as few as one-third of women would survive this critical stage of their lives.

Adults who did live to middle or old age were probably those lucky ones who had developed immunities to the epidemic diseases that were rife. Given the harshness of life, it is not surprising that in medieval times middle age was considered to be approximately the mid to late thirties and the age of forty-five was truly old. Little wonder that, in the widely adopted classical notion of the seven ages of man, the age of sixty-seven marked 'decrepitude'.

The Church Influence on Canongate

The church played a pivotal role in the lives of medieval people. In Canongate it was even more heightened. The constant presence of clerics on the streets of the town, the abbey dominating the skyline and an aisle of the abbey church functioning as the parish church meant that the burgh was permeated with religion and clerics. The prestigious housing of the clerics lining the main street was a further physical reminder of this presence. This picture is confirmed by evidence in surviving protocol books. John Wricht, vicar of Kirkcudbright and canon of Holyrood, inherited a property in 1489 on the south side of the Canongate from his parents, and the vicar of Baro (Bara) also held a tenement on the same side of the street. A 'great mansion' belonging to the church also stood on the north side of the High Street of Canongate, beside the gate to the monastery.

The church dominated life from birth and baptism, through 'handfasting' (an agreement to marry) and marriage, to death and burial in the burgh graveyard to the north of the abbey. Death was tempered by the teachings and support of the church. Death must have held less terror for the wealthier members of Canongate society who could afford to pay for masses, or even establish chaplainries, for the saving of their souls. Many of those who worshipped in the parochial aisle in the abbey could not afford this luxury; for them fear of death must have been more acute. For all the townspeople, the daily routine of work was marked by the sounding of the church bell at dawn and labour ended, and the town gates were closed, at curfew, again with the bell. The liturgical cycle also regulated the yearly secular life of the town, with the timing of head courts, at Easter, Michaelmas and Christmas/Epiphany.

Holy days were days for veneration of the saints, but also days of rest from routine, and religious plays and processions through the High Street must have brought not only the opportunity for reverence of the saints, but also for a bit of fun and amusement. The medieval plays of western Europe, such as the *Corpus Christi,* are amply recorded. In Scotland, it was usually in towns and at the royal court that such performances took place.[18] Canongate people probably witnessed many such events. The pertinents used by Edinburgh to celebrate their annual *Corpus Christi* procession correctly were loaned to the burgh of Dundee and give a small insight in to what must have been a spectacular occasion:

> sixte of crownis, six pair of angel reynis [wings], three myteris, cristis cott [coat] of lethyr with the hoses and glufis, cristis hed, thirtie one suerdis, thre lang corsis of tre [wood], sanc thomas sper, a cors til sanc blasis, sanc johnis coit, a credil and thre barnis maid of clath, twentie hedis of hayr, the four evangellistis, sanc katernis wheil . . . sanc androwis cros, a saw, a ax, a rassour, a guly [large] knyff, a worm [serpent] of tre, the haly lam of tre, sanc barbaras castel, abraamis hat and thre hedis of hayr.[19]

The church had influence over other areas of town life. A few fortunate boys benefited from attendance at the song school, run by the church. The principal aim of their education was to provide able choristers in the first instance. The emphasis was on music and the rudiments of Latin. In a few cases, entrants studied for the priesthood or monastic life at the grammar school. This was reflected in a typical curriculum as laid down by Edinburgh town council in 1520: 'grace buke, prymer and plane donatt', a book containing the graces for before and after meals, a primer to teach the alphabet and the rudiments of Latin and the 'donat', a grammar book based on the fourth-century *Aelius Donatus,* which appears to have been more popular in Scotland than other grammars.

The vast majority of the population, however, was not literate. Many could not even sign their own names, needing the assistance of a public notary to hold their hand and guide the pen. The invention of the printing press would go far to improve standards of reading. Scotland's first press, that of Walter Chepman and Andro Myllar, was set up at the foot of Blackfriars' Wynd in 1507. An agreement, formulated in 1610 between the four incorporated trades of Canongate – the hammermen, tailors, baxters and cordiners – is a firm indication of the literacy levels in Canongate, in so far as the ability to sign one's own name unaided is a crude indication of literacy. The signatures of the craftsmen of Canongate suggest that the ambition of the reformed church's *First Book of Discipline* of an educated, godly society was not yet a reality. Only one deacon, James Symsoun of the baxter craft, signed his name unaided. Of the hammermen, 11 signed; seven could not do so without assistance and two were missing; of the tailors, out of 25 five signed with their own hand unaided. The rest received the assistance of a notary public, marking 'with our handis at the pen led be the noteris undersubscryveand at our command becaus we cannot wreit our selffis'. Interestingly, the poor level of literacy is confirmed again in 1638. Those in Canongate who subscribed the National Covenant in March 1638 included many of differing social standing and educational background, from advocates, writers and schoolmasters to gardeners, coopers and stablers: 310 signed their own names; 330 could not write.

The church also supervised hospitals and almshouses. A hospital existed to the south of Canongate, at St Leonard's. Already in existence by the thirteenth century, it was granted to Holyrood Abbey by David II (1329–71). In 1493, Robert Ballantyne, abbot of Holyrood, reconstituted the hospital and established six beds for poor or old men in the almshouse to the south of the chapel of St Leonard. The manse of the chaplain of St Leonard's was sited within the burgh. It was referred to as 'the great mansion lying beside the gate of the monastery on the north side of the high street of the Canongate'. The *Treasurer's Accounts* in 1541 give some clues to its construction, which was probably similar to many of the prestigious dwellings known to have lined the Canongate. A total of 6s 6d was spent on 'grathing' [making ready] the house and breaking down two walls of mud and clay in it. Two locks for the doors of the manse cost 8s. In the following year, the manse was referred to as a 'tymmerhous', which implies a considerable quantity of wood in its construction, although it was undoubtedly a building of some standing, in close proximity to the abbey.

The nunnery of St Mary of Palcentia stood on the east side of the Pleasance, across Cowgate from St Mary's Wynd. An almshouse for poor women, dedicated to the Virgin Mary, stood in St Mary's Wynd itself; but though outside the Netherbow Port and Cowgate Port of Edinburgh, St Mary's Wynd fell within the jurisdiction of Edinburgh (*see* Chapter 3), and it is uncertain whether it would have been open to women of Canongate.

A poor hospital dedicated to St Paul had an adjacent chapel dedicated to St Mary and was founded, or probably refounded, in 1470. Its exact location is not certain, although Vincent Strathauchin's protocol book refers in 1521 to a land near the Hospital of the Blessed Virgin Mary, formerly called the hospital of St Paul, as being near to the port of St Andrew, with the stream of water called the Strand to the north, which at least places the hospital on the north side of the High Street. Other documentation suggests that it stood near to the Trinity Church, which would place it to the north-west of the burgh. Another hospital, also for the poor, in this case specifically twelve men, dedicated also to St Mary, occurs in the record in 1479. This probably united with the St Paul hospital, forming one establishment.

Around 1541 a further hospital, dedicated to St Thomas, was built. It stood in the Watergate. Its two chaplains served the altars of St Catherine and St Andrew; and the hospital was, as a result, sometimes referred to as that of St Andrew and St Catherine. The seven almsmen received annual rents from property in Bell's Wynd. These were all typical of medieval hospitals, which were, in reality, more in the nature of almshouses for a few poor people, or more often for select groups such as widows of important merchants or places of rest for pilgrims, housing very few beds.[20]

The church had a dominant and crucial role to play in the lives of medieval people. Life was tough and brutal. But the church gave some solace. Even if the ordinary person did not understand the Latin liturgy, the teachings through pictures and pageants offered some alternative to the harsh working life. It offered hope.

3

MAINTAINING ORDER

Canongate, as all Scottish burghs, was a specific legal entity. It was formally established and did not just evolve. Burghs were made legal entities by the granting of this status by the crown or by the giving of the right to found a burgh by the crown to an important magnate. The canons of Holyrood, with the permission of David I to have a burgh sited between their church and the king's burgh of Edinburgh, were, therefore, in a very privileged position. With the privileges came responsibilities.[1]

Burgh Law

The Abbot of Holyrood became the burgh superior; it was his duty, probably with the advice of the canons, to administer the new burgh of Canongate and dispense justice within it. How he initially did this is unclear, as little documentation survives from this early period. Later twelfth-century evidence shows that there was a body of law which applied to all burghs. Whether the *Leges Burgorum* – the Laws of the Four Burghs, probably the best-known compilation of laws relating to Scotland – were actually formulated as early as the reign of David I is less certain. Certainly, during the reign of David I's grandson, William I (1165–1214), royal recognition of a body of laws that applied to burghs was confirmed; and the *Leges Burgorum,* in fact, may well have begun to be compiled gradually in William I's reign. But it is also possible that this body of law, which was both legislative and customary, was partially based on the practices of the very early burghs, of which Canongate was one, since a charter of William I refers to three statutes of David I relating to burghs.

The *Leges Burgorum* reflect the mid twelfth-century 'customs' of Newcastle and, to a lesser extent, of Winchester, Northampton and

Nottingham. These Laws of the Four Burghs, perhaps originally drawn up for Berwick, became the general basic foundation for all early Scottish burghs, although as the Middle Ages drew to a close they were interpreted so liberally by some burghs as to be virtually ignored. Just as Scottish burghs borrowed and copied ideas from England, so they did from each other and from overseas. The proliferation of ideas from the little Norman town of Breteuil shows how widespread were new urban notions by the twelfth century. The resemblance of new boroughs, burghs and urban liberties throughout north-western Europe was not chance.

The Scottish *Constitutiones Regis Willelmi* were laid down in William I's reign. While they dealt with a number of wider issues, they were largely concerned with burghal regulations. Then, with the borrowing, or copying, of burgh charters one from another, there was also established a common code, which offered general guidelines, but which each individual burgh might adapt to its own circumstances. Various pointers suggest a high degree of inter-communication between burghs even into the fourteenth century. Dundee's charter of burgh foundation, for example, was lost, if ever it existed, by the early fourteenth century. An appeal was, therefore, made to Robert I (1306–29) in 1325 by Dundee to have its privileges substantiated by formal definition. A confirmation charter was granted two years later. Some of the sections of this charter were copied from the 1320 privileges confirmed to Berwick. These had been copied from Edward I's (1272–1307) original charter to Berwick. Specific use of wording from Aberdeen's foundation charter was also included and possibly also other sections that are no longer traceable were borrowed from lost charters of other burghs. The Dundee burgesses also appealed to burgesses elsewhere to confirm their knowledge that Dundee had possessed liberties since as long ago as the reign of William I. The important factor is that burghs had an accepted corpus of law and established practices from early in their history.[2]

Burgh Officials and Burgh Courts

To administer burghal law, officials called bailies presided over a burgh court. Very probably in the early years of the life of the new burgh of Canongate the bailies would have been appointed directly by the abbot and canons. But, gradually, these officers may have become more 'of the people' and representing their interests, rather than those of the superior. In Dunfermline, by the fourteenth century an abbot's burgh, appointments may have been totally free, at the discretion of the burgesses, or with the advice and consent of the abbot. The latter was possibly the case in Glasgow which was a bishop's burgh. In Arbroath, one of the two bailies was a town nominee, the other that of the abbot. Exactly how bailies were appointed in Canongate is not clear through lack of documentation.

In some burghs one man held the prime office. He was called either the *prepositus* (later in the vernacular 'provost') or the alderman. Lesser officers were also appointed, all with the purpose of maintaining order in the burgh. The sergeands' main function was associated with the burgh court. It was their responsibility to ensure that defendants appeared on the due day. They also assisted the bailies in the collection of debts in the town. The sergeands were appointed annually, as were the tasters of wine and of ale (*appressiatores cervicie*) and meat (*appressiatores carnium*) and bread pricers. The liners (*see* Chapter 2) may have been appointed for longer than a year at a time as their role required specific skills that not all burgesses would possess.

From the early days of Canongate's existence there probably was a form of burgh court to settle disputes within the town. From the thirteenth century, certainly, there were courts distinct from others in the realm to deal with specifically burghal matters; this jurisdiction covered all matters that arose in the burgh, other than the four pleas of the crown, which technically were dealt with by the burgesses acting as suitors before the royal justiciar. These burgh courts usually met fortnightly as the *curiae legales*. There were also the more frequent meetings of the court or assizes to deal with more minor matters and these were manned by the burgesses under the direction of the bailies. A further legislative and advisory body seems to have developed, possibly out of an informal grouping of the burgesses. This might loosely have been called a council. Its members were always burgesses. They were the 'best and worthiest' who were to rule for the benefit of the whole town.

Major legislative policy decisions, as well as some judicial, were taken at the head courts, held usually three times a year, at Michaelmas, Christmas/Epiphany and Easter. All burgesses were obliged to attend.

Canongate tolbooth

But how far the burgesses had any real power, other than ratifying the office-holders' decisions, is unclear. There is no evidence whether, even at the head courts, the burgesses could amend or reject the magistrates' decisions. The role of the burgess in the community might merely have been that of participation in consensus government.

What is clear, however, is that disenchantment with participation in burgh government was such that by the 1590s scores of non-attenders at head courts were listed. Public apathy eventually degenerated into ridicule. By the eighteenth and nineteenth centuries the right of sons of burgesses to claim their inheritance to freedom of the burgh had fallen into such disrepute that it was lampooned: the historic notion of the 'best and worthiest' had literally become an ass.

A medieval tron, as depicted on John Geddy's *c.*1580 view of St Andrews

Marketing and Trading Regulations

Market days were bustling, noisy occasions but a close watch was kept on selling and buying by the burgh authorities. Both quality and quantity control were carefully monitored, even amidst the seeming chaos. Tasters of ale, or *appressiatores cervicie*, checked on quality. If it was not up to scratch it had to be sold at a lowered price. Fleshers, or butchers, were under the surveillance of the *appressiatores carnium*, who checked that no meat came to the market 'blawn' or 'infectit with pokk or lung evyll' – another good reason for bringing the meat to market on the hoof – it would, at least, be fresh. Price, weight and quality of bread were also supervised. The only weights permitted at the market were those of the town, which were usually kept in the tolbooth and used on the town weighing machine – the tron. Anyone found abusing this ruling, or selling short measure was punished – usually with a fine and the 'dinging out' (banging out) of the bottom of the offending pot or barrel, so that it was of no further use.

So that all such dealings could be seen to be open and fair, selling was allowed only at the market cross or official booths and counters, not at the port in Leith or in 'myrk howsis and quiet loftis'; and there

Canongate market cross, as depicted by Gordon of Rothiemay, c.1647

were to be no dealings with 'straglaris and vagabondis'. The two greatest offences against the good rule of the market were forestalling (the purchase of goods before they reached market, so avoiding the payment of toll to the burgh) and regrating (buying in bulk and possibly hoarding in order to sell at an advantageous price when prices were high). Both met stiff penalties, either very strict fines or even banishment from the burgh.[3]

Keeping the Peace in the Middle Ages

In a small burgh with few inhabitants, deviant behaviour threatened the *status quo* of a close-knit community. Conformity was essential to the preservation of traditional values. Although there were burgh officers to maintain order, much punishment was, in effect, an expression of public disapproval as a whole. For this reason, offences against burgh society, such as slander, verbal abuse (particularly of a burgh officer), fighting and stealing, while often accompanied with a fine, resulted in the culprit being publicly ridiculed, where friends and neighbours might come to mock. The pillory, with holes to imprison the head and hands, stood beside the market cross, the most public space in the town. The cross itself held the 'jougs' on the shaft, a metal collar to hold the culprit fast. In many towns, it was also a practice to nail the ear of a culprit to the tron, again to receive the taunts of others. The girth cross also at times served as a place of punishment. This lasted into early-modern times: in July 1600 Jean Livingstone,

The later Canongate market cross

wife of Johne Kincaid of Wariston, had 'her heid struck fra her bodie' for the murder of her husband.

Two more common problems in medieval towns were drunkenness and 'nightwalking'. Many burghs imposed curfews at dusk, forbade the entry of outsiders by shutting the town gates and, as in Edinburgh, banned movement around the town after dark, other than for those carrying lanterns or on legitimate business.[4]

As well as housing the burgh court, the tolbooth was used as the town jail. Medieval towns were so small that often when committed to jail, the prisoner was given the key to let himself in. If he did not, or if he left before his sentence was completed, everyone would have known. There were few secrets in medieval towns. The prisoner had also to pay for his own keep while incarcerated. The tolbooth was replaced in 1591 and the site was probably identical to that of the medieval tolbooth. Still standing, albeit with later alterations, it was an important building, constructed of stone. Its roofing material was of wooden shingles, which were replaced with slate only in the late nineteenth century. A panel of the shingles was preserved at that time and is still in the keeping of the National Museums of Scotland. In spite of the sturdy structure of the new tolbooth, escapes were frequent. For serious breaches of the burgh's regulations the magistrates often resorted to branding and banishment, the ultimate punishment that could be imposed by the burgh.

Canongate's Regality

When establishing the burgh of Canongate, David I endowed the abbey of Holyrood with the barony of Broughton, the lands of Pleasance and adjacent areas and part of Leith, an extensive area, or regality. This was an important concession. Not only were those living in the regality obliged to attend the Canongate market, pay the market dues and obey its rulings, but also these people in the countryside could provide a workforce and assist the craftsmen of the town by taking on piecework.

These close physical and legal ties also forged other links. It is known from contemporary sources that the bailies of Broughton had certain official responsibilities within Canongate. In the sixteenth century, they acted alongside the bailies of the burgh in a variety of cases, such as petty debt, theft, assault, robbery and murder.

In spite of this, the burgh tried to set itself apart psychologically, if not physically. The ditch and small walling that enclosed the burgh, though punctuated with gates giving access to the fields outside, demarcated the town limits. By the later sixteenth century, it seems that the town was delineated with stone walls. The arrival at Edinburgh of James VI's (1567–1625) new queen, Anne of Denmark, in 1590, brought her along a route 'to the south side of the yards of the Canongate, along the party wall'. This gives the impression that, although there was no large walling surrounding the burgh, there was a very distinct demarcation. Already, by 1588, the wall to the north of Canongate was stone built. It was of sufficient structure for one William Stewart, a writer (notary), to have a privy built into the stone wall and an access route through the garden to reach it. This was well sited, as it could drain into the town ditch. This was probably not an unusual practice by the late sixteenth century and the same may be expected to have occurred on the south side also. Entry was only through the official ports, closed at night after curfew. Here, also, tolls could be paid

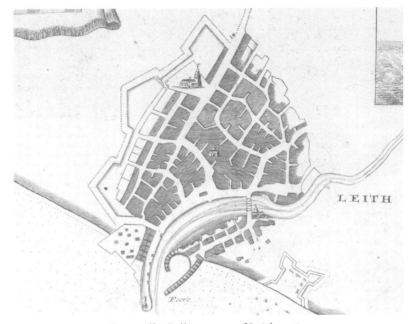

Greenville Collins, map of Leith *c.*1693

for attending the burgh market. The town ports were the legal and psychological barrier, but also the essential conduit.[5]

The grant of part of Leith gave the new landlocked burgh a sea port. This was called North Leith, the part of Leith that sits to the west of the Water of Leith. The shoreline in this region is now much changed: land has been reclaimed and developed. In medieval times, as has been shown by archaeological excavations, the shoreline was close to where Sandport Place and Sandport Street now stand. Edinburgh's port was in South Leith, on the east side of the Water of Leith. This physical proximity was a recipe for rivalry and dispute, particularly as the routeways to the respective ports meant each burgh traversing the other's path.

Sanctuary

There was a further jurisdiction in Canongate. The girth, or sanctuary, cross stood in the middle of the High Street of Canongate; it acted

1573 English engineer's drawing of Canongate showing the closeness
of the Girth Cross to Holyroodhouse precinct wall

as a marker. All who passed to the east of the cross and entered
within the sanctuary boundary, whatever crime they may have
committed, entered into the safekeeping of the abbey. The sanctuary
line ran southwards in a straight line from the Watergate until turning
westwards at the meadow at the foot of Salisbury Crags.

This time-honoured feature partially disappeared at the Reformation.
The right of sanctuary within the precincts of the girth cross became
restricted. A test case came in 1569, with a supplication to the privy
council by Adam Bothwell, bishop of Orkney, commendator of
Holyrood, and the convent and Mr John Spens of Condie, advocate.
William Barrie, messenger, had searched with armed men the houses
of Thomas Hunter, Andrew Chalmer and Sir John Stevenson, which
were all within the girth. It was, however, confirmed that the privileges

Holyrood Sanctuary

of right of sanctuary had been abolished at the Reformation. Only debtors might henceforth claim this protection.

Canongate and its Craftsmen

The growth of Edinburgh as a capital had a profound effect on Canongate. Nobles and their retinues, lawyers and their clients, and a growing infrastructure of service industries grew up from the increasing resort to the Court of Session after its formal constitution as a College of Justice in 1532, from the more frequent meetings of both privy council and parliament as well as from the requirements of the royal court. Both commerce and the trades or crafts in Canongate thrived. Food supplies from crafts such as bakers and fleshers and the services of tailors and seamstresses were essential to all. Less in demand, but necessary for the wealthier classes, were the makers of quality products. It is known, for example, that one Baldwin Glasinwright was living in the town in 1512. He may well have worked on the Palace of Holyroodhouse.[6]

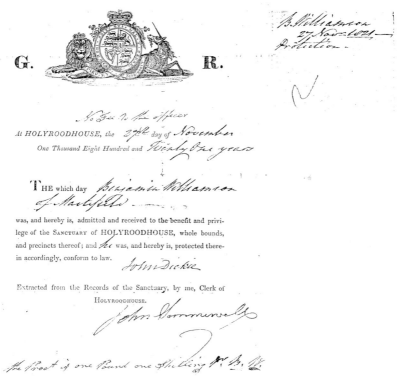

Certificate of admission to sanctuary at Holyroodhouse, 1821

During the sixteenth century there was a formalisation of the rights of a number of Canongate's crafts by the granting of seals of cause, or charters of incorporation, to their respective guilds. In 1538, the bailies of Canongate granted a seal of cause to the cordiners, or shoemakers, so bestowing on them all the rights and privileges enjoyed by similar incorporations throughout Scotland. This included the power to levy dues in Canongate from both shoemakers and cobblers, who were the vendors as well as repairers of old boots and shoes, but were not members of the incorporation. In 1554 this right was extended to outlying parts of the barony of regality, namely North Leith, the Pleasance or St Leonard's Gate, and part of St Ninian's Row – an extensive concession. Permisson was also given for them to build an altar in the parish church, dedicated to their patron saint, Crispin.

The earliest documentary evidence of the incorporation of tailors is their seal of cause granted in 1546 by Robert, commendator of Holyrood and bastard son of James V (1513–42), to 'Thomas Allanson, Dekyn and Kirk Master of the Tailzeiour craft within our brugh of Canongate and certain masters of the same craft'. As with the cordiners, rules were laid down and endorsed by the commendator in 1554. He also, at the same time, gave permission for the provision of 'augmentation of divine service at ane altar biggit within our said Abbey, quhair Sanct An, thair patrone now stands'.

The hammermen craft included many seemingly different trades, from wealthy goldsmiths and jewellers to blacksmiths, gunsmiths or dagmakers, cutlers, lorimers or harnessmakers, locksmiths, saddlers, pewterers and also coppersmiths, hookmakers, sheathmakers and braziers or whiteironmen, who were less wealthy. Armourers also were subsumed within the hammermen craft, but by the sixteenth century their skills were becoming almost obsolete; and it appears from the Book of the Hammermen that watchmakers were attached. As with the other crafts, a deacon was appointed to head the incorporation, in the case of the hammermen being elected at Beltane, usually 1 May, and from 1560 a treasurer also held office. The lists of apprentices show that young men from all parts of Scotland were sent to Canongate to acquire the secrets of the craft, with the intention of returning home to practise. The goldsmiths were the most prestigious members of the hammermen craft, their earliest mention in Canongate being in 1569. Amongst their numbers were James Gray and Adam Haw or Hall, and Jerome Hamilton, who rented his house in Canongate from a burgess of Edinburgh, John Achesoun, who for several years was 'master cunyear' (coiner) to the king. He had a son who was also a goldsmith. A clockmaker, Abraham Wanweyneburgh, was recorded in the craft in 1592.

In 1613 James Hart was a goldsmith master for one year at least; but after that no goldsmith appears to have been elected as a master for many years and during this period no freemen nor apprentices were admitted. The reason for this may probably be sought in the lack of trade, but it is also possible that Edinburgh, with its many goldsmiths, who were wealthy enough to serve as bankers as well, monopolised the trade. Clock and watchmakers were rare in both Edinburgh and Canongate. In fact, at one time, William Smith of Canongate was employed by Edinburgh since the larger town had no one of sufficient skill to regulate its town clocks.

One of the main advantages of the formalisation of the standing of the crafts was the authority bestowed on the masters to control all aspects of the craft, including regulations laying down requirements from apprentices, internal discipline, control of price and quality of goods produced, and protection of the monopoly and privileges of the craft. A further intrinsic character of guild life was the notion of fraternity linked to religion. All crafts supported their altars dedicated to their patron saints in the parish church; all processed, in order of importance, on saints' days carrying aloft their banners representing their saints and craft allegiances; and all worshipped together while living and escorted the bodies of members on death at their funerals in preparation for their journeys into the next life. This formal corporate worship would continue after the Reformation, albeit without altars dedicated to patron saints, but from pews or lofts allocated specifically to certain crafts where solidarity was expressed in physical form. 'Free' or privileged craftsmen were visibly set apart from 'unfree' members of what was still an intensely hierarchical society.

Holy days before the Reformation were not merely times to venerate the saints, but also occasions for revelries and fun. Of course, there were communal festivities that were a counterbalance to those in power. In the May Games, an 'abbot of unreason', 'lord of inobedience' or 'abbot of unrest' took charge and the conventional order and rule of burgh society was turned upside down. By the early fifteenth century, at least, traces of the cult of Robin Hood can be found intermingled in the May Games in many towns. The purpose of all these celebrations was to permit the lower members of society to enjoy a time of upturned rule, with the conventional order reversed, and their rule law.

But a closer look at the records gives a few hints that might indicate that the traditional view of the May revels as a time of upturned order was not all it was made out to be.

Most significantly, the occasion had the official blessing of the burgh authorities. In Aberdeen and Haddington, for example, the towns paid the abbots to fulfil their duties. In Edinburgh and Dunfermline the guilds merchant gave financial support to Robin Hood. And the choice of man to lead the common people in their time of unrest is very interesting.

The first page of *The Gest of Robin Hood*
among the Chepman and Myllar tracts

It was decided in Aberdeen in 1445 that, due to 'diverss enormities in tyme bigane be the Abbits of this burgh callit Bone Acorde', there were to be no such abbots. Rather, in future, the abbot was to be either the alderman or one of the bailies. In Ayr, it became the custom that the treasurers should take the part of Robin Hood and Little John. In Dunfermline the role of Robin Hood was usually filled by a member of the local gentry family – the Halketts. In Edinburgh, in 1518, the role of Little John was even offered to the earl of Arran – an invitation he stiffly refused.

It seems that, although the May revels may have served to release tension within burgh society, they were monitored by the ruling group. The parliamentary ruling of 1555 that there should be no impersonations of Robin Hood, Little John, the abbot or the queen of May, may be precise proof of this. As so often in legislation dealing with social matters in the fifteenth and sixteenth centuries, this act was probably a response to a particular problem in a particular town: in one of the four major burghs the annual ritual of supposed disorder and power in the hands of the underdogs had perhaps begun to display precisely these features. And it had to be stopped. In Edinburgh and Canongate, the association of Robin Hood and the lord of inobedience with civil disorder climaxed in 1561 when, it was claimed by John Knox, 'the raschall multitude war stirred up to mak a Robene Hude' by 'papistis and bischoppis'. A number were brought to trial for appointing a Robin Hood and a lord of inobedience. The traditional hierarchical order of society, including Canongate's incorporated crafts, had to be maintained at all cost.[7]

The old right giving permission to Canongate burgesses to use Edinburgh's lucrative markets still caused dissension. On 20 March 1595, the bailies and council of Canongate supported George Foullair, an armourer burgess, in an appearance before the privy council. The Edinburgh inhabitants had begun to molest Canongate men at their three weekly markets. Goods taken from Foullair were returned to him while the matter was considered by the Court of Session. Significantly, pending their decision, it was declared that there was to be freedom to Canongate people to trade in the Edinburgh market. This was only one incident in ongoing tensions and harassments between the craftsmen of the two burghs that was to continue into the next century.

An agreement was formulated in 1610 between the four incorporated trades of Canongate – the hammermen, tailors, baxters and cordiners or shoemakers. The hammermen included their deacon and nineteen master freemen, amongst whom were a pistol maker, a goldsmith, a pewterer, a cutler, an armourer and a blacksmith. There was the same number of tailors, but fewer baxters, possibly as they were still thirled to Canonmills. The representatives solemnly contracted 'for the haill remanent members and bodie' of their respective trades to maintain 'ane mutuall band of amitie luif and bretherheid'. It was agreed that there would be appointed annually a deacon convener, from each craft in rotation, and a convenery court was set up to maintain discipline. The fifth article agreed was that, on pain of a fine of ten shillings, all craftsmen would support their brethren at funerals. The sixth article of agreement forbade, under the pain of a £10 fine, that any craftsman dispossess another of the 'hous or buith quhairin he duellis or workis'. This may be hinting at an influx of artisans from Edinburgh and, in consequence, a class of unpropertied freemen.

Certainly, the increasing prosperity of the Canongate cordiners was a source of irritation to their Edinburgh counterparts. In 1568 the Canongate cordiners had already appealed to both the commendator

The Edinburgh Trades at Holyrood – the property of the
Incorporation of Wrights and Masons in the collection of
the Edinburgh Trades Maiden Fund

of Holyrood and to the privy council against their treatment by the
Edinburgh craft. Again, in 1607, the bailies of Canongate joined
with the deacon of the cordiners against his warding in the tolbooth
for buying hides at the public market and successfully obtained his
release. The Edinburgh records in this century do indicate that the
crafts of Canongate were a thorn in the side of the larger burgh, even
though numerically Canongate had market forces stacked against it.
This may have been because Canongate 'competed with Edinburgh
on quality rather than price'. Probably also resented was that, while in
Edinburgh the crafts had to submit to choosing their deacons from a
leet nominated by the town council, in Canongate the principal crafts
were strong enough to oppose their bailies and were, in consequence,
free to nominate their officers.

Canongate and its Neighbour

Tension between the two burghs was inevitable. Throughout the
Middle Ages, each was a quite independent jurisdiction. An anomaly
emerged, however, and it is unclear how this arose. A section of south-

west Canongate, in the area of St Mary's Wynd, became part of the jurisdiction of Edinburgh, although it seems that the frontage to the High Street remained within the remit of Canongate. This area became part of Edinburgh's north-east quarter, perhaps because it was the smallest of Edinburgh's four quarters. It meant, however, that Edinburgh had control of this area, which was one of the reasons why the 'creeping parliament' (*see* Chapter 4) could be held here in 1571, within Edinburgh's jurisdiction, but outside its gates. This anomaly probably also accounted for the fact that the so-called Leith stockings were, in fact, manufactured in the north-east quarter of Edinburgh.

The constant friction and geographical overlap between the two burghs were to come to a head after the Reformation removed the rationale of an Augustinian religious house. Its commendator until 1568 was Robert Stewart, one of the bevy of illegitimate sons of James V who had been appointed to major religious houses. Robert had been given the abbey in 1539 when he was only six years old. He took the chance to sell off the abbey's rights and jurisdictions. In a charter of 1565, Sir John Bellenden of Auchnoule, the justice clerk and a powerful figure at court, and his male heirs, were appointed as heritable justiciars and bailies of the barony and regality of Broughton and of the burgh of Canongate. On the resignation of the commendator and the convent, Sir John's son, Sir Lewis, obtained on 28 July 1587 a charter from the king of all the lands and barony, excluding the abbacy and the monastery and the district immediately adjoining them. This was to have far-reaching consequences for Canongate and its relations with its bigger neighbour, which had persistently throughout this period been attempting to challenge Canongate's jurisdiction.

The Bellendens of Auchnole were the maternal ancestors of the ducal family of Roxburgh, whose head in 1636 was Robert, earl of Roxburgh. Both Charles I (1625–49) and the earl of Roxburgh landed themselves heavily in debt to the town of Edinburgh, the former on account of loans by both the town of Edinburgh and the wealthy goldsmith George Heriot, 'Jinglin Geordie', the latter for loans by Heriot only. In commutation of these sums of money, in 1636 the whole superiority of Canongate and North Leith was transferred to Edinburgh, and the lands of Broughton went to the administrators of Heriot's legacy. These administrators consisted of the town council and the ministers of Edinburgh.

There was only one exception made in these transactions. The lands of Holyroodhouse had been disponed to John Bothwell, first Lord Holyroodhouse. By 1646 the second and last Lord Holyroodhouse had been dead for eleven years and, in consequence, a charter was granted by the crown in favour of James, duke of Hamilton, appointing him and his male heirs Heritable Keepers of Holyroodhouse. By virtue of this guardianship, Holyrood Palace and the abbey sanctuary appear to have become vested as hereditary in the Dukes of Hamilton.

This was little consolation to the burgh of Canongate. As superiors of Canongate and North Leith, Edinburgh no longer needed to fear the rivalry of its little neighbour. In 1856 with the Edinburgh Municipal Extension Act the corporate existence of Canongate as a burgh would cease. But until this time Canongate continued its existence as a separate burgh of regality – but with officials chosen by Edinburgh town council. It would, in effect, become a mere suburb of Edinburgh.

4

PALACE, PAGEANT AND POLITICS

Although only a small burgh, often dominated by its ambitious neighbour, Canongate saw many comings and goings of royalty. From David I's time, if not before, the area near to where the abbey was established was a royal hunting ground. The abbey complex was host to the crown on numerous occasions. A colloquium to discuss the remarriage of the king was held in the church of Holyrood in 1285, following the death of the heir of Alexander III (1249–86). Parliaments were held in Edinburgh in 1321 and in 1328, but although cited as taking place in Edinburgh, quite possibly the venue was actually Holyrood. If so, exactly where in the abbey the parliaments of Robert I met is unclear. The refectory, which was situated in the south cloister range, was possibly substantial enough to be converted in the sixteenth century into the great hall for the adjacent royal palace; there was also probably a late thirteenth-century chapter house of 39.7 feet (12.2 m) diameter. Either might have been able to accommodate parliamentary sessions; although a further possibility is that Holyrood Abbey church housed these meetings.

Edward Balliol also favoured Holyrood for his second parliament in 1334.[1] The abbey was the venue for the general council held in 1384, when royal justice was removed from the hands of King Robert II (1371–90) and entrusted to John, earl of Carrick, later Robert III (1390–1406), as guardian. Again, a number of the meetings of parliament recorded between 1373 and 1406 as being held in Edinburgh might, in fact, have been held at Holyrood. That held in 1389, for example, although initially summoned to Perth, concluded at Holyrood.[2]

Robert III stayed in the abbey guest house, as did all Stewart monarchs after him. This preference for Holyrood was exemplified by James II (1437–60), born in 1430 in the abbey, crowned there seven years later,[3] albeit as an expedient alternative to Scone, married in the abbey in 1449 and, ultimately, was buried there. It was also in the abbey that James III (1460–88) married.

It is not surprising that royalty preferred Holyrood with its spacious gardens and orchards to the windy castle, on a constricted site, a mile or so up the hill. Another major asset Holyrood had over the castle was its water supply. Water was scarce on Castle Hill. Initially, royalty and its entourage were probably accommodated in one of the abbey's guest-houses, as was the case in Dunfermline. Evidence from the 1470s onwards, however, suggests that there were official lodgings for the crown within the abbey precincts, maintained on a permanent or semi-permanent basis. Retainers and noblemen attending court probably took up residence in the many prestigious houses that lined Canongate's High Street.

A New Building Programme

Great changes were afoot for Holyrood and Canongate. With the reign of James IV the royal lodging at Holyrood was to be converted into what was called in 1503 'the king's palace near the abbey of Holyrood'[4] and, ten years later, the 'palace of Edinburgh'. The timing of the conversion seems to have been triggered by the forthcoming marriage of the king to his English bride, Margaret Tudor. This took place in Holyrood in August 1503; work on the palace was not completed until about a year after the wedding. As little now remains of this palace, it is difficult totally to understand the lay-out from contemporary documents. It seems likely that it was of a quadrangular plan, with all the principal rooms at first-floor level. A new chapel was constructed on the site of what would become the north side of the inner quadrangle of the palace. The queen's apartments seem to have been on the south side of that quadrangle, with her great chamber at the west end. As there is no mention of the king's apartments in the construction details, it is possible that the existing royal lodging, with the king's apartments, was incorporated into the new palace and stood at the west side of what would become later the inner quadrangle, affording communication with the queen's chambers. There was an outer court to the west and a forework mentioned in documents is probably the – still partially standing – gatehouse at the north-west corner of the present forecourt. This gate served both the abbey

The north-west tower of Holyroodhouse c.1650
[from *Old and New Edinburgh*]

and the palace. The complex contained a treasure house and a great hall – the latter large enough for the king to practise shooting there with his culverin in winter months. It is presumed that this was one and the same as the 'great hall of the monastery of Holyrood' and had been subsequently appropriated to crown use. It seems to have stood to the south side of the abbey cloister and was probably originally the refectory of the abbey.

The other advantageous feature was the water supply. Sited as the palace was beside the monastic buildings, it could utilise or adapt the abbey's water and drainage system. The canons of Holyrood had an excellent channelled water system, taking advantage of the two streams that ran behind Canongate's two Strands that were fed into the abbey complex. Probably the water was by now too polluted for culinary and brewing purposes; and it may have been at this stage that the spring called St Anthony's Well on the north slopes of Arthur's Seat was tapped and brought to the palace. It is known that the palace complex also had a good supply of fresh water from wells.

There was further construction work later in the reign. Towards the end of 1505 a tower was erected – possibly the one later known as the south tower. Then in 1511–13 there was the building, or rebuilding, of the queen's gallery and of a stone lion house. It is possible that the south garden of the palace was formed at this time, for it is recorded that in 1507 a loch in this vicinity was drained to make garden ground. It would have been in these gardens that the king cooped his hawks, readily available for falconry in the adjacent royal park. Partridges were also reared in the garden – probably for the royal table as well as for the hawks. Copious stabling and kennelling were also needed for the other necessities of hunting and hawking – horses and dogs. The policies housed the king's growing menagerie and the outskirts of the gardens also provided space for two other pastimes – tennis and bowls.

All of these extensive and elaborate building works meant masses of materials had to be carted into the burgh. Stone was probably quarried locally but timber had to be imported, mainly from the Baltic. Glass, both coloured and plain, came from the continent, but it is not certain from where, and plaster was shipped from France. Although craftsmen came from overseas to assist with the construction and decoration of the palace, many local men and women must have been employed on the more menial and cumbersome tasks.

In spite of all the vast expense of the building works and of the sumptuous tapestries and rich materials and cushions of royal beds of state and chairs, there were also touches of simplicity. Floors were timber and did not benefit from carpeting, but rather were strewn with grasses and rushes. The records show that the sand dunes in the Dunbar and Dirleton areas were excellent grounds for the growing of grass. This was then transported to the floors of Holyrood, where it was sweetened with intermingled herbs. Even though glass was increasingly common in the sixteenth century and the king had a glazier with a workshop and house within the grounds of Holyrood, glass still remained an expensive commodity. Some windows were covered in canvas. It is interesting also to note that, although the great furniture of state was luxurious, most of those attending the court were not offered the benefit of chairs, but had to sit on forms, as in medieval homes.

The palace was to undergo major remodelling and refurbishment in the reign of James V. After James IV's death at Flodden in 1513, the duke of Albany, as governor during the first ten years of James V's minority, undertook refurbishment and maintained the fabric of the palace well. Here it was that James V was crowned in 1524 and was buried in 1542. It was in the fourteen years from 1528, when James V took full control, until his death that a major reconstruction programme was effected. The first important works were the construction of a massive rectangular tower, rounded at the corners, at the north-west corner of James IV's palace. This was to become the new royal lodging. The king's quarters were sited on the first floor, with windows decorated with painted glass roundels bearing the king's arms. The queen's accommodation was on the floor above. The tower still stands, dominating the frontage of the present palace.

Scottish oak was used, but most of the timber – pine and oak – was imported from the Low Countries and the Baltic. To supply stone, several quarries had to be worked at the same time. Nearby Salisbury Crags provided unhewn rubble; freestone and ashlar for facings and dressings came from Leith Hill, Ravelston, Stenhouse, Niddrie and Culross. Lime from Gilmerton and Cousland was mixed with sand from Leith Links to make mortar, and oyster shells were collected and used as pinnings for ashlar masonry. Masons and wrights came from Lothian and Fife, Dundee and Perth; by the summer of 1535, there were more than eighty masons and twenty wrights on site. Internally, the main rooms were lined with Baltic pine and richly panelled. The floors were of local freestone and imported tiles.

Later, the west range was replaced by a new forework, designed to hold reception rooms and the north and south quarters were remodelled, the south containing a new chapel. There was also an ambitious architectural plan to give symmetry to the frontage, by the creation of a massive tower at the south-west corner, identical to that at the north-west. This was not, however, achieved until the reign of the king's great-great grandson, Charles II (1649–85).

Other expenses included £30 for timber to construct lists for jousting in 1527. Where they were placed is uncertain, but they were probably somewhere in the palace garden. It was probably these same lists that had further work on them in preparation for the festivities at the coronation of Mary of Guise in 1540. The weather was then so wet that 200 loads of gravel had to be brought from Salisbury Crags

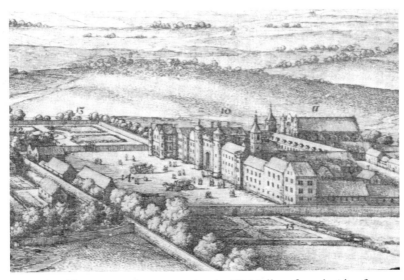

A mid seventeenth-century view by W. Hollar of south side of
Holyroodhouse [from *Old and New Edinburgh*]

'for drying of the saidis lists'. In 1537–8 a further £20 was spent on
the erection of butts for shooting practice with either the crossbow or
longbow. Two pairs of great butts and associated benches were made
and turf was transported from Liberton.

Politics and Religion Intervene

The untimely death of James V at the age of thirty on 14 December
1542, six days after the birth of his daughter Mary, heralded unrest
not only for Scotland, but also for Canongate. The king's body was
transported from Falkland Palace to Holyrood Abbey for the funeral
rites. Some forty years later, Bishop John Lesley would recount, with
the knowledge of hindsight, that the king might prophetically have
mused that 'Scotland suld be aflicted with the Inglishmen shortlie,
and sourlie'.[5] The young queen was to become a pawn in the political
and dynastic ambitions of Henry VIII of England (1509–47), in his
'rough wooing' of this child on behalf of his son Edward. Scotland was,

The English spy, Richard Lee's view of Canongate from Calton Hill, 1544. The troops may be seen in formation awaiting attack of the Watergate, before moving up the High Street with the intention of taking Edinburgh Castle.

indeed, 'sourlie' afflicted. In May 1544 a report on the expedition to Scotland by Edward Seymour, earl of Hertford, gives a flavour of the impact of national events on the capital: for three days 'neyther within the wawles, nor in the suburbs was lefte any one house unbrent . . . Also we brent the Abbey called Holy Rode, and the Pallice adjoynyge to the same'.[6]

This laconic understatement conceals a mass of misery and destruction for Canongate. Although Edinburgh Castle was the principal target, English intelligence determined that the weakest defensive point of the capital was from Calton Hill via the Watergate and then up Canongate High Street to the Netherbow and into Edinburgh. This route avoided the assault of cannon that would have greeted a more direct offensive on the castle. A contemporary plan, executed by Richard Lee, builder, architect and surveyor, who was knighted for his services in this campaign, or one of his staff, shows the massed ranks of Hertford's men assembled on Calton Hill, with one section already in the process of forcing an entry through the Watergate on 4 May. The troops then advanced up Canongate High Street, described in a contemporary account of the expedition as 'a brode strete', towards the Netherbow Port. The port proved impregnable; and troops returned the following day to wreak further incalculable damage on the lives and homes of the people of Canongate and the south side of Edinburgh, to pillage and to spoil.

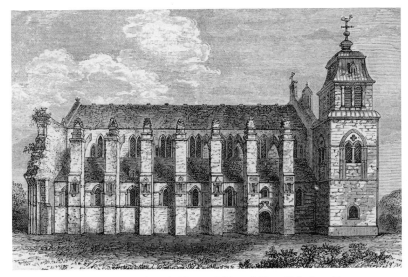

The Abbey Church [from *Old and New Edinburgh*]

The abbey was desecrated,[7] the lectern being carted off with other booty, and the palace was sacked, the one section that withstood fire being James V's new tower. The great hall of the Dominican friary, sited to the south-west of Canongate, was destroyed. Other smaller, but important, features of the townscape suffered. A great part of the Edinburgh leper house, possibly used by the Canongate populace, was laid waste by the English troops. Property belonging to the hospital of St Thomas – the tenement in Bell's Wynd, from which the seven almsmen received annual rents and the manses and chambers associated with the hospital – was destroyed.[8] The hospital itself, however, survived not only Hertford's attacks, but also the Reformation.[9] Hertford predicted ten days later that the destruction was such that 'the enemy shall neither recover these damages while we live, nor assemble any power this year in these parts, whatsoever aid come to them'.

Three years later, as duke of Somerset and protector to the young Edward VI (1547–53), Hertford defeated the Scottish army, under James Hamilton, earl of Arran, near Musselburgh, at the Battle of Pinkie. Leith was occupied; Edinburgh and Canongate awaited a

The Holyrood Lectern looted by English troops
from the old parish church in 1544.

further assault. The English leader, however, chose to turn south via
Soutra, avoiding the stronghold of Edinburgh Castle. William Patten,
a Londoner who was present with the English troops, recounted in his
diary, however, that Holyrood was not unscathed:

> Thear stode southwestward about a quarter of a mile from our campe,
> monasterie, thei call it Holly roode abbey. Sir William Bonham and
> Edward Chamberlayne gat lycence to suppresse it; whearupon these
> commissioners makyng first theyr visitation thear, they found the
> moonks all gone; but the church and mooch parte of ye house well
> couered with leade. Soon after, thei pluct of the leade and had doun
> the bels (which wear but ii), and accordyng to ye statute did somewhat
> hearby disgrace ye hous.[10]

As recorded some three hundred years later, lead from the roofs and bells 'that had frequently summoned to the exercises of devotion, were now removed by sacrilegious hands'.[11] The commendator of Holyrood at the time was Robert Stewart. He would join the Protestant Lords of the Congregation in 1559, which may have offered some protection to both the abbey and the abbot's burgh in the confusing years that were to follow the Reformation of 1560, but it probably also cast a good deal of ambiguity over the future of both.

The records of the burgh of Canongate confirm that properties that had once existed close beside the abbey had become derelict. In 1569 the bailies and council, with the advice of the minister John Brand, confirmed a charter of feuferme of 'certane waist houssis and landis callit of auld the Brewhous with ane croft of land lyand contigue thairto . . . on the south syd of the Abbay of Halierudhous'.[12] What the records do not clarify is whether these properties had become waste when fired in Hertford's raid of 1544 or, later, during the civil war of 1568 to 1573. What is clear is that Canongate burgh may have gained in prestige by the presence of royalty, but it was also to suffer from its proximity to Edinburgh, the capital of Scotland.

Further damage was done to the ecclesiastical fabric of the town, either in the name of religion or from neglect. As early as December 1520, Edinburgh town council granted a site at Greenside, north-west of Canongate, and the keys to the Rood Chapel there to the Carmelite friars of Queensferry, possibly with the purpose of caring for a leper colony in the area. They did not actually take possession for another five years; but their presence was not welcome to the monks of Holyrood. Whether this was because it was felt to impinge on the Holyrood rights in the barony of Broughton, or on the Carmelites' proximity to the important routeways to the Canon Mills and the port at Leith, the documents do not make clear. Friction became so bad that it resulted in the 'downcasting' of the house where the friars lived in March 1530.[13] The buildings were sufficiently adequately repaired, however, for them to be used as a leper hospital from 1591 until the site was cleared between 1652 and 1656.

A number of religious establishments in Canongate were affected in the Reformation crisis of 1559–60. In August 1560, parliament adopted a reformed confession of faith, rejected papal authority and outlawed the mass.[14] But, typical of the lukewarm conversion to Protestantism at the outset, even in the capital, was the selective damage to the religious fabric. Only a mile away from Canongate was Restalrig, a royal chapel, which was systematically dismantled. Within the burgh, however, initial damage was minimal.

The hospital of St Leonard stood to the south-west of the burgh. John Robesone, notary public, recorded on 17 March 1555, that on 1 January John Stewart had been admitted as a bedesman to the hospital.[15] He was allocated a place in the vestibule of the chapel, where he might put his bed and provisions, and a garden. This suggests that the chapel and the hospital were connected and that each bedesman had his own part of the two crofts of the chapel to tend. It is known that the chapel and hospital continued to function for a time after the Reformation. Six bedesmen were mentioned by name in 1561, the chapel was in existence in 1570 and reference was made in a deed of 1578 to a property bounded 'by the road leading to the chapel of St Leonard'. All the evidence, thereafter, suggests slow decline and ruin but not destruction at the time of the Reformation.

Another Canongate hospital to survive the Reformation was that of St Mary and St Paul. It still functioned in 1582 when new statutes were laid down for the master and bedesmen. It was apparently rebuilt in 1619 and developed in the seventeenth century as a workhouse or house of correction, and it continued in this role until 1750. Trinity Hospital was rebuilt anew in 1578 and bought by the town council of Edinburgh in 1585.

Although the official religion of the country had changed, many traditional, medieval features of burgh life continued. Canongate had a grammar school and a song school, run by the church, from the Middle Ages. The grammar school was probably sited close to the abbey, due to their close links. A reference to 'the school master', Master Hary Henryson, in 1529 might imply that there was then only one school functioning,[16] but it is possible that the person in charge of the song school did not merit the title of 'master'. In 1554 Master Robert Dormond was appointed to the post of master of the grammar school. In the 1568 ratification of his appointment it was specifically stated that he was still entitled to hold the school wherever he wanted in the burgh, although in 1606 the grammar school was specifically referred to as being 'beside the abbey', so it may not have moved from its medieval site. There were, however, other schools by now in existence, as in March 1565 the kirk session minuted that all masters of schools in the parish should convene.

For a short time in the summer of 1559, during the truce drawn up between Mary of Guise and the Protestant Lords of the Congregation, the Catholic mass continued to be said in the parish church of Canongate, while John Knox performed the new Protestant rite in St Giles' Church in Edinburgh. The return of the young Queen Mary (1542–67) from France in August 1561 encapsulated the religious problems facing both Canongate and Edinburgh. On the first Sunday after her return, the queen attended mass in her chapel of Holyrood; this was challenged the following Sunday with John Knox preaching at St Giles that one mass was more dangerous than a thousand armed enemies landing in the kingdom. Throughout Mary's personal reign (1561–7), the ambiguities of a realm which had a Catholic queen and a largely Catholic household but had also officially adopted Protestantism were closely mirrored within Canongate. The queen's private chapel within the palace became a haven for those disaffected from the infant Protestant church; and Canongate found itself in the odd situation of having a Protestant parish church next door to the only legal Catholic chapel in Scotland. Even legally, there were inconsistencies and lacunae: the Reformation parliament of 1560 had banned the mass, but not all seven Roman sacraments. Canongate, initially, became noted for a less zealous opposition to Catholics than its neighbour, Edinburgh. A number of Edinburgh burgesses and their wives took advantage of the absence of the queen to attend the mass in her chapel. If the Protestant Canongate kirk session proved difficult at times, those with the right credentials found protection within the households of significant members of the court or central administration.

Many people were, in time, prepared to conform to the new regime. There were 1,000 communicants in early 1564 and a further 200 two years later.[17] This, from a population that probably numbered between 2,000 and 3,000, including children not eligible to take communion, seems to indicate strong support for the Protestant order and may well also be a comment on the forcefulness of the Protestant minister, John Brand. Quite how much the ordinary, mainly illiterate, townspeople of Canongate understood the political and religious implications of the Reformation crisis is dubious and not documented. But much continued as it always had done. The same church building continued to function as their spiritual focus, although stripped of some of its altars and symbolic trappings. Queen Mary had the proclamation of her marriage to Henry Stewart, Lord Darnley, made by John Brand although her marriage took place in the chapel of Holyrood according to the Catholic rite. The following year, 1566, she attended the marriage of James Hepburn, fourth Earl Bothwell, in Canongate Church, according to the Protestant rite.

The celebrations at Holyrood of Candlemas 1566 (2 February) marked an attempt by Mary, which coincided with the formal investiture of Darnley into the French chivalric order of St Michel, to attract her Catholic nobility back to open celebration of the mass at court. The effect was explosive. Darnley and his drunken associates swaggered up the High Street of Canongate into Edinburgh, boasting that he had returned Scotland to the mass. But a month later, he was part of the gang of Protestant assassins who murdered the queen's Savoyard servant, David Rizzio, within the precincts of the palace. On the same night, John Black, the Dominican friar who had said mass in Canongate's parish church in 1559, was murdered by an armed Protestant gang. At Easter, some weeks after Rizzio's murder, it was reported that 9,000 Catholics attended the mass at Holyrood.[18] And at Easter the following year, Mary's own Spanish confessor claimed that Catholic worshippers exceeded 12,000. But this more open celebration of the mass by Catholics coincided with a slippage in the queen's own political position.

The mysterious death of Darnley at Kirk o' Field in February 1567 brought about a political crisis, which was exacerbated by Mary's marriage to Bothwell on 15 May. When the queen married Bothwell, Brand refused to publish the banns, a courageous move as Edinburgh was in the hands of Bothwell's supporters, but, even so, it was according to Protestant rites that the marriage took place on 15 May. Within a matter of a month, Mary had been confronted by the Confederate Lords, a formidable coalition of nobles, at Carberry, near Musselburgh. Bothwell was forced into exile and the queen was imprisoned on the island fortress of Lochleven. In July, she was forced to sign a deed of deposition in favour of her son. Just days after her imprisonment on Lochleven, the earl of Glencairn broke into the royal chapel and destroyed all its Catholic furnishings, statues and images.[19] This 'stripping of the altars' at Holyrood signalled the end of both Mary's reign and the possibility of a Catholic counter-reformation. With her escape from Lochleven in May 1568, subsequent defeat at Langside and ultimate enforced nineteen-year stay in England, the focus for Catholicism in Scotland was now lost. Canongate was no longer a Catholic haven.

Civil war raged in Scotland from 1568. By 1571, Edinburgh was its cockpit. Canongate inevitably was drawn in. The queen's men held Edinburgh, with a council and a kirk session, and the king's men, the young prince's supporters declaring him James VI (1567–1625), were based in Leith, with a rival council and kirk session. Dual government even extended to the holding of two parliaments. The Marian party convened a parliament in the Edinburgh tolbooth on 14 and 16 May. In response, the king's men held a parliament in the house of a William Cocker, geographically within Canongate, being to the east of the Netherbow Port, but technically within the precincts of Edinburgh (see Chapter 3),[20]

> at a place called St Johnis Croce; and fearing that soldiers of the town would disturb them thay forteifed two places, the ane at the 'Dowe Crayg' [later occupied by Calton jail] the other at a house belonging to Lawson in Leith Wynd; and there shot in violentlie at the east port and slew soldiers and inhabitants; which lasted all the time of that parliament, which was called the 'croping parliament'. After this those of the town sortit and burnt divers houses near the town walls where their enemies resortit.[21]

This 'creeping parliament', which lasted less than fifteen minutes, was little more than a brave show although it did enact mass forfeitures on Marian supporters in that time. In fact, 'Ther wes maney forfaulted at both ye Parliaments'.[22] Edinburgh's defences were now so strong that cannon and gun fire from Canongate could have little impact. But, in its turn, cannon fire from the castle bombarded the smaller burgh. It was claimed by some that the damage caused by both sides was even greater than that inflicted during the 'rough wooing'. The townspeople of Canongate with homes near the Netherbow Port paid harshly for the symbolic gesture of the creeping parliament.

The king's men, being stationed at Leith, were able to control both exports and imports and, consequently, prices. In this war of attrition, many mills and granaries, including those of Canongate, were burned.

Edinburgh was taken by the king's party in 1572, but it was only with the final fall of Edinburgh Castle in May 1573 that the young king's men gained control and some semblance of peace descended on the two neighbouring burghs.

The Transformation of Holyroodhouse

Queen Mary's short and troubled active reign allowed little time for building operations at Holyrood. Repair after the English attacks, and alterations and embellishment of the palace had been made in 1554 when the Queen Regent, Mary of Guise, restored Holyrood. The building works encompassed not only prestigious accommodation for royalty and its entourage, but also gardens and courtyards and the more mundane essentials such as stables, workshops and storerooms for hay for the royal carthorse. But there was to be a far greater investment in the palace, especially after the young king, James VI, took up near-permanent residence there in 1579.

A close analysis of sixteenth-century maps and illustrations gives very firm clues that a radical transformation, not only of the palace but also of the townscape, was in process at this time. The information they offer needs to be compared with seventeenth-century plans

Richard Lee's view of the east end of Canongate

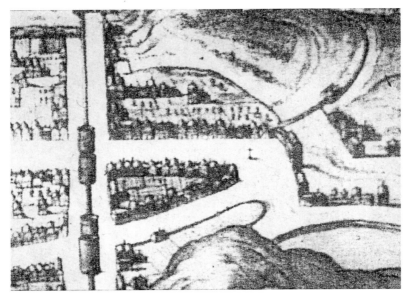

Braun and Hogenberg's stylised view of the Canongate *c.*1582

and views of Canongate. Reinforced with documentary evidence, it becomes clear that a major realignment of the east end of the burgh was in process in the latter part of the sixteenth century.

The 1544 view drawn from Calton Hill by the English agent, Richard Lee, is considered to be a relatively accurate portrayal of Canongate and Edinburgh, although certain small elements are stylised, produced as it was to delineate the best route for the English attack on Edinburgh Castle. Known buildings and topographical features of sixteenth-century Canongate are delineated. The Watergate is clearly noted, being as it was the main entrance into the burgh and the route the English troops used in 1544 to enter Canongate before passing up the High Street to the Netherbow Port. Holyrood Palace, the parish church, the girth cross and properties close to and associated with the abbey and palace appear accurately, as do the Salisbury Crags and even the routeways passing at their foot. Importantly, the plan suggests a distinct lack of development to the rear of properties at the east end of the burgh, both to the north and the south, and a definite narrowing of the building plan.

It is important to compare this plan with an English military engineer's drawing of the two towns – Canongate and Edinburgh – in 1573. This particular map has been proven to be very exact in features depicted in and around Edinburgh, such as the dry dock at Newhaven, used for the building of James IV's warship, the 'great' *Michael*, and it is not unreasonable to accept its accuracy for Canongate. This view is from the south and, because of this different perspective, the alignment of the routeway leading to Watergate in relationship to the High Street and other physical features may be viewed from another angle. The narrowing of the built extent of the burgh is portrayed again, as in 1544, at the east end of the burgh. This shortening of the length of the burgage plots at this east end was a relic of the town's geography, hemmed in as it was by the two water routes. The overall impression is one of a burgh that still retained many of the characteristics of an 'organic' settlement, which faithfully respected the geology and natural attributes of the site.

What is significant is that, delineated as it is from a different perspective, this 1573 drawing shows no building to the south of the Water Yett and girth cross. The line of sanctuary had from medieval times run through the Watergate, via the girth cross, and southwards into the 'King's meadows'. This lack of building south of the cross also supports the general accuracy of this drawing. What appears more clearly than in the 1544 plan is the siting of the girth cross in relationship to the west wall of the abbey and palace. The precinct wall is clearly delineated on the map, running north–south, beside the girth cross.

The 1573 view of the girth cross standing in isolation might seem to be supported by Braun and Hogenberg's map of 1582, but a number of other features on this plan are recognisably incorrect. The map is highly stylised, as are many of their town plans of Europe and, in consequence, little faith should be placed in it for these purposes. Nevertheless, the sixteenth-century cartographic evidence does, in general, support the theory that, well into the second half of the sixteenth century, development was marginal at the east end of Canongate; the girth cross probably stood in isolation and the precinct wall stood immediately to the east of the cross and the small routeway, the line of sanctuary, that gave access to the 'King's meadows'.

Cartographic evidence of the following century shows a totally

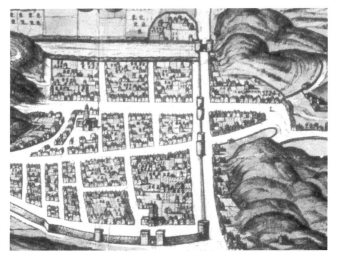

Braun and Hogenberg 1582 view of Canongate and Edinburgh

new picture. Gordon of Rothiemay's plan of Edinburgh of *c*.1647 has long been acknowledged as a highly accurate representation of site and boundaries. According to this plan, the girth cross, as would be expected, still stood in its traditional position, to the south of the Watergate. These are the only two urban features at the east end of Canongate that bear any relationship to the sixteenth-century topography. Most strikingly, the palace walls no longer lie immediately to the side of the girth cross. They are significantly distant. If compared with the sixteenth-century cartographic evidence and supporting documentary information, it can only be concluded that the medieval wall surrounding the abbey had been removed and replaced with another further east. Furthermore, the girth cross is now surrounded by properties with developed backlands and formally laid-out gardens. A radical reconstruction of the east end of Canongate had taken place. What is also highly telling is that Rothiemay's map retains, embedded, one further sixteenth-century feature – the imprint of the previous sanctuary precinct. Following a line through the Watergate and the girth cross, the delineating marker, the precinct line, may still be traced moving south through the seventeenth-century burgage plots, before skirting closely to the west wall of the erstwhile monastic gardens south of the Strand.

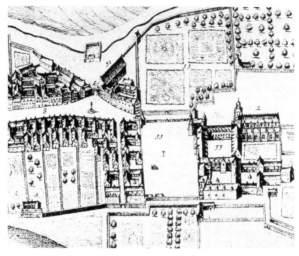

Gordon of Rothiemay's plan of Canongate, *c.*1647

There is no evidence of extensive building works at Holyrood Palace in the early seventeenth century, with the king largely resident in England from 1603; so it seems safe to assume that this transformation of the townscape took place in the sixteenth century, either during the minority of James VI or, more likely, in his personal reign some time after 1579. After the Reformation and the passing of religious houses, including Holyrood Abbey, into secular hands, King James and his agents were in a position to redefine Holyroodhouse and its associated lands. This secularisation of ecclesiastical property in the post-Reformation years probably served well James VI's elegant transformation of Holyroodhouse and its grounds. The Dominican friary, which stood near to the palace, had earlier in 1544 lost its great hall. The destruction of the friary itself in 1559 also brought problems for Canongate, for a regularly used royal guest house was lost. The court, as a result, had to find more accommodation in or near Holyrood itself.

A Royal Court with an Urban Precinct

Whether the realignment of Holyroodhouse occurred during the personal reign of King James VI or earlier, it was certainly during the latter part of the sixteenth century that this site became truly prestigious. The whole area became transformed into an urban precinct of grand and commodious housing for the royal court. Rothiemay's map shows clearly the insertion of a new roadway, later to be called Horse Wynd, possibly respecting an original pre-Reformation feature, whether abbatial or royal, through the newly established, very regular, burgage plots. These were to become the nucleus of a new urban court, along with the important housing to the east of Horse Wynd. They did not look to the wynd but, rather, were mostly furnished with courtyards opening into the outer courtyard of the palace.

The king's household, alone, numbered some 350, and nearer 600 by 1600, not counting the associated menial services of such as laundry women, cleaners and general labourers. These officers included masters of the wine cellar, ale cellar, pantry, wardrobe and stables (ten of the latter), keepers of the silver vessels (six personnel), great larder and small larder, an aviary man, a coal man, the tailor of the wardrobe and the cook of the court kitchen; all were supplemented by essential back-up staff.[23] The court would be swelled well beyond such numbers when the queen, Anne of Denmark, was in residence, or when visiting ambassadors and diplomats arrived with their entourages. Increasingly, prolonged attendance at court by nobles and their retinues became expected and the norm. Accommodation had to be provided for all of these, but outside the relatively small palace itself. Rothiemay's map of 1647 and Hollar's view of much the same date, but not published until 1670, define vividly the metamorphosis.

The result was a sophisticated royal court, focused, as it had been in the past, on Holyrood, but with a neighbouring urban enclave that offered a formal burghal setting of grand and commodious housing for the court. Significantly, for the twenty-first century, the eastern end of the site of the new parliament of Scotland lay within the earlier line of the abbey precinct and walls; thus it formed part of the prestigious abbey ground which had increasingly been taking on the characteristics of a royal residence.

It was not only the establishment of this urban court that characterised the latter decades of the sixteenth century, but also the transformation of the palace of Holyroodhouse itself. The fine detail of exactly how James VI brought about this transformation is largely non-existent for the earlier part of his reign – the Master of

Works Accounts are lacking for the pre-1579 years, but those extant for the following decade reveal much activity in and around the palace. There were extensive and ongoing repairs and minor building works from the autumn of 1579 to prepare the residence of the young king. Holyroodhouse itself and its extensive gardens received much refurbishment and repair work, but other necessities were not forgotten. The royal chapel alone needed 540 feet of glass, at a cost of more than £72. The 'dansing hous' was repaired, tennis balls were purchased, a billiard table recovered and sand was laid in Abbey Close for running at the ring. Hawks and hounds were purchased, a house with windows was repaired for the kennelling of the king's hounds and stables were prepared for the hunt horses.[24] They were to benefit from even more improvements between 1600 and 1601. In 1587, a door was made for the 'lyon hous'. As well as lions, a mini-zoo at the palace held lynx, tigers and gamecocks. All had to be housed and cared for, with their own keepers.

This was merely the beginning of an on-going process that resulted in the emergence of a sumptuous palace and a prestigious urban court frequented by aristocratic retinues. It also made Canongate a desirable place to live. Unlike crowded, cramped Edinburgh, Canongate offered urban space, gardens and light, as is clearly visible on Rothiemay's map. It is significant that Taylor, the water-poet who commented so favourably on the 'fairest and goodliest' Edinburgh's High Street in 1618, also reported that the 'gentlemen's mansions and goodliest houses' in the closes of Canongate were 'much finer than the buildings in High Street'.[25] It was here that the wealthier burgesses of Edinburgh and landed people from surrounding areas would choose to purchase property and take up residence, from lord provosts of Edinburgh and the swelling ranks of the legal establishment to wealthy merchants.

Civic Ceremony: Royal Entries and Civic Processions

A royal procession route through the capital was certainly laid out by the reign of James IV, but had perhaps begun a reign earlier. There are surviving texts for only two royal entries, that of Margaret Tudor, daughter of Henry VII (1485–1509) of England, at the time of her marriage to James IV in 1503; and of Charles I in 1633. It is, however, possible also to piece together what happened in the entries of Mary, Queen of Scots in 1561; of the young James VI, aged fourteen, in 1579; and of his queen, Anne of Denmark, in 1590. The difference between civic and royal ceremony was that the latter used both towns as its route. And the topography of Edinburgh and Canongate dominated all such performances. Although the royal court had used the residence next to the abbey of Holyrood as a 'palace' since the reign of James IV, it settled in near-permanent residence there for the first time from 1579 onwards. Urban theatre, as a result, did not end at the Netherbow Port, but extended into Canongate, which mounted its own pageants.

The overwhelming impression is one of grandeur, wealth and display. Formal entries of the monarch or his spouse into Edinburgh and Canongate reached the heights of splendour, magnificence and symbolism during the reign of James VI. It was Renaissance convention that the formal entry of a monarch, particularly to the capital, should be full of symbolism and display – of the splendour of the monarch and the obedience and love of the subjects. Margaret Tudor on her arrival in Edinburgh in 1503, for her marriage to James IV, set the tone of magnificence, to be emulated by Mary of Guise, Mary, Queen of Scots and James VI. Further undertones were at play with the extraordinary entry of Mary, Queen of Scots in 1561. The spectacular cost considerable sums. According to the *Treasurer's Accounts*, £334 14s 3d was spent on gowns for the queen and her ladies in waiting and trappings for their horses. By contrast, according to Edinburgh council records, the council expended the vast sum of 4,000 merks (£2,666 13s 4d) and doubtless Canongate contributed also. The queen was of the Catholic faith; some of her important subjects were no longer so. One of the significant gifts presented to the new queen was two books, a Bible and a psalter – a double insult, not only Protestant but English. More audacity was to follow – speeches were made on the abolition of the mass and effigies were burned (that representing a priest was avoided on the insistence of the earl of Huntly). The Edinburgh town council had taken the opportunity to press their political and religious propaganda into the customary displays of a Renaissance triumph. Canongate went even further: close to the palace the young queen was confronted with the tale of the three Israelites who defied the Law of Moses and were consumed by fire for their sins.

Mary's son, James VI, made his 'joyous entry' in to his capital on

Hollar's view of Canongate from the
Netherbow Port to east of the tolbooth

19 October 1579. But he had arrived at Holyroodhouse earlier, on 30
September, in preparation for a meeting of parliament on 23 October.
While waiting, the days were filled with feasting and festivities. Some
3,000 'nobility and gentlemen', eleven earls, thirteen prestigious
nobles, seventeen commendators and representatives of thirty-three
burghs assembled in the capital. The entry was the highlight. Many
of the conventional themes and imagery were portrayed – the canopy
of purple velvet, symbolising divinity; the judgement of Solomon
between the two mothers; the presentation of the town's keys by a
young cupid; four young maidens representing Peace, Justice, Plenty
and Policy – along with sermons on the duties of kings and singing

of psalms. A further station saw one final tableau – at the market cross of Canongate – where, perhaps as a none too subtle reminder of his mother's entry, the young king witnessed the abolition of the pope and the mass. The coronation of his bride, Anne, took place at Holyrood Abbey on 17 May 1590. She too was welcomed to the capital with a splendid entry. The supremacy of the monarchy was displayed to all – whether rich or poor.

Sumptuous display was an important part of ceremony. When parliament was held at Edinburgh it was preceded by the 'Riding of parliament'. The ceremony was redefined by James VI in 1587. The whole event was a great spectacle, protected by temporary railings and ropes. The route was even sanded for the benefit of the horses. Riding began with assembly in the forecourt of Holyroodhouse. Led by the king's commissioner, the procession was ranked in order of importance of the three estates, the purpose being to escort the monarch (or his representative, the commissioner, and the Honours) from the palace to the Edinburgh tolbooth where parliament met. This sumptuous riding of parliament was to continue until James VI and his court left for England in 1603; and the riding itself was to survive throughout parliament's life, the last occasion being in 1702.

The two neighbouring towns shared these prestigious spectaculars. They were, through their close association with royalty, unquestionably the twin capital of the realm. Royal government was mostly conducted in Edinburgh. But it was in Canongate that kings and queens made their main residence – not in Edinburgh. It was in Canongate that the elite came to stay. The small burgh was supreme as the elegant, refined choice of abode for the wealthiest and most important of the realm.

5

A CENTURY OF TURMOIL

With the Union of the Crowns, in 1603, James VI of Scotland succeeded to the throne of England. He and the whole royal court removed to London, capital of his new joint kingdom of Great Britain, as he insisted on calling it. Many Canongate people were upset at this move and considered that they had lost in status. In fact, some of the residents felt strongly enough to petition the privy council in 1629 to complain over their perceived poverty after the crown's departure.

This may not, however, have been the full truth. Although the crown and immediate court had left, Canongate was, in reality, not at all an abandoned town. The privy council itself was regularly meeting in the capital, sometimes in Edinburgh, but more often in Canongate. It is significant that, when James VI was preparing for a return visit to the capital and his palace at Holyrood in 1617, lodgings were sought in Canongate for his vast retinue as well as stabling for their horses. The bailies of Canongate replied that they were unable to offer such accommodation as 'Canongate was full of noblemen, gentlemen and officers of His Majesty's forces'. It was scarcely the response of an abandoned, poverty-stricken little burgh.

A Capital Without a King

A visitor's impression of Canongate in 1618 is also telling:

> the buildings on each side of the way [Canongate] being all squared stones five, six, and seven stories [sic] high, and many by-lanes and closes on each side of the way, wherein are gentlemen's houses, much fairer than the buildings in the High Street, for in the High Street, the merchants and tradesmen do dwell; but the gentlemen's mansions and goodliest houses are obscurely founded in the . . . lanes.

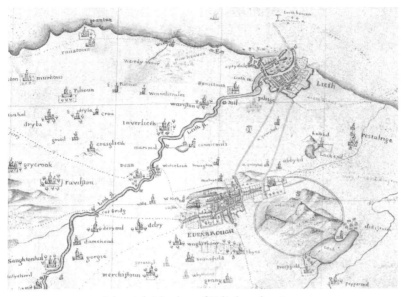

John Adair's plan of Edinburgh, 1690s

He continued to point out that so prestigious and solid were these properties that the walls were eight or ten feet (2.5 m or 3 m) thick.[1]

Such a view accords with what we know of the important noble houses that lined the Canongate. There are still standing reminders of the fine mansions that provided the town houses of the wealthy. Some tenements with High Street frontages were still bounded to the rear by orchards and gardens. Many of these, even if still possessing large gardens, might consist of several halls, chambers and vaults along the frontage to High Street.[2] While much of the evidence suggests an essentially rural atmosphere, there are also firm indications of the desirability of possessing property in Canongate and, in consequence, the development of repletion in the backlands of plots and the emergence of closes giving access to the properties to the rear of the forelands. Brodie's Close was one of the many closes that were to proliferate in Canongate in the modern period. It had its origins at least in the sixteenth century. Its earlier name was Little's Close, so named from the mansion of William Little, a future Lord Provost of Edinburgh, built c.1570. Bell's Close stood nearby and also dates to this time. Two such closes to the north of High Street were

Scott's Close and Pais' Close, named after one Pais with an unrecorded Christian name.

Inevitably, Edinburgh's role as the 'capital' of Scotland attracted aristocrats and lairds, as well as the personnel of government and those who supplied services and provisions. It was, for example, in 'my Lord Seytoun's hous in the Canegait' that the French ambassador resided as a guest in 1582. We know, also, from the details of the preparations in 1589 and 1590 for the marriage of the king with Anne of Denmark of the splendid furnishings that graced many of prestigious houses in Canongate.

Property transactions recorded in protocol books also give a clear indication of the desirability of residence in the Canongate from the previous century, at least. A 'great mansion' or 'great tenement' stood on the east side of Bell's Wynd. It was clearly highly prestigious as in 1580 it was raising an annual rent of 100 merks (£66 13s 4d) – a vast amount for the times – for Robert Pitcairn, the commendator of Dunfermline, and Ewfame Murray, Lady Rosyth, his spouse. Not only does this indicate the wealth of certain properties in the town, but also the desirability of investment here for people who lived across the Forth. A similar sum was raised the following year for John Murray, son of the late Andrew Murray of Blackbarony. Within five years, the property had been transferred to William Napier. He was a prominent merchant and a firm supporter of the king's party during the fighting between the young king's supporters and those of Mary, Queen of Scots. He had sufficient wealth to lend £1,000 to the king's cause. His investment in this tenement brought him an annual rent of £40.[3]

Thomas Marjoribanks of Ratho, a senator of the college of justice, also had interests in a dwelling house in the same wynd in 1581. A year later, it is recorded that William McCartnay, writer to the signet, and Marjorie Rolland his wife had a lodging within the back part of a tenement of St Thomas' Hospital in Bell's Wynd. A near neighbour in 1582 was Robert Chalmer, the fifth son of Alexander Chalmer, a burgess. He occupied the mid-lodging of Mr Alex Chalmers, vicar of the parish church of Liberton, within a tenement belonging to the Hospital of St Thomas, at the head of Bell's Wynd. David Crychtoun, the vicar of Auchtertool, had two chambers on the west side of the turnpike staircase of this tenement, now called the 'great tenement'.

Andrew Ferguson, a baker, and Margaret Haliburton, his spouse, had a booth in the same tenement.[4]

It is clear that Edinburgh merchants and tradesmen of some financial standing also had interests in Bell's Wynd. One such was Robert Smyth and his wife Katherine Norvell, the sister of the poet Robert Norvell, a close companion of John Knox. Smyth was assessed at £6 13s 4d tax in 1583. The average assessment was a mere 33s 4d. That a good return might be raised from rentals in Bell's Wynd can be seen by the case of Alexander Owsteane, an important Edinburgh tailor, who was deacon of his craft from 1580 to 1582 and a member of the Edinburgh town council from 1580 to 1581 and 1583 to 1584, and Jonet Anderson, his spouse. They received an annual rent of 25 merks in 1582 out of the lands in Bell's Wynd, once owned by the late Thomas Craig, a prominent lawyer and senator of the college of justice and cousin of Edinburgh's second minister, John Craig. Within a very short space of time, Owsteane was also in receipt of an annual rent from the lands of Robert Craig, on his resignation, also in Bell's Wynd. By the time Owsteane's wife died in 1602, she left £12,047; and two years later, on his own death his own estate was worth £9,152. This amount was approximately three times the norm for élite tailors; it shows a staggering rise in income for a man who was a relatively minor tailor at the time of the Reformation in 1560.[5]

Bell's Wynd was highly desirable because it was close to Holyrood Palace. But, equally, many other wynds were too, and the interest in property in Bell's Wynd was merely a cameo of what was happening in other parts of Canongate. Mr John Leirmonthe, the Edinburgh advocate, lived at the head of St Mary's Wynd. William Stewart, junior, the depute clerk of Edinburgh and son of the poet, and Jonet Neilsoun, his spouse, received an annual rent of 30s 4d from land on the south side of the High Street in 1580. John Owsteane and William Cokky, the prominent goldsmith, had interests in property on the High Street, as did Adam Fullertoun, a merchant and leading Protestant. Two years later, in 1584, also holding a tenement on the High Street was Mr Michael Chisholme, a very important member of Edinburgh society, who had been forfeited for treason by the queen's party for attending the king's 'creeping' parliament and had acted as a bailie in the King's party council exiled at Leith. He was sufficiently wealthy that, according to the *Treasurer's Accounts*, his was the largest loan to the king's party of any Edinburgh burgess. Another extremely prominent Edinburgh merchant holding property in Canongate, in 1587, was John Main. A councillor in Edinburgh from 1579, he died in 1596 leaving the substantial sum of £5,229. James Boyd of Kippis was a further example of the interest of people of standing in Canongate property.[6]

Canongate was becoming a known resort for important and expensive properties. One example was the mansion built for William Little around 1570, in what became called Little's Close (and would later be called Brodie's Close). This close may at one time have been called Tailliefer's Close, since William Little inherited land in Tailliefer's Close from his brother, Clement. Clement Little was a distinguished lawyer and benefactor of the town college.[7] But it is possible that William Little inherited more than one property on the south side of the High Street, coming as he did from such a distinguished, establishment family. He was also a cousin of the wealthy William Napier who financed King James's cause. Little himself reached the town council as early as 1567, immediately on being granted burgess-ship and guildry, and had a long career in civic office, culminating in his term as Lord Provost of Edinburgh. His position, and that of his family, in society is a good indication of the quality of this house and the desirability of Edinburgh establishment people to own property in Canongate. Little's house survived until 1836.

Many, naturally, settled near the palace not merely for social reasons, but to benefit their own livelihoods. Bakers, butchers, tailors, goldsmiths and many other crafts could find a ready outlet for their skills. It is not surprising to meet in the records less prolific crafts, such as Ninian Myllar, an embroiderer, and his spouse and Mr Gilbert Moncrief, the physician, or mediciner, to the king who had property on the High Street.[8] This intermingling of the extremely wealthy and those of more humble professions had long been a feature of life in Canongate.

The cordiners possessed a number of properties in the town; and it is clear from the rentals received, in 1647, that they varied from dwelling houses, some with lofts and cellars, to industrial premises, brewhouses, stables and yards.[9] One of their properties, which consisted of three tenements on the north side of Canongate, gave its name to Shoemakers' Close and Dark Shoemakers' Close. The

The Bible Land

eastmost property, built in 1677, was known as the Bible Land from the Bible carved below the insignia of the cordiners' craft. The insignia may still be seen on the renovated property in Canongate. In spite of owning property, until 1653, when the convening house of the cordiners was built, the annual meeting at which office-bearers were elected was still held on Calton Hill on Beltane Day (usually 1st May) or, if this fell on a Sunday, on 2 or 3 May. Other meetings took place in the Abbey Kirk, Canongate tolbooth or on MacNeill's Craigs (Calton Hill).

Another craft to see the potential for investment in property was the hammermen craft. Just as the cordiners, they met in the open air on MacNeill's Crags, or in Trinity College Church, the Abbey Church or Canongate tolbooth. On 23 September 1647, they, too,

The medieval market (SUAT)

A Residenter in an Ancient Burgh on his Way to procure a Burgess Ticket.

Sinclair. Lithograph, Edin.[r]

'A residenter on his way to procure a burgess ticket'. Even an ass might become a burgess, such was the disrepute of the freedom of the burgh, by the eighteenth to nineteenth centuries. (Royal Commission for Ancient and Historical Monuments of Scotland)

A typical backlands scene in the 13th/14th century, evidence from Aberdeen excavations. (Aberdeen Art Gallery and Museums Collections)

The horrors of the plague (Koninkjijk Museum voor Schone Kunsten, Antwerp, Belgium

Bell's Plan of the Regality of Canongate, 1813 (The Trustees of the National Library of Scotland)

'Superiority of the church being claimed'. The new parish church could not accommodate all. By 1692 only those with communion tickets and 'pensions of known quality' were permitted entrance. This lampoon shows the outrage of the ordinary parishioner. (Royal Commission for Ancient and Historical Monuments of Scotland)

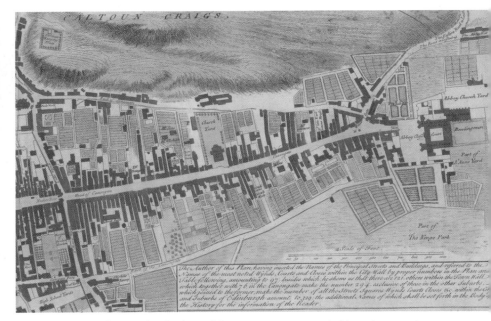

William Edgar's plan of Canongate, 1742, copied in colour, 1765
(The Trustees of the National Library of Scotland)

Aerial view of the parliament site (Royal Commission
for Ancient and Historical Monuments of Scotland)

Huntly House [from *Old and New Edinburgh*]

purchased property for letting out rather than for their own use. The following year, a decision was taken to make part of this property into a meeting room. In 1671 the hammermen employed Robert Mylne to consult with their masons and wrights to enlarge the premises. The tenement was raised by two storeys, with three broad gables to the street, jettied out above the eavesline of the existing building. It is very much in this original, converted, format that it is now known as Huntly House. Nearby Bakehouse Close was formerly called Hammermen's Close, recalling the close connection of the craft with this area of Canongate.

Sir William Brereton, an English visitor in 1636, drew attention to a characteristic of Edinburgh and Canongate houses that somewhat belies their beauty and suggests that not all homes were luxuriously commodious. Commenting on the height of the stone houses lining the main thoroughfare, he continued that they were

> lined to the outside and faced with boards . . . towards the street [which] doth blemish it and derogate from glory and beauty; as also the want of fair glass windows, wherof few or none are to be discerned towards the street. This lining with boards, wherin are round holes shaped to the proportion of men's heads, and this encroachment into the street about two yards [1.8 m], is a mighty disgrace.[10]

The high incidence of fire in the contemporary records, such as the diary of Robert Birrel, confirms that not all properties were totally of stone. Many were still built of wood, although some had a ground floor or solum of stone. To counteract the spread of fire, the townspeople were alerted by the ringing of the common bell and the beating of the town drum.[11] An account of 1608 gives a clear impression of good quality housing surrounded by smaller dwellings, all of which had suffered from fire. It is recorded that it 'being ane maist tempestuus and stormie nicht be accident yair arrais in ye cannongait ane grite and terribill fyre Be ye quhilk yair wes ane fair ludging distroyit and brunt with sum laich [single storey] houses and mekill insicht plenissing and mechand guidis quhilkis wer within ye said ludging for ye tyme.'[12]

The investment in property by many varying classes of society and the growing evidence of closes with multiple occupation was a result not merely of economic factors, but also of significant population growth. In spite of the complaints by Canongate at the departure of the king and court, the evidence suggests that this was a growing townscape. An unusual tax based on valued rents was imposed by the Covenanting regime in 1639. Not only is this probably a fairer indicator of size and prosperity than the more usual tax rolls, it is also important as it includes six baronial burghs not usually, as yet, subject to normal tax. One of these burghs was Canongate. While the rentals can give only a rough notion of population size, it is significant that, with a valued rent of £7,533, it might be suggested that Canongate had just over 4,000 people within its bounds, placing it within the top seven burghs in size, not counting the four large burghs of Edinburgh, Aberdeen, Glasgow and Dundee. This would have meant that Canongate was more populous than Ayr and Stirling; but, in truth, this was probably more a reflection of the high standard of

Acheson House

housing and the rentals that could be accrued than of the population size. This was no longer an insignificant town. But its constant sense of threat from its larger neighbour can perhaps also be better appreciated when Canongate's valued rent of £7,533 is compared with Edinburgh's £130,000.

Both Rothiemay's c.1647 map and Hollar's view of much the same date, while displaying clearly the closes running back from the High Street, also record that to the rears of the properties were largely open spaces, typical of the medieval backlands. These open spaces, capable of holding large gardens and orchards, were what attracted the building of several new and sumptuous dwellings.

Acheson House is a town house begun in 1633 for Sir Archibald Acheson, the Secretary of State. Its original frontage, still to be seen off

Moray House [from *Old and New Edinburgh*]

Bakehouse Close, is typical of many prestigious buildings that did not front the High Street. In fact, the present main entrance that may now be seen on the High Street was originally a side of the house and would have been invisible from the main road, being hidden by buildings on the High Street frontage. The entrance was from Bakehouse House Close via a small forecourt. The kitchen wing may still be viewed to the south of this forecourt and the entrance and rectangular stair-tower stand to the north. The pediment over the stair-tower door displays the Acheson crest of a cock standing on a trumpet, the date 1633 and Acheson's and his wife's (Margaret Hamilton) initials. Their initials may be seen again at the pedimented dormerheads, which display also their enthusiasm for the Union of the Crowns with rose and thistle finials.

Nearby stands Moray House, a further example of prestigious building after the departure of the court for London. It was built *c.*1625 by Mary, Dowager Countess of Home, who passed the property to her daughter Margaret, Countess of Moray, in 1643. The main west block was certainly built by Lady Home. With its tall gable and balcony set on massive carved corbels and Lady Home's arms on one of the strapwork pediments above the upper windows, the property appears very much as in her lifetime. The east wing to the street had been built by 1647 and Moray House in its entirety offers a fine example of seventeenth-century architecture in Canongate.

The gardener's inventory for the house in 1646 gives an interesting insight into the gardens of the wealthy in Canongate. It itemised two dozen apple trees, about sixty plum and eighty cherry trees, five apricot trees, a damson, a quince and a fig tree. Many of these trees were described as 'great', suggesting that some were quite old. Such prestigious policies throughout the town probably go far to explaining the relatively high numbers of gardeners in Canongate.

These were not the properties of an 'abandoned' burgh. Canongate may have lost its king, but not its desirability.

Worshipping according to the New Order

Canongate may now have been without a resident king, but it seemed to affect the lives of the ordinary people very little to begin with. The main preoccupations in life were still earning a living and enjoying a modicum of good fun. 'Good fun' was, however, somewhat circumscribed under the post-Reformation regime. May Games, Robin Hood celebrations and religious festivals and pageants were banned. Entertainment was to be seen to be more seemly, and not tainted with Catholicism, and the kirk sessions kept a close watch on the morality of parishioners. Even apparently petty breaches of the communal peace, such as swearing and slander, were dealt with firmly.

Of all sins, those of harlotry and adultery were the most strictly stamped upon. Culprits were to stand at the kirk door (adulterers in sackcloth and ashes) to be displayed before all attending church, and then committed to sit at the front of the church on cuckstools, facing the congregation, to listen to the ranting of the minister against them and their sins. Due contrition was to be shown by the penitent for his, or more likely her, misdemeanour and, after a suitable number of humiliating appearances, most were forgiven, unless further fault was found. The kirk session was especially vigilant about feigned repentance by using tricks such as putting snuff in the eyes to encourage weeping.

This placing of the penitent in the front of the church offers an interesting conceit on a problem faced by the post-Reformation church. It was no longer possible to display one's importance by processing in hierarchical formation in a religious festival. Other stratagems were found: rank could be displayed by where one sat in church – the allocation of seats determined a person's physical space and also social space. The well-to-do were, naturally, nearest the pulpit; the burgesses, their wives and older children a little further distant; apprentices, the poor and young children at the back and sides. The Abbey Church was undergoing a number of changes to make it more suitable as the parish church of the Canongate. In 1639 permission was given to erect seats, or lofts, for the populace. Rents for these seats in church were used, along with collections, to provide for the poor. On 20 November 1639, however, the kirk session minuted that some unscrupulous parishioners abandoned their seats just before the due payments were to be made. The session retaliated by ordering that, in future, payment would be in advance. This letting out of pews was quite lucrative. By 1649, the annual rents brought in £234 13s 4d Scots, the common yearly rent for a pew being £12 Scots. But there were those who wished to be seen to be above the ordinary parishioner and, in consequence, required more prominent and better seating. The earl of Lauderdale paid £13, the Laird of Scotscraig £20, while the earl of Angus parted with £26 13s 4d a year for his pew.

The incorporated crafts were also conscious of their status. In 1641 a deputation of Canongate hammermen appealed to the kirk session for space for new seats for their craft between the two pillars at the east end of what had once been the king's position of state. Two years later, a confirmation was given by the bailies and the council of the permission granted by the kirk session for a 'high loft' between the pillars east of the pulpit pillar, in addition to the low seat already possessed by the craft. This immediately prompted the tailors and weavers to ask for, and obtain, similar concessions. Although in a much changed format, with no altars to maintain nor religious pageants to take part in, the crafts were perpetuating an aspect of their pre-Reformation function – that of worshipping together and, in particular, offering spiritual and moral support at the funerals of their brother craftsmen, their wives, children or apprentices. Each craft was, thus, allocated lofts, where they might sit as a body and display their solidarity and rank. The best and most desirable lofts were those nearest the minister; there was much elbowing for these coveted positions. Canongate was not alone in this. After the Reformation the parish church of Dundee, St Mary's, removed altars and the trappings of Catholicism. In due course lofts were erected for the incorporated crafts. Permission was given that each craft might place a suitable homily above their loft. The baxters, or bakers, always conscious of their own importance, had emblazoned 'Bread is the Staff of Life'. Their rivals and neighbours, the fleshers, or butchers, countered with 'Man Shall not Live by Bread Alone'. There is no evidence in Canongate of similar actions to those of the Dundee craftsmen, but they would have been fully understood and approved of in Canongate.

Other pre-Reformation institutions found a new lease of life. The hospital of St Mary and St Paul was rebuilt in 1619 and it developed in the seventeenth century as a workhouse or house of correction. And on 2 February 1637 the magistrates of Edinburgh made over to the minister and kirk session of Canongate the ground annuals, pittances and pittance silver due from properties, including possibly some that had been mortified to St Leonard's chapel and hospital, for pious uses. In exchange, the minister and session undertook to pay 300 merks (£200) of salary to Mr Alexander Gibson, the master of the grammar school of Canongate. St Thomas' hospital was rebuilt in 1617 and from 1634 functioned as a house for the poor of Canongate.

James VI decided to make a return visit to his homeland in 1617. Amongst the many preparations for this royal homecoming, significantly, was included the transformation of the royal chapel in the palace. The Chapel Royal had been sited in the palace at Stirling, but was relocated from there to Holyrood in 1612. In readiness for the king, the chapel was now rearranged for episcopal worship and ornamented with woodwork and imagery by craftsmen brought from England. This was part of James VI's centralising ecclesiastical policy. A common church in his unified realm was to be a major step towards a reunited Christendom. Sectional differences were to be removed and conformity was the rule. Private baptism, confirmation by bishops, private communion, kneeling at communion and observance of Holy Days were all to be practised. These were the so-called Five Articles. They had been rejected by the General Assembly in 1617, but were pushed through at the next General Assembly, in Perth, in 1618. Their successful ratification by parliament in 1621 was achieved with only a

Chapel Royal, Holyrood

small majority. It was clear that the move towards episcopacy was far from popular. The seeds for major dissension in the reign of James's son, Charles I, had already been sown.

The Canongate minister, Henry Blyth, suffered various indignities at this time. He was accused of being a 'greeter theiff' than the minister of Dunfermline, who it was claimed stole from the church's coffers and took wheat that was allocated to the poor. The session, however, deemed him innocent. He was suspended in 1619 on royal instruction for giving communion to parishioners who refused to kneel.

Charles I's coronation in the abbey church of Holyrood on 15 June 1633 was conducted amidst much splendour. Preparations had been energetic to ensure that the town was in a seemly state for the event. The Canongate bailies had been instructed by the privy council to rid the town of 'sturdie, clamarous and raling' beggars before the king's arrival. Their response was that, while eager to comply, it would be a difficult task unless Canongate's own poor were removed from the streets and, to that end, a warrant was sought so that a collection might be made from the Canongate people to provide for the poor out of sight of the king. The reaction of the poor is not documented. Another group that felt the brunt of the king's presence were ministers, accustomed by now to plain black Geneva gowns, who were ordered to wear surplices and bishops' rochets, close-fitting surplices assigned to abbots and bishops. This assertion of the royal prerogative to prescribe apparel for clergymen was resented by many. One person who benefited from the arrival of the king was the provost of Edinburgh. He was knighted at St John's Cross, the marker for the extremity of Edinburgh's territory outwith the Netherbow Port.

For the coronation, Holyrood Palace was refurbished; the Abbey Kirk was once again transformed, its east gable being given its present giant traceried window and the west gable likewise dramatically altered, with a bell-cast cupola over the north-west steeple. But it was not in the kirk, but in 'his owne chappell royall' that Charles I held his devotions and that Archbishop Laud of Canterbury preached before him on Sunday 30.

In an attempt to further his father's desire for uniformity in church worship, a new prayer book was prescribed by Charles I. The Scottish response was the National Covenant of 1638. Those who subscribed to it bound themselves to maintain the forms of religion most in accord with the will of God – the Presbyterian road; and, if necessary, by force.

Revolution

It was not merely over religious matters that Charles I, as a largely absentee ruler, clashed with his Scottish subjects. From the late sixteenth century, parliament increasingly met in Edinburgh. But Edinburgh's tolbooth was becoming too cramped for parliamentary meetings and, in 1632, with encouragement from the king, the construction of the first purpose-built parliament was started, on a section of the former St Giles' graveyard in Edinburgh. The great hall with its impressive open-timber roof is a standing reminder of the grandeur of the building, which was originally adorned with paintings, tapestries and sculpture. The allegorical figures of 'Justice' and 'Mercy', two of the adornments, still survive. The parliament building was ready for its first session in 1639 and, significantly, at this same session, parliament quite specifically opposed the king's policies. This, and the aversion of the Scots to absentee and absolute monarchy, whether in religious or lay matters, would result in civil war and, ultimately, the deposition and execution of the king in 1649.

The effect of the king's execution by what became the English Commonwealth regime had the effect of drawing together many in Scotland who had opposed each other, and also opposed the king, for religious or political reasons. It also highlighted the discrepancies between the Covenanters (supporters of the National Covenant and the Solemn League and Covenant of 1643) and their English allies: the dead king's son was proclaimed Charles II by the Scottish parliament; the monarchy was abolished by the English parliament. By June 1650 the Scottish king was in Scotland, having signed the Covenants. With banners proclaiming 'For Religion, King and Kingdome', the king's new, heavily purged, army suffered a humiliating defeat at Dunbar on 3 September, with 4,000 Scots killed and 10,000 captured. The reaction in the capital was swift – Edinburgh's council and kirk sessions fled, the kirk's ministers fleeing to the safety of the castle. By December, the English troops of Oliver Cromwell, who had assumed power in the supposed absence of a king, took the castle, which offered little resistance. On 1 January 1651 Charles II was crowned at Scone amidst pressure to abandon his kingdom south of the Forth.

Summer and early autumn were to see the *denouement*. The Battle of Inverkeithing on 20 July and the capture of Perth on 2 August persuaded the new king to make for England, only to be run down by Cromwell. The king's men suffered an overwhelming defeat at Worcester and utmost devastation was perpetrated by the forces of Cromwell's senior officer, Monck, who remained in Scotland. Many towns, particularly Dundee, suffered appalling atrocities and the king fled to France. The Wars of the Covenant were over.

Warfare, revolution and occupation had a great effect on the lives of the people. Throughout all of the seventeenth century, there were grumbles in Canongate against the authorities for the practice of quartering troops on them. During the period of the Commonwealth, and of the Protectorate of Oliver Cromwell which followed, Canongate was particularly hard hit. Its magistrates in many ways made their own lives more difficult by their refusal to acknowledge the rule of Cromwell and his officers, as the Edinburgh magistrates did.

An indication of the troublous times came in 1651, when the hammermen expressed concern over the safety of their valuables. They ordered the titles of their new house to be built up in one of the rooms; confided other papers to the deacon, with the express condition that he was not to be held responsible in the event of their loss; and placed the craft mortcloths in the custody of another member. But on 26 May 1651 it is recorded that 'thair lockit book quhairin wes all thair acts and statuts for reiding of the traid and the samyne acts and statuts being reft spoiled and all lost' the said acts were to be rewritten and bound in the old boards. The book had been 'wronged by the suldiers'. But there is little evidence of interference in the life of the craft otherwise. Freemen continued to be admitted to the craft, swearing allegiance to uphold the king and government of the realm until 1658, when they swore obedience to the supreme magistrate of the burgh.

When visiting in 1648, Cromwell resided in 'Lady Home's Lodging in the Canongate', later called Moray House. The occupants of this house, and all other residents of Canongate, would see both victor and vanquished of the Covenanting wars. On 18 May 1650, James Graham, marquis of Montrose and king's lieutenant in Scotland, had been defeated and captured at Invercarron. He was brought from Leith via the Watergate and taken up the High Street of Canongate in a cart on his way to execution at the market cross of Edinburgh. At this very time Lord Lorne, the son of his enemy, Archibald Campbell Marquis of Argyll, was in Moray House for his marriage to Lady Mary Stewart, the sister of Alexander, fifth earl of Moray. The party watched the shackled Montrose from a balcony.

After his resounding success at the Battle of Dunbar in September 1650, Cromwell returned to Moray House and wintered there from 1650 to 1651. Town life was disrupted. The kirk session minutes note that: 'There was no session kept because of the defeat of the Scottish army at Dunbar by the Inglishe army. The ministers, elders, and whole honest men in the toun being removed.' Church life came to a halt for fully a year. The homes of many of the ordinary townspeople were also requisitioned. In November 1650, John Nicoll recorded in his diary that life was disrupted because of 'the body of the Englische airmy being quarterit in Edinburgh, Cannongait, Leith, and in severall uther pairtis of Lowthiane'.[13]

The palace was used as barracks during the Cromwellian era and, as a result, was accidentally almost wholly destroyed by fire in 1659. A nearby property was of sufficient size to house a military hospital for Cromwellian troops. On occupying Edinburgh, Colonel Monck, the leader of the Commonwealth forces, quartered his sick and wounded soldiers in the barely completed Heriot's Hospital in Edinburgh. In 1658, however, the governors of the hospital persuaded Monck to remove the troops, in exchange for other premises with all conveniences for sick soldiers, upkeep of the premises, grants towards the salaries of the physician, the surgeon apothecary, the surgeon's mate and the gardener. These premises were in Canongate. Certainly, there was in the possession of Heriot's Hospital archives, in an old inventory of writs, a document setting out an agreement 'betwixt my Lady Lauderdaell and the Commissioners for the Commonwealth of England for ane house at the foot of the Canongait, called Kinloch's Land, 20 December 1652'. A postscript added that 'Heriot's Hospital was taken into possession of by Cromwell for a barracks – the governors of the hospital memorialised for it being restored to them, and in reply they were informed that if they provided another barrack, their prayer would be granted'. Hence the agreement regarding 'Kinloch's Land'. A section of Brodie's Close was called 'of old' Kinloch's Close, after Henry and John Kinloch; and the governors of Heriot's Hospital are known to have owned property here into the eighteenth century. It seems very clear that the hospital was housed in property just to the west of Horse Wynd.

Life in Seventeenth-century Canongate

In spite of revolution, warfare and occupation, a semblance of normality was maintained in the burgh. Inventories and archaeological evidence indicate an increasingly high standard of living. In 1619, for example, the widow of Robert Tailfeir, a cutler, was ordered to give to a nephew certain heirship goods. Certainly, the fact that such a dispute had arisen would suggest relative wealth; but the documentary evidence offers an interesting insight into personal possessions. They included a copper cauldron of twenty-four gallons size and brewing utensils, valued at £100, a clear indication that more than the cutler trade was being pursued; a silver piece valued at £42; a furnished feather bed, a cupboard and a long oak settle, valued at £20; twelve plates and twelve trenchers worth £24; a suit of black clothes of Scots 'seybombasie', a brown cloak of English cloth, a pair of woven worsted 'shanks' (stockings) and a Scots hat with a crape (thin, twisted silk) band, all valued at 80 merks; twelve shirts, a sword and other arms, a chest, a chair, six stools, a brass pot of two gallons and a brass candlestick, together worth £20. This inventory serves to indicate the increasingly easy lifestyle for many, not merely the aristocratic, in Canongate.

But life was not easy for everyone. Natural disasters hit Canongate. Many of the medieval diseases, both endemic and epidemic, still afflicted the populace. Plague was, as ever, greatly feared and with reason, as it continued to hit randomly throughout the sixteenth and seventeenth centuries. The summer months were, according to the contemporary diarist Robert Birrel, when it hit hardest, as for example in the heat of July 1604.[14] In 1645 there was a devastating outbreak of plague, starting in Canongate in the June, which lasted almost a year. The authorities had major problems keeping the epidemic under control and such was the lack of manpower that prisoners were set free from the tolbooth. Many suffering from the disease were put in huts and tents in the park of Holyrood. The majority of the Canongate dead were also buried there, just as the victims from Edinburgh were interred in the Meadows, rather than in the churchyards. All of the residents in Trinity Hospital succumbed and died. The Canongate school could not reopen until March 1646 and the death toll, according to the kirk session, extended to 2,000. It is possible that mortality resulted also from typhus, hunger and hardship but this was a vast proportion of a parish which probably numbered less than 4,000.

The Return of the King

The restoration of the monarchy in the person of Charles II in 1660 meant far more than the return of a king. Also restored were the privy council, the Scottish parliament and the judiciary. Politics became even more closely intermingled with religion. By the Rescissory Act of March 1661 virtually all legislation passed since 1633 was declared void: the National Covenant and the Solemn League and Covenant were renounced; the official religion was once more episcopal. Significantly, as early as 3 September 1661, a letter was sent from Covent Garden, London, to Robert Douglas, the minister of Old Greyfriars, Edinburgh, informing him of the intended move of Jesuits to a house in Canongate. Clearly, after the restoration of Episcopalianism, the Jesuits felt the religious climate sufficiently calm in Scotland that even their presence would be tolerated.[15] With the new episcopal state religion would come confusion; opposition to religion might imply opposition to government and moderate dissent was conflated with radical Covenanting views. And, perhaps most symbolically for the people of Canongate and Edinburgh, a sign that times had indeed changed was the digging up of the disarticulated body of Montrose, the removal of his head from a spike on the tolbooth of Edinburgh, which it had adorned since 1650, and a reverential process down the High Streets of Edinburgh and Canongate to a formal state funeral at Holyrood.

For many, however, the return of the monarchy must have been a time of hope – an end to occupation by troops, an end to warfare and material loss, and an end to religious dissension. With the benefit of hindsight, these were, of course, unrealistic expectations. Normality and the Stewart monarchy had returned, though not necessarily having learned from the mistakes of its fathers.

The restoration of Charles II to the thrones of Scotland and England brought renewed activity to the east end of Canongate. Charles Maitland, Lord Hatton, brother of the earl of Lauderdale, a courtier, acquired 'ground and houses' there and then employed James Smith, mason, and Alexander Eizatt, wright, who were both involved

Slezer's view of Canongate from the north

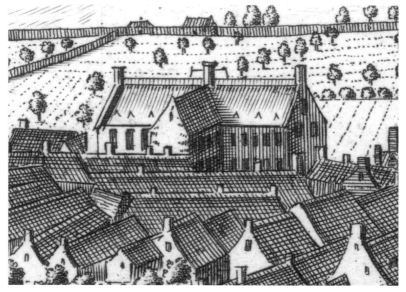

Detail from Slezer's view of Canongate, showing what appears to be a slated roof on Hatton House, surrounded by smaller properties with pantiled roofs

in refurbishments at Holyrood, to rebuild an existing house, probably incorporating earlier stone fabric, on a grand scale in 1679–81. The construction work involved a clash with the Canongate craftsmen, noted for their skills. Hatton employed country masons, who had no rights to labour in the burgh. The Canongate freemen, protesting that they would not even permit Edinburgh masons, never mind other outsiders, to work in their burgh, took their tools. The privy council deemed that Hatton could employ whom he pleased. Whether the fact that Hatton was a member of the privy council was of influence in this decision is not documented; but the craftsmen were cleared of the charge of rioting. The dwelling was completed, in spite of such setbacks, and may be seen clearly as a T-plan building on John Slezer's 'Prospect of Edinburgh from the north', drawn around 1690. Interestingly, a close-up of Slezer's view strongly suggests that Hatton House was slated, as one would expect of a prestigious dwelling, while lesser properties nearby were pantiled. It was to be largely remodelled

Queensberry House

and extended, again, in 1696–1700, to a design of James Smith, after
it passed to the first duke of Queensberry in 1686 and, subsequently,
to the second duke of Queensberry. A hint at the pretensions of the
Queensberry's may be seen in the belvedere they had constructed.
This look-out tower gave them an eye-to-eye contact with the nearby
palace. The grandeur of the building may be readily noted on Thomas
Sandby's mid eighteenth-century view of Canongate from the south.
This view, unfortunately, does not detail the gardens to the south of
the house, concealed as they are by trees. William Edgar's map of 1742
(reproduced in colour in 1765), however, gives a plan of the garden,
which may fairly reflect the lay-out established by the second duke.

When an assessment was made for a window tax in 1710–11, it
is not surprising that Queensberry House features as having thirty
windows or more, one of only fourteen such properties in Canongate.

The belvedere of Queensberry House

This compares with fifty-five such properties in the much larger burgh of Edinburgh. Canongate had twenty-two other houses liable to tax, since they had twenty windows or more, compared with Edinburgh's 147. As would be expected, given the difference in size, Edinburgh had more substantial houses than Canongate, but, significantly, Canongate had, at this time, proportionately a higher concentration of dwellings at the quality end of the market.[16]

The Hearth Tax records of 1691 give a further clue to the quality and size of properties in Canongate. Hatton's, later Queensberry House, had fifty-two hearths, compared with Moray House which had eighteen; but these were exceptional. If three 'lands' are considered, as test cases, individual dwellings were relatively commodious. In Ramsay or Reid's Land, eleven homes had an average of 3.7 hearths, one having seven (Sir John Cochrane), four having six and only three possessing single hearths. In Thomson's Land there were six dwellings. Their average number of hearths was 2.8, one having six hearths (Widow Maxwell) and two having single hearths. In Chalmer's Land ten properties averaged 2.5 hearths each, as many as five having single hearths, but one, that of Widow Gibb, having as many as eight hearths. In these three lands, 37 per cent of properties had single hearths; although the

Thomas Sandby's view of Canongate, *c*.1750. Queensberry
House appears almost as magnificent as Holyroodhouse.

percentage of single hearths for the whole of Canongate was as high
as 61.9 per cent. When compared with an annuity roll for Canongate
taken in 1687, however, it is clear that, while properties with multiple
hearths might raise the highest rentals, the rents paid for single and
two-hearth properties varied greatly, suggesting that wealthier tenants
were prepared to pay more for good- quality smaller properties than
for multi-hearthed properties of inferior quality. Although too much
should not, therefore, be inferred from hearths, when compared
with other towns the standing of Canongate becomes clearer. In
Musselburgh, for example, 72.5 per cent of properties were single
hearthed and its suburb of Fisherrow was as high as almost 78 per cent;
Stranraer had almost 64 per cent of dwellings with single hearths;
Linlithgow almost 70 per cent; Kirkcaldy 58 per cent; and Dumfries
63 per cent. Interestingly, however, when compared with two other
Edinburgh parishes, Canongate parish in the 1690s showed a higher
percentage of families without resident servants, which suggests a
lower socio-economic status for the smaller burgh.[17]

The craftsmen of Canongate continued to outnumber merchants
since the burgh by now functioned very much as a manufacturing
suburb of Edinburgh. In fact, a visitor to the capital in 1705 made
an interesting comment that Canongate was easier to navigate than
Edinburgh, as all the houses in the lower part of the town had the names
and trades of the occupants written on the doors. This preponderance
of crafts, as opposed to wealthier merchants, is reflected in the poll tax
returns of the 1690s. Fifty-three per cent of Canongate featured in the
lowest tax band, with only 4.9 per cent in the highest, indicating an
overall wealth considerably lower than central Edinburgh, but not as

poor as North or South Leith. The Canongate crafts believed that they continued to suffer from the oppression of the Edinburgh magistrates and crafts; the Edinburgh city councillors even attempted to impose a clerk of their choice on Canongate. It was also recorded, in 1677, that the Edinburgh merchants refused to annex Canongate to the royalty of Edinburgh, for fear that this might 'increase and strengthen' the Canongate trades, the Canongate craftsmen being considered superior to those of Edinburgh. Therefore 'out of a meir principle of malice [they] doe . . . hinder them from their freedome within the toune, and taxes them exorbitantly where they stay, and confiscats their work, if they apprehend it within the ports'. The Canongate bakers were probably a particular threat to those of Edinburgh, resulting in 1681 in the theft of Canongate bread; the council resolved that the Canongate bakers should have the right to trade in Edinburgh on three days of the week without harassment from the Edinburgh craft. In February 1683 the baxters of Canongate were fined £10 Scots by the magistrates of Edinburgh for importing 'bad light and insufficient bread'. On appeal, the magistrates were found to be within their rights. The brewers of Canongate, along with others from Leith, West Port, Potterow and Edinburgh also fell foul of the law.[18]

On the other hand, there developed also a fashionable interest in gardening and botany. The growing number of gardeners being entered as burgesses of Canongate attests to this. A 'medicine garden' was started in the 1660s or 1670s by Sir Robert Sibbald and Sir Andrew Balfour 'in ane enclosure forty foot of measure every way, obtained of John Brown, gardener of the north yardes in the Abbey of Holyrood'. This had a three-fold purpose: to teach the rudiments of botany; to instruct students of practitioners in medical plants; and to provide pharmacists with fresh plants. The venture was so successful that it was forced to move to larger premises and went to the garden of Trinity Hospital, where it became known as the Physic Garden. It remained there until 1766, when it was transferred to Leith Walk and was called the 'Botanical'.

The palace had suffered great damage during the Cromwellian occupation; it had been occupied by the English and seriously destroyed by fire in the 1650s[19] and plans were now set in place to bring Holyrood back to its former glory. Sir William Bruce was appointed as the architect. One of the seemingly small, but highly significant, schemes involved in this restoration of the building was that the private chapel of the king, the Chapel Royal, was to be removed and, in consequence, in 1672, the privy council decreed that the church of Canongate, the abbey church, was to be 'his majesty's chapel in all time coming'. The parish church granted to Canongate in the twelfth century was taken from the burgh.

Harsh though this may have seemed to the Canongate parishioners, suffering in the name of religion was greater in other parts of Scotland. The crudity with which episcopacy was reimposed caused about a third of the ministers in post to leave and gave rise to secret meetings in conventicles. Religious beliefs pushed many of the more radical Presbyterians into political rebellion against the perceived wickedness of episcopal government. Although the people of Canongate suffered little compared with other areas of Scotland in these times, Canongate tolbooth would see a number of prisoners incarcerated for meeting in conventicles, although in November 1685 five prisoners managed to escape from it. Many others would be martyred for their cause in these 'killing times'.

On the death of Charles II in 1685, his brother, the duke of York, became James VII of Scotland and II of England (1685–8). Signs of the times were already both openly and covertly in place. In 1681 James wrote to Lord Dartmoor from Holyroodhouse that 'I live here as cautiously as I can, and am very careful to give offence to none'. But he had already requisitioned the Long Gallery in the palace to serve as his private Catholic chapel. In December 1687 orders were given that the chapel royal, established in the nave of the Abbey Church since 1672, should be adapted to Roman Catholic worship and as a chapel of the Knights of the Order of the Thistle. The previous year, the king had also established James Watson as 'printer to our household in our ancient Kingdom' and from the Holyrood Press in a shop erected in the central court of the palace Watson and his successor Peter Bruce distributed Catholic books and pamphlets. A Jesuit college, also set up at Holyrood, offered free education to all.

This new college was probably resented by some as being in direct competition with the town college (later Edinburgh University). In reality, however, from his arrival in Holyrood in 1679 until the collapse of his personal government, royal patronage favoured not only the established college, but many other intellectual pursuits.

Canongate church

This patronage was not entirely innovatory. Many of the advances in learning he encouraged had their origins in the earlier part of the century and before; but as duke of York and as king, he responded to the demands and interests of the professional classes, in particular those of Edinburgh. New charters were prepared for both the college and the city of Edinburgh; the Royal College of Physicians, the Advocates' Library and the Order of the Thistle were established; the Royal Company of Archers and the Physic Garden were supported; and royal patronage was bestowed on varied intellectual pursuits from cartography, medicine, surgery, numismatics, mathematics and engineering to weather recording. Most of this intellectual activity was centred in Edinburgh and Canongate.

The people of Canongate, having lost their parish church and with no building in which to worship, found temporary accommodation at Lady Yester's Kirk, which was to become, in 1691, the parish church for the part of Edinburgh along the south side of Cowgate from Cowgate Port to Lady Yester's Kirk. But by 1688 the new Canongate parish church was completed, at a cost of 43,000 merks, with the great assistance of a bequest of Sir Thomas Moodie of Saughtonhall, with the proviso that all who had had the right to attend the Abbey Church of Holyrood should be certain of places in the new building. In spite of this proviso, accommodation was at times at a premium. After the Restoration, Canongate was again the hub of elite society. The kirk session and the trades met, therefore, to discuss 'the urgency of present accommodation of nobles and gentlemen now resident in the parish'. It was agreed that, for the meantime, the front two pews would be set aside for nobles and gentry. In 1692 the kirk session took the further measure of posting two elders 'to wait upon the kirk door and not to suffer any persons to enter but such as [had communion] tickets and pensions of known quality'. Lack of space, however, was to be a recurring problem into the eighteenth century. For over a year, from 1758 until 1759, the Canongate tailors were actually in legal dispute with the kirk session for depriving them of one of their pews.[20]

Other events impacted on Canongate at this time. James VII's efforts to gain toleration for Catholics and the apparent restriction of royal favour to those of this faith provided much opposition. Such was the concern that, in January 1686, rioting took place in Edinburgh at the celebration of mass in the house of Lord Chancellor Perth. The birth of James VII's son, James Francis Edward Stewart, bringing the possibility of another Roman Catholic monarch, tipped the balance against the king. Once the news of the landing in Britain of William Prince of Orange on 5 November 1688, with the intention of claiming the thrones of Scotland and England, reached Edinburgh, the Marquis of Atholl was swift to utilise the tumultuous Edinburgh rabble, with a view to removing the Catholic Lord Chancellor. In spite of the attempts by the Edinburgh provost to lock the town gates so the mob could not get out and attack the king's palace and the Catholic residents of Canongate, the mob set off for the smaller burgh. A picture of the earl of Perth was taken down from a building at the back of the Canongate weighhouse and the mob then marched down Canongate High Street, to the beat of a drum. Captain John Wallace and 120 men were defending Holyrood Palace; on refusal to disperse, the mob was fired upon, wounding many and killing a number – three or four, according to one source, approximately a dozen, according to another, thirty-six or thirty-eight according to a third. This merely inflamed matters. Holyrood Palace was taken, the Jesuits were driven out and their house plundered; the Chapel Royal was sacked and royal tombs were desecrated. After that, a contemporary letter relates, the chancellor's cellars were opened and the mob inflamed itself further with his wine. The next two or three days were then spent scouring the town, entering private houses, such as Huntly House, and plundering and harassing Roman Catholics, with the removal of rosaries, images and Catholic literature.

A New Order

In spite of the rabble-rousing in Canongate and Edinburgh, the 'revolution' of 1688 was basically peaceful. Largely instrumental in its success was the king's flight to France. Scotland declared that the king had 'forefaulted' the Scottish crown; he had broken 'the knoune lawes, statutes and freedomes of [the] realme'. [21] A monarch who ruled by divine right was replaced with joint rulers, William of Orange (1689–1702) and Mary II, whose authority was based on the power of those they governed. For Scotland, this meant a reassertion of the constitutional and political power of parliament and, almost conversely and perversely, the road to union with the English parliament. In Scotland, also, this was essentially a religious revolution. Presbyterianism finally ousted Episcopalianism.

How much the ordinary man in the street understood the political and religious changes afoot is difficult to assess. Mundane, routine matters were probably at the forefront of the mind. The kirk treasurer's accounts, for example, suggest that approximately thirty to forty-five poor received weekly financial support, as well as possibly ten or so being in receipt of monthly charity and a few individuals of one-off donations. The itinerant and begging poor would, on the other hand, not have benefited from temporary accommodation in the charity workhouse nor from regular hand-outs. Their numbers are difficult to calculate and the back alleys probably supplied homes to far more than were recorded. The poor were to be an increasingly growing problem in Canongate; these were the groups who had been most hit by the occasional, but devastating, forays of plague amongst the population and many, particularly children, were vulnerable to smallpox. But the town was relatively fortunate in the 1690s. Famine hit Scotland. It struck hardest in the north-east, however; the effects in Canongate were minimised by importation of foodstuffs via the harbour at Leith.

Overcrowding, by the poor and the wealthy, and congestion in the main street were causing problems. From 1675, in order to provide more room, the place for public execution in Canongate was moved from the High Street to Gallowlee; in July 1675 four witches from Culross were strangled here; and in 1681 six covenanters were executed at the same spot.

Attempts were made to improve the quality of house structures. In *c*.1676 it was laid down that houses were to be constructed of inflammable material, as wood and thatch posed too much of a fire risk, particularly given the increasingly close proximity of dwellings. To enforce this new ruling, a 500-merk penalty might be incurred. In 1676 the council insisted that chimneys were to be cleaned at least twice a year and this was increased to four times the following year. In 1707, it was enacted that it was 'strickly prohibited the keeping and using of privat furnaces . . . made use of in brewing distilling and melting of mettells and the like especially where the floor of these rooms . . . are laid with daills . . . without a speciall licence from the Dean of Guild'.[22] Much of the head of the Canongate burned down in 1696, including the school. Rebuilding after conflagrations did, however, give an excellent opportunity to upgrade and rebuilding and reoccupation took usually only a year or so. A fire of 1700 was exceptionally fierce, but even that damage had been repaired by 1704. The disadvantage to the residents, apart from the loss of possessions and homes, was probably the increased rents, which, of course, yet again, hit the poor.

In the seventeenth century fire was kept under control only with leather buckets of water hurled by the townspeople. Many improvements were to come in the next century. Firemen were employed and they were equipped with ladders as well as buckets and trained to a specific drill. By 1732 there were a hundred fire-fighters and the possibility of an engine that could deliver eighty pints of water a minute – a vast improvement on the seventeenth-century system.

Little is known of the feelings of the Canongate burgesses on the Union negotiations, and how far the 'pamphlet war' of late 1705 and 1706 actually influenced the Canongate mob is unclear. But for many, the influx of politicians and nobility would be of economic benefit, whether it came from sales of merchandise or paid services, legitimate or otherwise. In 1707 Moray House was occupied by Lord Chancellor Seafield, who took a prominent part in the negotiations leading to the union of the parliaments of Scotland and England, the signing of which some have argued may have been completed in the summer house of Moray House. The earl of Stair lived in Queensberry House during the negotiations; and the duke of Queensberry, himself, was Queen Anne's commissioner in Scotland.

If the true cost of the loss of parliament to Westminster crossed the minds of the man and woman in the High Street of Canongate it is not documented. This probably represented a microcosm of the state of the entire nation. Although almost all of Scotland was opposed to political union with England, bribery and corruption, and lack of political debate would secure the necessary votes to force through the agreement. Many were also acutely aware of the potential economic benefits. The burgh of Montrose was not alone in advising its representative to parliament to vote for union, for fear of losing trade. So, Scotland's capital would see its last parliament for several centuries.

6

A NEW CANONGATE?

Two of the last scenes in the slow, lingering drama marking the demise of the Stewart dynasty had Canongate as their stage. In November 1688, a mob had stormed the Palace of Holyroodhouse, ransacked the Chapel Royal and desecrated the tombs of some of the Stewart family buried in the Abbey Church. It was the beginning of the end for a dynasty which had ruled Scotland for over three centuries. The first of the major rebellions, in 1715, confined as it largely was to Scotland north of the Tay, left Canongate untouched. Thirty years later, however, the town became the headquarters of the court and tartan army of Prince Charles Edward Stuart, in the last act of the Jacobite challenge to the Union and Hanoverian Britain.

The capital surrendered almost by accident to the Young Pretender. Ironically, it was the coach which had conveyed Edinburgh's magistrates to an inconclusive meeting to negotiate a surrender which was the unwitting device that produced the city's fall. In the early morning of 17 September 1745, as the coach was allowed out of the port at the Netherbow, en route to its stable in Canongate, the gate was rushed by a force of Highlanders, who had skirted the south side of the town in silence under cover of darkness as far as St Mary's Wynd. By noon of that day, the capital was under the control of the Highland army.

The Palace of Holyroodhouse was occupied by the prince, but the Great Apartment, prepared some three-quarters of a century previously for Charles II, who never arrived, was showing the weary passage of time. So it was the old Queen's Apartments, now the residence of the palace's hereditary keeper, the duke of Hamilton, that were used by the prince. Here, for five weeks a Jacobite royal court was held 'with great magnificence', and many lavish balls for the local well-to-do.

Following the defeat of the government force under Sir John Cope at nearby Prestonpans on 20 September 1745, Canongate became a prisoner-of-war camp. Cope's officers were warded in Queensberry House, but permitted parole. His ordinary soldiers, on the other hand, were held under tight security crammed in Canongate tolbooth and church. Once autumn came, the Highland army that had been camping in the open at Duddingston was given forced quarter in Canongate, Edinburgh and surrounding areas. Many of the officers were accommodated in the White Horse Inn at the foot of Canongate. The strain of being prison, billet and field hospital for rival armies was considerable. The churches were silent on Sundays throughout the capital. Canongate's parish church could not be used, packed as it was with prisoners. The upper part of the capital, above the Lawnmarket, was an armed camp, with Highland sentries shooting on sight at any locals trying to take provisions into the government garrison in the castle. Bombardments and armed sorties from the castle, where some of Cope's force had fled, increased an acute but unreal sense of siege. Houses and shops in and around the Lawnmarket were pillaged and set on fire. Elsewhere, townspeople in both Canongate and Edinburgh suffered from incessant demands for shoes, clothing and water canteens. There were also some incidents of theft by the prince's men, though far less than the ritual plunder perpetrated by Highland auxiliaries along the roads to the south of the capital. But the five-week occupation produced a highly charged atmosphere in which fears and rumours proliferated. It was probably for this reason that the records claim that all the shops were 'closed'. This was probably an exaggeration, but closures of only a few must have made everyday living difficult. In general, it seems that the Highlanders acted with restraint. On the other hand, one of the reasons that the prince put forward for marching south was to avoid the temptations of drink and loose women which Canongate and Edinburgh offered in abundance. A winter spent amidst debauchery and a wet climate risked discipline and morale.

Prince Charles Edward left the palace on Thursday, 31 October and the whole Highland army was out of the town by the following day, en route to disaster at Derby. But there was ugliness to follow in Canongate. The government troops who had stubbornly held the castle against the Jacobite army raided the town two days later, ostensibly to search for arms. It became an excuse for pillage and the torture of Highlanders in the Infirmary. The duke of Perth's townhouse in Canongate was looted, as were those of other known supporters of the Jacobites. Holyroodhouse was also ransacked and the apartments and furnishings where the prince had lodged were plundered. Otherwise, despite the five-week trauma of occupation and the retaliation which followed, the experience of the Jacobite autumn of 1745 left little trace. In the cordiners' archives it is minuted that there was a postponement of an admission of a new member 'by reason of the late disturbances'. There was a complaint against Edinburgh's cordiners for searching hides in North Leith, which was the prerogative of the Canongate cordiners, 'during the late troblous times'. Otherwise, there is little reference to the occupation in the craft records, which rather suggests that life continued very much as normal.

The Changing Townscape

It was estimated that by 1775 there were approximately 4,500 people in Canongate. By the 1790s this figure had risen to about 6,200. Partly as a result of this and also as Canongate continued to be a desirable place to live, there was continued investment in property. But Canongate still had sufficient space for imposing large gardens and yards at the rear of many properties. Ainslie's and others' eighteenth-century maps and Bell's fine early nineteenth-century portrayal of Canongate show the townscape clearly before major change would come in the nineteenth century. Milton House was built east of Moray House in the garden of Lord Roxburgh by a nephew of Fletcher of Saltoun, Andrew Fletcher of Milton, in the first half of the century. By the nineteenth century the premises would function as a Roman Catholic School and this is now the site of Milton House Primary School. Fletcher's uncle would eventually own much of the land to the south of the Strand or South Back of Canongate, now called Holyrood Road, including the current site of Our Dynamic Earth. Lothian Hut was constructed in 1750, by William, the third marquis of Lothian. An elegant town house, described as 'finely built' and 'small but magnificently finished', it had a dining room that measured some 75 feet by 26 (22.8 m by 7.9 m).[1] It had a double access, from both Canongate High Street and Horse Wynd, and an imposing circular driveway. The records also indicate

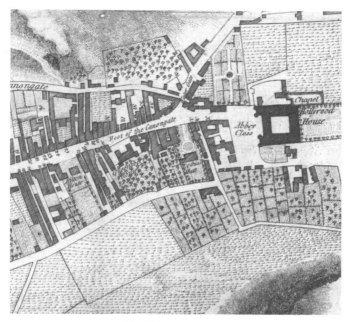

Ainslie's map, c.1780

clearly that, even after the building of their elegant town house, the
Lothians were still interested in purchasing property and made major
investments in Canongate. At the turn of the century, Lothian Hut
was the residence of Professor Dugald Stewart, one of whose most
notable students was Henry Temple, afterwards Lord Palmerston. A
further property, Lothian Vale, was added at the southern end of the
site, on the corner of Horse Wynd and Holyrood Road, with entry by
the Marquis of Lothian's Close.

   Another piece of land to be developed in this century was almost
opposite Queensberry House, the site of the town residence of the
Setons, earls of Winton. Here it was that Lord Darnley had stayed in
1564 and about eighteen years later Manzeville, the French ambassador.
This important house had by now been demolished and the land passed
through the hands of various owners, including Andrew Fletcher of
Saltoun, to John Grant, a Baron of Exhequer, who in 1766 gained
permission to build Whitefoord House. Sir John Whitefoord stayed
there for some years, before moving to the north side of St Andrew

Square. Later, for many years, until his death in 1833, it was the home of Sir William Macleod Bannatyne, who was raised to the Bench as Lord Bannatyne in 1799.

Whiteford House and Lothian Hut were evidence that Canongate still attracted wealthy residents. Much of this was due to the continuing importance of the Scottish law courts and the flowering of the 'Golden Age', when Edinburgh became, briefly, the hub of the civilised world in literature, philosophy and architecture. It was in Canongate that Robert Burns was inaugurated as the poet laureate of Canongate Kilwinning Freemasons Lodge, no 2. in 1787. This particular lodge was a favourite of the Edinburgh artists and architects of the eighteenth century. Panmure House was the residence of the economist Adam Smith from 1778 to 1790. He was visited here by Edmund Burke, the statesman and orator, in 1784 and 1785. David Hume, the philosopher, was one of the tenants in Jack's Land (Little Jack's Close) from 1753 to 1762 while writing his *History of England*. The graveyard of Canongate church itself testifies to the many 'worthies' who stayed in Canongate, including Adam Smith, Robert Fergusson, the poet, Dugald Stewart, philosopher, and 'Grecian Williams', the artist.

Although Queensberry House was flatted during the eighteenth century, it still housed people of high rank. In 1747 John Dalrymple, second earl of Stair died in the house; from 1761 to 1773 it was leased to the earl of Glasgow; and, in 1784, it was the residence of the first Scotsman to hold the office of Lord Chief Baron of Exchequer since the Union, James Montgomery of Stanhope.

An eighteenth-century house still partially standing until the late twentieth century was called Haddington House and later known as nos 8 and 10 Haddington Entry. This was reputedly built around 1700 as a town house for the earl of Haddington. It was accessed from Haddington's Entry to the east of Reid's Close, named after a brewer alive in the 1730s. Adjoining this property and possibly also forming part of it was 12 Haddington Entry, which was also later known as no. 99 Holyrood Road, built by Alexander Bredin of Rosemount, Fort Major at Edinburgh Castle. The standing remains of the property, before demolition, indicate that this was originally a quality building. In spite of this and its name, documentary evidence makes it clear that the earl of Haddington's House was not, in fact, on this site. The earl had built an elegant town house further west in Canongate opposite

St John Street

the parish church at Wilson's Court.[2] The court extended right down
to the South Back of Canongate. Here is further firm indication that
people of standing in society were still content to invest in property
and live in Canongate. When St John Street was constructed its first
residents were mainly aristocratic, and it was here that Tobias Smollett
lived in 1766. Canongate was still, in many respects, Edinburgh's
dignified and elegant social centre.

Holyroodhouse, on the other hand, became a sanctuary for debtors
and a refuge for a variety of squatters, exiles and ne'er-do-wells. It
even became the home of the exiled Comte d'Artois, brother of Louis
XVI, later to become Charles X of France. He arrived in January 1796,
three years after his brother was guillotined. A debtors' sanctuary
was considered by some to be suitable accommodation for him, as
it was believed that he was poor, because he had only one carriage.
Just how commodious a dwelling Holyroodhouse was by this time
must be doubted. The Hanoverian kings had little interest in it, so
it was permitted to fall into decay and many tenants of the property
sub-let to others. Even the debtors complained in 1753 to the duke of
Hamilton, the hereditary keeper of Holyroodhouse, that the common
sewer was stopped up, not having been cleaned since the union of the
two crowns. They argued that if it was not soon cleaned the palace

would be under effluent water. By now, Holyroodhouse resembled a crumbling doss-house rather than a royal palace.

The old palace was occupied for other purposes. In 1742, the constable of Holyroodhouse informed Canongate kirk session of the dealings of David Paterson. He was an ex-trainee minister who had fallen foul of the authorities for sexual misdemeanours and was already under the sentence of lesser excommunication. He hired a room at Holyroodhouse 'where he continued the practice to marry persons irregularly, and sometimes three or four Coupel in a Day'. The use of a room in Holyroodhouse by Paterson was a calculated flouting of the church's code of conduct.

The rise of irregular marriages, often conducted by ministers unemployed after the establishment of Presbyterianism, was one aspect of urban life that made kirk session control of the populace extremely difficult. Regular marriage entailed the reading of banns on three successive Sundays and a ceremony performed by a minister in the parish church. This very public form of marriage was designed to deter bigamy and protect women in particular.

After further dubious actions, it was deemed that 'the said David Paterson had been for many years not only a Reproach to the Ministeriall orders but had been and still continues to be a perfect Nuisance in the Town and City of Edinr and suburbs thereof while he still lurked notwithstanding of a Sentence of Banishment pronounced against him by the high Court of justiciarie'. In the twilight of his suspect career in the 1790s Paterson was in prison, from where he still continued to perform irregular marriages!

Canongate was both the home of the wealthy and reputable – noblemen, judges, generals, writers, doctors, bankers and the like – and, equally, the resort of the poorer elements of society. Property sales are a sure indication of the multiplicity of backgrounds of the people of the town, from prestigious professionals to craftsmen and the poor. Nobles, writers (lawyers), publishers, authors, poets, artists, surgeons, goldsmiths, merchants, brewers, distillers, painters, slaters, masons, wrights, baxters, tailors, candlemakers, soap boilers, coachmakers, harness makers, farriers, weavers, plumbers, blacksmiths, staymakers, letter-carriers, stablers, gardeners, seamstresses, shop keepers, beggars and prostitutes, and many others, lived in Canongate.

One wright, William Brodie, inherited a property in Horse Wynd

William Brodie

in 1782. He became the notorious deacon of the wrights. This man led a remarkable life as a pillar of society during the day and the leader of a gang of thieves at night. His downfall came while robbing the excise house, established in Chessels Buildings. This had been erected *c*.1745 as a speculative venture by Archibald Chessels to provide mansion flats for the well-to-do. Extension wings were built *c*.1765 and the building retains to this day many of its original eighteenth-century features. Brodie was ultimately executed for burglary by his own invention, an improved hanging machine, and his story is said to have inspired Robert Louis Stevenson to write *The Strange Case of Dr Jekyll and Mr Hyde*.

The presence of the wealthier classes continued to offer opportunities for the services of others, including women. Mantuamakers, who

Chessels Buildings

became called dressmakers by the end of the eighteenth century, were a new breed of women, usually from the upper and middle classes. Their production of mantuas, a woman's garment, to some extent superseded the role of tailors in making women's clothes. Miss Euphemia Elphinstone and her partner were advertising in the *Caledonian Mercury* in 1764 to the effect that they made garments without fittings, to the newest fashions from London, in their house in Canongate opposite the parish church. Louisa Cleghorn, spouse of Archibald Russell, a weaver in Canongate, worked as a sick-nurse; it was 'her business to wait upon sick persons' in 1775. Margaret Yorston, wife of James Yorston, a brewer, was functioning as a grocer in her own right in 1750, sending out bills for such commodities as candy, sugar, vinegar and whisky.

It is clear that not all properties were substantial. A complaint by David Bowie, cowfeeder, against a Mrs Straiton over the state of a thatch roof of a byre; and another by Alex Campbell, a brewer, against the widow of Hugh Cleghorn, distiller, for damage to his malt and maltbarn by the 'stopping' of the sewers, are reminders that routine life in Canongate was sometimes still very simple and rudimentary.[3] The Minute Book of Magistrates and Stent Masters for 1724 to 1742, listing monies received for poor relief, is a further small reminder that the less fortunate still rubbed shoulders with the moneyed classes.

Although, clearly, there were poorer properties in Canongate a claim in 1753 does seem to be an exaggeration. It was stated that Canongate:

> has suffered more by the union of the kingdoms than all the other parts of Scotland: for having, before that period, been the residence of the chief of the Scottish nobility, it was then in a flourishing condition; but being deserted by them, many of their houses are fallen down, and others in a ruinous condition; it is a piteous case!

Market Cross with knife grinder

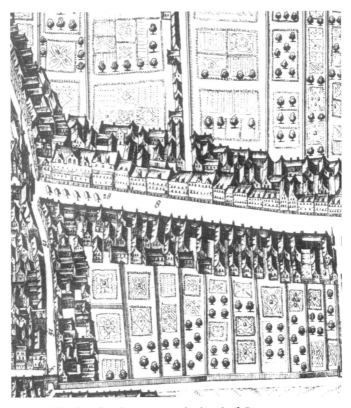

The butchers' stances at the head of Canongate,
taken from Gordon of Rothiemay's plan

Apart from the impressive dwellings that graced Canongate and
the poorer hovels that surrounded them, probably the outstanding
feature of the eighteenth-century townscape was the multiplicity
of closes that grew up in the backlands behind the street frontages.
One of the principal reasons for this was that the capital remained
very much confined to the narrow limits of the medieval burghs of
Canongate and Edinburgh, running as they did down the slim ridge
from the volcanic rock with the castle atop it. One visitor to the capital
commented that the closes were 'so very steep that it requires great
attention to the feet to prevent falling, but so well accustomed are

the Scotch to that position of the body required in descending these declivities that I have seen a Scotch girl run down them with great swiftness in pattens'.

The net result was congestion and uncomfortable accommodation for the growing professional classes, including the rapidly expanding class of lawyers who concentrated in the capital to administer criminal justice and civil jurisdiction. New streets were introduced into Canongate – New Street, for example, originally called Young Street from the house of Dr Thomas Young. It was intended initially as a private thoroughfare and remained so until 1786. Described as 'the boldest scheme of civic improvement effected in Edinburgh before the construction of North Bridge', it was designed to avoid the lack of privacy and squalor of the main street.

Being cramped into a narrow site, one solution to accommodation, as in Edinburgh, was to develop upwards. This tended to add to social stratification, with the poorer elements of society occupying attics and cellars. A further consequence of high-rise was the problem of carting water up many flights of stairs from the public wells in the street. This task was undertaken by water caddies, both men and women. All wore men's black hats and protected their backs with layers of leather, with a lip at the bottom, in the vain hope of spillage trickling sideways rather than down the legs. The water was carried in wooden casks on the back, held securely by a leather strap in front of the body. The inevitable result, a pronounced forward stoop, marked out the tribe of water caddies even when they were not carrying, so bent had their backs become. It would not be until into the nineteenth century, when the small reservoir on the north side of the Pentland Hills was supplemented by the Crawley spring on the south side of the hills, that better-class housing would have the luxury of water pipes.

Canongate was becoming a cramped, busy town. Market days inevitably brought greater congestion. Canongate's market was still held at the head of Canongate where there was a variety of stands selling numerous goods. But the market cross was moved from the centre of the road in 1737 to the churchyard wall 'for the convenience of passage in the street'.[4] The need for space on the thoroughfare was accentuated by the proliferation of horses and coaches; and the records, both documentary and cartographic, show clearly the growing number of coach houses.[5] The head of Canongate, it was said, was particularly congested, with butchers selling their wares. 'Coaches and carts [could not] go one by another' and local residents had trouble even accessing their front doors so great was the crush in the street with customers, fleshers and their scavenging dogs. This congestion continued even after the construction of a new north–south axis, the newly constructed North Bridge, designed to carry traffic over the old streets to the New Town of Edinburgh. Although this must have impacted on the traffic east–west along Edinburgh's and Canongate's High Streets the problem of negotiating the head of Canongate was not resolved.

New public buildings also joined the tolbooth, market cross, school and new church. Canongate Charity Workhouse was built in 1761 and was located in Tolbooth Wynd. Built through public subscription, it was occupied by the infirm and destitute of the parish. Contributions to the charity workhouse were made by the crafts, as well as support from church collections and private donations. The workhouse regulations included provision for nurses to tend both children and the sick.[6] The workhouse in large measure superseded the chapel and almshouse of St Thomas at the Watergate and the hospital of St Mary and St Paul.

St Thomas' almshouse had been converted into a hospital for the poor of the burgh in the early seventeenth century. Over its entrance were inscribed the Canongate arms, supported by a pair of cripples, an old man and an old woman, with the inscription 'Help here the poore, as ze wald God did zow. June 19, 1617'. The town magistrates had sold the patronage in 1634 to the kirk session by whom, it was claimed, its revenues 'were entirely embezzled'. By 1747 the buildings were turned into coach houses and in the 1770s or 1780s they were pulled down. The hospital of St Mary and St Paul was rebuilt in 1619 and it developed in the seventeenth century as a workhouse or house of correction. It continued as such until 1750, although the building survived longer. It was here, in 1805, that James Ballantyne established his press and that the Waverley novels were printed.

Hygiene

It was not only the poor who needed physical care. Disease was rife through all levels of society. Part of the reason for this was lack of cleanliness. From the beginning of the century, Canongate and Edinburgh had had the unenviable reputation of being the filthiest city in Europe. The growth of closes and high-rise flats with inadequate sanitation did nothing to improve matters. Streets were not properly cleaned; and the emptying of chamber-pots from windows with – sometimes – a belated shout of 'gardy-loo' added to the squalor. At the beginning of the century, one visitor, Joseph Taylor, gave a graphic description of the dirty streets:

> In a morning, the scent was so offensive that we were forced to hold our noses as we passed [along] the streets, and take care where we trod for fear of disobliging our shoes, and to walk in the middle at night, for fear of an accident on our heads.

Some tried to overcome this problem by wearing a type of metal frame lift under their shoes to raise them above the filth. But even this was useless when the passerby came across piles of human waste 'like mountains'.

With filth came flies. These proved a great hazard to health, particularly in warm weather. The ordure lying around the streets attracted swarms. They then walked and fed on the piles of dung. Any human food left uncovered soon received the attention of the filthy-footed flies. Meat, in particular, soon took on the appearance of being totally black, so thick with flies was it infested. Many in Canongate did not know how potentially dangerous fly-blown food could be and suffered seriously for this ignorance. Flies were also attracted to open wounds. Some of the poorer people did not dress wounds. Soon, particularly in the heat of summer, these wounds became infected by flies and began to suppurate; and, worse still, the flies laid their eggs in these warm nests and maggots hatched in the wounds. As long as the practice of leaving filth in the street continued, flies would have a field day.

The authorities were not insensitive to these problems and the records show that some attempts were made to clear the streets. In 1671 the bailies decided the cattle market and shambles should be removed from their traditional stance at the head of Canongate to 'some back-side and remote place'. The cattle market had been a notoriously noisy, dirty and extremely smelly feature of town life since the Middle Ages. And the authorities did make genuine, but usually fruitless, efforts to halt the throwing of human waste out of windows. The fact that such acts were constantly repeated is sure indication that they were having little effect. Measures included banning ejecting mess from windows, requiring homes to be equipped with chamber-pots large enough to hold waste for up to forty-eight hours, insistence on the right to seal up windows if matter was ejected, and laying down punishments for failure to obey these rules. Fines were imposed and servants were pilloried, whipped or even exiled from the town for persistently ignoring the rulings. But the old practices lingered on. Some efforts were made to clear the streets. Until the 1690s the individual householders had been expected to pay the cleaners themselves. Some did, others did not. After that, the clearing of the streets was auctioned and put out to contract. This was a potentially lucrative contract; ordure became manure, to be sold to gardeners and farmers. Even so, the streets were not clean in any sense that would be thought acceptable today.

Culture and Leisure

Triumphal entries and their dull parades,
Are chang'd for Op'ra, Balls and Masquerades;
No longer Sunday's dull employment cloys,
For Church we substitute politer joys.[7]

Operas, balls and masquerades were the mere tip of the iceberg as the capital became the fashionable role model for cultural activities. Theatres and dancing schools closed during the 'Forty-five', much to the chagrin of the regular attenders. And the sophisticated liked to be seen. They went to Leith to watch horse racing and archery contests or, later in the century, travelled to the farms between Edinburgh and Leith to eat curds and whey. Promenading, according to a contemporary, became customary for the well-to-do; they would 'drive in their carriages to the sands at Leith and Musselburgh, and parade back and forwards, after the manner of Scarborough'.[8]

Increasingly, the wealthy travelled far afield for their amusements and leisure activities. Horse-drawn carriages added to the congestion on the High Street of Canongate and inns for voyagers were opened. One of the earliest was the Coach and Horses, standing in 1712 at the

A stage coach at Canongate tolbooth

head of Canongate. From here the stage coach left for London. The journey took thirteen days and the fare was £4 10s. The White Horse Inn or White Horse Stables stood at the foot of Canongate, near the Watergate, and supposedly dated to 16–3 (the middle number is missing from the lintel). It was approached by Ord's Close, later called Davidson's Close, and then White Horse Close. The whole of the ground floor was originally used as stables, such was the demand for horse-drawn traffic. It was here, where his father had a blacksmith's forge, that William Dick was born in 1793. He went on to found the famous Royal (Dick) School of Veterinary Studies. John Somervell in the mid eighteenth century also had an inn at the foot of Canongate. He then opened a coaching business advertising, in 1754, a London stage coach as 'a new genteel two-end glass machine . . . drawn by six horses, with a postillion on one of the leaders'.

One of the most famous inns at the head of Canongate was the White Horse (not to be confused with that at the foot of Canongate). In the second half of the eighteenth century this was owned by James Boyd; and here it was that Samuel Johnson stayed in August 1773 on his tour to the Hebrides and first met the biographer James Boswell. The White Horse became the starting point for the Edinburgh–London Fly, Edinburgh–Aberdeen Fly and the stage coaches to Leith and Kelso. Another inn at the head of Canongate was the Black Bull Inn. From here the Edinburgh and Newcastle flying post coach set off every Monday, Wednesday and Friday at 6 a.m. It carried six passengers inside, at a fare of 31s 6d. In March 1772 it was announced that 'by this speedy convenience' passengers passed 'from Edinburgh to London in only four days at only five pounds stg per seat'. It was also advertised that at the Black Bull travellers could 'depend on clean beds and good entertainment and civil treatment'. In 1774, it was, moreover, offering the spectacle of 'a zebra (late Her Majesty's); a magnificent lion; a real Bengal Tyger and a Man Tyger . . . a young oran Outang; a miraculous Porcupine; a voracious Panther; a beautiful Leopard, with many others, all from the choice cabinet of nature . . . Price to the nobility 2/6, to ladies and gentlemen 1/-.'

James Clark, once 'farrier to his majesty' and owner of repository stables, proved even more entrepreneurial: he opened in 1781 'for the reception of the Nobility and gentry' 'Clark's Hotel, Chessels Buildings', probably the first hotel in the Old Town. Contiguous to the hotel were stables with 'a great number of stalls for horses, sheds and coach-houses for carriages etc'. Where, in 1763, 'a stranger coming to Edinburgh was obliged to put up at a dirty uncomfortable inn . . . there was no such thing as an Hotel; the word indeed was not known, or was only intelligible to persons acquainted with French'; by 1783 'a stranger might have been accommodated, not only comfortably, but most elegantly, at many public Hotels'.

Drinking rooms and drinking continued to be a popular pastime. Many of the drinking establishments were now larger and more commercial, with their landlords financing and marketing much of the entertainment. Inns became the prime venue for new entertainments, such as lectures, exhibitions, scientific experiments, sports, concerts, society meetings, as well as displays of animals, birds, human freaks, and acts by jugglers and magicians.

A contemporary in the 1770s noted that 'we have an elegant playhouse and tolerable performers; assemblies, concerts, public gardens and walks, card parties and a hundred other diversions'. Playhouse Close, opposite New Street, took its name from the first theatre opened there in 1746. Visiting companies of actors and performers had previously met in the Tailors' Hall in Cowgate. Before that, theatrical productions had taken place from 1681 until 1710 at the royal tennis court near Watergate. As early as 1664 there is mention in the records of a dancing master, a principal dancer, a trainee comedian and others in the entertainment industry. They were unfortunate enough to be remembered as their costumes were impounded to pay for their debts.

The city had its own school of artists, which included such prestigious persons as Allan Ramsay, Henry Raeburn and David Wilkie. The Norrie family were well known as interior house painters, living close to Canongate, at the head of Blackfriars' Wynd.

Societies proliferated. There were over two hundred and about forty different types, ranging from literary, to masonic, scientific, learned and political. And growing sophistication brought an interest in matters beyond Britain's shores. The tailors' minute book records in 1792 that the tailors unanimously joined with the other crafts in petitioning for the abolition of the slave trade; they thanked Wilberforce and his colleagues; and voted two guineas to their expenses.

There was also organised music-making in the capital by the 1720s. Poets and philosophers frequented the elegant salons of Canongate and Edinburgh, and also local taverns. Jenny Ha's Change House, on the north side of Canongate High Street, was a favourite resort of the poets, such as John Gay, author of the *Beggar's Opera*.

Newspapers, printers and booksellers were commonplace after the end of censorship. Although Edinburgh was well behind London in its output, it produced more than three times its nearest rival, Oxford, in its printed works. By the 1760s there were more than fifteen libraries in Edinburgh and the upper classes had an extensive range of periodicals, newspapers, novels and histories from which to choose. The principal booksellers were Bell and Bradfute, and Manner and Miller in Parliament Close, Edinburgh; Elphinstone

Jenny Ha's Alehouse

Balfour, Peter Hill and William Creech in High Street; and William
Laing in Canongate. The latter was particularly noted as a collector
of old books.

The French revolution produced a mushroom growth of periodicals
and journals and the first to claim to be a direct result of the French
situation was the *Edinburgh Herald*. This was followed soon after,
in 1802, by the *Edinburgh Review*, the first edition being edited by
Henry, Lord Cockburn. In 1782 there were only eight newspapers
in the whole of Scotland, and these gave mainly local news; by 1790
they had proliferated to twenty-seven and most of them were highly
political and increasingly outspoken.

By the 1790s, debating societies and radical political associations
were also spreading rapidly. Even though Lord Cockburn claimed
that 'everything rung, and was connected with the Revolution in

France . . . literally everything, was soaked in this one event',[9] many of the supposedly political societies of Edinburgh showed little desire for extreme radical change. The Edinburgh Revolution Society in 1790, while pledging to the cause of liberty throughout the world, actually failed to make specific reference to France. Lord Cockburn himself admitted that 'we had wonderfully few proper Jacobins, that is, persons who seriously wished to introduce a republic into this country, on the French precedent'.

Political events as a whole seem scarcely to have impinged on Canongate. Tom Paine's *The Rights of Man*, the failure of the government to repeal the Test Act, opposition from the government to burgh reform and the abolition of slavery, the use by the government of paid spies, and the sentencing of Thomas Muir, by the self-appointed tribune of the people in the Friends of the People, to fourteen years' transportation to Botany Bay in 1793, highlighted the fear of the government of radical subversiveness, but in reality, did not reflect political opposition in Canongate.

Adam Ferguson, the philosopher and historian, commented in 1759 that 'the wit and ingenuity of this place is still in a flourishing way, and with a few corrections . . . is probably the best place for education in the island'. Edinburgh University (the college) had approximately 1,000 students in 1700, which had risen to 4,400 a century later. The Scottish Enlightenment was firmly entrenched in the universities and academics took a prominent role among the literati. In particular, medicine was dominated by Scottish institutions, which produced as many as nine out of ten doctors academically trained.

It was documented that medical men were in need of suitable material to study. Fountainhall noted under the date of 6 February 1678, 'I hear the chirurgians affirme the toune of Edinburgh is obliged to give them a malefactor's body once a year for that effect; and it's usuall in Paris, Leyden, and other places, to give them also some of them that dyes in hospitalls'. This was a forerunner of what would become a lucrative business in the nineteenth century. By 1711 sensibility to the trade in bodies and grave robbing resulted in the publication of a poem *Account of the Most Horrid and Unchristian Actions of the Grave Makers*, which claimed that it was an affront to God and the relatives of the dead, a national scandal and a practice fed by the demand of surgeons. The trade continued, however, with bizarre occurrences, such as the prosecution of two chairmen in 1742 for attempting to smuggle a body through the Netherbow Port in a sedan chair.

Canongate's grammar school was in the first-floor flat of a tenement in Leith Wynd, but this burned down in 1696. From 1704 it was sited further east, set back from Canongate High Street, almost midway between Leith Wynd and New Street. There it stayed until 1822. By 1799 Canongate had 150 scholars, compared with Edinburgh's 489. In 1775 the master, Mr Inglis, as the authorities were looking for further pupils, argued that:

> the number of scholars in this school has of late increased considerably, but the number to each master is less than in many schools in Scotland . . . The grammar school of Canongate is placed in a very open, pleasant and healthful situation. It is large, well lighted and in every way commodious, having a large area in the front, and nothing but gardens in the back, as far as the bottom of Calton Hill.

In the *Edinburgh Courant* of 12 September 1778 it was stated that the school's grounds were 'in a very extensive area surrounded by walls which affords an ample space for the school games and exercise without being exposed to the danger of the public street'. This gives an interesting insight into the growing realisation of the necessity of exercise and fresh air, as well as book work.

The Comte d'Artois, while staying at Holyrood, was given English lessons by the grammar school master, then William Ritchie. Other schools began to proliferate in Edinburgh, some boarding, others charity, English or sewing schools. Many of these were run by women. It is highly significant, however, that by 1760 only 5 to 15 per cent of women and the poorer working classes could sign their names, although it is likely that many more could read – a very telling comment on the fact that the capital consisted of very divided societies.

Greater education and more leisure time meant that outdoor activities, as well as promenading, gained interest. Edinburgh had two golf societies by the 1740s and skating was a popular pastime. Canongate had a bowling green at the end of Shoemakers' Close, to the north of the High Street; and fishing tackle, shooting gear and children's toys could be bought at Thomas Henderson's shop at Cross Well in Edinburgh by 1759.

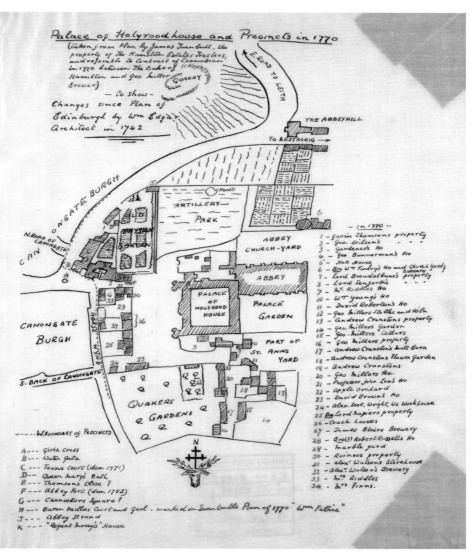

Holyroodhouse and its policies in 1770

There developed also a fashionable interest in gardening and botany. The *London Chronicle* of 3 September 1778 contained an entry on the Quakers of Edinburgh, one of whom was a 'Mr Miller who lives on a beautiful piece of ground near Holyroodhouse'. Their Canongate home was at St Ann's Yard, Holyrood, from 1760 to 1790. William Miller originally came from Hamilton to Holyrood as a nurseryman in 1689. His son and grandson continued the highly successful family business with extensive lands at Craigentinny. Their stock included 'prickly spinage', 'field turneep', 'cowcumber' and flowers such as Sweet William, Chinese Hollyhock, French marigold, lupins and asters. More adventurous still was the importation from Canada in 1775 of Canadian tree seeds, such as Canada oaks. A plan drawn of Holyrood House and precincts in 1770 shows graphically the interest in horticulture and allied skills. As well as the Quaker gardens and orchard to the south of the palace, nearby was Andrew Cranston's flower garden and to the north there was another gardener's house and a hot house.

From much of this entertainment and cultural activity the ordinary man and woman of Canongate were excluded. But traditional pastimes linked to the home and drinking houses remained. Celebrations and festivities meant bonfires, bells, flags and noise. Skittles, quoits, football, cards, gaming, gambling and boxing did not necessarily require great funds; and there was a new sport at which the spectator might bet. The first book on the subject in Scotland was published in 1705; and thereafter it proved very popular – cock fighting. Leith Links housed a cockpit from 1702, but the 'sport' proved popular in Canongate until 1869, when it was officially banned.

One section of Edinburgh society on the increase was that of the prostitutes. In 1763, it was claimed, there were only five or six brothels in the whole of Edinburgh; one might, apparently, have walked the entire length of the roadway from the castle to Holyroodhouse without being 'accosted by a single street walker'. Within twenty years the number of brothels had increased twenty times 'and the women of the town more than a hundred fold. Every quarter of the city and suburbs was infested with multitudes of prostitutes.' It is doubtful, however, whether this virtuous account of only five or six brothels in 1763 would stand up to much scrutiny. Privately published in 1775, *Ranger's Impartial List of the Ladies of Pleasure in Edinburgh* suggests a different story. Also probably masking the full truth was the difficulties the church faced when dealing with sexual services and the upper classes. One such unpleasant case in 1743 involved a girl of twelve in Canongate, who was procured by one Isobell Ivie, forced to drink ale and wine and then raped by a 'Sir William'. The kirk session deemed the offence a 'scandalous and heinous Iniquity', ordered the prosecution of Ivie by the civil magistrates for banishment from the town, but brought no action against Sir William, who was never named in full.

The level of concern over sexual misdemeanours resulted in Scotland's first non-statutory female penitentiary, or Magdalene home, being opened in Canongate in 1797 by the Philanthropic Society. Named the Edinburgh Magdalene Asylum, it originally housed all ages of women recently discharged from prison, but after four years it was concluded that a better success rate would be achieved if younger women were focused upon. Older women failed to turn 'from their inveterate habits' and younger women had probably not been on the streets long enough to develop serious drinking problems and contacts with the criminal underworld. It was also believed that they might benefit more from a strict regime of 'mild, wholesome, paternal and Christian discipline'. The only specification for admission to the asylum in Canongate was that the inmate 'be sincerely sorry for her past delinquencies and [was] desirous of being reformed'. The clientele was, therefore, not professional prostitutes with long criminal records, but rather young female petty criminals, vagrants and paupers. Women under twenty-four, with no disease and not pregnant were the prime target, but the records show that many could hoodwink the authorities, being susequently sent to hospital for a 'course of mercury', the treatment for venereal disease, or to the poorhouse when pregnancy became obvious.

A Slow Drift Becomes an Exodus

A telling comment on Canongate was made in the 1790s: 'a considerable change has taken place with respect to the rank and the opulence of the inhabitants. It was formerly remarkable for the number of noble and genteel families residing in it. But of late . . . the number of these has considerably diminished'.

For certain sections of society there were rising standards of living and a desire to display this growing wealth. Conspicuous consumerism and restricted urban space sat ill together. With a certain inevitability, and with the desire for improved living conditions and economic aspiration for profit, the greatest change in the capital's townscape would be set in motion from 1767. The building of the New Town was to ring the death-knell for Canongate. The slow drift of gentility away from the old town would eventually become a major exodus, leaving the once elegant town houses lining Canongate High Street and the newer thoroughfares to the poorer elements of society. But, in spite of this exodus of the wealthier classes, Canongate was not immediately deserted. St John Street, in particular, remained for some time a little haven. This was not a public thoroughfare and was regularly cleaned, supplied with water and a communal green and had a street porter to guard the entrances against all but residents and their guests.

But for many, the writing was on the wall and relocation became inevitable. By 1790–92, the earl of Haddington had moved from his home opposite Canongate parish church to the newly built George Street. He was merely one of many. Only two years after the opening of the prestigious Clark's Hotel in Chessels Buildings, it was found that the better class of patron was resorting to the luxurious establishments in the New Town and in 1783 it was advertised to be let. Canongate was no longer a desirable place to visit. The final blow for the town came in 1817, when a new road, Regent Street, was opened along the foot of Calton Hill. Canongate High Street ceased to be the principal thoroughfare into the capital from the east.

It was perhaps understandable that the New Town, Nicolson Street and George Square attracted many of Canongate's more notable residents away from the congestion and filth of the old town. With the development and establishment of the New Town, life in the old burgh of Canongate was to become irrevocably changed. Those who could not afford to move were the poorer elements of society. It was they who would come to dominate Canongate in the nineteenth century.

7

AN INDUSTRIAL SLUM?

The smell of brewing had been in the air of Canongate since the Middle Ages. The two Strands and the marshiness of the land at the east end of Canongate meant that there was a ready supply of water – an essential for brewing. By the seventeenth century, when the modern technology of brewing beer was replacing the old, primitive household method of making ale, the capital had become the hub of the brewing industry in Scotland. Not only was good, pure water at hand, but the agriculturally rich Lothian hinterland supplied a ready source of grain, and coal was easily accessible for the boiling process. Capital was readily available to finance the new technology, not least from the 'deep pockets' of George Heriot, 'Jinglin Geordie', goldsmith and moneylender. The local population provided an eager market.

Brewing

There were many small breweries in Canongate, but larger ones gradually emerged, either through internal expansion or by amalgamation. In 1726 the workings of Blair's Brewery were transferred from the west side of Horse Wynd to a new site to the east of the wynd. This would ultimately form the nucleus of what would be called the Abbey Brewery. Another famous brewing family was that of Younger. By 1789, out of seventy-two brewers in Edinburgh and Leith, Archibald Campbell Younger was paying the second-highest ale impost tax at £170 12s 2d. The family business was inherited by his brother William and in 1803 William Younger added to the breweries at Croftangry, within the abbey grounds, and at the Northback of Canongate by the purchase of Blair's Brewery. Over the next few years, other parcels of properties were leased or purchased as a large empire entered its infancy. In 1825, with the purchase of Lothian Hut, with its stable, byre and courtyard,

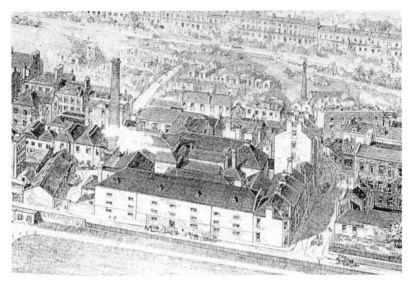

The Abbey Brewery in the late nineteenth-century

by William Younger II for the sum of £5,000, the brewery was set for vast expansion.[9] As a result, by 1840, the site of the Abbey Brewery stretched all the way from Canongate High Street south to Holyrood Road (South Back of Canongate) and the brewery's market reached as far away as Rio de Janeiro. The Youngers systematically bought property whenever the opportunity arose. Holyrood Brewery further west up Canongate was purchased in 1858. It stood near to where the St Mary's Brewery had been sited at the back of Chessel's Court. At the start of the twentieth century Abbey Brewery, with Holyrood Brewery, covered some twenty-seven acres, and their output accounted for a quarter of the entire quantity of ale produced in Scotland.

Contemporary illustrations reveal graphically the effects of large-scale brewing creeping and then galloping into Canongate. The view of Abbey Brewery and Queensberry House shows the depressing side to industrialisation. The tall chimney stacks, not only from the brewery but also from the Queensberry Hospital mortuary, are clearly seen belching out noxious fumes. It was Lord Cockburn's view that 'Holyrood, though not in such bad company as it lately was, is still polluted by the almost actual contact of base works and houses'.

The brewery maltings, once the exclusive Lothian Hut

The once magnificent Lothian Hut became the Lothian House maltings and the extensive dining room functioned as a growing floor for malt.[2] The *Guide to the Great Northern Railway* of 1861 extolled the virtues of Edinburgh ale, explaining that the success of Younger ale was 'partly owing to the adoption of all mechanical and other improvements, and also to the chemical properties of the water of which, by sinking to an immense depth, they get an abundant supply'.[3] The brewery was served by a series of wells supported by an integrated network of feeders and cisterns. By 1872, there were five wells in existence, the most recently sunk being 130 feet deep, and 400 feet of mines, most of the boring being through solid rock 150 to 300 feet below ground level.

In 1858, Andrew Smith, a partner in the growing Younger empire, kept a notebook on aspects of brewing, which was to become the property of his two sons. Of Blair's Brewery he noted that the 'water not good; they always thought there was some connection with the gas tank' – a telling comment on the closeness of other industrial activities.[4] Nineteenth-century views of the Abbey Brewery from Salisbury Crags are clear indication of the level of 'mechanical and other improvements' and industrialisation of the site, which housed all the accommodation necessary for the malting process, the brewing procedures, cooperage and stabling and smithies for the horses and drays.

Most breweries produced a variety of products, which included at least one stout or porter and pale ale. Scotland became renowned for its pale ale, particularly after the middle of the nineteenth century. One of the most renowned was India Pale Ale, brewed in the Holyrood Brewery. This plant alone was described in 1889 as 'an establishment as extensive as the Trentside breweries'.

On 5 March 1870 the *Scottish Standard* reported that 'The South Back of the Canongate of Edinburgh is more famous for breweries than any street in the United Kingdom.'[5] Canongate was almost one big brewery, interspersed with other heavy industry. The firm of Thomas and James Bernard had been brewing here since 1840, but gradually found themselves cramped for space, with no room for expansion, such was the congestion in Canongate. Just as James and Thomas Usher had been forced to move their plant from their original site in Chambers Street in Edinburgh to St Leonard's Street in 1860, Bernards in 1890 relocated to the more open spaces of Slateford to the west of the city. But in spite of the relocation of some plant, Robert Louis Stevenson wrote in 1896 that 'The Palace of Holyrood has been left aside in the growth of Edinburgh, and stands grey and silent in a workman's quarter among breweries and gas works.' It was a strange fate for a royal palace.

Unfortunately, brewing business archives – letter books and ledgers – reveal little about the working conditions or pay. If wage books were kept before 1850, these have now been lost. Labouring for the brewing industry also meant, for many, periods of no work. Brewing being a seasonal activity, labourers would often be laid off from late spring until early autumn. The season for brewing was the winter months; the crops of barley were gathered in and the weather was cool enough, even frosty, for the brewing process. By the late eighteenth century, large breweries, however, were managing to function all through the year, but this was not so with the smaller outfits.

Some of those employed would require specific skills, such as those demanded of the head brewer, the manager and numerous clerks, cashiers and book keepers. From the 1880s most of the big breweries would also employ a qualified chemist and equip him with a laboratory and scientific equipment. Skilled tradesmen were required for such tasks as malting, malt grinding, coopering and millwrighting. Much of the unskilled labour came from the local Canongate people. This was heavy and often hot work. Tasks varied from draymen, carters and hauliers to general brewery workers who would unload hundreds of sacks of malt and hops, stoke the furnaces, turn the mash in the kilns, fill the mash tuns, shovel up waste and draw off the ale and beer into barrels. For the majority, work in the brewery meant long hours and considerable physical effort; and there is no evidence of shift work before the twentieth century. By the early years of the twentieth century, Edinburgh, as a whole, employed approximately 45 per cent of the total workforce involved in the brewing industry in Scotland. By this time, women and boys were being employed in growing numbers, probably on a part-time basis, to cope with jobs such as bottle-washing, bottling and packing. This group was the lowest paid, earning ten shillings a week or less. Full-time, unskilled men might take home under twenty-five shillings a week. But the skilled workers, such as enginemen, coopers and mechanics might earn the princely sum of thirty shillings or more.

Glass Manufacturing

In 1815 William Ford of the Caledonian Glass Works, Canongate, proposed to convert premises to a Flint Glass Manufactory. An action was raised at the Dean of Guild Court on the grounds that a glass factory would be 'objectionable'. The defence against this complaint gives a clear insight into the level of industry on a relatively small site on the South Back of Canongate:

> Let him object as he may, it is quite clear that the Manufactory to be established is not one hundred part so Bad as the former Foundry, where Blast Furnasses, Coak Furnasses, Smelting Furnasses, Steam Engine, and no less than Eighteen Smiths Forges were kept constantly going on at one time.

There was also a glassworks at the North Back of Canongate, near to the Watergate, which was acquired by William Ford in 1819. The sasine details give an interesting insight into the changing topography

The elegant façade of glassworks on the South Back of Canongate

of this area. The land acquired prior to housing a glassworks had been
a coach yard, with stables to its west. This formed part of a piece of
ground that had previously been commonly called Brokies Bog. As
late as 1754 some of Brokies Bog was built on, but some was not. This
suggests that the east end of Canongate was still, as in the Middle
Ages, very boggy and wet. The water pond by the Watergate was still in
existence, and was probably still used for watering horses.[6] It appears
that by the nineteenth century, with the growth of manufactories
in the confined space of Canongate, land was being reclaimed from
bog. Cartographic evidence for the later nineteenth century gives no
hint of the abundance of water that once characterised the east end
of the town.

In 1838, John Ford founded the Holyrood Flint Glassworks, sited
on the South Back of Canongate. He had been employed by W.
Bailey & Co. of Midlothian Glassworks, at Portobello, as 'chief clerk
and traveller'. With his new prestigious premises, probably all of the

process was completed at the factory. The frontage of the glassworks factory on the South Back of Canongate was elegant, suggesting that industrialisation and its associated buildings were not all necessarily detrimental to the townscape.

Glassworking was a hot and sometimes heavy job, requiring labour from skilled blowers as well as unskilled carters of coal and packers of goods. Glass house furnaces were kept going night and day, unless essential repairs were needed, when the fire was put out. So there was a constant demand for raw materials. These were heavy and bulky. Coal, sand, lead and clay were trundled up from Leith. These endless processions made their way through the Watergate, past Holyroodhouse and up the South Back of Canongate. The hauliers also had to provide stables and hay stores for their horses. The noise, dirt and congestion at the narrow end of Canongate, in front of Holyroodhouse, must have been overwhelming.

Gasworks and Electricity

Another important industry in the locality was gasworks. For those who could afford more than simple candles, gas provided the essential supply for lighting. The Edinburgh and Leith Gas Company established itself on the north side of Canongate. But it was found, in 1890, as Andrew Smith had earlier predicted, that the chemicals involved in the production of gas were contaminating brewery wells.[7] It was the close proximity of coal supplies that made possible the rise of the gas industry. Under an 1818 act, the Edinburgh Gas Light Company undertook to light Edinburgh and its suburbs; and by 1840, when a further act for the better lighting of the city was passed, there was a second gas company – the Edinburgh and Leith Gas Light Company. Both of these were acquired by joint commission under the Edinburgh and Leith Corporations Gas Act of 1888. From then on it was their responsibility to administer the production of gas, until 1920 when this responsibility fell to the Corporation, until nationalisation in 1948.

Canongate was to benefit from better street lighting, which would eventually be a more efficient way of lighting than gas. The first steps to more modern lighting for the town came when the Edinburgh Corporation secured the right to supply electricity to the town under an 1891 order made according to the Electric Lights Acts. Leith had its own generating station under an 1897 order. Amalgamation in 1920 would lead to the construction of the large power station at Portobello and an efficient supply of power to the capital.

Railways

The introduction of railways to the capital brought not only the opportunity for employment, both skilled and unskilled, but considerable disruption and dirt, as well as many new workers looking for employment. Work began on a railway station in 1846. The North British Railway built its east-facing terminus for traffic to Berwick and Hawick. In the process, the city's Physic Garden was swept away, along with the historic Trinity Church. The church had been classified as 'one of the finest models of Gothic architecture that this country has to boast of'. Lord Cockburn described this demolition as 'an outrage by sordid traders, virtually consented to by a tasteless city and sanctioned by an insensible parliament . . . These people

Trinity Church and site of Waverley station taken
from Slezer's view of Edinburgh from the north

Trinity College with the railway under construction

Waverley Station under construction

More advanced stages of Waverley Station under construction

would remove Pompeii for a railway, and tell us they had applied it to a better purpose in Dundee.' Six weeks later, the Edinburgh and Glasgow brought traffic in from the west to the General Station (from 1854, renamed Waverley by Sir Walter Scott) and a year later the Canal Street Station was opened, tucked away in the north-west. In effect, three stations rolled into one were now about to change the face of Edinburgh and north-west Canongate.

Trinity Chapel and hospital were not the only properties to fall victim to the railways. After twenty years of procrastination, most of the stones of this medieval chapel, which had been laid aside for conservation and reconstruction, were lost. Many felt that the destruction of the chapel was nothing less than official vandalism.

But there was also a destruction that probably affected the lives of the people more – their homes. The clearing of working-class wynds and slums did indeed help to 'effect a sanitory [sic] improvement' but there were no plans to rehouse the homeless. Loss of housing to the railway, as well as the expanding breweries, merely added to congestion, deprivation and slum conditions in a town with an ever-growing population.

By 1902, almost all the fine New Street eighteenth-century mansions, once tenanted by such dignitaries as Lord Hailes and Lord Monboddo, had been destroyed by the North British Railway and the Corporation Gas Works. The building of Waverley railway station was deplored by many. It was ironic that the central vehicle of this destruction of a key part of the capital's medieval past was named 'Waverley', after Sir Walter Scott's novel of 1814 which looked nostalgically on what had been lost.

Other industries

Engineering and the metal industry occupied about 3 to 5 per cent of the population of Edinburgh. The clothing industry attracted most, accounting for 14 per cent of the city's workforce in 1841, falling to 7 per cent by the turn of the century. Building works in the New Town and the Union Canal, in particular, were a good source of employment, as was the growing transport industry. Traditionally, printing was also important in the capital. This and coach building were the biggest manufactures, as well as candle, soap and glass-making, brewing and distilling.

Panmure House felt the effects of industrialisation. It degenerated from an iron foundry to a ruin. To the north, the once impressive view towards Calton Hill was blocked by a large brick building about six feet from the mansion; unsightly buildings were also added to the east and to the south the one-time slender crowstepped gable had been disfigured. By 1881, according to the Ordnance Survey plan, the policies of Milton House, built by Andrew Fletcher of Milton in the early eighteenth century, had become a brass foundry. Whitefoord House was occupied by a large typefounding establishment.

It was claimed in 1859, perhaps with a little exaggeration, that 'Edinburgh cannot be called a place of much trade or manufacture, being chiefly supported by persons in the law and medical professions'. The Industrial Revolution of the nineteenth century increasingly set Edinburgh up as an administrative centre, with banking and insurance taking an ever-more prominent role, alongside the institutions of law, religion and the University. This presence of an unusually large professional and administrative middle class in the city as a whole drew many in Canongate into domestic service and also made Edinburgh very much a retail city, supplying the houses of the professionals and gentry. But there was also a high degree of manufacturing and this went on in the Old Town and Canongate, safely removed from the presence of the professional classes.

The Homes of the People

Although there had been an exodus of the wealthier classes, Canongate was not totally deserted by the well-to-do as an industrial wasteland. St John Street, in particular, remained, for some time, a desirable place to reside. Accessed from St John Close, the Close housed the oldest Masonic lodge room in the world – the Canongate Kilwinning Masonic Lodge. St John Street was home to Tobias Smollett, the earl of Dalhousie, the earl of Hyndford and Lord Monboddo.

Haddington House, as it was called until 1861, was still a relatively comfortable dwelling. The glassmaker John Ford chose to live here, before moving to St John Street. People of mixed social class lived nearby, however. In 1832–4, a John Ranken, letter carrier, was resident

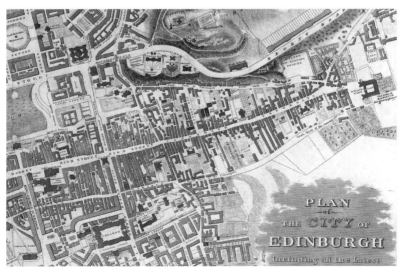

John Wood's plan of Canongate 1823

at Haddington Entry. In Reid's Close, at the same time, there were two teachers, a bricklayer and another letter carrier. In Queensberry House itself there was a manufacturer, a married lady of no stated profession and one Alexander Mackay, esquire. The Edinburgh and Leith Post Office Directories give an insight into other neighbours. In Cumming's Close were a victual dealer, a haberdasher and a dressmaker. In 1835/36, no. 56 High Street, Canongate was occupied by a Mrs Stevenson who ran an 'eating house' on the premises and by Miss Menzies, a milliner. No. 50 was lived in by a Miss Peat, a dressmaker. A John Lauder, victual dealer, lived at no. 48 in the 1830s and 1840s; with, nearby, at no. 44, James Alison (from 1830–3) and David Harley (from 1834), both haberdashers, and at no. 42, were A.& J. Crabbie, dressmakers. No. 40 Canongate were the premises of a surgeon from at least 1835. Another of this profession – Hugh Alexander – resided at no. 46 from 1839 until 1872.[8] This cameo of one small section in south-east Canongate was repeated elsewhere throughout the town. The occupations of those living on the frontage of Canongate suggest a certain level of gentility and indicate that people of at least modest means still lived in the old burgh.

But the 1841 census returns highlight the stark reality of living in Canongate. In this same south-eastern area, by now, no. 3 Horse Wynd contained sixteen households and seventy persons; no. 10,

Queensberry House, with its extra floor, built
to accommodate the military

eleven households and forty-four persons; no. 12 contained nine households and twenty-nine persons. There were twelve households in Reid's Close, eight in Haddington Entry and fourteen in Cumming's Close. Significantly, none of these fourteen households in the close merited a postal address. Indeed, from 1845, Cumming's Close is not even referred to in the postal directories. The close, however, is delineated and named specifically on the 1852 Ordnance Survey map. All this suggests that Cumming's Close was becoming the resort of the poorer elements of Canongate society. Added to this, its near neighbour, Queensberry House, became a house of refuge in 1834. Four years later a night refuge was opened. In the year to the end of September 1840, 4,334 people had been admitted to the night refuge, probably accounting for about fifty people a night. By 1853 the house sheltered 255 persons permanently.[9] Lord Cockburn described the once 'brilliant abode of rank and fashion and political intrigue' as 'now one of the asylums of destitution'. With its mortuary chimney stack adding to the fumes of industrialisation, it was, indeed, a great fall from grace.[10]

Queensberry House had served a variety of purposes. Not only did the house itself function as a hospital, but it had been occupied as a barracks, when it had acquired an extra floor. At right angles to Holyrood Road, on the east of the gateway, the officers' guard room was sited; and on the west was the soldiers' guardroom (quartermasters); there were also, separate from these, a canteen with a taproom and a large beer cellar, a bar, a kitchen and a staff room.

On the departure of the military, Major Nairne, the Inspector of Barracks in Scotland, gave permission for the use of Queensberry House and the enclosed area behind, once the formal gardens, then the parade ground, as a venue for the first general show of what would later be called the Highland Show, in December 1822. The shows continued here for the next three years. Between sixty and seventy cattle were exhibited. Former barrack buildings in the grounds seem to have been converted and pens were also constructed by Bailie Gordon of the Canongate, His Majesty's carpenter. An essential water supply was provided by the extant wells in the grounds. That cattle were well watered and provided for is somewhat ironic when the living conditions of many in Canongate are considered!

By the middle of the century, throughout Canongate, formerly spacious, well-furnished accommodation for persons of substance had become so subdivided that even a single room might function as a home for one family. It is difficult to imagine the destitution of some of these people. This density of occupation inevitably led to slum conditions in certain areas. The highest floors, it was said, contained hovels 'as destitute of furniture as the habitations of a savage islander or an inmate of a wigwam'. Cleanliness was generally 'somewhat at a discount' and the closes and stairs abounded with 'noisy urchins and little girls of astonishing strength of lungs and hair in much-admired disorder, whose hands and faces allowed you to draw an easy inference that they were addicted to dabbling in the neighbours' gutters'. So wrote Andrew Bonar, the minister of Canongate in 1850. Of Horse Wynd it was commented that where 'previously genteel families in most excellent houses' once lived, was now the haunt of 'auctioneers and pawnbrokers'.[11] The once gracious Acheson House now became home to fourteen families. And as late as 1937 the once desirable, single-family house, no. 1 St John Street, was home to 159 people.

Overcrowding and poverty

Overcrowding, poverty and high mortality rates were exacerbated by the influx of Highlanders and Irish into the Old Town, in all accounting for 66 per cent of the population increase between 1801 and 1831. The population of Edinburgh and its suburbs rose from 69,000 in 1801 to 161,000 in 1851, many coming to find employment in the expanding breweries of Canongate and Fountainbridge, in the legal and insurance offices of the New Town, and in the growing printing and publishing industries.

The 1840s were to see a further influx of Irish immigrants, exacerbating the overcrowding and potential for disease. By 1851, 29 per cent of the population aged between sixteen and sixty in the Old Town had been born in Ireland. Many Irish would continue to chose to live in Canongate and Cowgate throughout this century and the next, not merely because rents were cheaper, but also because they were near their place of worship – St Patrick's (affectionately still called St Pat's), the Catholic church at the foot of St Mary's Wynd.

It has been claimed that the Irish immigrants were 'in the almost impossible position of being unable to become Scottish . . . The

Watergate

essence of Scottishness was Protestantism and its culture of work,
thrift and sobriety.' George Bell, a doctor, noted that, in 1847, 379
out of 511 fever victims in Edinburgh Royal Infirmary were Irish. He
thought that the 'migratory Irish are a pestilence as well as a pest', but
admitted that the most destitute Scots were worse off than the Irish
poor, for one very simple reason: the Irish had a lifeline – a greater
attachment to religion. In reality, the only organisation that could
give the Irish cultural cohesion was their church. The Irish tended
to find employment where cheap labour had previously attracted
Highlanders, that was, in general service, domestic service, portering
and cleansing. A small but significant section moved into small-scale
retailing, dealing in provisions, spirits and old clothes.

Particularly under the Roman Catholic bishop of Edinburgh, Bishop
Gillis, self-help societies were established which provided assistance
in the form of funeral and sickness benefit and savings societies. This

helped to dampen fears of the Irish as a radical disruptive force, even though, during the tension of the threatened Chartist outburst of 1848, many Irish sided with the Edinburgh suffrage radicals and took part in the riots. Only once in the nineteenth century did the Irish-born become the largest 'outsider' or 'alien' group, and that was in the unusual census years of 1851 and 1861, after the Famine, when they accounted for 6 per cent of the Edinburgh population, compared with 4.5 per cent of English extraction. Otherwise, English immigration overshadowed the Irish. But their culture, their religion, their appearance – which was reputedly very slovenly and ill-kempt – and their nationality set them apart and made them an easily identifiable group. They also lived in certain distinct areas. Their plight was that they were living in the city, but were not genuinely part of it.

The year 1832 was to be a bleak one for the destitute; they were the group of society most affected by a wave of cholera that killed almost 600 people in Edinburgh between January and August. Inadequate efforts were made to counteract the attack. The authorities insisted that pigs were to be removed from homes; flannel clothing, woollen stockings and soup were provided for some of the poor; very basic facilities for washing and drying clothes were organised; and vagrants and beggars were excluded from the town. Not only did they add to the demand for food, but they also probably carried infection. The treasurer of Canongate Church reported that there were not enough coffins to bury the cholera victims. Because they were so overworked gravediggers were given one shilling per burial – a very respectable sum for the time.

A German visitor in 1842, Johann Kohl, was told of events during the outbreak of cholera. His account gives an interesting insight into the lifestyles and associated problems of some of the Canongate residents. The closes, he recounts, were so inaccessible to the sun that they were always wet. They were also almost equally inaccessible to the police, called in during the cholera epidemic to rid the town of pigs. Many Irishmen lived in these closes, or 'ruins' as Kohl calls them, and they were very attached to their animals. With no ground to graze them, they were kept in the homes. When ordered to remove them, the owners discovered that the pigs had grown too fat to be driven down the stairs; they had to be lowered on ropes, sometimes from fourth-floor windows.[12]

Low Calton

This onslaught of cholera was merely one of a number of major epidemics: influenza and typhoid came in 1837. The potato blight of 1845 had inevitable repercussions. By the following year, scurvy was making its presence felt as a result of lack of vitamin C and malnutrition. Epidemics of typhus and relapsing fever broke out in 1841 and again in 1843–4. Typhus and relapsing fever became epidemic again in 1846–9, with an outbreak of typhoid fever to intensify the misery. Cholera reappeared in 1848–9. Whooping cough, smallpox and scarlet fever hit regularly. Tuberculosis was so common that it was almost considered an inevitable part of life. Something very frightening and threatening was happening in Canongate in the 1830s and the 1840s.

Attempts were made in 1839 to clean up the environment. Sewers were causing problems and were likened to marshes. It was claimed that 'excrementitious matter of some forty or fifty thousand individuals is daily thrown into the gutters . . . or poured into carts which are sent about the principal streets'. Some have argued that the name 'Auld Reekie' conferred on the town was a reference to the foul odour in the streets rather than the smoke-screen over the city. This continuing practice of preparing manure, human and animal, by drying on the ground was prohibited. Plans were made to move the slaughter house a little distance from the town.[13] Even so, by the time of the publication of Edwin Chadwick's *Report on the Sanitary Condition of the Labouring Population* in 1842, Edinburgh's closes were considered the most debased living conditions in the country. His discussions of death rates, drainage and sewerage, housing conditions, lodging houses and water supply are vivid indication of the abject poverty and filth that many wretched souls had to thole.[14]

Two years later, Friedrich Engels wrote in *The Condition of the Working Class in England* of the 'foul wretchedness of the poor' of the Old Town of Edinburgh. The death rate by 1831 was calculated as being as high as one in twenty-two.[15] Other contemporary comments were equally damning: 'From their smoky beehives ten storeys high, the unwashed look down upon the open squares and gardens of the wealthy. Social inequality is nowhere more ostentatious than in Edinburgh.'

Gradually, many became convinced that there was a clear link between high death rates and certain areas of large towns – the areas that were crowded, poorly drained, inadequately supplied with water and inhabited by the poor. It was also suggested that when certain predisposing causes were linked with certain environmental conditions, disease would inevitably result. The predisposing causes were felt to include drink, immoral habits and poverty; the environmental conditions were linked to vapours and smells from putrid waste and sewage.

For many, moral, mental and physical disorder – the disintegration of the personality – represented in microcosm the symbolic disorder of society; control could best be effected by institutional care and restraint. Social order mirrored housing conditions; drunkenness was merely one symptom of disorder. While the Edinburgh *literati* might consume astonishing amounts of ale and claret, whisky had, by the late eighteenth century, begun to be, along with stout and porter, the drink of the masses – a potent combination that quickly and efficiently rendered the drinker senseless. The *Edinburgh News* of 1853 commented on the 'irrational expenditure' of 'constitutional drunkards'. Women as well as men indulged. One Adam Prophet Profit at the turn of the nineteenth to twentieth centuries stigmatised Canongate women as 'sly drinkers, taking on debt, dressing by instalments, deceiving their husbands; and many of their offspring are rickety, ill-bred brats growing up to fill their mothers' places and act like them'.

George Bell produced two reports – *Day and Night in the Wynds of Edinburgh* (1849) and *Blackfriars' Wynd Analyzed* (1850). He examined the almost inhuman conditions and destitution of many, particularly in Blackfriars' Wynd and nearby areas, where overcrowding was worse than in the town's prisons. His estimate was that there were around 1,000 people living in a wynd consisting of 142 buildings. He cited the case of one family at the foot of the High Street of Canongate which succumbed to typhus and starvation; because of abject poverty, they were forced to leave their miserable home and disappeared. Bell felt that there could have been fewer cheaper places to stay, other than possibly lodging houses – 'in themselves all horror and . . . situated in the vilest parts of the city'.[16] To consider overcrowding to be worse than in the prisons is a little ironic. Demand for room in Calton Jail was such that the tolbooth was used as an overflow prison for six years from 1842.

But overcrowding and inadequate housing lingered on. In 1861 the Canongate Registration District had 47 per cent of families in one-room dwellings. Conditions could be worse: the same census revealed that in the Old Town 121 families living in one-roomed houses did not have a window. Around 13,000 families, that was 66,000 men, women and children, lived in single rooms, of which 1,500 had between six and fifteen huddled together. There would have been little room for furniture.

In 1862, Dr Littlejohn was appointed as Edinburgh's first medical officer for health. A report of his gives a stark picture of Canongate. It had 220 people per inhabited acre – compared with Morningside's eight – or 140,000 per square mile. Between 100 and 200 people might share a common stair with no water and, in consequence, no water closets or sinks. Many improvements were proposed by Littlejohn: clean supplies of water were essential, the abandonment of the old cess pits was advocated and public hygiene education was proposed. Most of all, he criticised the foul burn system which was

Cowgate Port

peculiar to Edinburgh. The sewage of the old town was still used to irrigate meadows and open areas around the town, in particular fields just beyond Holyrood Palace. The stench must have been appalling; it was one of the reasons Queen Victoria disliked staying in the palace.

An 1877 account gives a vivid picture of life in the closes, which showed little improvement:

> An archway four or five feet wide leads through the breadth of the first 'land' into a close, not much wider, where the houses rise story [*sic*] above story till the light of heaven is almost excluded. A long, narrow, winding stair leads through darkness and dilapidation, to what is meant for a door . . . Here, then, is a room ten feet by eight, with what seems but a hole in the wall, dignified with the name of 'a dark bedroom'; the roof is cracked; the walls bear traces of damp and rain; the window is small, and the light admitted scarcely sufficient to reveal the faces of seven inmates – a father, a mother, and five children, doomed to this living death. In another apartment – or rather over the slender partition – four children and their parents, a son-in-law, and a lodger, who could find no other place, live together.

Ten years later, Canongate was still described as the 'nursery of disease and haunt of vagrants'.[17] The hospital sections of the poorhouses of Edinburgh were dirty, overcrowded and staffed by untrained, pauper personnel. Some of the lucky poor did receive treatment in the Royal Infirmary, which was intended for this group of society, as it was attached to the medical school. The infirmary was served by eminent medical men who worked without a fee, in the knowledge that prestige would bring students and private patients. In general, however, the sick were inadequately treated. Cholera, typhus and smallpox were being brought under control but the greatest causes of death were scarlet fever, diphtheria, measles, pneumonia and tuberculosis. The net result for the infant born towards the end of the nineteenth century was stark: by 1899 one child in five died before reaching the age of one year. For those lucky enough to survive, life was still grim and harsh.

8

CLEANSING AND CLEARANCES

In 1817 the 'Toon Rottens' were abolished. It was a sign of changing times. These 'old, hard-featured, red-nosed veterans', often from Highland Regiments, were the City Guard, founded in 1696. Disliked by the people, and particularly small boys who had a running war with them, they were obsolete symbols of a past age.

As early as 1761 the Canongate Charity Workhouse had been erected. But this did little to alleviate poverty in an area with so many poor. Begging became so rife that in 1812 a Society for the Suppression of Public Begging was formed. According to Lord Cockburn this 'materially promoted the subsequent institutions of Houses of Industry, Houses of Refuge, Savings Banks and many others'. But it really did very little about the causes of penury. The main aim was to force begging off the streets. This was assisted by the setting up of a new police presence. Policing with this new force went far to improve street life. But Canongate was suffering from far more than begging. The underlying causes of begging had to be faced.[1]

Attempts at Improvement in the Nineteenth Century

Some attempts were made to improve the squalid and unhealthy conditions that were home for the majority of the Canongate inhabitants. Many of the poor were at one point or another patients in Edinburgh Royal Infirmary (*see* Chapter 7); but there were times when overcrowding demanded other measures. From 1818 to 1819, when there was a fever epidemic in Edinburgh, Queensberry House was used for those who could not be accommodated in the Old Infirmary, a foretaste of its future use as a house of refuge and then a hospital.

A number of charitable ventures began to ease the lot of certain sections of society. The Edinburgh Institution for the Education of Deaf and Dumb Children was founded in 1810, and four years later

The Deaf and Dumb Institution

part of Chessels Buildings was purchased as a home for the children. There were initially about forty-five children being cared for. The boys were taught shoemaking and the girls sewing. By 1824, however, the institution had moved as the accommodation proved too restrictive and more space was needed.

Another 'charitable' institution was also to move out of Canongate. In 1864, the Magdalene Asylum, which had been built on the site of the eighteenth-century Bowling Green, at the foot of Shoemakers' Close, was moved to Dalry, into more pleasing surroundings. This move was partly the result of the suggested reforms of Dr William Tait. An attack on women's penitentiaries had begun in 1840 with the publication of his *Magdalenism*. He had recently been appointed as the secretary of the Edinburgh branch of the newly formed Society for the Protection of Young Females and the Prevention of Juvenile Prostitution. He launched an offensive on the adminstration of the asylum in Canongate for both its punitive management practices and its location. Violent control methods, such as head shaving, solitary confinement and corporal punishment were all practised. Tait argued that this led to a loss of self-respect and depression. As a result there was a high percentage of runaways, with young women finding themselves with little option but to go back onto the streets again. His comments on the location add an interesting insight into Canongate in the mid-nineteenth century. The asylum itself he likened more to a madhouse or a prison than a genuine refuge for the penitent. Its location in the centre of the city was counter-productive: there were temptations in a crowded town; it was impossible to run a full service laundry because smoke from the surrounding factories contaminated the clothes, leaving a foul smell; and there was no privacy, as it was surrounded by dwellings and the inmates could be watched and even shouted at as they walked in the yard. Tait argued that inmates should be free of the temptations of the city and have 'free exercise and employment in the open air'. Dalry, a rural location, was the solution.

A year later, a further measure to assist women came with the opening of Queensberry Lodge to the east of Haddington's Entry. This was intended for the 'safe accommodation and reformation of females addicted to habits of drunkenness'. As well as a bed and food, the women were provided with a flat roof 'for air and exercise without leaving the house' – and braving the temptations that Canongate offered.

The well-meaning efforts of those intent on reforming the habits of the masses, however, were incapable of dealing with the basic problem confronting Canongate and its inhabitants – abject poverty and all that it brought in its wake. Attempts were made in 1839 to clean up the environment of Canongate, but with little real effect – sewerage, drainage, water supply and housing conditions were, in general, foul.[2]

There was, however, a distinct group of working-class people who aimed to better themselves. Their social identity was created through a commitment to sobriety and propriety. The traditional drinking habits of the Canongate were rejected; temperance societies such as the Good Templars, the Band of Hope, the Independent Order of Rechabites and the Scottish Alliance-Edinburgh Council drew Canongate people into their ranks. Many of the skilled workers joined volunteer organisations which helped to promote their claim to be admitted to the ranks of civic respectability – a claim that would play a role in the Reform agitation of 1866–7. Allied to this went a belief in thrift and it was this group in its associations that supported such ventures as savings banks and co-operative societies. They, too, were the class of people who would benefit from shorter working hours after 1868. Walking, visits to the sea, golf, swimming, cricket and, in particular, football were soon popular pastimes. From the late 1880s, football developed as a mass spectator sport, with Heart of Midlothian FC even owning its own ground by 1881. The association of Hibernian FC with the community organisations of the Irish probably also brought in an element of unskilled participation in the sport.

Finally, it seemed as if the central authorities were to take some heed of the plight of the poor. The Royal Commission on the Scottish Poor Law in a masterly understatement found the Poor Law 'not adequate'. This resulted in a new Poor Law in 1845, with responsibility now shifted from the church to the state. Overseen by a Board of Supervision in Edinburgh, parochial boards were compelled to levy funds to assist the poor. But the act gave no right of relief to the able-bodied and did not require parishes to build poor houses. It also increased the residence qualification for help from three years to five. It remained at that level until 1898. The system thus left huge gaps in the provision of relief.

Poverty and inadequate housing, and the social problems these brought, increasingly became a concern of the church. Many radical Presbyterian ministers believed that through religious leadership would come economic, social and educational benefits for the people. It was disagreement on the exact method of how to deal with the poor, particularly in Edinburgh, that was one of the factors leading to the Disruption of 1843 and the founding of the Free Church of Scotland. One of the most forceful and vocal campaigners was Rev. Dr James Begg. In collaboration with other radical ministers, measures to alleviate poor housing conditions had been published in *The Witness*. In 1849 and 1851 Begg published two further pamphlets: *Pauperism and the Poor Laws* and *Drunkenness and Pauperism*. His intention was to deal specifically with improvements in Edinburgh. Following along very much the same lines as the evangelical leader Thomas Chalmers, formerly Moderator of the Church of Scotland, Begg proposed an eight-point charter: improvement in the quantity and quality of education; suppression of drunkenness; better homes for working people; public washing houses and bleaching greens; reform of the land laws; simplification of the transference of land; different treatments for crime and pauperism; and greater justice for Scotland in parliament.

Begg's address at the founding of the Scottish Social Reform Association the following year summed up the views of many: 'You will never get the unclean heart of Edinburgh gutted out until you plant it all around with new houses.' Such statements, reports and publications began to influence public opinion and there gradually developed an assumption, if not more, that the town council had the duty to take a more pro-active role in the state of the urban environment.

Demoralising poverty was such that one local butcher wanted urgently to provide quick and cheap food to sustain the poor. He himself had known poverty. Born in 1839 into a large family, he and his sister were sent away from home to live with relations in Canongate. They entered a butcher's household and in due course John Johnston became an apprentice. The plight of his neighbours disturbed him and, after some experimentation, he came up with a method of squeezing beef in order to extract and preserve its goodness. This he began to market as a quick and easy meal for Canongate people. He called his product 'Johnston's liquid beef'. As time went on and its demand increased, he went into partnership with a Canadian. This man, probably with a better sense of marketing, insisted that the name was not helping sales. It was to be called something else if it was to become a worldwide product. And so there entered into the culinary dictionary the well-known 'Bovril', as a direct result of the poverty of the people of Canongate.

Improvements were effected at the west end of Canongate, as in other parts of the Old Town, largely as a result of the Edinburgh Improvement Act of 1867. By using the private bill procedures of the Westminster parliament, specific local powers were created, enabling the city to remodel parts of the town in accordance with the needs of public health and communication. By 1879, the 'wretched old buildings' on the east side of St Mary's Wynd and adjacent closes, such as Home's, Boyd's and Gullane's, had been swept away and replaced with 'commodious tenements of an architectural character suited to the "Auld Toune"'. Leith Wynd, likewise, and the closes to the east – Old Fleshmarket Close, Shepherd's Close, Ramsay Court, Midcommon Close and Coull's Close – had all been demolished and were in the process of being replaced with decent housing. Blackfriars'

Wynd was also demolished and replaced with what is now called
Blackfriars' Street. Cranston Street, giving access to Market Street,
which originally functioned as a flesh market, but later became a fruit
and vegetable market and in 1876 a fish market, was named after one
of the town's bailies. It was constructed in 1867 as part of the city
improvement scheme and probably follows closely the line of the old
Leith Wynd.

Increased urbanisation on the peripheries of the city created new
working-class industrial districts; slum clearance reduced the density
in the older slum areas, although temporarily creating a housing
problem when tenements were demolished and not immediately
replaced and some chose to move 'spontaneously'. In consequence,
while the population increased throughout the city by 78 per cent in
the period 1861–1901, the increase in Canongate was only 49 per cent.
The resultant alleviation of pressure meant that the percentage of

Leith Wynd

families in only one room fell from 47 to 37. By the end of the century, the women of Canongate could avail themselves also of the facility of a 'steamie' and of the community spirit associated with these once well-loved establishments.

Canongate and Politics in the Nineteenth Century

The general election of 1830 brought the Whigs back to power. One of the main aims of the prime minister, Lord Grey, was to carry his Reform Bill into law. Throughout the country, various reform meetings were convened. That for Edinburgh was called on 26 April 1832 and was held in St Ann's Yards. The trades assembled in the Meadows and walked to St Ann's Yards in procession with banners and music. It was calculated that there were between 20,000 and 60,000 present; Lord Cockburn reckoned the latter was nearer the mark. 'No one thing occurred throughout the whole day to excite regret. All sorts of Reformers sunk their differences in the common object . . . not the slightest disorder either at the meeting or in the town.' Another meeting at the same venue was held on 15 May, with about 30,000 present.[3] In reality, the resultant Reform Act gave little further suffrage to the men of Canongate. By the act, the vote was given to £10 ratepayers – a level far beyond the means of the vast majority in Canongate.

A small extension of franchise, and a major symbolic victory for the working class vote, was gained with the Reform Act of 1867, the Scottish version being passed in January 1868, when household suffrage was established. Considerable support for the issue of votes for women had been growing and the contemporary feminist movement was represented in Edinburgh by the founding of Women's Suffrage Society in 1867. A lot of energy was put into petitioning the House of Commons for the extension of the franchise, and in the nine years from 1867 two million signatures were collected in Scotland. Campaigners were encouraged by the gain of some ground in certain representational capacities: the Education (Scotland) Act of 1872 established elected school boards and permitted women to participate both as voters and board members. The role of women on such welfare boards was becoming acceptable. Women officiated, for example, on the governing board of the Magdalene Asylum. In 1882 women were enfranchised for municipal elections (although in practice only unmarried women and widows might take advantage of this right); and in 1895 women gained the right to stand and to be elected to county councils and parish councils, although they were excluded from standing for town councils until 1907. The feminist movement was also given reinforcement by the attempt of the 'Seven Against Edinburgh' to obtain admission for women to medical studies. A group led by Sophia Jex-Blake succeeded in matriculating in 1869, but was then refused access to most classes in medical school. Jex-Blake returned to Edinburgh, however, and opened an independent School of Medicine for Women in 1886. The only working-class women's organisation formally affiliated to the suffrage movement was to be the Women's Co-operative Guild, the first socialist and labour organisation to show such support.

The suffrage movement would later in the twentieth century resort to sabotage, but the 1914–18 war efforts of such women as Dr Elsie Inglis, the founder of the Scottish Women's Suffrage Federation, went far to ensure that in an ambitious post-war reconstruction programme, which included electoral reform, women were given the parliamentary vote. Essentially a middle class reform movement, the impact on working-class Canongate women was probably not immediately obvious.

Probably of more importance to Canongate were local affairs. Legally, Canongate ceased to exist as a burgh in 1856, when Canongate and Portsburgh were absorbed into Edinburgh. But the signs of the times were already present. The incorporation of tailors had already resolved that they no longer felt it necessary for their members to be burgesses of Canongate unless they lived in the burgh. Although technically unconstitutional, clearly many members lived and worked outwith the burgh. This was merely one aspect of the change of times and attitudes; the building of the New Town and other suburbs and the encroachment of the railway and factories impacted particularly on Canongate. These factors, allied with the influx of migrants from the Highlands and Ireland, went far to undermine the old sense of community and identity, which was so bound up with the rights and privileges of the craft incorporations.

For those who enjoyed the franchise, politics were dominated by complaints about civic debt and the delays in civic improvement or their cost: the Usher Hall was first mooted in 1896 but the foundation stone was laid only in 1911. Municipal salaries seemed to be rising out of control and the cost of improving the water supply threatened new levels of expenditure and debt.

Learning in the Nineteenth Century

With the gradual exodus of the more genteel classes out of Canongate, the old grammar school began to suffer. An academy had been opened by 1788 in Hanover Street, where, according to the *Edinburgh Evening Courant*, 'the method of education so successfully practiced [*sic*] in the English Academies' was adopted and the New Town Grammar School was opened in Register Street in the same year. The master of Canongate grammar school was forced to supplement his slender income by taking in as boarders pupils who attended the High School or the university. He further offered to tutor them in classical studies and at their 'leisure moments their attention will be directed to the study of Geography and history . . . by way of recreation and amusement'! Worse was to follow. In 1820, the schoolmaster, Mr Cumming, attached to a glazier's account the note: 'None of the above windows were [*sic*] broken by the boys attending the school, therefore I hope you will pay the bearer the above and adopt some effectual measures for preventing the school yards from being constantly invested [*sic*] by blackguards.' In 1822 the following advertisement appeared in the *Evening Courant*: 'To be sold or feued – that large tenement in which the High School of Canongate has long been taught.' There was no longer a demand for this once so successful school.

The Disruption in the Church of Scotland in 1843 was also to have far-reaching consequences. The Free Church initiated a programme of setting up a second network of churches, ministers, manses and schools. With its resources so seriously curtailed, the established church found difficulties coping with the provision of poof relief and parish schools. Gradually this role would pass to the burgh authorities and out of church control.

With the sale of Trinity Hospital and College Church to the North British Railway Company, Francis, tenth earl of Moray sold Moray House and it became a place of accommodation for the former inmates of the hospital. The governors of Trinity Hospital then sold the house to the Free Church of Scotland in 1846. It, in turn, with the assistance of the town planner Patrick Geddes, converted it from its dilapidated state into a Normal College for training teachers. The Normal Training College of the Church of Scotland, which had first been established in Chambers Street, relocated to Canongate and became the precursor of Moray House Training College.

Edinburgh did, of course, have its renowned college (university), but there was growing concern in Britain by the early decades of the nineteenth century over the conditions within universities, in terms of low standards of entrance, poor achievement, the shortened university year, standard of professorial teaching and financial regulations. An 1830 report, resulting from a Royal Commission, went far to address these worries on paper, but politics within Scotland, the Reform Acts and changes in government and ministry delayed action. John Stuart Blackie, professor of Humanities in Marischal College, New Aberdeen, spearheaded action for reform in the 1840s; but it was not until 1858 that the government, as opposed to individual colleges, took action and implemented some of these recommendations.

Further education did not enter into the most fanciful of dreams of the vast majority of the Canongate populace. The desire for the advancement of medical knowledge in the college and associated institutions, however, did impact on Canongate when William Burke and William Hare began their notorious search for bodies for medical research. They murdered sixteen people by perfecting a method of killing by suffocation, which left no evidence of violent struggle. By initially searching out victims who were nomadic, disappearance went unnoticed. The poor, the unknown and the unwanted in Canongate provided rich pickings.[4]

A new school, Milton House Public School, was built on the site of Milton House in 1842.[5] In due course a modern burgh school was set up just to the east of the parish church. The Edinburgh Free Kindergarten, the first in Edinburgh, was established in Reid's Court in the early twentieth century, but could cater for very few children. Before compulsory education was laid down in 1872 most working-class children received their basic schooling through the Sunday School. Just how much education, in reality, the average child in Canongate received is very much open to question. It is known that many parents in this period of industrialisation realised the potential

Washing dolls' clothes in the free kindergarten

So the first lessons learned are not only the three R's, but also that there are such things as truth, honour, love, cleanness of speech & unselfishness of life – is that not infinitely worth while?

First lessons

of their children as a workforce. Of those who did attend school, many did not stay until they could write, although some achieved a basic reading ability. Edinburgh may have been renowned for such literary figures as Walter Scott, John Galt and James Hogg, periodicals such as the *Scots Magazine*, *The Edinburgh Review* and *Blackwood's Magazine*, and the *Scotsman* newspaper, published weekly as the first respectable opposition to the establishment from 1817, but they had little impact on the mass of Canongate people.

Housing Improvements

In 1897 the management of some of the housing at Chessel's Court was taken over by the Edinburgh Social Union. A philanthropic organisation, it was founded after Patrick Geddes visited Octavia Hill in London to learn about her work in slum clearance. The aim was not just to provide decent living accommodation but also to promote craft activities. The union did not purchase the properties, but by making agreements with the owners they ensured that the rents were ploughed back into property maintenance. Fitted up as comfortable homes for the 'humbler classes of the community', it was also the aim of Geddes to attract new residents into the Old Town and diversify the social mix. Chessel's Court was also furnished with gardens and a children's playground at the back under the same scheme. Another similar initiative took place at White Horse Close, which was restored by the Social Union in 1902, after it had been purchased by Dr Barbour and his sister, both active members of the Union.

A local historian in 1906 could still claim that 'the once fashionable suburb of the Canongate is now degraded to a slum and brewers surround the ancient palace of the Scottish kings'. The townscape, however, was vastly upgraded, particularly in the middle of the century. Frank C. Mears had renovated the timber-clad seventeenth-century projections in Bakehouse Close in the late 1920s. E.J. MacRae had worked in Chessel's Court and New Street in the 1930s, as did Tarbolton and Ochterlony across the road at the Old Sailors' Ark. In Bakehouse Close, Acheson House was bought by the Marquis of Bute in 1935 and the property was renovated two years later. From 1946–1953 the exterior of Canongate Church was cleaned and the interior restored. The old market cross was yet again moved, this

Chessel's Court, Arcade, a view from north after restoration

time from the pavement to inside the churchyard. The Tolbooth Area Redevelopment by architect Robert Hurd started at no. 197 with Shoemakers' Land. This was the rebuilt front of half the tenement reconstructed by the cordiners in 1725, the other half having disappeared in 1882. The panel above the door at the east (originally the centre), moved here in 1882, remains – with the cordiners' emblem and inscribed with 'Blessed is he that wisely does the poor man's case consider' – a slightly ironic statement given the condition of Canongate at the time. Nearby, stands the almost completely rebuilt front of a double tenement erected by the cordiners in 1677. Above the door this, too, has the original cordiners' emblem of a crowned shoemaker's rounding-knife flanked by cherubs' heads. Below sits an open book with inscription, giving the tenement its name, Bible Land. From its reconstruction in 1954, the property has housed flats. In 1956–7, Hurd also redeveloped Morroco Land, at no. 267. The half-length figure of a Moor on the left front accounts for its name. Numbers 202–254 on the south side of the street were also redeveloped by Robert Hurd and Partners.

White Horse Close in derelict condition

Ian G. Lindsay and Partners, Basil Spence, Glover and Ferguson and Frank Mears and Partners all had a hand in the upgrading of the frontages of Canongate High Street and its closes. Lindsay and Partners were responsible for restoring Reid's Court as the Canongate Manse in 1958–9. The arcaded canopies at nos 139–11, unfortunately blocking eighteenth-century Cadell House and Panmure House, were the responsibility of the Spence partnership. Panmure House itself, built for the Earls of Panmure *c.*1691 and occupied by Adam Smith, author of *Wealth of Nations*, was restored by the town council in 1957 with a donation from Lord Thomson and used as the Canongate Boys' Club and, later, a social training centre for young people. It is now approached through Lochend Close. Moray House had been the headquarters of two training colleges for Protestant teachers from 1907. By 1959 the College of Education spread as far back as Holyrood Road, some of the houses in St John Street being demolished to accommodate this expansion. There was by now both a primary and secondary school attached to the college. The house at the head in St John Street, where Smollett lived above the opening to St John

White Horse Close renovated

Close, was restored in 1955. Between 1963 and 1964 the town council renovated Chessel's Court as flats, but the building still contained the Saviour's Child Garden until it closed in 1977. Bakehouse Close was, again, upgraded, along with Huntly House in 1968–9. And at the foot of Canongate, the approach to Holyroodhouse was renovated and a garden was laid out to include Queen Mary's Bath House. White Horse Close, nearby, restored almost as a Hollywood fantasy, was the remit of Frank Mears and Partners in 1972.

Many other properties were demolished. A big campaign tried to save Golfers' Land, standing beside Whitefoord House, but in spite of all efforts it was destroyed. It was traditionally said to have been built with John Paterson's share of the stakes in a golf match on Leith Links when Paterson and the duke of York, later James VII and II, beat two English noblemen. Paterson was a shoemaker who made the leather golf balls then in use. The property, however, may have been even older than late seventeenth-century, possibly having been purchased by Paterson's father, Nicol Paterson, in 1609. Little Jack's Close, which

Golfers' Land [from *Old and New Edinburgh*]

was sited next to Shoemakers' Land disappeared. General Dalyell, persecutor of the Covenanters and victor at Rullion Green in 1666, had lived here, as well as notable people such as David Hume. From 1753 to 1762 David Hume was a resident while writing his *History of England*. From the rebuilding of 1956–8 there has been no trace of the close. The entry to St John Close also disappeared in 1966. And some areas changed out of all recognition. New Street, built *c*.1760 as a private roadway on the site of Kinloch's Close, was the home of the Lords Hailes and Kames. In 1786 the street was declared public and became so by 1819. By the later twentieth century it housed on its eastern side the Eastern Scottish bus garage and then an indoor car park.

The Life History of a Slum Child.

This is "a nameless lassie nursed by her unhappy mother's unhappier mother in a room which was not untidy & which contained.

A chair-bed with old coats for covering

A chair.

A box for a second seat.

A table.

A lamp.

A pot & kettle.

A strip of old worn-out carpet.

A few dishes & odd (indeed odd!) ornaments (sic).

And literally Nothing else.

This was the <u>HOME</u> of the Father (who was in prison when the child was born) & the Mother who was just <u>16</u> years of age.

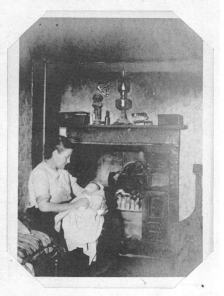

"Those are, not the actual parents of this child, but others of the same class & age — irresponsible, self-indulgent — bold — to whom alas too often, Love . . . is the lamp of the tomb."

'The Life History of a Slum Child'. The commentary says as much of the observer as of the observed.

Reid's Court Kindergarten

How did the people live behind the façades of all this upgrading? Ambitious housing programmes had two main impacts. Firstly, rehousing outwith the central core of the Old Town helped to reduce the reality of depredation, while renovation and rebuild improved, though did not totally remove, the air of depredation. Although there were a number of families who maintained spotless homes, most were sparsely furnished, with linoleum on the floor and few rugs to soften the feel, and box beds with sometimes clean, sometimes unclean, bed covers occupied the living rooms and kitchens. But new council housing in the 1920s and 1930s did provide, for some, water closets inside individual homes rather than on common stairs. But in many tenements at least six families still shared one w.c. and a water tap. Significantly, the son of the caretaker of the kindergarten in Reid's Close from 1939–49 remembers that many of the locals were a bit jealous, as his family was provided with a bath on the premises. This was a rare luxury. Some women did have small sinks to do their washing; others did theirs in a metal tub. A clever way to move the laden, heavy tub when it created an obstacle in a confined space was to keep it in the frame of an old pram and push it out of the way. Other housewives went to the steamie at Abbeyhill. Private double sinks for washing were put into some houses, so overcoming the need to go to the communal washhouse. Even though this was a great luxury, many women missed the community spirit that the steamie provided. The last one closed in 1977.

By 1946, 80 per cent of families were still housed in one or two rooms. Even with a kitchen being classified as one room, 28 per cent were in dwellings of one room, 52 per cent in two rooms and just over 8 per cent had three rooms. There were only eight dwellings in Canongate with four rooms and these housed only a fraction more than 1 per cent of the population. Only three dwellings had the luxury of five rooms. Canongate compared badly with Glasgow, which had over 70 per cent dwellings of single or two rooms in 1901 and was stigmatised as the most overcrowded city in the United Kingdom. The miserable state of Canongate becomes clearer if it is compared with Paris or Berlin in 1901, which had 57 and 35 per cent respectively in this category. By 1949, there were 4,369 people resident in Canongate, making it the area of highest residential density in the whole of Edinburgh; it also had the highest concentration of industry, apart from only Granton, Newhaven and Leith.[6] By the 1951 census, 20.6 per cent of the people of Holyrood still lived at a level of more than two per room. St Giles, central Leith and Craigmillar were only marginally worse. The equivalent percentages for Morningside and Murrayfield-Cramond were 1.9 and 1.5 respectively.[17] The middle classes had inevitably relocated to more commodious suburbs, leaving the Old Town to the working classes.

Health and Welfare

Although much had been attempted in the previous century to clean up the townscape and improve the overall health of the inhabitants, there was no room for complacency. One project established in 1893 continued into the twentieth century – the work of the Sisters of Charity. In 1893 they came from France and set up home near the head of St John Street. Their big white hats soon became a common sight in Canongate. Not only did they give to the poor but they also performed many acts of charitable kindness. In a basement beside the convent

The back view of 73 and 73a Canongate (Malloch's Close 2), immediately prior to the City of Edinburgh Improvement scheme

the nuns opened a dispensary. It was soon in great demand. A Sister Gabrielle was in charge of the dispensary and here she prescribed, cleansed and bandaged. Ointments for chest complaints and strains were sold for two pennies a tin and embrocation and medicine were three pennies a bottle. The mother superior was known for her generosity to the poor of Canongate. She must have known Canongate well; she was a member of the Younger brewing family.

In 1906 the local Charity Organisation Society published a *Report on the Physical Condition of Fourteen Hundred Schoolchildren*. The survey, conducted over the winter of 1904–5, had as its main purpose the heights, weights and general health of the children, but information about family background was also noted. North Canongate School

231–237 Canongate immediately prior to the City
of Edinburgh Improvement Scheme

was one of the schools analysed. While it was noted that the school was
in the old working-class area and serving the poorest in the city, 'yet it
has also an admixture of the children of the substantially comfortable
and thoroughly respectable working class'. Recent analysis of this
report on the school and the heads of households concluded that the
less prosperous sections of the working class were heavily represented;
and that, apart from shoemakers, all of the skilled trades of the city
were under-represented, compared to the industrial population of the
city generally as returned in the 1901 census. Clearly, Canongate was
essentially a working-class area.

Tuberculosis remained a constant threat, with advances in its
control coming only very slowly. Even in the late 1920s cows were
kept in dark barns in the middle of the city, and little was understood

North Canongate School – dinner hour, 1914

of how dangerous milk could be when cows were reared in insanitary conditions. It was not until the 1930s that tubercule-free cows were brought into the city from Colinton Mains Farm – a major innovation. In 1936, 1941, 1947 and subsequently until 1959 small outbreaks of poliomyelitis, another disease difficult to eradicate, occurred. These were not successfully controlled until after the mass vaccination scheme of 1956 began to take control.

Although conditions were not yet acceptable, the comparison of figures from 1863 to almost one hundred years later does show the advances being made throughout Edinburgh as a whole. In 1863, for every 1,000 of the population there were 36.24 births, 25.88 deaths, infant mortality of 145 and 6.23 deaths from TB. By 1961, the comparable rates were 17.7 births, 13.1 deaths, infant mortality of 23 and 0.03 TB deaths. But Canongate was probably not as healthy as these wider Edinburgh statistics suggest.

Care of the People

As the century progressed it became clear that the destitution and poverty in Canongate were such that many needed outside help to improve their lot. Queensberry House acted as a house of refuge. Its principle was that those who could afford to do so should contribute towards the cost of their upkeep, while the wholly destitute contributed in the only manner available to them, by working in the house. By 1938 the rates ranged from 16s 6d to 22s 6d per week. Attached to the institution was a hospital with sixty beds for aged and infirm women, enabling those whose circumstances did not admit of proper care and attention in their own homes, a safe and caring environment. There was also a small hospital of about fifty beds for men. A medical officer was in daily attendance and a visiting chaplain held regular Sunday services. These were supplemented from time to time with services conducted by clergymen of different denominations. In 1937–8 there were 190 inmates.

The Queensberry House complex provided other facilities. There were separate night shelters for men and women, in addition to the regular inmates. Here, in Reid's Close, accommodation was provided free, everyone was washed, and a meal was given in the evening on admission and a further meal in the morning. In a twelve-month period in 1937–8, 6,627 people were sheltered and fed here – a significant comment on the poverty of the area. Such was the demand that people began to queue from four in the afternoon.

Another life-saver was a soup kitchen. This was open between the hours of eight and nine in the mornings and from twelve noon to one o'clock. For a penny a basin of porridge and milk could be had in the morning and a quart of soup and a roll in the middle of the day. Destitute applicants were given their meals free. Over the same period, in 1937–8, 8,024 meals at 1d were served and 14,183 free meals were given out.

It was reported that applicants for admission to the house often arrived in a state of complete destitution. The directors appealed for donations of clothing and shoes and indicated that they would happily collect from any address in Edinburgh. The public gave donations and the town council an allowance. Many, including the Religious Tract Society, the Scottish Liberal Party, the British Red Cross Society and Edinburgh Public Library, supported the house's library with books and magazines. Messrs Chambers supplied copies of their *Journal* and Mr George Robertson, the station master of London and Eastern Railway, brought a daily delivery of newspapers.

An old lady resident at Queensberry House

The house's neighbour, Scottish and Newcastle, provided free steam for the laundry and gave the residents Christmas presents.

When Mr Calcott became governor of Queensberry House in 1939 his remit was to move the establishment out to Ingliston. The Second World War intervened and the National Health Service took over administration of the Institution. In spite of improvements, even into the 1950s, conditions would have been considered Spartan compared with modern standards. A communal television, a Christmas tree, concerts by the choirboys of Canongate parish church and others were genuine attempts to relieve the harshness of life in the house.

Concern was raised over the living conditions of certain ex-servicemen. During the winter of 1909 between seventy and eighty ex-sailors and ex-soldiers were huddled together in a shelter in a vennel off Grassmarket. They had merely straw for their beds and covering. Brigadier-General Sir John Hanbury Williams visited the men and, with the Lord Provost, it was recommended that better housing should be found. Whitefoord House was purchased to accommodate them. The new premises meant that not only would the men have a better

Whitefoord House

night's sleep, but those who could not afford to pay for their keep, were offered employment, such as wood-chopping, sorting paper, gardening, painting and window-cleaning in the house and garden and attached workshop.

The Old Sailors' Ark offered warmth, company and food, not only to retired sailing men but also their families. One family visited every week in the 1930s. The father had been medically discharged from the navy but, with the Depression, failed to find work for five years. As Monday was wash-day and mother was occupied at the steamie, the two children were given a ha'penny each to go to the Ark in the lunch break from Cranston Street School. With this ha'penny they could each buy one ball of mashed potatoes, covered in gravy. After a while they realised that for one penny they could get three balls of mash. So, what luxury, they bought one pennyworth plate of three balls, picked up two spoons and tucked in. Other once-local children remember the pleasure of buying steamed pudding for a penny, rather than spending it on school lunches.

Hungry children could be inventive. Ears were kept close to the ground when gossip of weddings came up at the 'stairhead' or local shops. One group of boys had a successful technique for maximising their takings. Working as a group of four, they positioned themselves strategically beside the wedding car in readiness for the arrival of the bride and her father and the money he would throw from the window. One boy stood in front so the car could not speed away before the distribution of pennies took place; another positioned himself beside the bride's car door, in case father lent across and threw money that way and two waited on the father's side – one to scoop up quickly, the other to push off competition. Even with a few 'poor oots' no one got rich, but some Saturdays, the pickings might rise to two fourpenny fish suppers and a plate of peas and vinegar for each of them, or maybe just a penny bag of chips from Glennie's chip shop.

Although not well off, many children enjoyed themselves. Schooling had come a long way since the nineteenth century and youngsters were not forced into work at such a young age. Even with compulsory attendance at school there was still time for fun. At the turn of the nineteenth and twentieth centuries the High Street rung to the calls of street vendors – second-hand clothes, fruit and nuts, baked potatoes, bits of coconut and roasted chestnuts were all for sale. The hurdy-gurdy man added to the pleasure with his wheezy old organ and the children loved his little monkey dressed in a red hat and coat. And if they were very fortunate, they might even be able to afford to do a deal with the balloon man.

Life could be fun in other ways. 'Guiders' were a favourite toy. Usually propelled on pram wheels, sometimes but not often with the luxury of a piece of wood attached to the rear wheel as a brake, they were an ideal mode of transport and enjoyment in hilly Canongate. The only problem was the shortness of the runs. The more adventurous progressed to a 'Cresta Run'. Starting in Regent Road, passing the Royal High School on the left, then the bowling green on the right a quick turn at Abbeymount was achieved. A swoosh under the railway bridge at Abbeyhill, then past the Edinburgh City Mission Hall was all brought to an abrupt end opposite the Queen's Bath House, where there was a break in the pavement.

A great time could also be had playing football in the street. The ball was not always leather. Paper was screwed up tightly and held with a string. This makeshift equipment gave pleasure to many; anyone could join in and there were on occasions hundreds on each side.

Even the fights between gangs of boys over caches of wood for bonfire night are recalled with pleasure. One boy remembers with intense satisfaction going to the shandy shop beside Huntly House on a Sunday with a mug to collect a kind of stout for his granny. Pubs were shut on a Sunday and women were not permitted in pubs, anyway. A few sly sips went down well with the youngster. One of the greatest games, because of the necessity to outwit the watchmen, was to creep into the grounds of Holyroodhouse through railings that had been noted to be loose and could readily be moved and replaced without detection. A spree of apple-stealing then began. In spite of purloining royal property, the children enjoyed singing round the fountain in the forecourt of the palace on Saturday nights when the king and queen were in residence and watched them from a balcony.

The years after the Second World War years saw increasing attempts to deal with the deprivation in Canongate. Boys Clubs helped to occupy, educate and entertain the young. Rev. Selby Wright, well-loved minister of Canongate parish church, ran a boys club and encouraged activities such as camping. The Boys Brigade attracted a number and some joined the Scouts, Cubs and Guides at St Giles'. Milton House School had a playground with a gym and children of all ages seemed to play there.

The Council of Social Services made visits to homes to give financial support, after assessing the home circumstances. Many residents were so poor that applications were made for clothes. Dorcas Societies, largely run by the churches, supplied hand-knitted layettes and other goods. Turnbull and Wilson, once located in Infirmary Street, provided cheap parcels of soft goods to the Dorcas Societies to distribute to the needy. Social workers, often based in the Pleasance and functioning as church-based charity workers, knew that they were visiting what many called the worst slums in Europe. The poverty was such that when the 1937 coronation was broadcast on the radio the people of Canongate were invited to go to the parish church to listen; very few had radios. Those fortunate ones who did would send their children off to the garage to get the 'accumulator' charged. The minister of the church recalls visiting a house in the 1930s and finding it absolutely bare of any furniture.

Many Canongate residents were relocated with the intention of offering a better future. Although the moves were made with great faith and hope, many missed the closeness that Canongate had offered. Mayfield Church specifically sent mission work to assist in Craigmillar. Housed out in Craigmillar, Niddrie, Redhall, Broomhouse, Sighthill, Oxgangs, Saughton Mains, Prestonfield and elsewhere, all were not happy. Many felt isolated from friends and family.

A New Canongate

As the twentieth century progressed the people of Canongate became more and more depleted in numbers and a shadow of the former close-knit community. Two world wars and the savage force of the Depression took their toll. Canongate became increasingly a backwater, a rather unimportant suburb of Edinburgh made up of a largely unskilled working class and an underclass. Rationalisation of Younger's brewing empire had a profound effect on the area. In 1931 William Younger's combined with William McEwan's to form Scottish Brewers Ltd. In the same year, the old brewery buildings on the north side of the site were demolished, to be replaced with a new brewhouse and tunrooms, in typically contemporary style, with granite plinth, red brick superstructure and narrow mullioned windows. Dray horses were still used to pull the loaded beer carts up Holyrood Road. The most popular were Sam and Sally, whom the local children were allowed to feed with locus, which looked rather like black flat bananas with seeds inside, which the horses loved. Local people remember the horses at the Market Street Fruit Market also. These were apparently the best fed, as fruit and vegetables were thrown at the children if they gave cheek. If they were not lifted quickly and taken home to the mother's soup pot, the horses gobbled them up. But further impact on the townscape and the life of the locality came in the 1950s, with the ceasing of brewing operations at Scottish Brewers; and by 1961 the general offices were extended eastwards and northwards up Horse Wynd, culminating in the mid-1960s with the conversion of the brewhouse, in 1968 with completion of a new computer block and in the 1970s with modifications and alterations along Horse Wynd.

In the nineteenth century Canongate had become an industrial zone. Now, even this was lost. Brewing, printing and engineering have mostly been closed or relocated from the Canongate area, and there is little left now to remind the passer-by of this important cultural heritage.

Just as the rich industrial past of Canongate has been erased, so has the deprivation. Much of Canongate had by the end of the twentieth century been sanitised. Overcrowding, slums, poverty and dirt are largely things of the past. But under the surface, mingling with the visitors and 'ghost' tours, there is much that remains of the old Canongate. Huntly House and the old tolbooth now function as museums, recalling the town's past – both its illustrious and poverty-stricken moments. Other buildings continue very much in their former roles. Canongate parish church still ministers to the people and to the royal family when in residence at the palace. Whitefoord House is a welcome shelter for ex-servicemen and women. And the Ark still stands at the top of New Street. Most of the residents of Canongate may no longer need the financial help of charities, but there is a new group in the capital in need of support – the homeless. The Ark, partially supported by the Queensberry House Trust, still provides moral and practical back-up, warm clothes and hot food. Unchanged, also, are the memories of so many people of the old days in Canongate. There was deprivation and poverty. Times were hard. But with this went a closeness, a pulling-together and a feeling of community.

9

CANONGATE REBORN?

By the end of the twentieth century the sense of loss of the close-knit community that was once Canongate was still keenly felt. But Canongate was, yet again, as so often in its history, to experience change of fortune. May 1997 brought to power a new Labour administration pledged to deliver home rule for Scotland. A referendum of 11 September resulted in an overwhelming 74 per cent approval. This ensured that the political aspirations of the vast majority of Scots would at last become a reality. Scotland would once again have its own parliament. For some, as Winnie Ewing declared on Wednesday 12 May 1999, when parliament met, 'The Scottish parliament, adjourned on the 25th of March 1707, is hereby reconvened.' For others, this was the culmination of a campaign for home rule which was barely a century old. It was a new parliament for a new millennium.

The choice of a permanent home for this parliament produced lively and, at times, acrimonious debate. Various sites were considered, both in Edinburgh and beyond. These included Leith, now beginning to lose its industrial image and becoming upmarket, and Calton Hill. The site of the old Royal High School on Calton Hill, its premises long vacant, was the choice of many. Doubtless Lord Cockburn would have agreed. His disgust at the placing of the nineteenth-century prison on Calton Hill, so demeaning the great potential of such a wonderful site, had been obvious: 'The year 1808 saw the commencement of our new jail on Calton Hill. It was a piece of undoubted bad taste to give so glorious an eminence to a prison. It was one of our noblest sites, and would have been given by Pericles to one of his finest edifices.' But, for others, the strong association of this site with Scottish nationalism placed it at a political disadvantage. There were other, more eccentric, suggestions, including a brownfield site at Haymarket, Donaldson's

A view of the Parliament building

School for the Deaf, and a site at the Gyle, no doubt convenient for escape along the M8 corridor to the west. The Canongate Scottish and Newcastle Brewery site was a late runner. But the debate concluded with the selection, by a few on behalf of the many, of this historic site at the foot of Canongate.

Canongate was – yet again – about to be transformed. The brewery buildings were all demolished and the site was cleared. But under the ground there remains a rabbit-warren of capped shafts and wells, awaiting future archaeologists to complete the unfinished investigations. Excavation work had started at the west end of the site, revealing tantalising clues to the site's past – wells, storage pits, drains and sewers all had their own stories. Most have now gone, preserved only in recording and photography. Health and Safety rulings meant that one of the most potentially rewarding areas – the bottoms of the deeper well shafts – could not be examined. But Queensberry House revealed within its shell the older Hatton House and beneath the floor medieval closes and structures. As archaeological work progressed eastwards a more pressing timescale was imposed and detailed excavation was the victim. Old vennels, such as the sixteenth-century Brodie's Close and Cumming's Close, have now disappeared within the new parliament complex. The site is still bounded, however, by two historic closes – Horse Wynd and Reid's Close, the old delineating the new. Queensberry Lodge, the refuge for 'women given to habits of drunkenness', was taken down stone by stone and stored ready for re-erection as part of the complex – a plan that never came to fruition – in effect another Trinity Church. The one building that survived on the site was Queensberry House.

It is one of history's little ironies that the very house where many of the negotiations took place which resulted in the loss of Scotland's parliament in 1707 should now feature so prominently in the parliament complex. It has undergone vast refurbishment and now bears few reminders of its past roles as prestigious dwelling, barracks, house of refuge and hospital. Not all of this refurbishment has been welcomed. The belvedere, still extant within the body of the building, was not restored. Excuses for this ranged from cost – modest, in fact, given the overall bill taxpayers footed – to the fanciful: the tower might be used by a sniper as a vantage point to fire on the royal family when in residence at Holyrood Palace! Also inappropriate is the new roofing material. It seem that in all probability, Hatton House, the precursor to Queensberry House, had been slated (*see* Chapter 5). But, against the overwhelming advice of architects, archaeologists and historians, Queensberry House was roofed with pantiles rather than slates, which would have been authentic and more suitable.

In spite of the parliament project being deemed a 'management failure of massive proportions', Canongate has now gained a prestigious, architecturally ambitious suite of buildings, designed to reflect the towering Salisbury Crags that have watched over the small burgh's many turns of fate. This home of the new Scottish parliament is built partly on the very ground that once housed James VI's urban court and, before that, the precincts of the abbey. So, yet again, the great and the good will resort to this ancient burgh. Canongate, once more, is to be the meeting ground of the elite. Historically, this was an excellent choice of site.

In other ways also, history may be seen to be repeating itself. Once again, the 'Royal Mile' has become the processional route of kings and parliament. On 1 July 1999, Queen Elizabeth II rode in state to open Scotland's parliament – 'a moment anchored in our history' for First Minister Donald Dewar. The route was the same as devised in the 1580s – from the Palace of Holyroodhouse, up the High Streets of Canongate and Edinburgh, the ancient spine running down from the volcanic rock, to parliament's temporary quarters in the General Assembly Rooms of the Church of Scotland. In spite of tight police security, some of it armed, and the presence of the Household Cavalry and members of the armed services, four protestors were able to climb over the safety barriers and rush the queen's carriage. Was the medieval thoroughfare still a suitable processional route? Encroachment of buildings onto the roadway has made Canongate High Street narrower than its medieval predecessor. Was the urban space now too confined?

Otherwise, the topography of the Royal Mile remains unchanged. At the lower end of the ceremonial route visitors can still see the footprint of Canongate's two ancient Strands, now no longer back lanes but main thoroughfares – Calton Road and Holyrood Road. But they are still aligned as the old Strands and curve in towards each other in a pincer-like pinch-point, exactly as they did in the Middle Ages. The new parliament, of palatial proportions, at least in terms of its cost – estimated in 2001 as £195 million but ending up over £430 million – threatens to reinforce the natural focus of the capital at a topographical dead-end. Yet again, just as the carts carrying essential supplies from Leith had to trundle through the Watergate, past the front of the Palace of Holyrood, congestion of more modern vehicles will impact. History was evinced in the choice of Holyrood and Canongate as the site of the new parliament, but geography and geology still control the townscape. The capital may be about to embark on a topographical traffic nightmare.

So Canongate is to become the home of the elite. Yet again, history is repeating itself. Mingling with the great will be the ordinary man on the street. Canongate will again house, as it always did before the nineteenth century, a multi-layered society. But what of those depleted numbers of the old residents of Canongate? What have they gained? Our Dynamic Earth, on what was Fletcher of Saltoun's land, the new *Scotsman* building, expensive hotels and a supermarket on Holyrood Road probably offer little compensation for the turmoil that this small burgh has had inflicted upon it. Souvenir shops abound but there are few general stores. Public transport is poor, but there are sight-seeing buses aplenty. Little wonder, for there are ambitions to attract 750,000 tourists a year to the new building. The cost of becoming a tourist icon is a loss of the community that once was. Plans to infill the gap sites between Canongate High Street and Holyrood Road with mixed housing – both private and public and large and small – to reflect the old Canongate, have been abandoned. Few can now afford the exorbitant prices of this newly prestigious residential area.

Canongate is once again the desirable place to be and to be seen. Exiles from Canongate, and those who remained, must look upon the developments with mixed feelings, as must the residents of Reid's Close, encroached upon by the massive structure of the new parliament. Yet, the little burgh has once more proved itself to have greater cachet than its larger neighbour. But there is still lingering in the minds of many a sense of loss for the old days – good and bad. It is a sense of loss that has yet to be compensated by a sense of future. Part of that future, of course, will be the renewal, once again, of an ancient burgh that has seen so many different phases in its long life. Canongate has entered its next era, as the new residents of this ancient burgh – the MSPs – show themselves worthy inheritors of the historic site of Holyrood.

NOTES

These endnotes refer to primary source material. For secondary sources, consult 'Select Bibiography'.

Chapter 1

1. G.W.S. Barrow (ed.), *The Charters of King David I* (Woodbridge, 1999), no. 147; *Liber Cartarum Sancte Crucis* (Bannatyne Club, 1840), p. lxxxvi.

Chapter 2

1. G.S. Pryde. *The Burghs of Scotland; a Critical List* (Oxford, 1965), 3; *Registrum de Dunfermelyn* (Bannatyne Club, 1842), no. 26.
2. *Liber Cartarum Sancte Crucis*, 6.
3. There are no extant charters to burghs before 1160, and many of those known to have existed soon after this, such as those to Edinburgh, Perth and Berwick, are lost or destroyed. It is, therefore, necessary to extrapolate from surviving evidence, such as the charters to Inverness or Rutherglen, reiterating the rights bestowed by David I: *RRS*, ii, nos 213, 224.
4. *Leges Burgorum*, c. ic, for example, in C. Innes (ed.), *Ancient Burgh Laws* (SBRS, 1869).
5. *Protocol Book of James Young*, no. 533.
6. *Ibid.*, no. 1120; MS. Protocol Book of Vincent Strathauchin, i, no. 37.
7. A. C. Lawrie, *Early Scottish Charters prior to 1153* (Glasgow, 1905), no. 169; *Charters and Other Documents Relating to the City of Glasgow* (Glasgow, 1894–7), i, pt. ii, 5; *Prot. Bk Young*, nos. 35, 221.
8. *Prot. Bk Young*, nos. 207, 990, 1041; Prot. Bk Strathauchin, i, no. 51.
9. *Prot. Bk Young*, no. 82.
10. *Ibid.*, nos. 71, 50, 410, 836, 404, 754, 1120.
11. Prot. Bk Strathauchin, i, nos. 866, 867, 774, 1061.
12. Dundee Archives, MS. Dundee Burgh Head Court Book, 4 June 1521; 12 June 1521; 13 July 1552; 19 Oct. 1554; 22 Dec. 1556; 13 July 1552; 4 Feb. 1557.
13. *Prot. Bk Young*, no. 72.
14. *Liber Cartarum Sancti Crucis*, 6.

15. *RMS*, ii, 217.

16. I.B. Cowan and D.E. Easson (eds), *Medieval Religious Houses. Scotland* (London, 1976), 175–6.

17. *Extracts from the Council Register of the Burgh of Aberdeen* (Spalding Club, 1844–8), 177; *Edin. Recs*, i, 71–2.

18. D. Laing (ed.), *The Booke of the Universall Kirk of Scotland* (Bannatyne Club, 1839), i, 375; *Edin. Recs*, iv, 172.

19. 'The Book of the Kirk' in MS. Dundee Burgh Head Court Book, vol. i.

20. Cowan and Easson, *Medieval Religious Houses*, 177.

Chapter 3

1. *RRS*, ii, nos 213, 224.

2. *Leges Burgorum*, c. ic, for example, in Innes (ed.), *Ancient Burgh Laws*; *Leges Burgorum*, c. xciv; A number of manuscripts survive, the earliest being BL, Add. MS. 18111.

3. MS. Dundee Burgh Head Court Book, 5 Oct. 1556; E. Beveridge (ed.), *The Burgh Records of Dunfermline* (Edinburgh, 1917), 64, 81, 33, 184; E.P.D. Torrie (ed.), *Gild Court Book of Dunfermline, 1433–1597* (SRS, 1986), fos 2v., 3v.

4. *Edin. Recs*, i, 75, 190.

5. *Papers Relative to the Marriage of King James the Sixth of Scotland, with the Princess Anna of Denmark, AD MDLXXXIX and the Form and Manner of Her Majesty's Coronation at Holyroodhouse, AD MDXC* (Bannatyne Club, 1828); 'Extracts from the Records if the Burgh of Canongate', *Maitland Miscellany*, ii (Maitland Club, 1840), 356–7.

6. Prot. Bk Strathauchin, no. 111.

7. *APS*, ii, 500; D. Laing (ed.), *The Works of John Knox* (Bannatyne Club, 1846), ii, 157; R. Pitcairn (ed.) *Criminal Trials in Scotland from 1488 to 1624* (Bannatyne Club, 1833), i, 409.

Chapter 4

1. *APS*, i, 500.

2. *APS*, i, 556–7.

3. *APS*, ii, 31.

4. *TA*, iv, 528.

5. J. Dalrymple (ed.), *The Historie of Scotland, wrytten first in Latin by the most reverend and worthy Jhone Leslie, Bishop of Rosse, and translated in Scottish by Father James Dalrymple 1598*, eds E.G. Cody and W. Murison (Scottish Text Society, 1888) i, 259.

6. D. Laing, 'On the state of the abbey church of Holyrood subsequent to the devastations committed by the English forces in the years 1544 and 1547', *PSAS*, i (1851–4), 102.

7. J. Dalyell (ed.), *Fragments of Scottish History* (Edinburgh, 1798), 6–7.

8. *RMS*, v, no. 1242.
9. Cowan and Easson, *Medieval Religious Houses*, 178.
10. Dalyell (ed.), *Fragments*, 82.
11. W.S. Daniel, *History of the Abbey and Palace of Holyrood* (Edinburgh, 1854), 5.
12. 'Extracts from the records of the burgh of the Canongate', 9 June 1569. Protocol books refer to other waste properties in the Canongate: a tenement on the south side of High Street, Canongate was 'waste and burnt' in 1549, for example (MS. Protocol Book of Alexander King, 11 Dec. 1549).
13. *Edin. Recs*, i, 203, 222; *Protocol Book of John Foular, 1501–28*, eds W. Macleod & M. Wood (SRS, 1930–53), iii, no. 461; *Acts of the Lords of Council in Public Affairs, 1501–54*, ed. R.K. Hannay (Edinburgh, 1932), 325.
14. *APS*, ii, 523 –35.
15. MS. Protocol Book of John Robeson, 1551–7, fo. 94v.
16. *RMS*, iii, no. 918.
17. *CSP Scot*, i, no. 967.
18. *John Knox's History of the Reformation in Scotland*, ed. W. C. Dickinson, 2 vols. (Edinburgh, 1949), ii, 5; *Papal Negotiations with Mary Queen of Scots during her reign in Scotland, 1561–1567*, ed. J. H. Pollen (SHS, 1901), 496.
19. Knox, *History*, ii, 213.
20. Dalyell (ed.), *Fragments*, 19.
21. 'Historie and Life of King James the Sext, 1566–1596', *BOEC*, xvi (1928), 18–19.
22. Dalyell (ed.), *Fragments*, 19.
23. NAS, E21/63, MS. Treasurer's Accounts, 1582, fo. 130.
24. NAS, E21/63, fo. 82v; NAS, E22/6, fo. 131v; NAS, E21/64, MS. Treasurer's Accounts, 1585, 71.
25. 'Extract from John Taylor the Water Poet's Pennylesse Pilgrimage to Scotland in 1618', *Bannatyne Miscellany*, ii (1836), 403.

Chapter 5

1. 'John Taylor the Water Poet's Pennylesse Pilgrimage to Scotland in 1618', 403.
2. Prot. Bk Strathauchin, 1507–1525, no. 50.
3. MS. Protocol Books of Alexander Guthrie snr, 1579–81, 117, 159; 1585–87, 135.
4. *Ibid.*, 1579–81, 171; 1581–82, 143, 182, 136, 134.
5. *Ibid.*, 1585–87, 116; 1581–82, 151; 1582–85, 147; Register of Edinburgh Testaments (NAS, CC8/8/1), quoted in M. Lynch, *Edinburgh and the Reformation* (Edinburgh, 1981), 270.
6. Prot. Bks Guthrie snr, 1581–82, 143; 1579–81, 88; 1581–82, 123, 162; 1582–85, 147; 1587–88, 134.
7. *Ibid.*, 1579–81, 89, 100; 1587–88, 134.
8. *Ibid.*, 1581–82, 60; 1585–87, 13.

9. NAS, GD 1/14/1, Minute Book of the Cordiners of Canongate, 1584–1773.
10. P. Hume Brown (ed.), *Early Travellers in Scotland* (Edinburgh, repr. 1973), 139–40.
11. Dalyell (ed.), *Fragments*, 55, 61.
12. NLS, Wodrow Ms. Quarto ix, fo. 50r.
13. 'The diary of John Nicoll, 1650 –1667', *BOEC*, xvi (1928), 36.
14. Dalyell (ed.), *Fragments*, 61.
15. NLS, MS. Wod. Fol. xxvi, ff. 137–8.
16. ECA, 'Burgh of Canongate, Window Tax, 1710–1711', shelf ref. 64; indexed at page 74.
17. ECA, Annuity Roll 1687; NAS, Hearth Tax, E69/16/3, fos. 53, 62.
18. ECA, Moses Bundle 118 (no. 4762); V, bun. 18/4762.
19. *Register of the Privy Council of Scotland* [*RPC*], iii (1669–72), 594.
20. NAS, CH2/122/4, fo. 324; NAS, CH2/122/9, fo. 55; NLS, MS 1961, 122–3, 138.
21. *APS*, ix, 33–4, 38–40.
22. *RPC*, iv (1673–76), 182; H. Armet (ed.), *Edin. Recs, 1689–1701*, 83; H. Armet (ed.), *Edin. Recs, 1701–1718*, 144.

Chapter 6

1. University of Glasgow, Scottish Brewing Archive, MS. 'Messrs Wm Younger & Co., Ltd, Abbey and Holyrood Breweries Ltd, report' (undated), 15.
2. NAS, MS Minutes of the Town Council of Edinburgh, 11 Sept. 1782; *Williamson's Directories* (Edinburgh 1889), 1782–3, 1786–7; NAS, Register of Sasines, P.R. 322.245 (2797; 21 May 1787; 30 May 1788); *Williamson's Directories*, 1790–99.
3. ECA, MS. 'Dean of Guild Records', xv, 1 Oct. 1746 & 14 Jan. 1747.
4. W. Maitland, *The History of Edinburgh from its foundation to the present time* (Edinburgh, 1753), 156.
5. MS. Minute Book, Particular Register of Sasines, 1726–1733 (RS71/10), fo. 133v; Lib. 109, fo. 394.
6. *Regulations for the Canongate Workhouse, 1761*, 24.
7. *Epistle to Mrs M*ll*r . . .* (Bath, 1976), 6.
8. E. Topham, *Letters from Edinburgh Written in the Years 1774 and 1775* (London, 1776), 38, 51, 84, 256, 94.
9. H. Cockburn (ed.), *Memorials of His Time, by Henry Cockburn* (Edinburgh, 1910), 73.

Chapter 7

1. Scottish Brewing Archive, MS. 'Outer House, 7 March 1826'.
2. *Ibid.*, MS. 'Abbey and Holyrood Breweries Report', 15.

3. *Ibid., Guide to Great Northern Railway* (1861), 217.

4. *Ibid.*, MS. 'Notebook of Andrew Smith'.

5. *The Scottish Standard*, 5 March 1870.

6. NAS, RD12/131/4 Sasine John Walker, merchant, 1754; NAS, RS27/861 Sasine William Ford, 1819.

7. ECA, Black Index Book, no. 1/5; 84, no. 27.

8. *Edinburgh and Leith Directory, 1835–36*, 160; *Ibid., 1836–37*, 169; *Edinburgh and Leith Post Office Directories, 1830 – 1850, passim.*

9. ECA, 'Census 1841, district no 685–3; area nos 11, 12'.

10. Cockburn, *Memorials*, 176.

11. *Ibid.*, 99.

12. J. G. Kohl, *Reisen in Schottland* (Dresden/Leipzig, 1844), part i, 53.

13. ECA, MS. 'Journal of correspondence regarding slaughter houses', shelf ref. 48, page index 54.

14. E. Chadwick, *Report on the Sanitary Condition of the Labouring Population* (Edinburgh, 1842), 13, 233, 247, 78, 106, 282, 59–60, 120–24, 97–99, 198, 277, 281–22, 397, 366, 416, 138, 162.

15. F. Engels, *The Condition of the Working Class in England* (Stanford, 1844), 41–3, 113, 119.

16. G. Bell, *Day and Night in the Wynds of Edinburgh* (Edinburgh, 1849); *Idem, Blackfriars' Wynd Analyzed* (Edinburgh, 1850), 4–5.

17. ECA, MS. 'Dean of Guild Records, burgh engineer's drawings', 14. vii. 1887.

Chapter 8

1. H. Cockburn, *Journal of H. Cockburn, being a Continuation of Memorials of His Time, 1831–1854* (Edinburgh, 1874), *passim.*

2. ECA, MS. 'Journal of correspondence regarding slaughter houses'.

3. Cockburn, *Journal*, i, 28, 29.

4. Macnee, J, writer, taken in short hand, 'Trial of William Burke and Helen McDougal before the Justiciary at Edinburgh on Wednesday, December 24, 1828 for the Murder of Margery Campbell or Docherty' (Edinburgh, 1829), *passim.*

5. *Edinburgh Pictorial*, 19 March 1954.

6. P. Abercrombie and D. Plumstead, *A Civic Survey and Plan for the City of Edinburgh* (Edinburgh, 1949), 86.

7. *Census* (1951).

SELECT BIBLIOGRAPHY

PRIMARY SOURCES

Dundee District Archive and Record Centre.
Dundee Burgh Head Court Books.
'The Book of the Kirk' in Dundee Burgh Head Court Book, vol. i.

EDINBURGH CITY ARCHIVES

Black Index Book, no. 1/5. 'Census 1841, district no. 685–3; area nos 11 & 12'.
Burgh of Canongate, Window Tax, 1710–1711, shelf ref. 64; indexed at page 74.
Census 1951; Report on the Fifteenth Census of Scotland, vol. i, part i, City of
    Edinburgh.
Dean of Guild Records.
Dean of Guild Records, burgh engineers' drawings.
'Journal of correspondence regarding slaughter houses', shelf ref 48, page index 54.
Minute Book of Magistrates and Stent Masters for 1724 to 1742, Canongate, shelf
    47.
Moses Bundle 118, III, IV, & V.
Roll of the Superiorities of the City, 11.1.1740.

NATIONAL ARCHIVES OF SCOTLAND

Accounts of the Lord High Treasurer of Scotland, E21/61–64; E22/6.
'Canongate Church', CH2/122/4.
'Canongate Church', CH2/122/9.
Hearth Tax records, E69.
Leges Burgorum, PA 5/1.
Minute Book of the Cordiners of Canongate, 1584–1773, (GD 1/14/1).
Minute Book, Particular Register of Sasines, 1726–1733 (RS71/10).
Minute Book, Particular Register of Sasines, 1733–1739 (RS71/11).
Protocol Books of Canongate and Edinburgh notaries public
Protocol Book of Vincent Strathauchin, i (1507–1524/25), B22/1/5.
Protocol Book of Alexander King, 1548–50, B22/1/14.
Protocol Book of John Robeson, 1551–57, NP 1/14.

Protocol Book of James Logane, 1576/7–1580/81, B22/22/25.
Protocol Book of Alexander Guthrie snr, 1579–81, B22/1/29.
Protocol Book of Alexander Guthrie snr, 1581–82, B22/1/30.
Protocol Book of Alexander Guthrie snr, 1582–85, B22/1/31.
Protocol Book of Alexander Guthrie snr, 1585–87, B22/1/32.
Register of Edinburgh Testaments, CC8/8/1.
Register of Sasines, P.R. 322.245 (2797; 21 May 1787; 30 May 1788).
Sasine, John Walker, merchant, RD12/131/4.
Sasine, William Ford, RS27/861.

National Library of Scotland

Account of the Most Horrid and Unchristian Actions of the Grave Makers, 1711,
    S302.b.2[68].
MS. Wod. Fol. xxvi.
MS 1961 Kirk Session disputes over seating in Canongate Church.
Wodrow Ms. Quarto ix.

Royal Commission for Ancient and Historic Monuments Scotland Archive

'Design for the Canongate which was ratified by parliament and dated 22 March
    1661'.

Archive and Business Record Centre, University of Glasgow

'Abbey and Holyrood Breweries Report'.
Guide to Great Northern Railway (n.p., 1861).
'Inventory of titles and properties belonging to Messrs William Younger & Co,
    Ltd', MS. WY2/1.
Licensed Victuallers Guardian, x, no. 337 (London, Saturday 15 June, 1872).
Messrs Wm Younger & Co., Ltd, 'Abbey and Holyrood Breweries Ltd, report'
    (undated).
Notebook of Andrew Smith, partner of William Younger, which includes notes
    on brewing and was bequeathed to his two sons.
'Outer House, 7 March 1826'.

PRINTED PRIMARY SOURCES

Abercrombie, P. and Plumstead, D., *A Civic Survey and Plan for the City of
    Edinburgh* (Edinburgh, 1949).

Accounts of the Lord High Treasurer of Scotland, eds T. Dickson and Sir J. Balfour Paul (Edinburgh, 1877–1914).

Acts of the Lords of Council in Public Affairs, 1501–54, ed. R.K. Hannay (Edinburgh, 1932).

Acts of the Parliaments of Scotland, eds T. Thomson and C. Innes (Edinburgh, 1814–75).

Anderson, A.O. (ed.), *The Chronicle of Holyrood* (SHS, 1938).

Armet, H. (ed.), *Register of the Burgesses of the Burgh of Canongate, 1622–1733* (SRS, 1951).

Barrow, G.WS. (ed.), *The Charters of King David I* (Woodridge, 1999).

Begg, J., *Drunkenness and Pauperism* (Edinburgh, 1851).

Begg, J., *Pauperism and the Poor Laws* (Edinburgh, 1849).

Bell, G., *Blackfriars' Wynd Analyzed* (Edinburgh, 1850; reprinted Leicester, 1973).

Bell, G., *Day and Night in the Wynds of Edinburgh* (Edinburgh, 1849; reprinted Leicester, 1973).

'Birrel, Robert, Diary of', in J. Dalyell (ed.), *Fragments of Scotish [sic] History* (Edinburgh, 1798).

Bonar, A., *The Canongate, Ancient and Modem* (Edinburgh, 1856).

Brereton, Sir William, 'Account of visit to Edinburgh and Canongate, 1636', in P. Hume Brown (ed.), *Early Travellers in Scotland* (Edinburgh, 1891: reprinted 1973).

Calderwood, A.B. (ed.), *The Buik of the Kirk of the Canagait* (SRS, 1961).

Chadwick, E., *Report on the Sanitary Condition of the Labouring Population* (Edinburgh, 1842).

City of Edinburgh Charity Organisation Society, *Report on the Physical Condition of Fourteen Hundred Schoolchildren in the City* (Edinburgh, 1906).

Cockburn, H., *Journal of, being a continuation of Memorials of His Time, 1831–1854* (Edinburgh, 1874).

Cockburn, H., (ed.), *Memorials of His Time, by Henry Cockburn* (Edinburgh, 1910).

Cockburn, H., *Memorials of His Time*, edited by W.F. Gray (Edinburgh, 1946).

Cowan, I.B. and Easson, D.E. (eds), *Medieval Religious Houses. Scotland* (London, 1976).

Dalrymple, J. (ed.), *The Historie of Scotland, wrytten first in Latin by the most reverend and worthy Jhone Leslie, Bishop of Rosse, and translated in Scottish by Father James Dalrymple, 1598*, eds E.G. Cody and W. Murison (Scottish Text Society, 1888).

Dalyell, J. (ed.), *Fragments of Scotish [sic] History* (Edinburgh, 1798).

Daniel, W.S., *History of the Abbey and Palace of Holyrood* (Edinburgh, 1854).

Dunfermline, The Burgh Records of, ed. E. Beveridge (Edinburgh, 1917).

Edinburgh and Leith Directories, 1830–37.

Edinburgh and Leith Post Office Directories, 1838–1850.

Edinburgh Evening Courant, 11 August 1788.

Edinburgh Evening Courant, 12 October 1822.

Edinburgh Evening Courant, 30 August 1788.

Edinburgh Pictorial, 19 March 1954.

'Edinburgi Regiae Scotorum Urbis descriptio, per Alexandrum Alesium Scotum, S.T.D., 1550', *Bannatyne Miscellany*, i (1827).

Engels, F., *The Condition of the Working Class in England* (Stanford, 1844).

'Extract from John Taylor the Water Poet's Pennylesse Pilgrimage to Scotland in 1618', *Bannatyne Miscellany*, ii (1836).

*Epistle to Mrs M*ll*r . . .* (Bath, 1976).

Extracts from the Burgh Records of Edinburgh (SBRS, 1869–92).

Extracts from the Records of the Burgh of Edinburgh, 1589–1718, ed. M. Wood *et al* (Edinburgh, 1927–67).

Extracts from the Records of the Burgh of Edinburgh, 1665–1800, ed. M. Wood (Edinburgh, 1950).

Extracts from the Records of the Burgh of Edinburgh, 1689–1701, ed. H. Armet (Edinburgh, 1962).

Extracts from the Records of the Burgh of Edinburgh, 1701–18, ed. H. Armet (Edinburgh, 1967).

Extracts from the Council Register of the Burgh of Aberdeen (Spalding Club, 1844–8).

'Extracts from the records of the burgh of Canongate near Edinburgh, MDLXI–MDLXXVIII', *Miscellany of the Maitland Club*, ii (1840).

'Fountainhall's [Sir John Lauder of] historical notices of Scotish [sic] affairs', *BOEC*, xvi (1928).

Grant, J., *Old and New Edinburgh* (Edinburgh, 1881–83).

Innes, C. (ed.), *Ancient Burgh Laws* (SBRS, 1869).

John Knox's History of the Reformation in Scotland, ed. W.C. Dickinson (Edinburgh, 1949).

'John Nicoll, diary of, 1650 –1667', *BOEC*, xvi (1928).

Kohl, J.G., *Reisen in Schottland* (Dresden/Leipzig, 1844).

Laing, D. (ed,), *The Booke of the Universall Kirk of Scotland* (Bannatyne Club, 1839).

Laing, D. (ed.), *The Works of John Knox* (Bannatyne Club, 1846–64).

Laing, D., 'On the state of the abbey church of Holyrood subsequent to the devastations committed by the English forces in the years 1544 and 1547', *PSAS*, i (1851–4).

Liber Cartarum Sancte Crucis (Bannatyne Club, 1840).

Littlejohn, J., *Report on the Sanitary Condition of the City of Edinburgh* (Edinburgh, 1865).

'Londini, The Late Expedicion in Scotlande, made by the Kynges Hynys Armye, under the conduit of the Ryght Honorable the Erle of Hertforde, the yere of oure Lorde God 1544', in J. Dalyell (ed.) *Fragments of Scotish [sic] History* (Edinburgh, 1798).

Macnee, J, writer, taken in short hand, *'Trial of William Burke and Helen McDougal before the Justiciary at Edinburgh on Wednesday, December 24, 1828, for the Murder of Margery Campbell or Docherty'* (Edinburgh, 1829).

Maitland, W., *The History of Edinburgh from its foundation to the present times* (Edinburgh, 1753).

New Statistical Account of Scotland; Edinburgh (Edinburgh, 1845).

Papers Relative to the Marriage of King James the Sixth of Scotland, with the Princess Anna of Denmark, AD MDLXXXIX and the Form and Manner of her Majesty's Coronation at Holyroodhouse, AD MDXC, collated by J.T. Gibson Craig (Bannatyne Club, 1828).

Paton, H.M. (ed.) *Accounts of the Masters of Works for Building and Repairing Royal Palaces and Castles, i, 1529–1615* (Edinburgh, 1957).

Patten, W., The Expedicion into Scotlande of the Most Woorthely Fortunate Prince Edward Duke of Somerset set out by way of Diarie', in J. Dalyell (ed.) *Fragments of Scotish [sic] History* (Edinburgh, 1798).

Pitcairn, R. (ed.), *Criminal Trials in Scotland from 1488 to 1624* (Bannatyne Club, 1833).

Protocol Book of James Young, 1485–1515, ed. G. Donaldson (SRS, 1952).

Protocol Book of John Foular, 1501–28, eds W. Macleod and M. Wood (SRS, 1930–53).

Protocol Book of John Foular, 1528–34, ed. J. Durkan (SRS, 1985).

Pryde, G.S., *The Burghs of Scotland: a Critical List* (Oxford, 1965).

Ranger's Impartial List of the Ladies of Pleasure in Edinburgh (Edinburgh, 1775; reprinted Edinburgh, 1978).

Regesta Regum Scottorum, eds G.W.S. Barrow and others (Edinburgh, 1960).

Register of the Privy Council of Scotland, eds J.H. Burton and others (Edinburgh, 1877-).

Registrum de Dunfermelyn (Bannatyne Club, 1842).

Registrum Magni Sigilii Regum Scotorum, eds J.M. Thomson and others (Edinburgh, 1882–1914).

Taylor, J., *A Journey to Edenborough in Scotland, 1705*, ed. W. Cowan (Edinburgh, 1903).

The Scottish Standard, 5 March 1870, British Library Collection, Colindale, London.

Topham, E., *Letters from Edinburgh Written in the Years 1774 and 1775* (London, 1776).

Torrie, E.P.D. (ed.), *Gild Court Book of Dunfermline, 1433–1597* (SRS, 1986).

Williamson, P., *Edinburgh Directories* (Edinburgh, 1889).

Withrington, D. J. and Grant, I..R. (eds*), Statistical Account of Scotland, 1791–1799*, ed. Sir John Sinclair (Edinburgh, 1975).

The Witness (Edinburgh, 1840s).

Wood, M. (ed.), *Court Book of the Regality of Broughton and the Burgh of Canongate, 1569–73* (Edinburgh, 1937).

Wood, M. (ed.), *Book of Records of the Ancient Privileges of the Canongate* (SRS, 1956).

SECONDARY SOURCES

Anderson, A.H., 'The Burgh of the Canongate and its Court' (Unpublished PhD thesis, University of Edinburgh, 1949).

Anderson, A.H., 'The regality and barony of Broughton', *BOEC*, xxxiv, part 1 (1974).

Anderson, H.M., 'The grammar school of the Canongate' *BOEC*, xx. (1935).

Aspinwall, B. and McCaffrey, J., 'A comparative view of the Irish in Edinburgh in the nineteenth century', in Swift, R. and Gilley, S. (eds), *The Irish in the Victorian City* (London, 1985).

Birrell, J.F., *An Edinburgh Alphabet* (Edinburgh, 1980).

Blaikie, W.B., 'Edinburgh at the time of the occupation of Prince Charles', *BOEC*, ii (1909).

Boog Watson, C.B., 'Notes on the names of the closes and wynds of old Edinburgh', *BOEC*, xii (1923).

Boog Watson, C.B., *The Notes of Charles Boog Watson: History and Derivations of Edinburgh Street Names* (Edinburgh, 1996).

Boog Watson, C.B., 'Moray House, Canongate', *BOEC*, xii(1923).

Boog Watson, C.B., 'Queensberry House, Canongate', *BOEC*, xv (1927).

Cameron, A.I., 'The Canongate crafts: an agreement of 1610', *BOEC*, xiv (1925).

Catford, E.F. (ed.), *Queensberry House and Hospital. A History, by M. Hume and S. Boyd* (Edinburgh, 1984).

Chambers, R., *Traditions of Edinburgh* (Edinburgh, 1980).

Clive, J. (ed.), *Henry Cockburn's Memorial of His Times* (London, 1974).

Cooke, A., Donnachie, I., MacSween, A. and Whatley, C.A. (eds), *Modern Scottish History, 1707 to the Present*, vol. 4: *Readings, 1850 to the Present* (East Linton, 1998).

Daniel, W.S., *History of the Abbey and Palace of Holyrood* (Edinburgh, 1854).

Daunton., M. (ed.) *Cambridge Urban History of Britain*, vol iii (Cambridge, 2000).

Dickinson, W.C., 'Burgh life from burgh records', *Aberdeen University Review*, xxi (1945–6).

Dingwall, H.M., *Late Seventeenth-Century Edinburgh* (Aldershot, 1994).

Donnachie, I., *A History of the Brewing Industry in Scotland* (Edinburgh, 1979).

Dunbar, J.G., *Scottish Royal Palaces: The Architecture of the Royal Residences during the Late Medieval and Early Renaissance Periods* (East Linton, 1999).

Dupree, M., 'The provision of social services', in M. Daunton (ed.), *Cambridge Urban History of Britain*, vol. iii (Cambridge, 2000).

Edwards, O.D., *Burke and Hare* (Edinburgh 1993).

Ewan, E., *Townlife in Fourteenth-Century Scotland* (Edinburgh, 1990).

Fawcett, R., *Scottish Abbeys and Priories* (London, 1994).

Forbes Gray, W., 'Panmure House, Canongate', *BOEC*, xiii (1924).

Forbes Gray, W., 'The musical society of Edinburgh and St. Cecilia's Hall', *BOEC*, xix (1933).

Forbes Gray, W., 'St John Street: an early civic improvement', *BOEC*, xxviii (1953).

Geddie, J., 'Sculptured stones of the "Royal Mile"', *BOEC*, xvii (1930).

Gibson, J.S., *Edinburgh In The '45; Bonnie Prince Charlie at Holyrood* (Edinburgh, 1995).

Gifford, J., McWilliam, C. and Walker, D., *The Buildings of Scotland. Edinburgh* (Edinburgh, 1984).

Goodare, J. and Lynch, M. (eds), *The Reign of James VI* (East Linton, 2000).

Gray, R.Q., *The Labour Aristocracy in Victorian Edinburgh* (Oxford, 1976).

Gray, W.F., 'An eighteenth-century riding school', *BOEC*, xx (1935).

Gray, W.F., 'Manor of Canonmills, Barony of Broughton', *BOEC*, xviii (1932).

Hannah, H., 'The sanctuary of Holyrood', *BOEC*, xv (1927).

Harris, S., *Place Names of Edinburgh and Their Origins and History* (Edinburgh, 1996).

Home, B.J., 'Provisional list of old houses remaining in High Street and Canongate of Edinburgh', *BOEC*, i (1908).

Houston, R., 'Fire and filth: Edinburgh's environment, 1660–1760', *BOEC*, new series, iii (1994).

Houston, R.A., *Social Change in the Age of Enlightenment: Edinburgh, 1660–1760* (Oxford, 1994).

Hume Brown, P., *Early Travellers in Scotland* (Edinburgh, 1978).

Jamieson, J.H., 'Some inns of the eighteenth century', *BOEC*, xiv. (1925).

Keir, D., *The Younger Centuries* (Edinburgh, 1951).

Keir, D., *The Third Statistical Account of Scotland*, vol. xv, *The City of Edinburgh* (Glasgow, 1966).

Kerr, H.F., 'Map of Edinburgh in the mid-eighteenth century', *BOEC*, xi (1922).

Kinnear, W., 'The Canongate, Edinburgh', in Salmon, R.B. (ed.), *Field Excursions in Eastern Scotland* (Edinburgh, 1969).

Laing, D. 'Proposals for Cleaning and Lighting the City of Edinburgh in the Year 1735', *PSAS* (1858–9).

Law, A., 'Teachers in Edinburgh in the eighteenth century', *BOEC*, xxxii (1966).

Leneman, L. and Mitchison, R., *Sin in the City, 1660–1780* (Edinburgh, 1998).

Lynch, M., Spearman, M. and Stell, G. (eds), *The Scottish Medieval Town* (Edinburgh, 1988).

Lynch, M. (ed.), *The Early Modern Town in Scotland* (London, 1987).

Lynch, M., *Edinburgh and the Reformation* (Edinburgh, 1981).

Lynch, M. (ed.), *Mary Stewart: Queen in Three Kingdoms* (Oxford, 1988).

Mackay, J., *History of the Burgh of Canongate, with notes of the Abbey and Palace of Holyrood* (Edinburgh, 1879).

Mackay, J., *History of the Burgh of Canongate, with notes of the Abbey and Palace of Holyrood* (Edinburgh, 1900).

Mackie, A., *An Industrial History of Edinburgh* (Glasgow, 1963).

Mahood, L., *The Magdalenes. Prostitution in the Nineteenth Century* (London, 1990).

Malcolm, C.A., 'The Incorporation of the cordiners of the Canongate, 1538 –1773', *BOEC*, xviii (1932).

Marwick, W.H., 'Municipal politics in Victorian Edinburgh', *BOEC*, xxxiii (1969).

Marwick, W.H., 'The Incorporation of the tailors of Canongate', *BOEC*, xxii (1938).

McCallum, R.I., 'Historical Notes on Chessels Court', *BOEC*, new series, iv (1997).

Merriman, M., *The Rough Wooings: Mary Queen of Scots, 1542–1551* (East Linton, 2000).

Minay, P., 'Eighteenth- and nineteenth-century Edinburgh seedsmen and nurserymen' *BOEC*, new series, i (1991).

Mitchison, R., *The Old Poor Law in Scotland, The Experience of Poverty, 1574–1845* (Edinburgh, 2000).

Morris, R.J., 'Death, Chambers Street and the Edinburgh Corporation', in A. Cooke, I. Donnachie, A. MacSween and C.A. Whatley (eds), *Modern Scottish History, 1707 to the Present*, vol. 4: *Readings, 1850 to the Present* (East Linton, 1998).

Mullay, A.J., *Rail Centres: Edinburgh* (London, 1991).

RCAHMS, *An Inventory of the Ancient and Historical Monuments of Edinburgh* (Edinburgh, 1951).

Reid, H.G., 'Modern Dwellings of the People', in *Edinburgh Past and Present: its Associations and Suburbs* (Edinburgh, 1877).

Robertson, F.W., *Early Scottish Gardeners and their Plants* (East Linton, 2000).

Rodger, R., *Housing the People* (Edinburgh, 1999).

Ross, T., 'The Tailors' Hall, Canongate', *BOEC*, xi (1922).

Sanderson, E.C., *Women and Work in Eighteenth-Century Edinburgh* (Edinburgh, 1996).

Salmon, R.B. (ed.), *Field Excursions in Eastern Scotland* (Edinburgh, 1969)

Selby Wright, R., *An Illustrated Guide to the Canongate Kirk, Parish and Churchyard* (Edinburgh, 1965).

Selby Wright, R., 'The School of the Royal College of Holyrood House', *BOEC*, new series, ii (1992).

Sinclair, J., 'Notes on the Holyrood "Foir-yet" of James IV', *PSAS*, xxxix (1904–5).

Smeaton, O., *The Story of Edinburgh* (Edinburgh, 1905).

Smith, J., 'The story of Craigentinny', *BOEC*, xxii (1938).

Smith, J. and Paton, H.M., 'St Leonards lands and hospital', *BOEC*, xxiii (1940).

St Ann's Reminiscence Group, *'Ah Mind Fine'* (Edinburgh, 1993).

Thin, R., 'The old infirmary and earlier hospitals', *BOEC*, xv (1927).

Wilson, D., *Memorials of Edinburgh in the Olden Times (Edinburgh*, 1891).

Wood, M., 'The hammermen of the Canongate, parts 1 and 2', *BOEC*, xix (1935) and *BOEC*, xx (1937).

Wood, M.,'The work of the Canongate Court', *BOEC*, xx (1937).

Wood, M., 'Survey of the development of Edinburgh', *BOEC*, xxxiv, part 1 (1974).

INDEX